GW00360055

HEALTHY PRACTICE FOR MUSICIANS

Elizabeth Andrews

R·

RHINEGOLD PUBLISHING LIMITED
241 SHAFTESBURY AVENUE
LONDON WC2H 8EH
TELEPHONE 0171 333 1721
FAX 0171 333 1769

First published 1997 in Great Britain by
Rhinegold Publishing Ltd, 241 Shaftesbury Avenue,
London WC2H 8EH, Great Britain.

Cover design by COLOPHON

British Library Cataloguing in Publication Data.
A catalogue record for this book is available from the British Library.

___   ISBN 0-946890-73-0
Printed in Great Britain by Perfectaprint, Byfleet, Surrey.

CONTENTS

AUTHOR'S PREFACE

Although the contents of this book come from experiences in both my professions as Freelance Musician and Chiropractor, I could not have accomplished nearly as much without the guidance, nurturing and teaching I received.

I shall always regard the playing of Peter Schidlof, William Pleeth and Vadim Borissowsky with reverence and awe and I have enormous respect for the inquisitive and generous minds of George Goodheart DC, John Thie DC and Sheldon Deal DC in their teaching of Applied Kinesiology.

For reading through my manuscripts the common sense, patience and support of Tibby Pilcher, Hilary Greaves, Bayan Northcott, Frances Fernyhough, Joseph Goodman and Marianne Barton were invaluable and I am indebted to Peter Cox for his clear line drawings.

I am extremely grateful for Lord Menuhin's generosity in consenting to write the Foreword and, last but not least, I would like to thank Keith Diggle, Richard Thomas and Sarah Davies, at Rhinegold Publishing, for having the vision and dedication to bring this book to fruition.

Elizabeth Andrews
May 1997

FOREWORD

Lord Menuhin OM KBE

I must congratulate Elizabeth Andrews on the best book on the many obstacles, impediments, and challenges to a musician. She has covered the ground with admirable thoroughness, practicality, and sympathy.

This book will remain without doubt *the* reference book not only for musicians but for people in general who have aches and pains which may be tolerable or do not impede their daily life but become intolerable when perfection and absolute balance of mind and body, of limb, of ear and eye are indispenable. Her advice is first-rate and comes from great, first-hand experience and much study and an all-encompassing mind.

I would give this book my full and heartfelt endorsement as one of the most important gifts for all our colleagues.

Yehudi Menuhin
London
April 1997

ix

CHAPTER 1

Introduction

Musicians' expectations and attitudes
The purpose of the book
How to use the book
Standard medical treatment
Alternative and complementary disciplines
Visiting a practitioner
Self-help
Five-minute wonders

Musicians' expectations and attitudes

This book is about musician management. Regretfully it won't get you out of scales, practice or rehearsals, but it will help you to make the most of the time spent doing them, and to sit in the 'front row' of your life.

Music can be described as a language without words. Carried to its logical conclusion, this means that music is worthless if it doesn't communicate. This is a book about removing the barriers to that communication, and allowing musicians to play whatever 'game' they choose: an exploration, a reflection of life, a vehicle for self-expression, an Everest of technical gymnastic achievement, or just a surrogate voice to hide behind. At best, as a career, music brings with it empathy, respect, travel, and perhaps even glamour and adoration. At worst there is fear, deep pain, boredom, loneliness and a discipline as hard as any I know. It can devour you or just be fun, depending on how you think about it and how you 'live' it.

It's curious that you are trained to wear your heart on your sleeve, be a perfectionist and yet at the same time be expected to take rejection and misunderstanding in your stride. It's no joke that you have to have the 'heart of an angel and the hide of an elephant'. To get from the dreams and the song in your heart to world fame is a long and arduous journey which only partly depends on you. The other side of the partnership – the recipients, be they listeners, academics, examiners or critics – all have you at their mercy and, beyond that, modern methods of electronic reproduction have changed the pressures on successful performers out of all recognition, both for good and bad.

Wilhelm Kempf is supposed to have said 'Music is not a profession but a mission', and this sums up an attitude very common amongst soloists. As a musician, your teaching and expectations have been technical (how to produce sounds out of the machine you own), and interpretative (how to turn the dots on the paper into a bridge between the composer's concept and the audience's ears). Very few musicians, however, will have much idea of how the body (which has to produce this miraculous bridge) works.

The purpose of the book

This book is addressed mainly to instrumental musicians, with a bias towards string players. Statistically, their problems and injuries far outnumber all others, and a simple translation of the help offered here can be made by other instrumentalists in terms of their own art. The book may also be of use to practitioners treating musicians, broadening their understanding of the stresses impinging upon a musician's life. Music making is probably the most complex of all human neuro-muscular activities, necessitating movement of the hands within a very specific range and angle, with great precision and accuracy. It means, too, that the muscles used to carry and hold the limbs up against gravity are subjected to prolonged effort. Both precision and stamina are, therefore, needed in a way required by few sporting activities.

The problems and pitfalls discussed are those which mostly arise when musicians are on their own 'out in the field'. Each instrument requires its own special mechanical asymmetrical use of the body, and normal tolerances can easily be exceeded by overwork, unaccustomed repertoire or adverse playing conditions. The build-up of extra muscle can cause nerve traction or compression, and this can cause sensory deficit, muscular weakness and atrophy beyond the entrapment site. There may be coordination problems, jaw dislocation and joint instability, all kinds of arthritis, swelling and inflammation. Any of these can be combined with chronic anxiety problems and depression to make a destructive spiral.

Of course these problems also occur in the ordinary population, but there is a well-documented much higher incidence amongst musicians, such that these diseases are considered an occupational hazard. The risks may be due to several factors: the specific shape, one-sided or one-handedness of the instrument; the amount of physical effort and stamina required during the long hours of practice; to congenital, physiological, or pathological predisposition; and to environmental conditions such as poor lighting, chair slope and height, and on-stage conditions, as well as the stress of touring and constant performance. This all adds up to a very heavy load which greatly decreases physical and emotional tolerance, so that quite a small injury will push the musician over the rubicon into pain and misery, which is compounded by an heroic 'the show must go on' attitude.

3

There's no way I can revolutionise car seat design in the motor industry or the furniture trade and convince them that very few people are actually 'average' shape, nor can I alter the slope on so many theatrical stages, but I can suggest ways of adapting the performing world to fit you. A musician's life should not be 'a tussle with the muscle' but about the 'space within' and its powerful communication through sound.

Via Medline I have scanned the latest articles and papers in medical and other reputable alternative and complementary journals, and have been horrified by the published statistics. Owen (1985, see References at end of chapter) studied 110 musicians and reported 20% to be on muscle relaxants; Lederman (1989 and 1991) found 29% had peripheral nerve disorders; and in 47 symphony orchestras studied, there was a significant relationship between occupational stress and psychological and physical medical problems. Mandel (1990) talks in terms of 50% injury or over-use syndromes.

What carnage! This is the tragedy I hope this book will help to prevent, for, contrary to some people's belief, pain is not the inevitable accompaniment to playing at *any* standard from beginner to international artist. Moulton and Spense say that 'it remains unclear why certain individuals develop pain problems when others do not, given the same work practices, and similarly why some individuals recover relatively quickly following the onset of pain'. One wonders how many lucrative recording sessions or insurances were around! Either that, or no one has looked closely at *all* the factors involved from the beginning, because they cover so many medical disciplines as well as instrumental. Regrettably, perhaps because musicians feel their needs are not thoroughly understood, there is a distrust of the medical profession. It arises from many doctors' lack of understanding of a musician's drive to keep practising and performing, a drive characterized by ever increasing effort as performance ability dwindles, thereby aggravating injuries. A musician will modify muscle use, and adopt defensive postural habits, rather than seek advice and be told to stop playing for a while and lose work contacts.

There is always the question of how much to include and explain in a book like this. It is not intended as a scholastic tome, nor can it offer a panacea for all ills. The aim is to forestall most of the specific problems that beset musicians, and to fill some part of the gap between the 'Try and relax and play it this way, dear' (which displays a low level of knowledge), and the abstractions from medical treatise on anatomy, physiology, neurology, pathology and pharmacology, which musicians are unlikely to read. Too much information leads to a floundering reader and bewilderment, resulting in nothing being done; too little, and people make assumptions and bad mistakes, the source of help becomes a five-minute wonder, and is put aside.

I have decided to use plain english throughout, and banish medical jargon wherever possible. The aim is (a) to give only safe information for use as self-help (on the understanding that there is a great deal more available which requires hours of precise and devoted study); (b) for the book to be used as a resource for asking good, searchingly useful questions of practitioners of whatever school of thought.

Twenty-five years freelancing in music, and twelve as a practitioner in various sorts of complementary medicine, have taught me two things. First, that there is so much that could be and needs to be discussed between musicians, doctors and complementary medicine practitioners; second, that there are many things that can be done by musicians to smooth the way for themselves before resorting to professional medical help of whatever sort. It is equally important to recognise when you *do* need help, and to this end I have included some guidance as to the best avenue to follow. Even more can be done if the musician and medic understand each other's terminology. Then good communication is possible, damage is limited and the minimum of time wasted.

In humility I offer some of the solutions I have garnered from many sources. I know, from experience, that they work. I have also intentionally left out any suspicion of instruction in instrumental technique. Everyone has good and bad technical abilities, good and bad luck, and each of us tends to think that others have it easier. Actually there is no 'normal' life. There is a fulfilled life if we can be responsible for ourselves, have an awareness of all the chances, opportunities and choices there are out there, even if they are not decked out in Piccadilly-bright lights.

I hope my suggestions are helpful, that they will dissuade readers from the inappropriate philosophy of 'no pain, no gain', will curtail the need for excess alcohol and Beta-blockers, will encourage the provision of alternatives to coffee in rehearsal breaks and will otherwise encourage musicians to be responsible for their bodies as well as their instruments. I aim to widen knowledge, so that, knowing the possible future problems, musicians and teachers can adapt instrumental technique themselves *before* problems arise and become locked in so tight that steroids or surgery seem the only solution and the career is in ruins. Here are tools to adapt to your own use. I want to inspire you to climb out of any hole you may have dug for yourself in the name of 'doing it' more/better/faster. I want to enable you to be in charge and sort out your problems before they become chronic and you become their victim. I want to set you free to love what you do and communicate it, rather than living under the tyranny of 'playing the right note, at the right time, in the right place'. Prevention is always far better and cheaper than cure. This book is a treasure trove. The intention is not, however, that everyone should do *everything* in the book, but that those with a weakness or problem may find helpful ideas within its chapters.

The most important thing to remember, in whatever aspect of self-help you choose, is that you live with yourself 24 hours a day and are the only person inside your own skin. *You* know how you feel, better than anyone else can. That alone makes you some sort of an expert on yourself. However, I have to include the **all-purpose disclaimer** that 'before following the advice given in this book, readers are urged to give careful consideration to the nature of their particular health problem and to consult a competent physician if in any doubt. This book should not be regarded as a substitute for professional medical treatment, and while every care is taken to ensure the accuracy of the content, the author and the publishers cannot accept legal responsibility for any problem arising out of experimentation with the methods described.'

None of the techniques in this book will harm you if used as described and in moderation. (Nor will it harm you to ask professional advice. Whether or not you take that advice is *still* your choice, whatever anyone may say.) I hope it will bring to your attention the nature and purpose of pain, and the cost of ignoring it. This is certainly not a book for those who don't want to be responsible for their own health, who want someone else to 'fix' their problems, so that they can repeat the same destructive pattern which caused the problem in the first place. It is a book for those who, despite the occupational hazards, want to go on doing their job successfully, and look after themselves in an environment that is physically, mentally and chemically as benign as possible. *You* are your greatest asset. Never forget that.

Although it is essentially a self-help book, you may need another person to help you with muscle testing to find out what you need to know (such as exactly which muscle isn't functioning correctly). You do the corrections yourself. If you follow the correcting techniques as described here, your innate survival mechanism and healing ability then is able to do an expert job, if left alone to get on with it. These methods are also particularly good at removing that last residue of hesitancy and doubt in performance left following rehabilitation from injury or surgery, and for broadening your performance. You will therefore find scant mention of strapping and bandaging, or analgesics, and nothing that conflicts with modern medicine and physiotherapy. The techniques here come way before or way after all that.

How to use the book

1. Read the contents page to see how the book is laid out, and where the main blocks of information are. This will save you valuable time later.
2. Flick through page by page. This will only take a few minutes and will give you an overview of what is available, the format and diagrams.
3. Skim read (but beware of relying on this for memory), marking the pages relevant to you.
4. Read the rest of this chapter carefully.
5. Do the above four things NOW!!
6. At leisure, read each chapter *thoroughly;* especially read about what you can do if the only time available is a 15-minute rehearsal break, or the odd few minutes stuck in a traffic jam.
7. If none of the techniques in the book work for you, then either you are not following instructions carefully enough, or you need professional help from a doctor, physiotherapist, chiropractor, osteopath or dentist.

When looking for a practitioner of any description, understand that passing exams does not necessarily make a good practitioner; it only makes a good academic (who may live in an ivory tower). Exams do nothing to contribute to a practitioner's understanding of, or sensitivity to, a musician's needs, nor do they prevent mistakes being made (experience does that), but exams do guarantee a certain level of knowledge and code of ethics. Don't judge a practitioner either by the politeness of the receptionist, the decor or the numbers of machines with flashing lights. 'Some patients equate the use of advanced technology with "good" care and may be disappointed surprised or concerned if a thoughtful physician does not order a battery of tests'(Parmley, 1995). What you need is someone who understands what you are talking about. Get a local practitioner's name from the professional lists available or from British Association for Performing Arts Medicine, and then make your own enquiries as to what s/he is like.

Whatever advice you take, you will not derive the full benefit from it unless you follow it 100%. Don't half do it, or mess about doing a bit of this and a bit of that. Certainly don't double up what you have been advised to do either, in the hope that more equals better/faster etc. If you are dissatisfied with the treatment you have been given, before you change your treatment remember that there will have been good reasons for the prescription being given you exactly as it was. Perhaps you have now progressed beyond it. By all means ask for a second opinion, look things up, and ask *lots* of questions, but don't go around collecting opinions and 'rubbishing' all the previous practitioners you have visited. They will have done their best for you, particularly if you are as clear and specific as possible when you see them for the first time.

Standard medical treatment

If you think you need professional help, it's useful to know who is good for what. Ask around locally, but realise that your friends are not experts on your problem, only on theirs, and they may not be musicians. Understand, too, that doctors, because of the way they have been trained, tend to look only at the problem area and not at the whole person; they may perhaps also fail to realise the problem's special significance to you as a musician, so it's wise to take your instrument with you, if possible, to demonstrate what's wrong.

Generally speaking, **family doctors** only have time to treat you as Mr Average, not as the specialist artist that you are. They tend to deal with the problem mainly from a chemical point of view, with the aim of suppressing the symptoms chemically rather than getting at the cause of the symptoms. Whilst drugs are usually effective for damping things down, it's as well to remember that there isn't a drug in existence that doesn't have side effects for *somebody,* and to which you may or may not be susceptible. (See how to check these later.) Doctors are, however a good source of referral to specialists such as surgeons, physiotherapists, counsellors and some alternative practitioners such as chiropractors and osteopaths. You may then be able to claim fees on your medical insurance if you have one. Check first. Some GPs may not be interested in, or approve of, anything other than formal medicine, and you might have to do some educating! BAPAM (see References) have a Helpline, and will help you find a musicians' specialist.

As far as **surgeons** go, most are brilliant, but remember that surgeons have had years of training with a vested interest in using knives. Once you have something surgically cut or removed, it can't be replaced or returned to its original state. There will always be inelastic scar tissue to cope with. Please, try a chiropractor or an osteopath first. Surgery is often effective but must be considered a last resort, as surgeons 'often have a reputation for being knife-happy, insensitive and crude'. . . 'The surgeon should be right at the bottom of the filter' (I. Winspur FRCS FACS, 1995). Surgery is 'salvage' work.

Physiotherapists have a range of machinery, massage techniques and exercises developed specifically for pain removal, strengthening muscles and joints, and for improving breathing function. They are wonderful in the first stages of rehabilitation after injury or surgery. They are also limited to the area that the doctor specifies they may treat, rather than being able to treat the whole body. Treatment tends to be in blocks of six sessions followed by a reassessment. They don't usually have time to observe how your playing is being affected.

Alternative and complementary disciplines

There is contention as to whether disciplines are 'alternative' or 'complementary' to conventional medicine. Each discipline has its advocates and its limitations. My preference is to think in terms of 'complementary', as I do not believe any one discipline to have all the answers for everyone. Whatever type of treatment is first selected, it frequently proves to be an 'entry point' for the patient, from which, given a sympathetic practitioner, other avenues of help may open. The most important thing for *all* practitioners is to be open to new ideas, as well as knowing all they can about their own discipline. Beware the bigot who tells you 'Nothing can be done to help you, you will just have to live with it' when what they mean is 'I don't know how to help you'. Where possible I have included a book list at the end of each chapter (see References) for you to investigate each of the techniques further yourself.

There are some conventionally trained medical doctors who have also studied **homeopathy.** They will usefully give you an opinion based on both disciplines. The traditional, but superficial level of homeopathy I suggest is discussed later in the chapter.

The techniques of most **osteopaths** and **chiropractors** overlap with those of physiotherapists, but are more wide ranging and don't need a doctor's permission because their training is deemed to be alternative and primary. Most also have a 'licence to diagnose' and can take and read X-rays. They are not limited to treating just backs either (despite popular belief!) and may also look at your diet and gut function, ergonomics and work stresses, and even at your family background from the point of view of stress.

What's the difference between osteopaths and chiropractors? Originally quite a lot on the theoretical side. Now there is less difference, and, to allay any nonsense you may have heard – please note – there are rough and gentle practitioners in both professions. I've met brutes and butterflies, frogs and princes in both worlds. What matters is how good they are for *you*. I personally believe that minimum force should always be used. Often the better the practitioner, the less force is needed to get the same result because of better body positioning. Therein lies part of the artistry of adjustment; it shows greater respect for the patient's body by working with it, persuading, coaxing, but not imposing a new 'correct' alignment on it or overloading the system, which causes withdrawal, tension and pain. However, having said that, some people don't feel they have had a treatment unless they have been bashed about and wrung out like a dishcloth because they adhere to the 'no pain, no gain' fallacy.

In a nutshell:

1. Osteopaths look at the body as a mainly fluid medium (you are, after all, 70%+ water), and talk about the 'supremacy of the artery'. Chiropractors believe that everything is controlled by the nervous system, a bit like a printed circuit or a communications network. Both believe that these systems can be upset or affected by tissue tension or by hard objects such as bony malalignment or other space-occupying lumps and bumps getting in the way of free flow. The body will work optimally and efficiently when everything is in good alignment for the purpose for which it was designed, i.e. 'Structure equals Function'.

2. What do they do about it when things go wrong? Osteopaths slacken off muscle tension by massage, and then use the long levers of the body (e.g. by pulling the top half of your spine against the lower half, to lever the bone in the middle of your back (which is the cause of the problem) into alignment). Chiropractors go straight to the spot and use precise alignment of drive, and employ speed of adjustment to overcome muscle tension by surprise. Both methods are concerned with control of adjustments to minimise risk of injury, and they borrow techniques from each other.

3. Both have interesting adjunctive techniques which are somewhat parallel and deal with cranial work, and both have contributed to Applied Kinesiology – of which more later.

Dentists have far more effect on our lives than even some of them admit. Obviously any wind or brass player will be aware of how important they are to embouchure and teeth alignment, but string players, pianists, percussionists and others may not realise that what goes on in your mouth can affect jaw alignment and head balance. They can even affect the balance of the rest of the body through the muscles of the neck and back. (For instance it's not uncommon for a proud or ill-fitting filling to cause back pain! More of this later as well.)

Visiting an alternative or complementary practitioner

Practitioners of all disciplines vary enormously in the way they treat patients. It depends on the nature of your problem and the time both you and they have available. Whenever possible, *take your instrument with you,* so you can explain and, if necessary, demonstrate your problem precisely.

On the first visit you should have a thorough history taken of your complaint and how it affects your playing. You may also be asked about your near family, and a whole lot of *seemingly* irrelevant questions (such as a question about fat digestion when you have come about a shoulder pain.) Such questions are not asked for fun, but because they may have a bearing on your problem which is not obvious to you (in the instance given, gall bladder malfunction occasionally refers pain to the shoulder). A physical examination may be given, and also various orthopaedic and muscle tests. Urine sample and X-ray are sometimes taken and, much more rarely, a blood sample.

If no samples were taken, then you may be told immediately what the findings and recommended course of treatments are. Where samples are taken you may have to wait a few days for these to be analysed, and then return for a full diagnosis. You will often not get actual treatment until this second visit. You may be asked to sign a consent form and a letter may be sent to your GP. If X-rays were taken, anything abnormal that can be seen should be explained to you. You should be given an idea of how many treatments you need, how long it will be before you can play again (if applicable) and the cost.

Now is your chance to ask all the questions you want, so come prepared. Ask what you can do to help yourself. Ask if the ideas and exercises suggested in this book are appropriate, or need to be adapted or extended for you in a way you hadn't thought of. Make sure you have all these details clear before you sign the consent form, and then do, properly and conscientiously, all homework exercises you are given. Ring up later and ask if you are not sure of some details. Meanwhile cosset yourself with Tender Loving Care (TLC). Keep warm, eat sensibly and don't push yourself to do things you find a strain.

Self-help

So far I have decribed the available professional medical treatments. What follows is a description of some of the main techniques used in this book. These are those that you can safely do for yourself or with your nearest and dearest. They are not the only techniques available, nor are they the only techniques I advocate. Although mentioning them, I have not, for instance, included Alexander or Feldenkrais techniques or acupuncture; you need a trained practitioner for these. I might, however, suggest the use of traditional five-element acupuncture law without needles within Applied Kinesiology. Because of this, if you go to an alternative or complementary medicine practitioner, do tell them what you have been up to on your own, so there can be no misunderstanding or conflict of treatment.

Applied Kinesiology. This is the umbrella technique I use which combines ideas from chiropractic, osteopathy, cranial work, dentistry, acupuncture law, soft-tissue work and lymphatic drainage, nutrition and anti-stress techniques. To be a recognised practitioner you must have had four years full-time training in basic sciences, and have a licence to diagnose (as ICAK – International College of Applied Kinesiology – law stands at the moment), but there are many allied therapists of lesser standing, and techniques the general public can use (consult La Tourelle/Courtenay, *Thorson's Introductory Guide to Kinesiology* – see References). AK holistically views the body as being affected by the mental/physical/chemical triad (which is also affected by environment and heredity). When one side of that triad is distorted, e.g. by emotional stress, the other two sides are affected also, and you may get head and backache, plus indigestion as well! AK also considers the five factors that affect the supply of energy to nerves, blood vessels and their derivatives within the body. AK uses the diagnostic tool of simple muscle testing, which bypasses the logical brain, to reach the deeper causes of pain, dysfunction, weakness and poor coordination of which you may not be consciously aware.

What is portrayed in this book is but the tiniest fraction of what is now available to fully qualified ICAK practitioners, and what has been researched and presented for peer review. Don't be dismayed! Although the research is high powered, most of the techniques and instructions here are child's play. You only need a pair of hands.

Spontaneous positional release. Muscles move bones. The smaller muscles can have a devastating effect, but because they are often not on the surface of the body and not obvious, they get forgotten. Those most frequently in trouble are the ones between the bones of the spine, especially in the neck, between the shoulders and in the lower back. They can go into cramp just as easily as the big back and shoulder muscles. This technique, by using accurate positioning, then holding with slight pressure and waiting, allows each small muscle to undo itself and release the tension on the bones to which it's attached.

Behavioural barometer, goal balancing, visualisation, reframing and affirmations. These are all ways by which you can replace negative thoughts, attitudes and actions with positive ones, so that you can be successful at what you want to do with the minimum of stress. They allow you to break down the barriers and subconscious sabotage with which you surround yourself, and align the conscious with the subconscious will, so that you attack life with *all* systems on GO.

Inner game. This is another method of getting people to perform to the best of their ability rather than the worst, by displacing concentration away from themselves and from success/failure so that the body's natural coordination is not short-circuited and can perform naturally.

Bach flower remedies. These are flower essences at homeopathic strength. They are wonderful at changing your mood, and with it the energy available to you, especially when combined with the behavioural techniques outlined in the previous two paragraphs.

Homeopathy. This is a way of treating ailments, which is recognised by a few GPs. It works by subtly encouraging the body's strong natural healing processes specific to your ailment by the administration of incredibly small doses of a substance which may cause the same symptoms in a healthy person. Symptoms are regarded as the overt sign that the body is in action, healing and defending itself e.g. by burning up (fever) or throwing out (rashes) the offending foreign body or substance that has invaded it. The character of the whole person is considered and encouraged, not just the symptoms of the rash or the fever. In this way homeopathy beautifully compliments AK and the gentler forms of chiropractic and osteopathy, whereas the blanket suppression of symptoms practised in conventional medicine seems more aligned to the imposition of the bio-mechanical model of the tough manipulators.

Reflexology. This foot massage is generally diagnostic by highlighting specific points on the feet which seem to have reference to specific areas of the body. When there is malfunction in a specific body area, painful deposits of urate crystals occur on the corresponding area of the foot. Diagnostically it may not be nearly as pinpoint accurate as conventional medicine, but I tend, when working on a specific area, to include the relevant reflexology point as a bonus. In any case, people often find a good foot massage very relaxing, which is beneficial in itself.

Bates eye method. At the end of the last century and the beginning of this, W. Bates, an oculist, put together a series of eye relaxation and exercise techniques. Although they improved vision so much that, for some, glasses became redundant, they were extremely boring. This meant that people often didn't persevere with them and, sadly, gave up. Bates' ideas have recently been modernised and made more user-friendly by various practitioners. Since reading music demands both good near and far vision under stress, especially in the orchestral world, these techniques seem to me to be essential as an auxiliary to general fitness and stamina. They take little time and no special equipment, but do need persistence.

Five-minute wonders

Here is a short list of self-help techniques and things to do on a train or bus, in your hotel on tour, or in that odd five minutes when you can't do any thing else to stop being bored. You may need to be alone! Chapter numbers in parentheses refer you to a more detailed description of a particular technique.

1. Stretch and wriggle to stop cramp.
2. Recharge your (meridian) energy by meridian running (Chapter 15).
3. Head, neck squeeze and facial massage for relaxation (Chapter 15) and then wring out your face flannel or hand towel in as hot water as you can find and put it over your face, or brush you hair 100 times with a bristle brush to wake up.
4. Give yourself a foot massage and then pop your feet into warm water.

5. Isometrics, eye and breathing exercises.
6. Lymphatic drainage points, or massage points (Chapter 10).
7. Visualisation and/or similar techniques; self-talk (Chapter 7).
8. Memory rehearsal (Chapter 3).
9. Technique clarification (Chapter 7).
10. Leisure planning (Chapter 5).
11. Take a five-minute holiday (Chapter 8).

Main point summary

1. You are a human being as well as a musician, a dot interpreter, technician and gymnast.
2. You have an inside and an outside environment.
3. There are many alternative and complementary medicine techniques to help you. Know which technique is best suited to which problem, and then give yourself the best you can afford – you deserve it!
4. Don't be frightened to ask for other expert advice if you need it.
5. Be ready with all the questions you want to ask when you visit a practitioner for the first time – write them down, and the answers too, since it's surprising how inaccurate the memory is when you are under stress.
6. Ask! Ask! Ask!, and then remember, you are also your own body's expert. Trust your own judgement! Be responsible.

REFERENCES
1. **Beighton P.** (1990) *The Ehlers-Danloss Syndrome,* William Heineman Medical Books, London
2. **Chaitow L.** (1974) *Osteopathy,* Thorsons, Harper Collins
3. **Connelly D.** (1979) *Traditional Acupuncture: The Law of the Five Elements,* Centre for Traditional Acupuncture Inc., Maryland USA
4. **Courtenay A.** (1987) *Chiropractic for Everyone,* Penguin
5. **Goodheart G.** (ed.) *The Acceptance of Applied Kinesiology* (a short monograph of articles limited to those outside the chiropractic profession)
6. **Goodheart G. and Schmitt W.** *Applied Kinesiology,* 20567 Mack

Av., Grosse Pointe Woods MI 48236 USA

7. **Lambert C.** (1992) *Clinical Review. Hand and Upper Limb Problems of Instrumental Musicians* (British Journal of Rheumatology 31: 265-271)

8. **La Tourelle M, Courtenay A.** (1992) *Thorson's Introductory Guide to Kinesiology,* Harper Collins

9. **Lederman R.** (1989, 1991) *Peripheral Nerve Disorders in Instrumentalists* (American Neurological Assn. Journal of Occupational Health and Safety)

10. **Mandel S.** (1990) Overuse Syndrome in Musicians (Vol. 88/2 Post-Graduate Medicine)

11. **Moulton B, Spense S.** (1991) *Site-specific Muscular Hyperactivity in Musicians with Occupational Upper Limb Pain* (Vol.30/4 p375-386, Behavioural Res. Ther.), Pergamon

12. **Norris R.** (1993) *The Musician's Survival Manual: A Guide to Preventing and Treating Injuries in Instrumentalists,* International Conference of Symphony and Orchestral Musicians

13. **Owen E.R.** (1985) *Instrumental musicians and repetition strain injuries,* Journal of Occupational Health and Safety 1, p135-139

14. **Parmley W.** (1995) *The Decline of the Doctor-Patient Relationship* (Journal of the American College of Cardiology Vol. 26 no.1 July p287/8)

15. **Ramsell J.** (1989) *Questions and Answers Clarifying the Basic Principles and Standards of Bach Flower Remedies,* Albry Printing Co.

16. **Winspur I.** (1995) *The Professional Musician and the Hand Surgeon* (Performing Arts Medicine News, Vol.3 no.3, Autumn), BAPAM

ORGANIZATIONS

British Association for Performing Arts Medicine (BAPAM), 18 Ogle St, London W1P 7LG. *Tel:* 0171-636 6860; *fax:* 0171-636 6880; *helpline:* 0171-636 6960

CHAPTER 2

Musician versus Instrument I

Fitness to play
Freaks, facts and fallacies
Physique, beginners' methods, prostheses
Teachers and selection
Ossification
How you grow
Muscles and joints
Posture, imagineering and mirror imaging

Fitness to play

This chapter is directed not only at hopeful parents, but also at professionals so that they can look back and understand where things started to go wrong for them. At all levels of playing, it is curious how little notice is taken of fitness to play. In the UK, beginners are frequently chosen by teacher availability, because a specific instrument is required in the school orchestra, the family heirloom was found in the attic, or because of some other, equally serendipitous reason. Later, once school and college are survived, the general expectation is that you will fend for yourself. This happens at a time when you suddenly go from playing for an hour or so a day to six or more as a budding professional. Any athlete similarly placed has a coach, physiotherapist and sports medicine clinic to attend to all acute and chronic injury needs. The only exception to this situation seems to be singers, and even they tend only to have musical coaching with some acting and language tuition. However, because they are usually older when they are really under performance strain, they can cope better.

When the damage has become chronic because the early-warning signs and symptoms have been ignored, musicians usually have to attend rheumatology clinics or have surgery. Very few GPs have any idea of the degree of precision and dexterity required in instrumental playing; they are only trained to know what 'normal' requirements are for everyday life. This means that early-warning signs are missed, ignored or put down to neuroses. There is an almost universal inability amongst musicians to recognise signs of damage in the early stages and the possibilities available for help across the board (both conventional and alternative). Only through reading medical research papers did I discover the Performing Arts clinic in Edinburgh, and that was after 25 years in the music profession! In London there is the computerised British Performing Arts Medicine Trust, who send you to a practitioner via your GP, so that expenses are defrayed by the National Health Service, but this is after the damage has been done.

The average conservatoire appears to have no instruction in the field of injury prevention, chronic stress reduction and prevention, self-help, performance anatomy, physiology and bodily awareness, diet, sleep patterns, ergonomics and posture, and the art of instrument carrying. All these have been available as part of the curriculum for the past eight years in Trondheim, Norway. Facilities there include a preliminary student assessment, effective practice-habit building, and a basic training in self-observation and self-knowledge, all of which is obligatory. Students have an awareness of available facilities, communication and follow-up. There is also a built-in 'quiet time' (for just as music is composed of notes and the spaces between them, so should a musician's life be). Their advanced programme is voluntary, it can be a degree course module and is particularly relevant to future teachers.

Recently the Alexander and Feldenkrais methods have been virtually the only preventative techniques known at music colleges in this country, and there's almost nothing written about predisposition to mechanical malfunction and subsequent disease in musicians. This is sad because so much pain and so many over-use syndromes could be prevented by the simple techniques and methods of tension reduction discussed here. It's odd that we have had to wait for the advent of VDUs for the public to become aware of repetitive strain injury and the like. Musicians have been suffering from these for years. They have been finding out the hard way, having to undo damage by backtracking to first principles and by unlearning bad habits and retraining. What a waste of time, money and effort!

Basic body awareness has many benefits, but is so rarely taught. Maximum efficiency should be improved by increased consciousness of how well our bodies can work with minimum effort. We can learn to organise the relationship between different parts of our bodies when we become aware of the existence of those different parts, then direct the work through to a part of the brain which has instinctive patterns and reflexes. Emotional energy can flow unblocked through a free body once we know where these blocks are. Both Alexander and Feldenkrais techniques are excellent for this.

One of the best ways to start exploring body awareness is to do all the activities of normal daily living the other way round i.e. clean your teeth with the other hand, cross your legs the other way, change hands on a broom, write with the other hand. Of course you will feel awkward, but most of the ineptitude is inexperience not inability, and you gain insights as to how, when and where you hold unnecessary tension. Do some imagineering (see below). The next stage is to observe your playing in the same light.

The Feldenkrais method – awareness through movement and functional integration – enhances spontaneity and pleasure in natural human movement by awakening body intelligence. Your posture improves as you learn to adjust your response to gravity, and enhance the cooperation between all parts of the body. You actively experience the choice, range and ease of motion available to you, rather than just intellectually understanding it. The Alexander technique also teaches you self-awareness so that you can return to appropriate body and muscle tone when you finish using those muscles. There are now teachers attached to most music colleges.

Nobody stresses general medical and bodily fitness to a musician, although it is self evident to any athlete. All thought and effort go into instrumental technique and interpretation and almost none into *that specific human-being who has to perform that specific task,* and yet, surprise, surprise, we all differ mentally and physically, in general bodily stamina and agility. This is before we even consider the vagaries of make, layout and size of the specific instrument which is to be played.

Freaks, facts and fallacies

No consideration is given to the fact that often the heights of instrumental technique and the heights of artistry are invented by people with unusual anatomy. Paganini almost certainly had Ehlers-Danlos disease, an inherited syndrome which, in a person with normal-sized limbs, gives extreme laxity in the joints and very loose skin (amongst other things). This diagnosis agrees with contemporary medical accounts rather than the caricature drawings which exaggerate his finger length (as in Marfan's disease, see below).

Paganini's compositions, particularly the Caprices, created for and by such extra free movement to astonish and amaze, are now considered normal fare for any aspiring violinist. They are *de rigueur* for international competitions, despite the fact that violin neck-lengths, pitch and string tension have all increased, leading to even greater mechanical difficulty. All is sacrificed on the altar of a brighter sound. I don't mean that one should never play Paganini's compositions, but although the average player may have developed some extra flexibility with modern violin methods, the fact remains that Paganini had abnormal joint mobility. Violinists with normal anatomy will only store-up trouble for themselves by judging themselves by such standards. Player beware!

Pianists are usually more sensible, and few with small hands will attempt Rachmaninoff or Brahms without some judicious editing for performance. Both composers had physical abnormalities. Rachmaninoff inherited Marfan's Syndrome, which causes all the bones to grow very long and thin and also causes joint laxity. Looking at Brahms, he shows the signs of acromegaly – over-activity of a growth hormone which causes a large forehead and jaw and large (often knobbly) hands.

Conversely, looking at his piano music, Mozart had small, neat hands. How he coped with playing the viola I can't imagine, unless his instrument was under 16 inches or had a very small stop. Schumann had normal-sized hands but there is the theory that he had extra tight binding ligaments across them, and between the base of the fourth and fifth fingers, and that it was in trying to overcome this with a finger hoist that he did permanent damage to his hands. Posterity benefited by his concentration on composition, but I wouldn't advocate following his example!

Most instrument sizes are fixed, but where they are not (e.g. the viola) there is a tendency to play an instrument that is too large or has too long a stop, because the lower timbre is preferred or because small musicians subconsciously compensate for their own small stature. Sacrifices are inevitable in one area or another; usually it is the human-being that pays (or his technique). Whereas one can build stamina to cope with an instrument that is too heavy, there is little one can do to alter arm-length and hand-size without inviting retribution physically or mechanically, and usually both. Instruments which are too heavy invite poor posture, eventually limiting technique, because although, with time, the musician gains strength, the adapted posture becomes, through habit, the one which 'feels normal' and it never gets changed to what is now appropriate. Such musicians are consequently shocked when they see themselves on video or are 'corrected' by an Alexander teacher.

So, what is the ideal shape/size of person as opposed to instrument? What about children? What are the guidelines?

Physique, beginners' methods, prostheses.

As a very broad generalisation, small people move faster than large, young girls are more dextrous than young boys, the bigger you are the stronger you are, and men are more logical and one-track-minded and less flexible than women in the joints – especially in the wrist and elbow. Men's strength tends to be in the upper part of the body and women's in the lower. The same goes for the centre of gravity. According to Lederman (1994) 'Women are more likely to report musculo-skeletal problems than men'.

I know I'm stating the obvious, but certain instruments require physical size and even brute force; others require far more stamina and fine, fast motor movement. Whatever the type of movement required, it's always between certain very precise parameters governed by the technical dynamic abilities of that particular instrument (not to mention style of playing). It helps to have long arms if you wish to play the trombone, bass, harp or percussion; to have a wide palm if you chose the cello, viola, guitar, tuba, bassoon or piano. Hands that are 'square', with all the fingers of similar length, help enormously with coordination for all keyboard and upper string instruments, because the brain has less computation and adaptation to do to regulate finger fall. Long, flexible thumbs help keyboard players and bassoonists, and strong thumbs are essential to cellists, clarinet, oboe and cor-anglais players. Good pads at the ends of the fingers help most instrumentalists, giving airtight covering of the holes in a wind instrument, and making double-stopping easy on stringed instruments for example. Wide finger-tips, however, can get stuck between the black notes on a keyboard, and make playing in tune in the high positions on a violin very difficult.

Good sideways movement of an index finger that's not too long helps flautists and all string players, and there isn't a violinist who hasn't complained that his or her little finger is too short! Good wrists are as essential for percussionists as good lungs and diaphragm are to a wind player. Thin lips don't help brass playing, and good teeth are essential to any instrument that goes anywhere near the mouth.

Double-jointedness brings its own problems. Obviously, great flexibility lends itself to dexterity, but there is a greater need for extra stability, support and strength, or adaptation becomes inevitable. Once the tendency of a joint to collapse is controlled then the musician has the best of both worlds. Some double-jointedness may be acquired through years of playing, but regrettably this usually succumbs to arthritic conditions in later years as the body tries to support itself by growing extra bone or other fibrous material around such joints. Clicking and trigger-finger effects may be observed, with an eventual decreased range of movement.

Any professional musician out in the field will know most or all of the above, but children starting out at school won't (and their adoring parents may not either). Attracted by a specific sound an instrument makes, or by the media hype around a star on TV, a child may be quite the wrong size to have any chance of success at playing the chosen instrument. Even if a teacher is found, the child gives up because it's all too difficult and the dream is shattered. Guidance and patience is needed.

You have to wait until a child can easily stretch far enough to play some instruments. By 'far enough' I don't mean *just* reach, but reach with ease. For example, if a child can curl his or her fingers round the scroll of a violin when held under the chin in normal playing position, then there will be enough arm-length for the fingers to reach first position and still have some flexibility and range of movement to spare, so that playing will be relatively easy physically. Where the 'stop' of an instrument is unchangeable (as in an oboe, clarinet, bassoon etc.) the child should start on a similar, smaller instrument, like one of the recorder family, to develop dexterity, coordination and musical expression, and should (if applicable) wait for the second teeth to settle down. Ideally an orthodontist or periodontist should be consulted to assess the dental appropriateness of a woodwind or brass instrument, and for advice about teeth mobility and receding gums.

With the piano, either start the child on a spinet if you are lucky enough to get near one, or on an electronic keyboard where at least the action is lighter, using a low chair and table. If using a piano, find an old, light- action piano like a Bechstein, use a footstool for the child's feet (and don't worry about pedalling, which can be learned later). A lot of pop keyboard players play standing, so this is another, perhaps less classical, temporary solution. What's important is that the child's hands shouldn't tire or be stretched too far, and the forearms should be roughly parallel to the ground. (Yes, I know some people think otherwise because of their 'method' or 'school' of technique, but I am not concerned with any such method. Mechanical efficiency is what's important in this discussion and that should be to place the wrists in the middle of their range of movement i.e. level. Children have soft, pliable bones, of which more later in the chapter.)

Stringed instruments have the advantage of having smaller sizes made. Obviously quality of sound suffers, but I beg you not to be seduced into straining on an instrument which is too large in order to overcome this. Better a little less quality of sound now than aches, problems and pains later. The main disadvantage of starting small, and changing as the child grows, is that accuracy of intonation suffers at each change of instrument size, causing some insecurity. Mostly this is very short lived.

Gypsies got around the problem of violin size by learning everything in the high positions first on a full-sized instrument, resting the wrist against the body of the instrument, and only gradually progressing back to the first position as the child grew and could cope with both the greater stretch of the 'stop' distances, and leverage in the weight of the instrument. (This accounts for their amazing agility and technically brilliant bird imitations up in the snows of the rosin.) Starting that way either forced the traditional very low position of the violin on the chest, or the instrument was held with the scroll higher than the tailpiece so that the weight of the instrument fell inwards towards the neck as it sat on the collar-bone.

Most professionals have found their own compromise. However the combination of extreme methods or schools, added to the strengthened agility required, plus the stress of modern playing, all mean that the unfortunates who started in these methods are among the most frequent casualties who end up having to have surgery. Left hand and wrist dysfunction are the most frequent injuries of all among musicians.

Gripping *any* instrument – 'hanging on for dear life' to the one stable thing around, your instrument, while playing under stress – causes disruption of coordination, and over-use or misuse of muscles, tendons and their sheaths. This leads to inflammation and swelling of soft tissues, pain and compression of any nerves and blood vessels which are near by, or which supply the area in question. This then causes altered sensation and function of the area supplied by that nerve. I will go into more detail later, but examples here might be leg problems from Saphenous nerve compression in cellists, bass players and harpists, or perhaps right hand muscle spasm in wind and brass players, and of course the well-known ones of repetitive strain injury and brass player's lip.

Various *prostheses* or artificial supports have been developed for all sorts of needs, from simple pads to mechanical contraptions. There are dozens of shoulder-rest designs for the violin and viola, notably the Australian device which has a V-guide and socket attached to the middle bouts and an adjustable, curved, steel support which fits into the waist band, thus removing the weight of the instrument from both neck and left hand. I would add my own suggestion of using one of the more decorous forms of non-slip carpet underlay between the legs and lower bouts, to stop a viol that has no end pin slipping down as you play and causing ever-increasing hunched shoulders and knee tension. Tortelier angled end-pins were invented to stop this problem in cellists.

Wind players can use a post support to remove the weight of the entire instrument from the thumb, or a thumb-rest to move the weight of the instrument on to a part of the thumb nearer the hand. Saxophonists have clipped the lower part of the instrument to a key-toggle attached to the belt to relieve neck-strap strain, and for flautists, an angled headjoint to alleviate neck and shoulder problems has been invented; some adaptations in wind instrument keys, and thumb-rests for short fingers, are also available.

There have been various attempts at ear-plug and -shield design to protect against decibel damage, and the dental profession is slowly becoming aware of the incredible effect a filling can have on a brass player's career. Wheels are often attached to various heavy instrument cases to prevent back injury.

Aural and visual problems are also discussed later. Suffice to say that, if the child is musical and has a good sense of rhythm but a poor sense of pitch, don't suggest an instrument where every note has to be pitched (like any of the violin family), but select a 'ready made', such as most brass, wind and keyboard instruments. There's nothing worse than putting your heart and soul into playing only to have your effort dismissed because it is 'out of tune' (the assumption being that you are, therefore, a bit 'tone deaf').

Teachers and selection

Having decided what instrument, the next hurdle is which teacher. In these days of educational cutbacks there may be little or no choice, or nothing at all, at school, so a private teacher must be sought. If the child shows any sign of reading and learning problems, then before starting I suggest you contact the British Dyslexic Society, which has a lot of information and lists of specialist music teachers.

The first priority is to find someone who still loves music and isn't just going through the motions to earn a living. Next, this teacher must love *people*. The teacher must be a good, inspiring communicator with the patience of Job and an affinity for children, so as not to terrify the child out of playing before the first lesson is through. It takes a special sort of teacher to teach a beginner. A sound technique is important of course, but so is instilling a love of playing and knowing when to pass the bright child on. The older the child, the more important it is that the teacher should have the same body type as the child and thereby understand the physical problems inherent in being that shape and playing that instrument. Don't make the mistake of choosing for a teacher a technical genius who has never had to struggle to acquire technique, since such teachers are less likely to understand what ordinary mortals have to suffer to attain what comes naturally to them. Anyway, teachers who are *that* good are likely to be away on tour too much to give their pupils the necessary continuity. The worst you can do is to subject the child to your own, or the teacher's, Dickensian despotic terrorism, which comes from lack of respect and trust in the child's precious potential. This is, after all, 'a fire to be lit, not a pot to be stuffed full of facts'. Give a child a Dickensian 'Gradgrind' and he or she will end up a bundle of nerves and/or hate playing for ever more.

Teachers so often teach the way they were taught. They haven't really thought things through, and continue the faults of that method, adding to it their own shortcomings, so that the unfortunate pupil gets a double dose of unhelpful 'teaching'. Typically, XYZ scales and studies are taught, or exam syllabuses followed, no matter what the child's need. No real thought is given to that child's individual anatomy. The idea that an early start means good adaptation is ridiculous: such a child simply becomes 'adulterated'. Children have less bad postural habits early on, agreed, but the emphasis should be on *integration with the instrument* not adaptation to it, which simply builds future problems. (See bone ossification below.) With some teachers, the dots and dynamics on the page are so slavishly followed in the rare piece the child plays, that this, too, is treated like a study, and all musical communication is squashed out or shattered. In contrast, some teach no technique at all, with resultant sloppy playing. Both methods, unremedied, lead to failure later.

The most memorable lessons for me were when technique was not in question and we were inspired to create a picture or a story for the audience. I was able to share my enthusiasm, joy and glee with the other members of my ensemble at what we were learning together. We played 'out of our skins' and communicated it in no uncertain terms. We *played* in all senses of the word, and playing is the best way of learning.

It is also worth noting that if children are to achieve a high standard of orchestral playing, they have to be able to see both their music and the conductor clearly at the same time. Two sets of glasses, or music stands which are too high or too low, won't do, and place a child at an unfair disadvantage!

When considering children's potential, parental size and general environment should be taken into account *before* a teacher is sought and financial commitment entered into. How much is each child likely to grow, and will they get the parental support that they need?

When I was in the USSR, the selection (both for sport and music) of potential international competition winners for propaganda purposes, took place before the children were sent to school. For music, children were chosen for intelligence, coordination, flexibility and dexterity, aural acuity and ability to distinguish pitch and rhythm, their physical attributes and those of their parents. They were assessed for their main attitudes in respect of 'success achievement' (their determination to succeed when playing games with other children) or 'failure avoidance'. The type of personality (explosive/stable, sociable/loner) and degree of speed/stamina etc. were also assessed. The children were then matched with appropriate instruments to see which appealed most.

Specialist training followed, and the best went to the special schools and on to the conservatoires, where they led privileged lives compared to everyone else. The hard side of this for them was that they were subjected to continuous competition. As soon as they reached the minimum eligible age they competed at local level, proceeding later to home county, country, region, federation and national levels. Winners were awarded a highly coveted international passport. This meant that, by the time they actually competed internationally, they had been perfoming the required repertoire from memory for almost a year, and were totally 'competition proof'. The far better living conditions that they experienced when abroad as compared to those at home, meant that they thought they were in clover, and were very certain that at least one of the delegation would win first prize. There was the underlying pressure that not to do so was rather a disgrace, but what a grooming and no wonder they won so much at the rest of the world's expense! These performers were expected to have an excellent instrumental technique completed by the time they *entered* the conservatories, not as a result of being there (as it tends to be in the UK). Their breadth of repertoire, therefore, was enormous. It was studied with the professors, who were probably international artists. Any remaining technical weaknesses were worked at with the assistants, who were tough as old boots because they were answerable to the professors. Lessons were normally master-class style. Exams (once a term) were always played from memory and judged by *all* the professors, so everyone knew how you played. There was no hiding! You might also be made an assistant for a while, especially if you only came second in a competition! What a hothouse! Officially you aimed at being a soloist for the 'Glory of Communism'. Unofficially it was to get an international passport, and any thought of chamber music and ensemble playing was regarded as being rather a waste of time!

To return from such giddy heights, the above goes to show how important temperament is to the performing artist, but to begin in the right place also helps. Look for the winner in whom everything fits. An extrovert with a fast, facile mind would enjoy the challenge of the violin, flute, cornet or percussion. A more musically introspective mind might prefer an instrument less given to pyrotechnics, speed and brilliant gymnastics, and is usually less exposed, such as the horn, clarinet or viola. Make no mistake, however: to get to the top in any aspect of music you have to have a killer instinct and a really tough hide to cover the sensitive part that makes you a good musician. You must have self-discipline, single-mindedness and determination, and not mind the hours of loneliness, practice and travel which get worse as you get better.

Ossification

With age and size we must also deal with heredity and bone ossification (or calcification). Whilst most children seem to outgrow their parents, it is unlikely that four-foot-six, short-armed parents will produce a six-foot-six, long-armed professional bass player for an offspring, no matter how keen and supportive they are! Having said that, it's as well to remember that children grow in spurts. I was short for my age at eight and was considered for special ballet lessons. My mother had the sense to say that as my father was six foot two and she was five foot nine I would probably grow. I did, and I'm now six foot, so she saved a lot of money and I a lot of heart-ache!

As children develop, their musculo-skeletal system alters dramatically. Changes in angulations, rotations and longitudinal growth of the long bones of the limbs, and concurrent changes from soft cartilage to hard bone are still continuing. Whilst I laud the Suzuki method of teaching children by a natural 'osmotic' process, together with their mother in the same way they learn to speak, great care should be taken. First, attention should be paid to the way a child will copy posture, body use and muscular tension from its parents, mimicking without knowledge or understanding their faults, with consequent future damage. Second, remember about ossification, especially before the age of seven. Everyone knows about the baby's soft spot, but few realise that it's not the only area that hasn't fully calcified and hardened. All the shapes of a new-born's bones are there, but in soft, malleable, cartilaginous form. The process of calcification and mineralisation needed to make the bones strong and hard continues until the age of 25. (In some people a few bones, such as parts of the breastbone, never become fully hardened and joined.)

Bones calcify and harden in various ways. Most commonly, a series of centres within the cartilage will calcify first, subsequently spreading and joining up, often around the age of puberty. In long bones, like the thigh and shin, plenty of space has been left for growth, but problems can occur where muscles, attached to these areas of bone which are still growing, are trained to be too strong too early. They then pull the growing area of the bone out of shape, maybe permanently, and certainly cause misalignment problems, mechanical inefficiency and pain at the time, and arthritis later on. Osgood-Schlatter's disease is where this happens in young footballers' knees, but musicians can also suffer in their own special way.

So, which bones, and the ages at which they calcify, are relevant to a musician? When do they stop being bits of rubbery cartilage and join up? Read carefully both the descriptions and line drawings provided at the end of this section. It is all rather technical, and you may want to skip this bit, but the more you understand how the body grows, the better you will be able to look after it, and prevent future problems.

The ethmoid. This bone fits into the front of the skull behind the nose. It's like a walnut shell with wafer-thin, very easily broken divisions, giving passages through it. Ossification begins between the fourth and fifth years. It's an unusual bone in that it is one of the few with no muscle attachments, yet it often gets damaged in school sports such as boxing, football and rugby. Its shape is vital to singers and wind players to allow free airflow and resonance.

The occiput. This is the bone that forms the lower back part of your head, and through which your spinal cord passes to reach your brain. At birth this will still be in anything from four to eight parts, becoming one bone by the age of six.

The temporals. This bone includes the ear hole. You have one each side of your head, shaped like two wobbly wheels. Each is in two parts at one year but it's all one by puberty.

The sphenoid. Shaped like a big butterfly, this bone can hardly be reached from the outside of the skull, as it works like the supporting cross-struts inside. It's made up of 10 to 12 bits which unite early on. The sphenoid and occiput then join, but there is still some movement between them up to 25 years.

The maxilla. This is the upper jaw. It starts as two bones joined at the back by the soft palate. Initially its shape is longer from front to back, changing to wider from side to side in adulthood, and finally reverting to front to back length in old age.

All the large bones and the head (cranium) interlock with those surrounding them, having either tongue-and-groove or bevelled joints. This means that misalignment or torque on one bone is transmitted to all the others, and can affect the shape of the holes in the cranium through which the nerves pass from brainstem to ears, eyes, nose, mouth, tongue and neck.

The mandible. This is the lower jaw, which starts its ossification before birth, the two halves uniting in the first year. The upper and lower jaws in themselves are not usually a problem, whereas jaw dislocation, teeth mal-positioning and poor dentistry can be, as we shall see later.

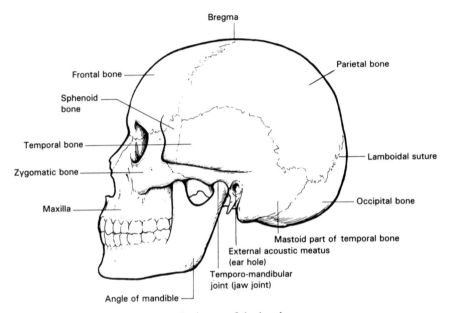

The bones of the head

The sternum. This is the breast bone and it starts as six bits. Total join-ing and ossification between the top two is rare except in old age. Bones two to five ossify from the top down between puberty and 25 years, and the sixth, the small pointed bone between the ribs, usually remains cartilagi-nous and can easily break off, protrude or be pushed in or to one side caus-ing breathing stress.

The ribs. These are formed from three centres each, and the parts finally unite between the ages of 16 and 25. The angle at which they are set can vary enormously and, as a consequence, so can the space within them, which houses the lungs and other essential organs such as the heart.

It is therefore important that they are not squashed by poor posture or a tightly held instrument.

The clavicles. These are the collar-bones. They are amongst the first bones to be calcified enough to be seen on an X-ray of a foetus. However the middle two ends don't finish calcifying until somewhere between 18 and 25 years, and can become misshapen by a badly fitting shoulder-rest.

The scapulae. These are the shoulder blades, which unusually calcify from the edges and corners, with most bits joined between 14 and 20 and the final bits by 25, though occasionally the tip of the shoulder stays separate.

The humerus. This is the upper-arm bone, which may be made from seven or eight bits. The lower end, by the inside of the elbow, joins up at five years but the outside doesn't join till 14, and the whole bone is not complete till 20 years.

The ulna. This bone makes up the elbow, the funny bone and the little-finger side of the forearm. The upper part near the elbow appears on X-ray by age ten and is usually complete by 16 years, and the lower end by the wrist appears at four years and is complete by the age of 20. The lower end is therefore more vulnerable in musicians.

The radius. This is the other bone in the forearm and is on the thumb side. It rotates round the ulna. The upper part appears on X-ray at five years and joins at puberty, whereas the lower part appears at two years and doesn't finally join until 20.

The carpals. These are the seven wrist bones, and they are all cartilaginous at birth. You can tell the age of a child by the number visible on X-ray – roughly one per year of age. Thus if a child starts to stretch to play a large instrument too early, damage can be done.

The metacarpals and digits. These are the bones that make up most of the palm of the hand and the fingers. They are calcified enough to be visible on X-ray as a series of small straight bones with little round bits in between, which don't all join up into the familiar three bones per finger until 20 years.

As can be seen from the above, very many of the bones are not properly formed until well into the 'teens or even early twenties. Cartilage is malleable, and live, young bones are pliable and plastic, with their honeycombed interiors well supplied with blood. This means that they are easily pulled out of shape by over-developed muscles, or compressed by pressure of an instrument that is too heavy or is gripped too hard rather than just supported. The teeth may already be very hard, but these other bones haven't developed that hardness yet. Notice that many bones are not properly hardened until puberty, or perhaps not until late twenties, yet there is an emphasis on starting to learn an instrument earlier and earlier – sometimes even at three years old. Children's bones break in splinters like a green stick. They don't snap across like an adult's. A joint pulled out of alignment in childhood will grow like that and is far more likely to be troublesome in later life. The extra wear and tear of all those years practising will simply make matters worse.

It would be interesting to do a study in 15 to 20 years time to compare the physical and mental stress problems experienced by children taught by the various methods (e.g. Suzuki versus Russian or European) who are now professional musicians of many years standing, and see if method, racial type and flexibility, or home background, made a big difference to the size and type of the emerging casualty list.

How you grow

Having described to you how bones grow, let us go back a stage and take a global view of *homo sapiens*.

The foetus starts off as two cells uniting and then dividing again and again till there's a blob of them that has no particular form. It then goes about getting a shape by differentiating the soup of contents in each cell. Those with more calcium in their soup get together to form cartilage shapes which later become bone. These act as spacers in the blob, to give it some stiffening, provide places to hang things on and protect the important vulnerable bits, such as the heart etc.,which move to the middle of the blob. Other bits develop lines of tension through movement and become muscles and ligaments. Calcium content also governs pliability. The less calcium, the more floppy; the more calcium, the stiffer and less elastic. The body continues this movement of calcium around for the rest of its life, as part of the replace-and-repair service which should be balanced according to need. (An example of the balance getting out of hand is to be seen in the family of arthritic diseases.)

35

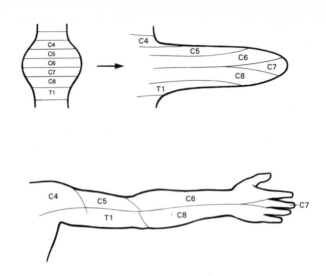

Arm growth and consequent neurological development

To go back to our blob – properly speaking our foetus. At one stage in its development the skin and the nervous system are one and the same. The rule is that once there is a nerve supply to an area it never changes. In general then, this means that the bits that stick out at the top are served by the nerves at the top of the spine and those at the bottom end by the bottom of the spine. How amazingly obvious, you will say! Well there are a few exceptions, because the foetus folds up on itself, bits grow at different rates, and a few of the internal organs decide to migrate. The lower limbs twist so that they bend the right way, and then finally the foetus decides after all that it wants to stand upright. Ah well, you can't always get it right first go, but it does help to understand what's happened to the nerve supply when you are trying to unravel what has gone wrong.

The main thing to remember is that, if you were to slice the body up like a loaf of bread, each slice would have its own nerve and blood supply plus a bit of overlap from the next door slice for safety and togetherness. It's also slightly pulled upwards because the spinal cord grew slower than the rest. So, the arm, elbow, wrist and fingers are supplied by nerves from the lower neck area, and the legs down to the toes from the middle to lower back, with the rest mostly pro rata in between. This is why problems in the lower back can show up as a foot, calf or knee problem, and neck problems can similarly affect any part of your upper limbs. It also works the other way round (by a referral system to be discussed later). Suffice it for now to say that, if any of the harder tissues such as the 'spacers' (bones) are out of alignment or are misshapen or scrunched up too close, the softer nerves and blood supply will be squashed or stretched, and you get starvation or a flood in the areas they supply, which does not make for good functioning. The diagram above shows you how the arm grew and therefore generally how its nerve and blood supply work.

Muscles and joints

Now let's look at the areas outside the bones, along those lines of stress that move the bones – that is **muscles.** They are comparatively simple things at heart. They are bundles of bundles of bundles of fibres, and each bundle is wrapped in its own a sausage-like skin. The ends of the bundle skins join and become tendon and the tendon then attaches to the bone's covering skin in a way that resembles Velcro. There are usually two ends to each muscle, one anchored to the stable bone or part of the body, the other end attached to the bone that is to be moved. Muscles only have one main function, to contract. They are not able to stretch by themselves, but need an opposing muscle pulling the opposite way to stretch the first muscle out again (known as agonist and antagonist). Muscle contraction is done at microscopic level by an electro-chemically operated ratchet system rather like the hand brake in a car. The electro-chemical fuel of raw materials (mainly sugar, oxygen and calcium) is supplied by the blood which also removes the waste products afterwards. This is why, when the supplies have run out, and the rubbish is uncollected after an unexpected game of tennis, the muscle gets tired and is stiff; you ache next day in places you didn't know you had! The only difference between the muscles of a slob and those of an athlete is not to do with quantity, but with training. This increases the throughput of goodies and waste collection from an athlete's plumper, stronger muscle fibres.

The next thing to consider, back on a larger scale now, is how muscles move bones. They act as levers, often against gravity. It may help to know the generally accepted range of muscle movement:

0 = No discernible movement or evidence of contractability

1 = Trace – a discernible twitch, but no real contraction and no joint movement

2 = Poor – a complete range of movement as long as gravity is eliminated

3 = Fair – there is complete range of movement against gravity but not against any extra resistance

4 = Good – the limb is moved against gravity but can only withstand a slight extra resistance

5 = The limb moves against gravity with full resistance

This last is considered the level of normal muscle strength. When our muscles feel weak they are mostly at grade three to four. Lower than this means there is some injury or disease.

Often hospitals, doctors and physiotherapists will get you back to four, or four-and-a-half, and assume you will do the rest yourself in your own good time. Sports coaches assume no such thing; they will have a graded ladder of exercises that you must be able to perform before you are allowed back on to the field, because they know that, if you go back too soon, the chances of re-injury are very high. There is nothing, as yet, available specifically for musicians, let alone specifically for any one instrument. I have provided a blueprint in Chapter 15, but you can easily construct your own with a book of relevant exercises and studies compiled from those already extant for each instrument, together with a medic or alternative practitioner who plays the same instrument.

Sometimes a musician's 'four-and-a-half' will be considered acceptable because it compares with a five in a normal person not trained as a musician. Beware. This is where other muscles are then subconsciously tensed to provide support during playing. A different/less appropriate set of muscles is used, or a postural change is made in some way to compensate. After a while these new muscles, which were neither built, nor trained for the job, start to complain too, and are more susceptible to injury; so again, without consciously realising, yet more muscles are recruited and a chain of events is set up. Frequently it's only the last lot of muscles which are painful, but trying to remove the problem by concentrating the treatment on them will do no lasting good. This is because, in themselves, they are not the main causative problem. They are merely trying to compensate for the previous unsolved injuries, and will go on being painful, or the pain will recur, until the original problem is sorted out.

You can see this easily in everyday life if you carefully observe the way a child of three walks and then a person of over 70. The gait and posture of the old person will more probably be due to a large collection of unresolved problems than to age itself. In the same way, a practised eye can spot, a mile off, people who play any one-sided instrument such as the flute, violin, guitar, horn etc., because their one-sided posture has now become their 'normal' posture.

Between any two adjacent bones there are **joints,** allowing varying degrees and direction of movement. Usually they are like hinges, held together by ligaments and having muscles that work them. Often several muscles work together as a group to flex or bend the joint, with an opposing group to extend or open it out. They are called the flexor group and the extensor group. (There are also rotators – pronator and supinator – and opposers, and I will deal with the other types of joint that occur in the upper limbs in Chapter 9.)

All muscles have Latin names which explain what they do, their shape or where they are. Take *extensor pollicis brevis* as an example: literally 'the extensor of the thumb that is short'. By logical deduction, there must also be a longer one somewhere nearby that does something similar, and there is: the *extensor pollicis longus.*

Coordination is not a local event. It happens in the brain in conjunction with your visual input, which is why some people give themselves an extra sense of security by looking at their hands when they play. Within muscles and joints there are also specialised nerve endings which tell you how contracted the muscle is, and where the joint is in relation to the body and in space. They are called *proprioceptors* and have set levels which protect you from over-flexing or over-extending. However, ligaments, muscles and their tendons can tear, which upsets the proprioceptive setting locally, and that has the effect of shutting down the muscles around the joint until it has healed. Occasionally they then don't reset properly. I will explain how to reset them with Reactive Muscle technique in Chapter 15.

Sometimes, too, you find that these joint proprioceptors are more useful than touch to judge distance, because they register larger movements.

For instance when changing position on the violin or viola, I found it more helpful to judge accurately with the angle of my elbow flexion than by the feel of the string as it slid under my fingers. Strings, fingerboard and the thickness of skin on the end of my fingers all change minutely (and are therefore less reliable), my elbow doesn't. Of course I backed it up with all the other contact points one has between hand and instrument, but the change of emphasis made all the difference to my intonation. Suffice it here to say that you have potentially as good a muscular (kinaesthetic) memory as mental or visual, and it will remember and replay both good and bad happenings physically, and sometimes a bad muscular memory needs to be defused after an accident. It also means you need to be careful how you practise! This will all be dealt with in Chapters 3 and 15.

No joint works on its own. It is always part of a chain of joints called the kinematic chain. Some chains are closed and form a circle, like all the joints in the shoulder or pelvic girdle; some are open like the joints of the arm or leg; but in all cases, what affects one joint – if deviant enough – will eventually affect all the other joints in the chain. At first sight a foot problem being the cause of a headache may seem a little unlikely or at least far fetched! But let me explain.

If you have a foot problem, you will either hobble or not put it down flat on the ground because it causes pain. This causes a twist in the knee joint which will make your hips unlevel, because your stride becomes uneven. Uneven hips mean your spine has to curve sideways (a scoliosis), and the back muscles compensate, causing your shoulders to tilt. Your eyes, however, like to look horizontally at the horizon, so the muscles that attach the uneven shoulder to the head must then have unequal tension on them, to compensate for the shoulder tilt and level the head, and therefore pull unequally on the back of the head. Immediately under those neck muscles, where they attach to the back of the head, is the greater occipital nerve which goes up over the top of the head. Squash this through extra muscle tension and there's your chronic headache. Knock-on effects like this happen all the time, but we don't always spot them, and the temptation to do a neck massage and take an aspirin (which is symptom treating) rather than to find and treat the cause at the other end of the body is all too understandable.

Speaking generally again, you have a bony support all the way up the back of your body – your spine – but there is a gap in the front. There's nothing bony in the front between your pelvis and your ribs to support you. The tendency, therefore, is to collapse forwards. Yet we have to stand up straight against gravity, so front and back must balance each other. Strong back muscles will hold the front of your ribs out of your pelvis, but if your stomach/abdominal muscles are weak and stretched, or you have a 'beer belly', your back muscles have to take up the abdominal slack, and so go into spasm – if they didn't you would fall over! You then complain of lumbago or some such. About 90% of the 'back' problems I see that are muscular, are actually *front* problems. If the victim is a physically well-endowed female who insists on wearing high heels all the time, then the natural body-balance is thrown to the winds and she is a back problem waiting to happen.

Posture, imagineering and mirror-imaging

Posture works against gravity and musicians must work with, and integrate their bodies and instruments with, the same forces. 'Proper posture is a way of blending with gravity, just as proper attitude is a way of blending with life.' Ideally it should be done with the minimum of effort. Some people take this to mean that we should be completely floppy. This is a misunderstanding. There has to be some muscle tone to counteract gravity or we would fall over. It's all a matter of how much tone or tension. Normal muscles never have no tone! Postural muscles pull against gravity all the time, but you don't normally get cramp because not all the fibres are involved at any one time. They work in rotation – as you will find out if you try to stand on one leg with your eyes closed.

Without your instrument, the perfect posture from the front is that your nose, chin, top of the breast bone and belly button are all in a vertical line which continues down between your knees and ankles. Eyebrows, earlobes, shoulders, elbows, hips, knees and ankles should all be level and horizontal. From the side, a plumb-line should seem to fall through the ear hole, the middle of the shoulder, just in front of the top of the thigh-bone, through the middle of the knee and end just in front of the ankle.

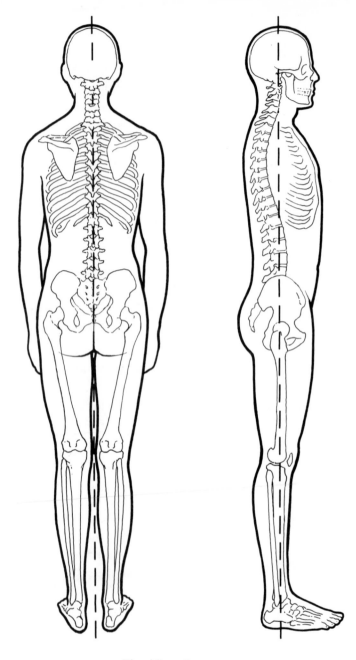

Plumbline alignment

To check your own posture, stick cotton on a long mirror with tape. Use one central piece as a plumb-line by tying something to swing on the end to get a true vertical before you stick it down, then stick several pieces horizontally as markers at shoulder, waist and knee height. Next put a line on the floor about three feet in front of the mirror and parallel to it and place your heels, shoulder-width apart, on that line. Now shut your eyes and wriggle till you feel you are standing straight. Don't cheat by looking: *Feel* what feels straight and right. When you are sure you have got it, don't move but open your eyes. Now check yourself against the lines on the mirror, both horizontal and vertical. Be critical.

Are you surprised by what you found? Everyone is. Remember that what you feel is right *is what you have got used to*. It is not necessarily right! Your posture is the sum of your unresolved past experience. We also copy the faults of our 'elders and betters'!

Wriggle about and correct what you see. Feels wrong? Well you can see it isn't. Don't try to force your body into the correct position or say to yourself 'Stop this' or 'Stop doing that'. Allow the tense bits to relax. You need to re-educate those feelings.

Do a spot of '**Imagineering**'. Starting at the ground, and with your eyes closed, check that both your feet are equally balanced weight-wise on the floor, from front to back, inside to outside the foot and between the feet. When you are satisfied they are, move up to the ankles and, in your imagination, twiddle the dials till your ankles are equally relaxed. Pop back down in your mind and recheck the feet. If all's well, move up to the knees and alter the dials here until they are balanced. Check below again and then move up to the hips. Employ the same process with the back, the shoulders and arms, and finally the head. Now open your eyes and check once more against the lines on the mirror. Your posture will be straighter and should feel easy and relaxed.

Now fetch your instrument (or move the mirror to it) and, as near as you can, repeat the first exercise and play a little before you open your eyes. Now where are you out of line? Is that really what you want, or are you contorting yourself unnecessarily? Now take up your instrument, think yourself into whatever is, for you, a very frightening situation, and play the most difficult solo you know with your eyes shut. Open them and see what's happened to your posture now and, while you were at it, what happened to your breathing? Unless you're a wind player or singer, ten-to-one you stopped breathing too! So when you have the hardest things to play, in the worst conditions, you also starve your brain of oxygen! Does that make sense? Of course not, yet 90% of musicians do this unless or until they are taught otherwise, or go to an Alexander or Feldenkrais teacher. Don't lose heart if you seem to be all out of alignment for no reason. You may just have to unlearn some habits that you originally acquired because it was the best you could do at the time. Now you know better, and can do better, let's look at how these postural habits are set up, and why.

There are two main factors to consider. The first is adaptation to your instrument – are you playing a one-sided instrument? If so, then look and see if you twist the top half of your body against the lower half unnecessarily, or are you raising your shoulders 'to give yourself room to play'? We do an awful lot of sitting about rehearsing. What's worse, the instrument may require one-sided muscle *training,* which then pulls unevenly on the spine. You get so used to it that it stays that way all day, and the build-up of muscle strength in particular areas means you are probably fit to play your instrument, but certainly not fit overall. Are you a pianist sitting at the wrong height at the keyboard and hunching to compensate, a bassoonist with a poked forward head position, a harpist who twists the spine to reach the bottom strings, or a cellist who thinks the cello must be vertical at the cost of bending your spine to the right, rather than with the peg box to the left?

We all 'warm up' to get our fingers moving, but who ever heard of a musician 'warming down' or doing some contra or mirror-image exercises? It's usually who can get out of the stage door and away first! Yet all serious sports people do warm-down exercises or stretches.

The second main factor is the emotional output and input. We are taught to 'wear our hearts on our sleeves', 'give our all' and 'put out 120% so the audience gets 100%'. At the same time we have our own load of personal emotional input, which has to do with survival and the building of defence mechanisms. These were probably essential in the beginning, but are now merely habit. Because they worked for us once, such habits are not dropped when they are no longer needed because we become psychologically addicted. Such habits can be anything from curling your feet round the chair on which you sit when you play, to grimaces, alcohol and beta blockers.

Posture is a life-long sport. If I say: A negative thought → a negative attitude → muscle tension → habit of body use → a specific poor posture → stresses/strains on the other body systems → dis-ease → predisposition to specific diseases → chronic disease . . .

Need I go on? There is such a connection between habitual emotional states and posture that we have taken them into our language. For example 'he's a push-over' describes an over-eager person who walks leaning forward or very unassertive person who leans back; someone 'weighed down by anxiety' will walk with bowed back or rounded shoulders; a 'stiff-necked or stiff-upper-lipped' person can't be seen to give way to his feelings, or is very inflexible in his thinking and has to be right all the time; children with learning difficulties, whom others describe as 'round the bend' or 'off their rocker' frequently have the top bone in the neck (which has rockers!) out of place, affecting blood to the brain; they need cranial osteopathy and help, not ridicule. There are many, many more examples.

This is the collection of postural baggage we build up and carry around without thinking because it feels 'safe'. We have practised it for many years and built it into our playing. However, if it is wrong for the body, that poor body will revolt or break down in the end, and we then experience chronic neck, shoulder or back problems and a host of other ills that can diminish or even wreck the rest of our lives, long after we've despaired of playing again. And often we don't know how they started.

This is the real purpose of this book: prevention. It's much easier than trying to reverse tissue damage, and it's about people's lives, because being a musician isn't a five-minute wonder, or a disease symptom, it's a way of life.

The simplest and most powerful antidote there is, before and after checking everything else, is **mirror imaging.** You can practise it everywhere and anywhere in everyday life – indeed you should. Most people are either right or left handed, and they do everything that way. This 'handedness' was, in the first instance just preference, then it was trained in, by learning to do everything that way, and by learning dexterity and precision with the dominant hand, but not with the other. In fact, it is only strictly necessary to do things that require particular safety or precision that way. There is no real reason why you can't sweep the floor, clean your teeth, hold the phone or put on your coat the other way round. Of course it will feel funny, because you have never tried it the other way round! It will feel just as funny as when you tried to learn to write; something you now do automatically. It isn't that you can't, you just haven't. Try it. Be silly for once. Have fun, then teach yourself as you would teach a child.

Obviously there are jobs that you can't swap round because that is the way the machinery is built. In this case when you have finished the job, do the opposite. In other words, if the job requires a twist to the right and a forward bend with one arm palm down and the other palm up (as in sitting playing the violin in long black dress) when you finish have one really good long stretch in the opposite direction – reverse your arms and twist to the left and backwards to bring your body back into the 'midline'. Otherwise it will assume you still want to keep the previous posture, particularly if you spend many hours a day set in it. Believe me, after that good stretch it will thank you, with a new sense of relief and relaxation. So, analyse what you do (i.e. if a harpist, bassoonist, cellist or horn player, do you also twist back to the right, or if a bass player, twist to the left) and make sure you also do the opposite for your body's sake. You don't have to match time in one direction with time in the other direction, you only have to remember to stretch and undo the knots into which you have tied your body, so you don't end up with an arthritic cat's cradle for a spine!

REFERENCES
1. **Barlow W**. (1973) *The Alexander Principle*, STAT Books
2. **Fry H**. (1986) *Overuse Syndrome in Musicians: Prevention and Management,* The Lancet, (September 27 p728-731)
3. **Gray H**. (1901) *Osteology, development* (Anatomy, descriptive and surgical 15th ed. p 1-170), Bounty Books
4.**Lederman R**. (1994) AAEM Mimiograph 43: *Neuro-muscular Problems in the Performing Arts* (Muscle and Nerve, June 1994)
5. **Smith D**. (1982) *Paganini's Hand* (brief report in Arthritis and Rheumatism Vol. 25 no. 11 p1385/6)
6. **Spaulding C**. (1988) *Before Pathology: Prevention for Performing Artists* (Medical problems for Performing Artists, December p135-9)
7. **Szende O., Nemessuri M**. (1970) *The Physiology of Violin Playing,* Collet

ORGANIZATIONS

Feldenkrais Guild UK. PO Box 370, London N10 3XA (also via BAPAM, see Chapter 1)

Society of Teachers of Alexander Technique (STAT). 20 London House, 266 Fulham Rd, London SW10 9EH. *Tel:* 0171-352 0666

CHAPTER 3

Musician versus Instrument II

Memory, sight reading and practice
Excess cold and heat
Skin problems
Calluses and varicosity

Memory, sight-reading and practice

Memory and practice are closely related. *How* you practise can determine how good your memory is. If you always stare at the music as you practise and never attempt to play from memory until you have 'learnt' to play the piece, then the chances are you will find it more difficult, because you have been using a crutch that's difficult to let go of and your mental cleanliness will have left something to be desired. (By this I mean the random way you will have skimmed some bits and worried away at others.) You will have to memorise on top of all that. Much easier with a clean slate!

There are some fundamental tenets here for efficient 'note crunching' which will cut down on the hours, and you will not be so exhausted.

1. Never even try to learn when you are tired. Do 50 minutes hard work then take a complete break for 10, but put on a timer or the 10 will stretch, momentum is lost and you will have to start up all over again. Children will need graduated practice time-lengths, maybe only 15 minutes' work with a five-minute break, working up to three sessions in an hour per day.

2. Invent games that make it *fun* when you practise. You learn better that way. As you play, integrate some of the Green-Gallwey 'Inner Game' techniques, by watching where your hands, arms or posture are, visually enjoying the look of your efficiency; by listening for tone quality next game; by observing bow pressure, speed or articulation in the next, and so on. This adds interest each time you repeat a passage, and you end up memorising it without even trying to.

3. There are several types of memory: ultra-short (used in sight-reading), short (used in aural tests), medium- and long-term memory.

4. There are several ways of remembering: aural, kinaesthetic, visual and structural. Know which is your best method and enjoy using it, but always back it up with your second-best method.

5. You remember best the first and last things you do each session, so always end with a correctly played phrase.

6. Practise efficiently. 'Garbage in equals garbage out.'

Memory types

Ultra-short term memory is used in **sight-reading.** If you are bad at it you are committing one of the following sins (assuming there's nothing wrong with your vision and you are not dyslexic): (a) You are looking at the actual note(s) you are playing instead of looking ahead. Try looking at the step your feet are on when you run down stairs and you'll see how you trip up over your own feet. The mind needs processing time for the information to get in to the brain via the eyes, compute the necessary movements and then send messages down to the muscles that are to do the job. (b) You see notes singly instead of recognising groups. This causes congestion and slows the computing down enormously. Try to see shapes of phrases rather than individual notes. (c) You are too much of a perfectionist. Such an attitude is inappropriate here until you are a 'master sight-reader'. Save perfectionism for practice time. Getting the 'sense of it' is what's required in sight-reading at first. (d) You waste time by looking back at what you've done. This is a scanning habit we all have that's useful elsewhere, but not here.

The best way to help yourself to learn is to make friends with a teacher who has a large repertoire of graded beginner's pieces and borrow them in difficulty order. Use sight-reading practice as a fun reward, to 'bash through' something and giggle at your howlers, when you've done all your other work. Read a book or two on speed-reading, and apply some of the techniques as they suit you. Enrol a friend who is as bad at it as you, and as you play get them to cover up first one, then two, then three bars ahead to *make* your eyes look ahead to pick up the note patterns, rhythm and accidentals. Then you can turn the tables on your friend. Give each other positive, helpful feedback, don't both wear hair shirts about it!

Sight-reading ability is something that one tends to lose if it isn't indulged in regularly, because of the speed of mind required to translate dots into sound. Dyslexia is discussed in Chapter 4.

Regrettably, those good at sight-reading often don't bother to memorise and vice versa. This is a pity when both are available. A good instrumental memory is also conducive to improvisation and experiment. This is something that's far too little encouraged, or even actively discouraged as 'time wasting' by many classical musicians, because of the race to stardom and the sheer amount of repertoire to learn.

Short-term memory is where you remember things for a few minutes only, and is the sort of memory needed for aural tests. It can be activated if you play or hear a short phrase three times. You can then repeat that phrase from memory. But do this with a long passage and you will remember bits only – the beginning, the end, and a few salient points in the middle – because they are more remarkable in some way than the rest. Short-term memory will only last for about ten minutes, or less if there is further intervening input. It fades quickly and needs to be reinforced by repetition two or three times. After this it will then be good for about an hour before it starts to fade again.

Medium-term memory lasts anything from a day to a week. So the phrase held in the short-term memory will need to be repeated after a day, when it will then last a week. Reinforce it again then, and it will start to become *long-term memory* and will last about a month and when further reinforced will last six months to a year. Each repetition causes a larger and larger memory connection in the brain, provided it is done before fading sets in. You also seem to remember things in chunks rather than scraps at this stage.

All the above time lengths are generalised, but they give an idea how normal memory works. There are some lucky individuals who only need to hear something once to remember it forever, but us average mortals need reinforcement, and a few of us will need even more frequent reinforcement. However, it is in the nature of being a musician that we need to practise technically difficult bits far more than is necessary just to remember them.

Ways of remembering

While it is rare to use only one form of memory, it is as well to know and use that which comes easiest to you. Do you remember the tune *(aural)*, remember how it feels as you play *(kinaesthetic)*, where it is on the page *(visual)*, or the structure of the piece – sonata form or whatever *(analytical)*? Use your strongest memory-type and back it up consciously with your second strongest. Don't assume that because you are musical, your aural memory must be best. Aural memory is enhanced by constantly humming the piece to yourself when away from the instrument, kinaesthetic memory by fingering it through soundlessly, visual by writing it out, and analytical by putting the salient points on a postcard that you carry about in your pocket and looking at in odd moments.

When you really know a piece well, it 'plays itself' rather like Zen. Then your limitations, and those of the instrument, are no longer apparent and you are communicating directly. That is a height to aim at.

Can you *finger a piece through* and see the music away from both music and instrument and hear it in your head? As soon as you can do this, you start to make the piece musically 'your own', because you are untrammelled by instrumental difficulties. This kind of reinforcement memorising can be done anywhere, such as in the bath or on a train.

Can you alter speed and play it faster or slower than it should be with equal ease? To be able to manipulate the speed of a piece means that technically it is in your control. Playing it at the right speed will therefore be so easy and assured that you will have the brain power left for the music itself to speak.

If you have a brilliant technique anyway, then use your memory to be absolutely clear about each technical trick as it flashes by, so that there are no fuzzy edges in your mind and your instructions to your fingers are therefore clear and precise. I happen to prefer the 'musician' to the instrumental gymnast, but in reality both have their value in developing instrumental playing.

GIGO (garbage in equals garbage out) is a computer term that applies equally well to your instrumental computer, namely your mind. If, whenever you take a run at a passage, you always break down at the same place, this becomes a memory well rehearsed and reinforced. So what happens in performance? You break down, or at least wobble, on cue, as rehearsed.

Take a difficult section apart. Analyse it. Is it a right-hand or left-hand problem, a coordination, rhythmic or distance-judgement problem, or a combination of these? Does the same passage appear elsewhere in the piece – exactly the same or slightly different, or in a different key? Get one problem right at a time and then the next. Practise the join and, when it all runs easily, congratulate yourself.

Some people find it hard to sustain stamina in a long technical passage. If this is the case, do the end first and get that secure. Then add the bar before and practise its approach, then add two earlier bars. This has the effect of the *end* getting a large amount of work and so it becomes easy.

When you perform the whole passage it then becomes *easier and easier* as you go through it, rather than harder and harder. If the passage is fast, practise it until you can cope at 120% of the speed necessary. Then the correct speed will have the same ease as the rest of the piece.

Other useful games to play with yourself are (a) to see if you can play the passage ten times correctly in a row, starting slowly and pushing the metronome up one notch each time you get it right; (b) to practise it with different rhythms, thus improving the speed between a few notes at a time, then put it all together in its correct rhythm in order to build up to the next level. Meanwhile you may have played it at least 100 times right and are still not bored. (I once knew someone who was only sure he could play some thing if at the same time he could walk round the house, up and down stairs and even lying on the floor! It was one way to freedom but I'm not sure I'd recommend it with a valuable instrument!)

In all your endeavours, I implore you not only to make it fun, but to keep breathing! This applies particularly to string players, whose instruments may press down on their chests. If you practise holding your breath in a difficult passage, guess what you'll do under performance conditions – you will starve your poor brain of oxygen. Under stress, in a hot concert hall, you need all the oxygen available, so build proper breathing into your playing from the beginning. If you are a wind player you may do the opposite and hyperventilate, or find your breath doesn't last as long as it did when rehearsing. Take that into consideration when you work out your original breathing marks.

In all you do with memorising, *always end with a faultless example* which is up to speed if you can, but slow and correct if you can't. Begin slowly, carefully and correctly too – maybe even going through it once or twice in your head first before you touch your instrument, so you know clearly what you mean, and so your brain can give your fingers clear instructions from the outset. This is important because you remember best what you start and end with. Above all don't practise *in* your mistakes by constantly playing through from the beginning until it falls to bits like a musical Mr Micawber, hoping something will turn up and it'll go right!

If you do make a mistake, it's not the end of the world; you are human and do not deserve to be castigated for being so. Stop and think. Be clear about what went wrong. Don't just baldly bash away at it again. Do some mental preparation and repair; be certain about how it will go when it's right; reinforce the elements that fell to bits and then put them back into context. Finally, put the whole passage back into its context and approach it from a musically sensible place so that the flow is not disrupted. Do as much mental as physical practice. Coax and cajole, rather than castigate yourself like some awful strict teacher you might once have had. Treat your clever fingers with the respect they deserve.

Playing through a piece is *not* practising it, but self indulgence and a way of avoiding having to face your mistakes. It has no goal except to get to the end somehow. Practice *must* have a goal: aim for faster, clearer, better intonation, better gradation of a crescendo, speed of bow, breath control, balance with the accompanist, and so on. Of course playing something through for the sheer joy of it is also a valid reason, but that should be reserved as a reward when the work is done, to put it all together, reinforce what's right and rejoice in the progress you have made.

My reason for stressing mental practice is based not only on experience, but also on experimental sports psychology tests done with three teams over a season of matches. Team A worked hard physically, with practices every other day. Team B met the same amount but worked on theory, match tactics and visualisation, only meeting for a short warm-up before each match. Team C also met as Team A, but spent at least half the time, each meeting, visualising and getting mentally clear about each aspect of technique, and then went out on the field to practise with specific aims in mind. In the results at the end of the season, Team A did slightly better than Team B because, although they made plenty of mistakes, they had the stamina to see them through. Team C far outstripped the other two even though the teams had been matched for ability. This was because they were fit, had stamina, and their technique and tactics were well worked out. Because they had spent time together and were not exhausted or bored, they could play to one another's strengths, and were inspired by one another. By the end of the season not only had the tactical ground rules been sorted out, but they could be inventive on the field and keep a sense of fun. Their performance was well above their class.

Excess cold and heat

After memory, sight-reading, speed and stamina problems, perhaps the most frequent other complaint of musicians is of temperature extremes. Unfortunately the situation is also made worse by the stress of performance. Most people suffer from frozen fingers or intolerably sweaty hands, which are an enormous bugbear, both to player and instrument. Cold hands are caused by a cold environment, such as playing in an unheated church, and by poor circulation. Defence against cold buildings consists of a thermos of hot soup or herb tea, long johns, thermal underwear, thick-soled shoes, fingerless gloves and pocket hand-warmers (obtainable in golf shops and chemists), and the knowledge that the audience, who are sitting still, are probably as cold as you.

The best you can do about air temperature is to avoid sitting near the draught from open doors and the organ bellows in old churches, and endeavour to schedule the concert around a church service (so the clergy will feel more inclined to put the heating on early) or borrow a commercial hot-air blower (such as farmers use for grain drying and for their sheep in winter) for use in the interval.

I have not suggested alcohol, hot sweet tea or coffee, or other stimulating drinks for good reason. The yo-yo effect caused by suddenly dumping a lot of quick-release sugars plus a stimulant into the system is counter-productive. What happens is that the body doesn't know how much more may be coming down the tubes into your stomach and so over-reacts by producing extra insulin, and an hour or so later you have a blood-sugar *low* and you feel colder and more tired than ever. Much better to stoke up beforehand on whole grains in the form of brown rice, wholemeal bread or a muesli bar (even though it may have honey in it). These release the sugars you need for warmth and energy in a slower, more controlled way, so there is no yo-yo effect.

I have found the problem of cold fingers worse when playing the viola than when playing the violin. This is because the violinist's fingers tend to move faster and more often, and are closer together, so that less heat is lost. None of the larger instruments have these advantages, so players suffer more.

If your fingers regularly go 'dead', lose feeling, go white, blue or red for no apparent reason, check with your doctor that you haven't got Raynaud's syndrome (most common in young women), or that it's not a side effect from a drug that you may be taking for some other condition. (Anti-migraine ergot and Beta blockers are known for this.) Otherwise, causes of micro-circulatory spasm in the extremities are: general poor circulation (as for instance with smoking and diabetes); postural or neck and shoulder problems (causing impingement of the nerves controlling the width of the arteries); or constriction of the arteries themselves as they pass through these areas on their way to your hands.

Poor circulation in the hands can be helped by (a) alternate hot and cold water rinses to stimulate the circulation of blood, (b) swinging your arms round and round, fast and hard to drive the blood into your hands by centrifugal force – not advisable in confined spaces!, (c) pouring warm water over your wrists to warm the blood where arteries come near the surface, (d) keeping your fingers constantly moving, or clenching and unclenching your fists during bars rest, (e) by massaging one hand with the other, especially between the bones (which is where the hand and finger arteries lie), (f) by putting a hand warmer in your pocket, (g) by lightly sitting on your hands or putting them in your arm pits, (h) by visualisation (this last works by closing your eyes, relaxing and imagining that your arms are a foot longer than they actually are and concentrating on sending the blood down to your fingers – which are also an imagined extra foot further away).

Incidentally, smoking also causes vasoconstriction and even gangrene to some, so don't even think about it! You can get drugs to help Raynaud's syndrome, but they may also cause side effects such as depression – ask your doctor about this and then the choice is yours whether to take them or not.

Draughts are a pest. If you can't move your seat even a couple of feet, then you could become chilled, especially if you get very hot playing. Side draughts from open doors and windows, which you may have to put up with for the sake of the rest of the population, are morally difficult to combat – again try to swap seats with someone who longs for 'fresh air', or put some sort of baffle, curtain or shielding between you and the draught, at least in the interval if not before. Your only other resort is to shut the offending door or window firmly and promise faithfully to open all to the four winds during the interval, after which only leave those open which are on the opposite side to the prevailing wind for the rest of the performance – fair's fair after all!

Down draughts are the worst, because they are usually from cold air-conditioning and most often occur in recording studios. Here your only defence is to say that it is affecting your instrument's tuning or tone, and thus will wreck the recording. (Remembering that you are judged by the sound you make, not your comfort or your pretty shade of blue!) Engineers will take note if you talk in terms of a wrecked recording, because re-recording time costs money. They will ignore human suffering, which costs them nothing, heedless of the fact that it may cost you in work lost if you are ill the next day.

Excessive heat is worst if it is damp heat. Obviously instruments will react here, but I am concerned with humans. Hyperhydrosis (excessive sweating due to over activity of the sweat glands), can be a nervous-system reaction to stress. It is also a reaction to excess stimulants such as alcohol, tea, coffee, a high red-meat diet, and excessive extraneous movement during playing. Glandular disorders, fever and menopause will also cause this reaction and may need medical advice.

Aluminium chloride 20% solution and an alcohol derivative of some sort are the basis of most over-the-counter underarm antiperspirants. Use an antiperspirant on your hands, let it dry before playing and shield your instrument if it is valuable. *Do not stop drinking fluids.* It won't make you sweat less, and there is little real connection between these two functions. Abstention will only cause dangerous dehydration and kidney problems later if persisted in.

A supply of wet wipes and sawdust in pockets helps, but do empty your pockets before putting the garment in the wash! Talc is more socially acceptable than sawdust, but tends to clog delicate instrument parts. The other side of the coin is to practise with wet hands and get used to it! This will make you less nervous about dropping the instrument and more secure when skating about, and thus more relaxed about the whole idea. The result will be less nervous over-stimulation and therefore, eventually, less sweating. If your fingers swell because of the heat (as opposed to long-term water retention problems about which you should talk to your GP), soaking them and exercising them in very salty water will help.

If you sweat excessively under your arms and in the crotch, sew or clip pads in to soak it up and cut down on dry-cleaning bills. The new, thin sanitary towels work very well and are unobtrusive. This was taught me by a famous lady cellist who moved about a lot as she performed. It reduced the unsightly marks on her dresses.

The smelliness of sweat really only occurs in the armpit and intimate places. All other sweat (from feet, head, back etc.) has a different consistency and chemical make-up and does not contain pheromones which cause the smell. This means that if there is a smell, it is due to bacterial growth which needs to be showered off in frequent, lukewarm showers. Wearing natural rather than man-made fibres helps. Hot or cold showers will only make matters worse.

Skin problems

Skin problems for musicians are miserable. They are an awful nuisance because it seems as though the more you play, the worse they get. There are two main types of problem, which at first look similar. One arises from contact with an allergen – known as contact dermatitis, the other happens to have erupted in one specific place, but is the result of something you ate, and usually takes the form of eczema or a rash. This is then exacerbated by acid perspiration and friction. The area may be scaly, highly coloured, and may also have little blisters, pustules, cysts or even scarring in severe cases (Zimmers, 1994).

There is a curious idea amongst medics that has persisted since Greek times, and which is diametrically opposed to the ideas of Hippocrates. It is that 'symptoms' are definitely *not* normal and *must* be suppressed chemically, to return the body to a symptom-free, supposedly healthy, state. In fact, symptoms are usually evidence that the body is very healthily busy with very normal protection and repair procedures (see Homeopathy and Naturopathy in Chapter 6).

The body's survival depends on a natural and very efficient garbage disposal system. Mostly it throws rubbish out via the urine, faeces, breath and skin. That which it can't get rid of, it seals off, or stores in your fat. Urine and faeces everyone knows about, the others are not so obvious. Toxic chemicals can give rise to gases which are expelled through one end or other of the digestive tract as burps, farts or smelly breath. Toxic chemicals that are still in the bloodstream or tissues, and haven't been filtered out by the kidneys, are collected together and thrown out with sweat through the skin. If they are still too toxic there may be skin inflammation, and you get rashes or boils and other skin eruptions. If the toxicity can't get to the surface, and affects the soft, inner parts, there is another mechanism for dealing with it – mucus. To explain: if you use a spade in the garden a lot, you build up protective calluses on your hands against wear and tear and corrosive or irritant materials. You can't do this inside your body because it needs to stay soft, so it coats itself, and the toxic substance, with a lubricant – mucus – which we cough up as phlegm.

Because rashes and mucus tend to occur in warm damp places they attract bacteria which thrive in such environments. Bacterial detritus is an irritant, causes swelling, makes proper function of the area painful and difficult and will send you to your GP, whose only resource is to suppress chemically the very waste-disposal system that is trying to help you. Such short-term treatment only builds up underlying problems which appear later, often in another form. The sorts of warm, damp places where musicians get problems that interfere with playing are hands, chin and mouth and, in organists and pianists, between the legs.

If the reaction is obviously due to contact with an allergen, then there are a few simple options. Protect yourself with chamois leather or similar, lacquer your instrument with a substance which will not damage it, or use another brand if the offending substance is rosin or reed. My husband used to sweat a lot on his head when stressed, and then got a very sore chin. His solution was to make several chamois leather chin-rest covers and wash the leather frequently so there was no bacterial build up. Another friend with very sweaty palms lacquered the upper bouts of his violin. A third found his sweat was so acid, that he came off the concert platform with a blue right hand until he lacquered the inside of the bell of his French horn.

These were comparatively easy to remedy. Where the symptoms are not caused by contact, only exacerbated by it, and do not respond to protection techniques, then the causes are much harder to find and I refer you to the section on diet and allergy in Chapter 15.

The most common household substances which can cause contact dermatitis are: very acid or very alkaline solvents, detergents and washing powders (especially the 'biological' sort), metals and fungus. Certain drugs you might take on tour with you, such as anti-malarials, may be activated by the sun or sunbeds (i.e. ultraviolet light) into becoming a skin irritant.

Once there is inflammation, and it is itchy, infection may follow if you scratch it. Rescue Remedy cream will sink in immediately, leaving no sticky mess, and will soothe the area so you won't want to scratch. You can protect injured skin further by wearing rubber gloves that have a sprinkling of talc inside (to prevent acid sweating, as a reaction to the rubber, making things worse) whenever you wash up, or have to use the strong materials listed above. Use a toilet soap that is adjusted to match the natural skin acidity (the label will say pH 5.5).

Don't assume that the reaction against the irritant is always immediate. It may take a few days to appear, and occasionally months to go, after the irritant has stopped. All you can safely do is keep the area scrupulously clean, protect it, and hunt for the cause by thinking of everything you have touched in the past week.

Calluses and varicosity

Calluses occur through excess wear and tear. In musicians they usually appear on the fingertips, pads, thumb sides, palms or under the chin. If they are annoying you, or they are so thick you can't really feel where you are going, then check the fingerfall pressure you use, the gauge of the wrapping on your strings (which may be too rough and wide), the fit of your chin-rest, and the padding on the thumb-piece if you are a wind player.

Normally there is just a slight extra thickening or grooving of finger pads that doesn't really affect feeling. Lack of pads after a holiday shows you just how fast these wear and are replaced. Wiping them with methylated spirit is said to help toughen them up.

Problems happen when there is cracking or splitting as well as thickening, because the thick sides chafe and ooze. Cracking is usually due to an ingrowing nail, an allergic reaction or eczema, fungus infection or psoriasis. To keep the area supple use Vaseline or similar thick ointment under a plaster during the day, then clean and pumice it night and morning to lessen the rough edges and let it heal naturally. 'New skin' or a non-allergenic plaster will help to hold the crack together in an emergency.

If you are lucky and have good pads to the ends of your fingers, don't cut your nails too short. If, however, you have tapered fingers and poor pads, and even short nails interfere with your playing (such as in vibrato) you have to be meticulous about cleaning underneath the nail and pushing the flesh gently back *before* cutting to prevent nicks, and then filing along the nail, never across it from front to back.

Varicose veins cause fatigue, aching and even painful legs, and are something young professionals usually only come across if they are pregnant. However with advancing years, and thousands of hours sitting or standing playing, they are more and more common.

They occur because of gravity and lack of movement in the legs, or because of constant breath holding, which inhibits venous return in the chest. Blood would pool in the legs if it were not for non-return valves in the leg veins, combined with muscular movement which siphons the blood back up against gravity. Being still for hours, whether sitting or standing, means the blood gets stuck down there in the legs and the valves in the outer leg veins stretch and balloon, which is why you get that wriggly, knobbly appearance. Sitting has the further effect of squashing or inhibiting the flow in the surface veins at the back of the thigh, compounding varicosity in the calf. (How often do you go numb in that area after sitting for a long time on a hard chair?) Unfortunately the tendency to get varicose veins is also often inherited.

You can help yourself considerably by exercising your legs as much as possible – ideally as much as you exercise your arms by playing. Keep-fit, swimming and walking are the best help when not playing, and wearing support hose when standing still, sitting or playing. You can activate the siphoning, pumping mechanism of your muscles by standing on your toes frequently, and by toe pointing and ankle flexing when you are sitting. Wriggle unobtrusively to keep the circulation going in your thighs while counting bars rest. It may also help to put a brick under the foot of your bed to raise it three to four inches, to walk, run or use a cycle instead of the car where possible, and walk upstairs instead of taking the lift at any chance you have.

Haemorrhoids are ruptured varicose veins around the anus. Sitting on a hot radiator will dilate them and cause throbbing and is to be avoided, but avoiding constipation by a high-fibre diet is the best remedy of all, because it keeps the bowel contents soft. Haemorrhoids are ruptured and produce blood during straining to eliminate. However, *any* blood in the lavatory pan, other than the normal female menstruation, should send you straight to your GP as it can be a sign of all sorts of things, both trivial and serious, that need checking. Haemorrhoids can be removed surgically quite easily, but are best avoided in the first place by a proper diet. According to naturopath Paavo Airola (1981), added vitamins E and C complex, pineapple juice and buckwheat in the diet (amongst other things) are helpful.

REFERENCES
1. **Airola P.** (1981) *How to Get Well,* Health Plus Publications, Phoenix, Arizona.
2. **Berkow R.** ed, (1992) *The Merck Manual of Diagnosis and Therapy,* 16th ed, Merck Research Lab. Merck and Co., Inc. Rathway N.J.
3. **Green B.** and **Galwey T.** (1986) *The Inner Game of Music,* Pan Books Ltd.
4. **Zimmers P.** and **Gobetti J.** (1994) *Head and Neck Lesions commonly found in Musicians,* (Journal of the American Dental Assn. Vol.125 Nov. p1490)

CHAPTER 4

Above the Shoulders

Eyes: how they work; spotlights; driving
Bates eye exercises; nutrition
pinhole glasses
AK visual help
near/far vision defects
dyslexia

Ears: how they work; pitch, range and
volume; shields and ear plugs
tinnitus

The neck, mouth and tongue;
the teeth and jaw
dental and orthodontic treatment

The eyes

How they work

Your eyeball is like a small ping-pong ball with a slight bulge in the front. It is kept clean by a steady flow of moisture from your tear ducts, spread by blinking. It is moved by six external pairs of muscles attached around its vertical 'equator': two for up and down, two for right and left and two to swivel. The optic nerve pierces the back. It spreads out to cover about two-thirds of the inside like an onion skin and forms the retina which contains 130 million light-sensitive cells reacting best to general and black and white vision round its outside. Almost in the centre, there is a small specialised bit, the size of a fivepenny piece and with seven million cells, which is for acute, detailed vision and colour.

The inside of the eye also has muscles: those that control the size of the pupil, affecting how much light comes in; and those that control the thickness of the lens for focus. The eyeball is kept pumped up to the right pressure by transparent fluids in front of and behind the lens.

Light comes through the protective outer covering or cornea, then through the pupil and lens, hits the retina, and causes a chemical change resulting in a tiny electrical charge which goes at 300 mph down the optic nerve to the back of your head. (This is the main optical brain centre which interprets the charge as the pictures you call vision.) The internal eye muscles move more than 100,000 times a day to react to light and focus. You see with your brain not your eyes, which is why a bang on the back of the head causes you to see stars. At birth, vision is only light and shadow and distance, but it reaches its peak at eight years.

The most common defects of short and long sight are due to the shape of the eyeball being wrong, or the ability of the internal muscles being reduced. If the eyeball is squashed top to bottom, the retina is moved further back from the focal point, and you will be short-sighted. Conversely, if it is squashed front to back you will be long-sighted. Flattening at one point will cause astigmatism (visual distortion). Occasionally, in an attempt to improve your vision, you may find yourself screwing up your eyes to try to see something better that is out of focus. What you are doing, instinctively, is temporarily changing the shape of your eyeball to bring the retina to the focal point.

Eye muscles, whether external or internal, are like any other muscles, and need to be fully used or they deteriorate. They will also get tired in the same way if you stare, which holds one level of contraction for a length of time. In just the same way too, they need good blood and nerve supply to function properly. Of course there are genetic predispositions to eye shapes as there are to anything else. However, weak external eye muscles will not hold the shape of the eyeball properly and it becomes horizontally egg-shaped. Over-tense eye muscles will cause it to go egg-shaped vertically. Astigmatism is where there is an uneven pull on one part of the eyeball. All these conditions can be helped by exercise, as set out at the beginning of the century by Bates.

In their natural state, the internal eye muscles controlling the lens are set for distance vision, but if, instead of using the full range, you constantly only use a small part of the range for near vision, their action becomes unbalanced and they 'forget' that the whole range is available and gradually lose the ability, and you are told you need spectacles. In fact glasses and contact lenses are crutches which simply hasten the process of disuse of the full range, and you gradually need stronger and more pairs – reading, music, driving and distance – or put up with awful combinations such as bifocals or varifocals. What you need for healthy eyes is not glasses but a regular eye workout. Such an activity only has one disadvantage, you may have to get another weaker prescription pair of glasses which, if you persist with the exercises, you will probably eventually throw away.

Spotlights

The times when your near/far range of vision is restricted are when reading, when reading music, when driving and when, if you sit in a permanent seat in an orchestra, you do a lot of your work always looking at the same angle to and from your music and the conductor. Sitting on a platform too, you may be beset by glaring spotlights: as often as not just behind the conductor, which cause you to screw up your eyes tensely. You may also be fobbed off with poorly written music with leger-lines, and you again have to screw up your eyes to decipher it. This is followed by long motorway and night driving before your poor eyes can rest for the night.

If you can't lose the light behind the conductor, ask if it can at least be shielded. Often the lighting is done by theatre lighting engineers who think it more important that the audience sees you, than you the conductor. Orchestral playing is not primarily a visual spectacle. If the worst comes to the worst, play with your section leader and don't look at the conductor – but don't let the conductor know that!

Poor copy is a legitimate cause for complaint. It just means that someone has written the part out themselves instead of employing a professional copyist. They deserve any wrong notes they get.

Driving

Motorway driving, day or night, causes you to keep a steady, high speed. This means you (a) probably fix or lock your neck muscles, and may even hold them more tensely still if visibility is poor; (b) your eyes have a fixed focal length like a stare, which they find extremely tiring.

Try these exercises while driving:

1. Whilst you drive, *without* taking your eyes off the road, *gently* turn your head 45° each way, right and left, tip it right and left towards your shoulder, and raise and lower your head. This will softly exercise and free up both neck and eye muscles.

2. Talk to a companion or, if you are alone, sing loudly to break down neck and facial tension.

3. Keeping your head looking forward, safely but randomly flick your eyes to one side or the other and see what you notice of the roadside flora. There are some beautiful mini nature reserves to be seen.

4. Blink a lot.

5. Focus close in front of your car bonnet and then let your vision slide out to the horizon and back.

6. Where possible, avoid driving for miles on roads with evenly spaced trees in bright sunlight; it's very tiring and has even been known to trigger epileptic fits. Being an epileptic might disqualify you from driving.

7. Stop at least five minutes for every hour you drive (remember the world lost a wonderful horn player in Dennis Brain who fell asleep at the wheel and drove into a tree) and do some 'palming' (see home eye exercises below).

Night driving, when both you and your eyes are tired, and you've probably had a coffee to keep you awake, is definitely not good news for your eyes. They are probably feeling 'grainy' from your evening's work, especially if there were spotlights or strip lighting. The coffee might keep your brain awake, but will cause constriction of the arteries supplying the eyes, and although the caffeine will help your hypoglycemic state if all you had to eat was junk food five hours ago, it's far better for you and your eyes to keep a packet of unsweetened oat biscuits and an apple in the car to nibble.

If you have to drive longer than an hour on an out-of-town gig, don't resort to glucose tablets which will drain you, and I do mean *drain!* All quick-release sugars gobble up vitamin B in order to be metabolised into useful energy, and vitamin B is the one you will be needing most for steady nerves, plus vitamin A for night vision.

Whilst we are on the subject of driving, be aware that it's an unfortunate biological fact that (a) one in eight men are colour blind in total or in part, and may well see red as green (this inherited tendency is ten times less in women), and (b) people of either gender may be unaware that they are slightly night blind. Because they have always been like that, they assume it's the same for everyone. It isn't, so allow for it.

A clean windscreen is easier to see through. Clean it on *arrival* whilst it's still light and you can see what rubbish you have collected. You will be too tired later to bother. If oncoming headlights are painful, or have halos, you need to get your eyes checked. Take some extra vitamin A too. In any case, never look at blazing headlights; the glare will temporarily blind you, more so if you are tired. Concentrate on the nearside kerb and, with luck, you won't hit it, be blinded, or wrap yourself round a tree.

Bates eye exercises and nutrition
These exercises are basically those advocated by Bates at the beginning of the century (see also Chapter 1), which I have made more relevant.
1. Rest your elbows on a table and cup your chin in your hands.
Now, without moving your head, let your eyes trace/write huge
letters of the alphabet. Use capital letters and write as big as your eyes
will let you so you use the full range of movement possible, *but do it
without strain.* This will exercise all ranges of movement and isn't so
boring as 50 circles right, 50 circles left. You may need to start with

half an alphabet if it makes your eye muscles ache. If you get fed up with the alphabet, trace or draw imaginary outlines round the edges of everything you can see without moving your head.

2. Hold your arm out in front of you at shoulder height. Stick your thumb up. Look at your elbow crease, your thumb and a distant object in line with them in quick succession and back, but no faster than you can focus on each as clearly as possible. You may need to remove your glasses if they stop you focusing on one of the three. Make friends with your blur, and watch it disappear as your eye muscles get stronger.

3. Keep your head and eyes facing front, and spread your arms wide at shoulder height, until you can no longer see your fingers (waggle them to be sure). Now take them over your head. You should be able to see almost 180° in all directions except across your nose. A wide range of vision is essential for chamber music as well as for driving safety.

4. 'Palm' by covering your eyes with your palms, pressed against your eye sockets not your eyes. Shut out all light. Total darkness is very therapeutic for your eyes. Closing your eyes alone is not good enough, some light still gets through closed eyelids. Breath deeply and relax for five minutes. Then do exercise 1. above, with eyes closed under your palms. Finish with another five minutes' deep eye relaxation.

Get yourself a copy of Goodrich's *Natural Vision Improvement*. It's a great *fun* book for children of all ages.

Good nutrition is as important for eyes as for anywhere else in the body. Eat wholefood, and avoid junk food, as much as possible. Eyes particularly need vitamins A, B complex, C complex, zinc and calcium. Check on their sources in Chapter 6, and eat these foods as fresh as possible.

Trayner pinhole glasses

Difficulty in focusing causes the image to fall either behind the retina (long sight) or in front of it (short sight). This means that each point of vision is a blur circle. The greater the error, the greater the area of blur. The effect of introducing an array of pinholes in front of the eye reduces the blur circle proportionately, enabling the brain to recognise what it needs to do to focus correctly, and give a sharp image, so improving lazy brain-eye coordination and flexibility. These are exercise glasses and come with a training programme. They also cut down VDU eyestrain, and reduce glare like a form of sunglasses, but should never be used in situations that require good peripheral vision such as driving. They work well in conjunction with *Natural Vision Improvement*.

Visual inhibition and AK visual techniques

Eye direction is very important to the balance of the head on the body, and you should not lurch to one side or fall over if you stand still on one leg, or with your feet together, and close your eyes. If this happens to you, go and talk to your doctor. If you are accustomed to muscle-testing (see Chapter 10), you should not notice your muscles go weak when the eyes are turned in a particular direction. This is less serious but very tiring.

If you find you trip over curb stones a lot, you may have a foot problem, but this, or feelings of insecurity when going up and down stairs or on and off concert platforms, or feeling tired when you look at a piece of music or at the conductor, is a sign that you may be suffering from **visual inhibition.** It could be that you have learned so much stress while you were using your eyes in a specific way that your natural 'switch off' defensive mechanism has come into play.

To correct this problem, you could try an **Applied Kinesiology (AK) technique.** (If you have not already done so, reading Chapter 10 at this point will help you to understand what follows.) Show someone else as Tester how to find an indicator muscle which is strong when the Testee (you) is looking straight forward. Retest, as the Testee looks up, down, right, left and in all the diagonal directions too *without moving the head.* It's also worth swivelling the eyes clockwise and anti-clockwise and right-left-right-left as in reading. Whichever direction weakens the indicator muscle, that is the one that needs treatment. When the Tester watches the Testee's eyeball it appears to jump rather than move smoothly through that area and that's where the Testee should be asked to look while either person massages the Acu-point K-27 and the tummy button. K-27 is immediately under the collar bone either side of the breast bone. Massage firmly for 30 seconds. The points may be tender, and at first the Testee may try to look away from the direction you are treating. Pay attention. Re-testing the direction of gaze plus the indicator muscle should now produce no weakening.

If you trip over curb stones or find going down stairs perilous, it could be that the foot muscles are reactive (see Chapter 15) to the eye muscles, and only go weak when you look down, causing the foot to drop slightly and you to miscalculate the step height. In this case the eye muscles are set too high and you need to switch them off temporarily by firmly rubbing points on the head, that are on a line extended back behind the head from the top of the eyebrows, and diagonally above and behind the ear, in a little dip; and reset the foot muscles while the Testee looks downward. The foot muscles should now not become weak or drop. Although the correction only takes one person, it is helpful to have someone else there as Tester to test foot muscle strength and observe the drop.

Sometimes a specific focal length needed for reading music or looking at the conductor causes a problem. This will be obvious when a previously strong indicator muscle becomes weak at that, and only that, focal length. Correct this similarly as above, reproducing that specific focal length by setting up the music stand and chair and a person or marker on the wall at the distance of the conductor, and while looking rub K-27 and the tummy button (see above), firmly.

Near/far vision defects

Another cause of weakening muscles or tiredness occurs in moving between near and far focus. Changing focal length is the cause of the problem, and occurs as you flick your focus from your hands to the music, to other players, to the conductor and back to the music. It can be a nutritionally related problem. Test for it by asking someone to find an indicator muscle (see Chapter 10) and focus on something close, e.g. your hands in playing position. The indicator muscle should remain strong if you are normal or near-sighted. Now move your focus to a more distant object, e.g. the music, another player or the conductor, and immediately re-test. If the indicator muscle now becomes weak you may need to increase intake of foods containing vitamins B1, B3 and B6, and support your adrenal glands by cutting down on substances which drain them, such as those containing caffeine.

If focus on a distant object causes no indicator muscle weakening, you are probably normal or far-sighted. If bringing your focus to a near object, e.g. your hands, and immediately re-testing causes weakening of the indicator muscle then you may need an increase of foods containing vitamins B2 and B5. Again you may help yourself by supporting your adrenals as above. In either case, boosting your intake of the required vitamins will eliminate the indicator muscle weakness as you change your focal length; cutting out as much stress from your life as possible will also help. Should the above prove ineffective, and you are sure that a simple change in your spectacles prescription is not what is required, then an applied kinesiologist will help you.

The actual movement of the eyes from side to side in reading can also cause weakness. As before, while doing this, test a previously strong indicator muscle, which will now be weak if this technique is needed. Correct the problem by rubbing K-27 and the tummy button (see above) firmly for 30 seconds. It may also be important to do the correction while looking up and moving the eyes side to side, and again while looking down with side to side eye movement, or even at an angle if you share a music desk, or the conductor is not directly in front of you.

Dyslexia and music

Although this is not actually a visual problem but an interpretation problem, I have included it here because this is where the problem is often first recognised, and because the unsuspecting music student may be asked to teach a dyslexic child, simply because they require more time and patience than a lot of professional musicians have available.

At pre-reading age suspect a problem if: (a) the child missed the crawling stage and went from shuffling along on its bottom straight to walking, and doesn't swing its arms properly when walking; (b) the child is very clumsy, late with learning to dress and tie shoe-laces and doesn't seem to be able to learn right from left, up from down or back from front; (c) the child has poor memory and concentration although apparently very intelligent.

These children need special help, or they will be discouraged and find themselves on the scrap heap of life. They can either use left brain for logic and calculation or right brain for spatial awareness, colour and sentient things, but cannot use both together or integrate them. They get locked into one or the other mode. Unfortunately the world of music needs and uses both together. What we take for granted they have to work at and 'overlearn'.

All aspects of learning music hold traps for dyslexics:

1. *Reading music:* learning that G is followed by A, not H; words and music together; different clefs and score reading; enharmonic equivalents; groups of notes which are beamed together for instrumentalists, but broken up for singers; leger lines; crotchet and quaver rests that are mirror image of each other; whole-bar, minim and semibreve rests.

2. *Left/right confusion:* 'up and down' a keyboard (vertical) is actually right and left (horizontal); hand-pattern reversal (playing fingers 1-2-3-4-5 with the right hand on a keyboard moves 'up', but the same pattern in the left hand moves 'down'); why is it 'higher' to the right side anyway on a keyboard?

3. *Rhythm:* poor coordination in clapping, even though the rhythm is clearly felt.

4. *Language:* confusion with American/English terminology (quarter note equates with crotchet rather than quaver); use of Italian, French and German terms.

5. *Accuracy:* missing out complicated bits, and words like hemi-demi-semiquaver; poor sight-reading; counting bars rest.

6. *Conductors:* when watching the conductor, and then when looking back at the music, being unable to find their place again on the page.

With luck, by the time dyslexic learners come to take exams, these problems will have come to light and can be allowed for. Solving them requires great tact, patience, consistency, repetition and multi-sensory learning, with care that new things are never sprung on the children, since this causes panic. The choice of an instrument which uses only one stave and one clef may be 'make or break' for dyslexic children, and a wrong choice could rob them of a lifetime's pleasure. Specific help can be obtained with specialist teachers via the British Dyslexic Society and with techniques set forth in the books *Natural Vision Improvement* and *EK for Kids* (see References). These dramatically reduce the stress around dyslexic problems with simple 'fun things' the children can do to help themselves.

The ears

How they work

There's a tradition, especially amongst advertisers, that spectacles are more than respectable; they give you an air of erudition and make you an authority on the object being advertised. It's a curious thing that there is no stigma attached to an artist wearing spectacles, but a musician wearing a hearing aid is immediately suspect, and it is assumed that with loss of hearing goes musical ability. Thank goodness Evelyn Glennie is changing all that. Perhaps it is because poorly sighted people have to make the effort almost entirely themselves and wear a badge (the aforementioned respectable spectacles), whereas the hard of hearing mostly have to depend on a poorly hidden aid, and on others speaking clearly and directly *at* them. People with poor vision have a choice over the direction of their gaze, but those who are hard of hearing cannot control the direction of the source of the sound. The populus at large forgets that poor hearing is not the same as low IQ and poor understanding, but can cause it.

The flap on the side of your head – most people's idea of an ear – is merely the sound collector which directs sound into the inch-long channel towards the tenpenny-sized ear drum. Hair and wax in the channel protect it and also warm the air. Behind the drum is the middle ear, the real business part of the ear. Here three tiny bones pick up the slightest deflection of the drum caused by sound waves and amplify it 22 times. This vibration is then passed through to the fluid-filled inner ear via the oval window. In the inner ear is the cochlea, which is like a snail-shell-shaped, covered spiral staircase. It contains thousands of tiny hair cells, each one responding to one specific speed of vibration or pitch. Playing middle C will excite the middle-C hair and it sends a tiny electrical charge down the acoustic nerve to the main hearing centre in the brain which is three quarters of an inch away. The brain translates the signals into meaningful sound (middle C), so you hear *with* your ear, but *in* your brain. People who can recognise a sound, and put a name to it straightaway have Perfect Pitch.

You also hear by bone conduction. Lightly strike a tuning fork and put it on top of your head in the centre. Even if the sound it makes is so soft you can't hear it via air transmission to your ears, you will still hear it easily, because the sound is conducted via the bones of your head. You should hear it equally in both ears. If you only hear it in one ear, then that ear needs investigation. Usually the trouble is only impacted wax (see below).

The other function of the ear is direction detection. Three fluid-filled canals in the inner ear measure up/down, side to side and front/back movement of your head in space. The fluid they contain is very turgid and pulls on sensitive hair cells which send messages to your brain. However the messages from these hair cells are also sent by the *same* nerve as those for sound, so when the nerve is affected by disease *both* functions are affected as in Menier's disease which causes tinnitus and dizziness and eventually deafness. Unfortunately it is quite a common problem in later life.

Pitch, range and volume

Pitch definition is not the same as **range** or **volume** definition. Women and children can detect higher notes than men. They can hear bats, but bass notes, which to them just sound like a noise, have a distinctly recognisable pitch to men. Both men and women can have very fine pitch definition, which is the ability to differentiate between two sounds that are maybe only one or two vibrations apart e.g. 440 and 442 for A. Neither of these has anything to do with volume.

People think they can accommodate an excess of volume but they can't. If the decibels are too high there is always damage, particularly in discos where the sound level is so high that you *feel* it rather than hear it. Unfortunately one man's music is another's noise pollution, and many modern composers seem to go for 'the big effect'. Noise levels are measured according to factory regulations and must not go above a prescribed level for more than a specific length of time; they are usually measured in a venue as the overall effect of continuous sound levels, not from the seat of the nearest musician who may be sitting just in front of the brass section.

Your hearing changes throughout your life. Tissues lose elasticity and what starts as a hearing range of 16-30,000 cycles per second is down to 20,000 by teenage and around 4,000 by aged 80. At this last level, conversation in a quiet place with one person is quite easy, but very confusing in a crowded restaurant, worse if there is the noise pollution of 'background music'. Decibel loss occurs too, and 'virtually all executant musicians have had their hearing capacity reduced to some degree over the years by the mere fact of playing any instrument', says Anthony McColl (1995). Typical excessively noisy places such as a machine shop cause rapid hearing loss because the levels are continuous, but what about in the middle of a full symphony orchestra belting away *fortissimo*? It's just another machine shop after all! The effects are also multiplied when in a confined space such as a theatre pit. This is also why most conductors, who stand in the middle of all this volume, and to whom it is directed, suffer from hearing loss, even though very few will admit it publicly. Road diggers are issued with ear muffs, and in a recording session one has cans, but can you imagine a conductor wearing ear protection on the concert platform?

When excessively loud, *low*-pitched noises like thunder hit the ear-drum, a tiny protective muscle tightens the ear-drum as a reflex. There is **no** protection against loud, *high*-pitched sounds, as most rock musicians know to their cost in later life (but by then they are millionaire 'has-beens', not in the public gaze any more, so they don't worry about it). All you can do at these concerts is to wear ear plugs, but that looks 'chicken', and gives you a distorted sense of the sound balance of your own contribution. Extra string and woodwind players, who always sit at the back of their section right in front of trumpet and trombone players, suffer in the same way. A *fortissimo* on a trumpet, the bell of which is a few inches from your ear, is extremely painful, even when respectably played, and you can hear nothing for ten minutes afterwards until your ears finally stop reacting, just as you are temporarily blinded if you look at the sun. Unfortunately some brass and percussion players seem to believe that *ff* means 'obliterate everything else'.

Shields and ear-plugs
Various attempts at shielding have been tried, such as the 'Acoustishield'. Others have been tried by the CBSO and the BBC Philharmonic. They take the form of a perspex screen, free-standing or fixed to the back of the sufferer's chair. They reflect the sound back to the player who then is at risk, but at least has control over the volume produced.

Ear-plugs have both merits and demerits. Gunshot ear-plugs are not generally suitable as they remove all sound, and with it contact with the others playing round you. All you can hear is yourself via conduction through the bones of the skull. Cotton-wool or wax can be used in emergency, but still don't give the protection that's needed at the same time as allowing you to hear everyone else. Some of the problem is overcome with the new MU Ultra Tech. ER 20 ear-plugs available from Central London Branch (see end of chapter). Wearing these raises permitted daily exposure to loud noise from 15 minutes to eight hours. Drum punctures are not a matter for this book (they usually heal themselves or are repaired surgically).

Tinnitus

Tinnitus, however, does concern us. Constant ringing or rumbling in the ears is exasperating to any musician, and very difficult to track down, as it can be caused by excess noise levels, inflammation, fever, circulation changes, tumours on or near the acoustic nerve, some antibiotics, allergies and alcohol, and cranial or jaw-joint misalignment. It can also be a sign of the beginning of Menier's disease, but then there will be extreme dizziness too. Nicotine, caffeine and stress will constrict the inner ear arteries, making the condition worse, as will the common aspirin derivatives and sucrose or other simple sugars. Abstain from them and alcohol, and reduce animal fats and salt, while increasing intake of foods containing vitamins A and E , zinc, magnesium and potassium. Assuming there is no fever (see your GP or a naturopath) or tumour (get an X-ray done), visiting a cranial osteopath, or chiropractor who also practises cranio-sacral technique, is the best course of action. It is also worth investigating your jaw-joint (see later), especially if you have had a lot of rough or heavy dental work done lately. Reduce your toxic metal load if hair analysis shows mercury, aluminium and/or lead. Homeopathy will help you with this. A herbalist might also prescribe Gingko biloba (*What Doctors Don't Tell You* Vol.5 no.8 (see References) has further researched information).

Excess wax can be removed by first using a little almond oil at blood heat in the ear and then, next day *very gently* cleaning it with a cotton bud. Beware though, as it is so easy to push the wax still further in, when it becomes impacted on the drum. Don't try to remove this impacted wax yourself. It's extremely easy to puncture the drum even with a cotton bud if someone startles you and makes you jump at the wrong moment. Get your ears professionally syringed by a sympathetic doctor who will take care about things like a comfortable water temperature. Wax formation is always worse when there is a cold wind, when you have a cold, or you are tired and tense after a long tour. The same is true of temporary deafness from flying. There, all you can do is to keep swallowing and yawning, both of which move or open the Eustachian Tube (that runs between your inner ear and your throat), to equalise the pressure to allow you to hear again. Don't try to force it to clear by sticking your fingers in your ear and pulling it about; it will clear in its own good time even if it is painful. And don't blow your nose too hard; that just forces mucus up the tube against the inner ear.

Overgrowth of bone inside the ear can cause early conduction deafness, probably shown up by the tuning fork test I described earlier. In children the Eustachian Tube is much more horizontal than in adults which means that it does not drain so easily and fluid builds up. 'Glue ear', from which children fashionably suffer at the moment, is usually treated by inserting grommets to ventilate the area behind the drum. This can cause scarring and sclerosis later, whereas the fluid problem will often resolve itself if left alone. When it doesn't, the build-up is usually in response to an allergen. Try an allergen elimination diet (see Chapter 6) before submitting the child to surgery which will only deal with the symptoms not the cause, and may result in scarring. Follow this up with cranial osteopathy. Misalignments of cranial bones and the vertebrae at the top of the neck can sometimes cause partial deafness by interfering with nerve- or blood-supply to the ears.

Aural inhibition

Occasionally turning the head round to the left or right as you might do when holding a violin, viola or flute will make a previously strong indicator muscle (see Chapter 10) become weak. This means that any other normally working muscle that is being used at the same time as you turn your head will also become weak. Not useful in performance conditions!

To correct this, take hold of the Testee's ears, especially the curled over top, and pull firmly away from the ear hole, uncurling the curled bits as you go and working from the top round to the earlobe. Always pull away from the ear hole, e.g. pull the earlobe downwards. Retest with the head turned as before, and the indicator muscle should now stay strong and with it all other normal muscles. This technique will also improve balance.

The neck, mouth and tongue

The ear, neck area, jaw, face and the mouth are all closely associated. While many may think they are the province of singers, wind and brass players, they affect us all in at least a secondary fashion. Because your head is the heaviest part of you, and furthest from the ground, any imbalances here are exaggerated in their effect. So, just as foot problems could eventually cause headache via the body's attempts at compensation, poor head posture or a poor bite can cause head, neck and back pain or even walking difficulties.

The neck
Because our muscles tend to become tense when we are mentally tense, the neck suffers particularly. If the body emotionally wants one thing, and the head logically wants the opposite, then the poor neck in between doesn't dare show its feelings and we become literally mind- (psycho) body (somatically) 'stiff necked'. The English language is full of such phrases that the body takes literally – more of this later.

The musician is a real hostage to this area. There seems to be a built-in tendency in musicians to take the head *to* the instrument rather than take the instrument to the head. This causes raised and rounded shoulders, a neck that sticks forward, and a pain between the shoulder blades because that's where the weight of the head is now being carried. Later, tingling and loss of strength in the arms may appear from the same cause. This 'poked forward' posture of the head also happens where the music is difficult to read, the light is poor, vision not so good, or you do a lot of driving. If you wear bifocals, these regulate your head position by forcing you to look through one particular part of the lens in order to focus. Poking the head forward has the effect of increasing the bend in the neck at its very top and then the chin has to jut forward to keep our eyes looking forward. If only we could leave the neck alone and *bring the instrument to us*. It doesn't suffer aches and pains after all! Who is in control here, you or it?

Check in Chapters 11 and 15 if your neck muscles are tight, remembering that where the neck muscles attach to the back you may get back pain, and where they attach to the back of the head you may end up with a headache.

You can feel most of the bones in the spine by the line of bumps that go up the middle of your back. However you can't feel the very top one at the back at all and may only just be able to feel it under your ear, behind your jaw. When this bone and the next few below are even slightly out of alignment, they affect the inner and outer blood supply to the head.

Whereas the nerves supplying the ear and the eye never leave the skull, those affecting the tongue, pharynx, larynx, upper neck muscles and digestive organs can be dramatically affected by misalignments of the top four bones of the neck. The lower three neck bones will affect the nerves that go to your entire arm. This is why chiropractic, osteopathy and their cranial studies and Alexander technique concentrate so much on making these areas freer and more efficient, and why misuse due to instrumental playing can lead to all sorts of problems.

Your neck is an amazing area! You can easily fit your hands round it, and yet through it goes all the air you breathe, food you eat, blood supply and messages to and from the brain and the whole of the rest of the body, hydraulic and bony protection for the spinal cord, and muscles to support the heaviest bit of you with a secondary balancing system. At the same time it must be flexible enough for you to look over either shoulder and tip your head up and down and from side to side, without compromising a single one of the vessels which pass through it.

The last thing it needs is to be used as a G-cramp to wedge a violin in place – particularly if you use no shoulder- or chin-rest and have a long neck! (A sure sign of tension and friction is an area of callus on the neck under the left side of the jaw.) Most players usually have a high shoulder-rest and low chin-rest in a effort to keep the left shoulder-joint free, forgetting that this means they have to lift the right arm higher. Menuhin suggests the instrument should be like a bridge supported at both ends. Certainly, if you can have the freedom to clap your hands over your head and walk round the room at the same time as holding a violin or viola under your chin, or play a four-octave scale with your chin off the instrument you will not feel the need to clamp it into position.

The neck may be twisted or side-bent when holding a flute, or poked forward to fit round a mouth-piece, thus constricting the vital nerves and blood vessels because the arms are too lazy to lift the instrument appropriately. Tilting the head to one side will cramp the Triple warmer meridian which governs the thyroid and can therefore decrease the immune system efficiency (according to John Diamond, 1981). Pianists hunch and cramp the shoulder muscles in order to play loudly or express an illusion of continuing musical tension (Russian pianists are taught to lean forward over the keyboard, which is better mechanically for using the weight of the arm for powerful playing). But pianists often forget to put their shoulders back down again when they have finished using them for such a specific purpose. Necks are also hostage to wrongly positioned or wrongly adjusted music stands – a common difficulty where desk partners have different length backs and visual abilities.

The mouth

The mouth is an interesting area. The main components of interest to a musician are the cavity containing the tongue and teeth, the facial muscles (and lips), and the jaw joint.

The internal or buccal cavity varies enormously in size and opening, and may, together with the shape and contents of its adjacent sinus cavities, affect, or be one of the main constituents of, the tone you make, if you blow or sing for a living.

Constantly blocked sinuses are usually the result of a recent heavy cold or flu that hasn't cleared yet; chronic infection, allergy or drugs causing too much mucus to be formed; polyps if you are on long-term steroids for asthma; or even an infected tooth root. Unfortunately the sinuses are not well designed for easy drainage. If you happen to do yoga headstands, or want to use acupressure points, you can help to clear them. These points are all round the inner rim of the eye-socket and under the middle of each cheek bone. Seek out and massage the tender spots. Better still, find the cause of the extra mucus first, eliminate it if you can, then use the acupressure to finish the job.

The tongue

Because of the high density of nerve-endings in the lips, tongue and hands, they all have a disproportionately large share of the motor cortex in the brain. This allows you to be very sensitive to extremely fine gradations of sensation, and this is what you as a musician train and trade on. A tiny piece of food, for example, when caught between your teeth, will give you far more annoyance than its size warrants, and the inside of your mouth feels much larger than it actually is because you are acutely aware of every nook and cranny due to tongue hypersensitivity.

The misconception of most people is to think of the tongue as a taste mechanism and not much more. They are wrong. Observe the enormously complicated movements made in tonguing (single, double and triple) and in speech. The tongue has a memory too. Have you noticed that some 'foreigners' *always* speak with an accent? They may hear the difference between 'd' and 'p' or 'ze' and 'the' but, because the sounds don't occur in their own or first language it's very hard to learn new muscular tricks in later life. You may be the same. Beware of this as a singer – some people don't even *hear* the difference.

Your tongue is as individual as eyes or ears (as any wine-taster will tell you) and while of course dentures or a heavy cold change the taste of things to most people, so do nutritional deficiencies such as of zinc (see Chapter 6). If you don't need it, it tastes disgusting, if you do need it, it has no taste at all. The tongue can also indicate states of health. A beefy-looking, red, very smooth tongue is a useful early-warning sign for anaemia; a fiery-red one can mean B vitamins are very low; if you have liver problems it could turn yellow. Black tongue, though alarming, is usually only a comparatively 'harmless' fungus problem. If in doubt, consult your GP.

The idea that a coated tongue indicates indigestion is not always correct. It can be due to alcoholic overdose or to particles of food and old cells caught between the natural little bumps on the tongue surface. If you stick out your tongue and it won't go straight, that's another reason to see your chiropractor, osteopath or doctor, but that's not a likely problem until you reach old age or suffer brain injury.

Mouth infections are common and can be caused by borrowing instruments from others who may not even know they have a problem. Herpes can be transmitted in this way, dismissed as chaffing due to contact with a metal mouthpiece or reed brace. (Herpes = cold sores). Once you have this virus you have it for life. All you can do is keep your immune system functioning as well as possible with fruit juices and alternating vitamin E with vitamin C and iron. Try to eliminate food sensitivities which lower the effectiveness of the immune system. A homeopath will be able to help.) Gum boils and mouth ulcers between the lower lip and on the tongue are usually short lived and self-healing if you can refrain from irritating them with too much playing. Candidiasis or mouth thrush often follows a course of antibiotics and may make playing brass or wind instruments uncomfortable. All of the above are indicators of general poor health, over-tiredness and being 'run down', because that's when these infections get the upper hand. Homeopathic help is available (see Chapter 6). Try it before the more heavy-handed conventional medicine, which may often only deal with the symptom not the cause.

Even if, because your playing depends on them, you brush your teeth regularly, use mouth washes, special toothbrushes, floss or interdental brushes, don't be lulled by advertising into thinking your mouth is clean. It is still a zoo of microbes. You take them in by the million with the air you breathe and every mouthful you eat. Plaque is an ideal warm, wet medium for them to multiply in, and as it picks up minerals from the saliva, it hardens and pushes the gums away from the teeth leaving yet more nicely protected breeding grounds and inflamed and bleeding gums. Another cause of bleeding gums is lack of Vitamin C, but in this affluent society that is less likely than lazy dental hygiene, particularly if you follow a good diet and exercise the teeth with crisp chewy foods like apples and celery. Those teeth that don't get exercise may be due to a poor 'bite'. They will also be the ones that are most likely to need your dentist's attention.

Teeth and jaws
Why do I worry about this for musicians? Malocclusion, teeth extraction, braces and bridges can all have a devastating effect on your playing and can cause headaches, neck ache and upper and lower back pain. This underlying cause is often impossible to find unless you know where to look.

Malocclusion occurs where, when you put your teeth together in your 'normal' way they do not meet evenly all round. The usual dental solution to this in childhood, is to extract teeth where wisdom or eye teeth have no room or grow sideways, or to prescribe a brace, bridge or plate to pull the teeth straight, fill in the gaps, or widen the jaw. Braces and plates stop all movement of the upper and/or lower jaw, and consequent jamming of the cranial bones needs to be remedied at the earliest opportunity after removal, when the straightening work is complete, by a cranial osteopath. Regulatory and reparative dental work may be essential to professional wind players, but needs to be done with great understanding and care for the exact embouchure needs of that player and that instrument. Not knowing this, it might not occur to the parents of an aspiring and talented child to take the head of a flute or clarinet mouthpiece to the dentist too. According to Pamela Zimmers (1994) 'Less than 100 grams pressure is required to orthodontically move a tooth, and the forces of a musical instrument (up to 500 grams) can harm the occlusion and teeth.'

Everyone holds tension by clenching some part of their body, be it shoulders, buttocks or teeth. Grinding the teeth while sleeping can be stopped by a guard, but clenching jaw muscles whilst playing is a not uncommon habit amongst pianists and cellists, and is the source of many headaches and dental problems. 'Equilibration', which is to file the teeth down professionally to 'improve' the bite, without looking at the alignment of the jaw-joint or the muscles that hold it in place, is an all-too-frequent 'crime' commited with the best of intentions. It locks in the jaw problem for life.

What can you do about it? First, go and look in the mirror. Look really carefully.

1. When your eyes are level, are the following also level : your eyebrows, ear lobes and cheek creases and mouth corners?
2. Is the tip of your nose in a straight line above your chin and the notch between your collar bones?
3. If you were to measure from the outer edge of your eyebrow to the back edge of your jaw under your ear, is it the same distance both sides?
4. Bare your teeth. Notice how much the top layer overlaps the bottom. It should do so by about a third of a tooth, or is there a gap? Did you suck your thumb as a child to push the middle front teeth forward?
5. Open your mouth slowly. Does your chin drop straight down or

does it waver about on its way down or way back up?

6. Now gently stick your fingers in your ears (or just place them in front of your ear hole on the side of your face) and slowly open and close your mouth. (It may help feeling to close your eyes.) Do both sides move evenly and together? Do you hear crunches or clicks? Chances are you will have one of these problems. Most of it will be due to an imbalance of strength and tension between the following muscles and from cranial problems.

7. If you do clench your teeth or chew your tongue when you play, a video of yourself will soon show you how you look. You then only have to find an 'anchor' to remind you to let it go, and add it in to your practice routine.

The muscles that close the jaw are *temporalis, masseter* and *medial pterygoid,* one on each side. The jaw openers are *lateral pterygoids* and gravity. The main muscles round the mouth are *buccinators* (cheeks), *risoris* (for smiling), *levator* and *depressor anguli oris* (for the mouth corners) and *orbicularis oris* round the mouth used in whistling (see Chapter 10).

The lower jaw is suspended by two composite joints each side, in front of the ear. One joint is like a hinge and just lets the jaw drop, the other, next to it, lets you open even wider by sliding the jaw forward. Because of this, the jaw is quite easily dislocated if opened too wide in yawning or heavy dental work. Normal opening should allow you to put three fingers sideways in your mouth and maybe four with the jaw's forward slide movement. Tight muscles one side means that the other side has to be extra loose to compensate, and this causes headaches, a lopsided face and the mouth opening crookedly. This is common amongst violinists and violists, smokers who constantly dangle their cigarette or pipe out of the side of their mouth in order to speak, and singers who sing out of one side of their mouth only.

Unfortunately the jaw-joints are not the only joints affected. The bones of the skull all fit closely together, like tightly knit cog-wheels, which move microscopically on average 12 to 18 times a minute. They pump the protective fluid in which the most delicate parts of the brain sit. So, where there is strain, clamping, or unusual movement, this is transmitted to all the other bones of the skull as a torque which upsets the whole hydraulic system. This affects the brain, the brainstem, the spinal cord and the roots of the nerves as they come out of the spine, thus having a bearing on your entire health, equilibrium and general well-being. Cranial techniques can help these problems specifically.

You can put some of the muscle problems right yourself (see Chapter 10), but because teeth and jaws are so important to all wind and brass players, please go and see a dental kinesiologist or a dentist who works closely with a kinesiologist, before you have your teeth irretrievably ground down. Remember that grinding could simply lock the problem into the system and have unpleasant side effects if inaccurate.

Dental and orthodontic work

Braces pull your teeth straight in order to lessen plaque problems and improve bite. They may also cause you embouchure problems until you get used to them, and the inside of your lips toughen up. They also have the effect of jamming the hydraulic system described above while they are worn. When they are finally removed go and see a cranial osteopath to get the system going again, and you will find your general health improves and a lot of niggling symptoms clear up too. Dentists may not tell you to do this because usually they are primarily concerned only with your teeth.

It is important, if you have a tooth removed, that you get a plate made to fill the space. The other teeth will otherwise migrate to fill that space, change the bite and set up another strain in the cranium. Also, if the back teeth are removed, it can change the angle of air flow if you are a wind player and upset your technique. If you have a family history of poor teeth and a lot of extractions, get an impression made while you still have them all. It is far easier to fit spares later if you already have a model. Your embouchure may affect your teeth over the years. Lower front teeth tend to get pushed in by the mouthpiece of single-reed instruments, flute and piccolo, and both upper and lower teeth by brass instruments. To correct this:
1. When you finish playing, gently pull them forward again in a 'mirror image' of the way they were pushed in playing. You won't loosen them any more than normal eating does.
2. If you play professionally and still have your own teeth, have a photo taken by your dentist of both front and side view, with and

without your mouthpiece, so that in later years when replacements are needed, they can be exactly matched and you won't have to alter your embouchure completely.

3. Make sure you either go to a dentist recommended by BAPAM or that at least your dentist has a copy of Porter's *Dental Problems in Wind Instrument Playing* (see end of chapter).

4. Always take your mouthpiece to the dentist so that any rough edges left after treatment are immediately obvious to you and can be removed before your lips become sore and scarred.

5. If you have to have dental surgery, stop smoking at least while the wound is healing. The nicotine from more than 20 cigarettes a day causes serious constriction to the blood supply to the area and healing slows dramatically and will keep you off work much longer.

Interestingly, just like there is on the ear, there appears to be a holographic correlation between specific teeth and specific acupuncture meridians. The upper and lower jaws compliment each other. Removal of that tooth will upset the associated meridian and the organ it serves; you might find it helpful to 'run' your meridians (see Chapter 15).

Teeth are identified either by name or number. Avoid having them extracted if you possibly can, because of their meridian associations which are as follows:

Incisors (1,2): Kidney and bladder

Canine (3): Liver and gall-bladder

Pre-molars (4,5): Lung and large intestine (upper teeth); Spleen and stomach (lower teeth) stomach (lower teeth)

Molars (6,7): Spleen and stomach (upper teeth); lung and large intestine (lower teeth)

Wisdom (8): Heart and small intestine.

The muscles that will be affected are:

Upper teeth:

1: middle *trapezius;* 2: abdominals; 3: *latissimus dorsi;* 4: diaphragm; 5: *pectoralis major clavicular;* 6: *coracobrachialis, popliteus, deltoids* and *serratus anterior;* 7: *subscapularis;* 8: neck flexors and extensors.

Lower teeth:

1: *psoas;* 2: *quadriceps;* 3: *sartorius* and *gracilis* (front

and inner-thigh); 4: *pectoralis major sternal;* 5: hamstrings;
6: *quadratus lumborum;* 7: *gluteus maximus;* 8: *piriformis,* adductors,
gluteus medius.

If you check the descriptions in Chapters 11-14, you will see that most muscles are involved in playing some musical instrument. Whatever your embouchure, head/neck position when you play, just as you have a mental memory of stressful times, you have a physical/muscular memory too which builds up. If you can use positional Injury Reversal Technique (Chapter 15) you will be able to lose that subconsciously built-up stress, relax and play much more easily.

When amalgams were first introduced to fill teeth, the mercury content was very high – as much as 50%. Now it is much less. However your old fillings may leak mercury, and having an old one drilled out causes mercury vapour and you can't help absorbing some as the dentist works. Have them replaced with the new plastic compounds available whenever possible; make sure your dentist uses a proper dam to stop you swallowing the drilled out amalgam and breathing in all the vapourised mercury, and take homeopathic Merc. sol 6 for at least a week before and afterwards to help eliminate residual mercury from your body. Symptoms of mild mercury poisoning are dizziness, depression, stress and poor concentration, and a general feeling of being unable to cope normally with life. None of that is helpful to a musician's already stressful lifestyle.

REFERENCES
1. **Dennison P.** *EK for Kids,* Educational Kinesiology, PO Box 5002, Glendale, California, USA
2. **Diamond J.** (1981) *The Life Energy in Music,* Archaens Press, NY, USA
3. **Fitton J.** (ed.) (1995) *Acoustic Shields – a practical solution that may be provided by managements to help players endangered at work,* (Pan Vol. 13/2)
4. **Goodrich J.** (1987) *Natural Vision Improvement,* David and Charles Pub., Newton Abbot, Devon
5. **McColl A.** (1995) *Hearing Damage to the Musician — A Review of Audiometric Studies in Orchestras and Their Practical Conclusions,* (Pan Vol.13 no.3 p24/6)

6. **McColl A.** (1995) *Advances in Earplug Design – A Survey of the Options Available to the Practical Musician,* (Pan Vol.3 no.3 p26/7)

7. **Porter M.** (1978) *Dental Problems in Wind Instrument Playing,* The British Dental Association.

8. **Ratcliff J.** (1975) *I am Joe's Body,* Reader's Digest, Berkley Books NY, USA

9. **Skeath J.** (1994) *Hard to Learn,* (Music Teacher, Oct, p8-11)

10. **Wale J.** (ed.) (1987) *Tidy's Massage Massage and Remedial Exercises in Medical and Surgical Conditions,* 11th ed. John Wright and Sons Ltd.

11. *What Doctors Don't Tell You,* 4 Wallace Road, London N1 2PG *tel:* 0171-354 4592

12. **Zimmers P. and Gobetti J.** (1994) *Head and Neck Lesions Commonly Found in Musicians,* (JADA Vol. 125 Nov. p1487-1496)

ORGANISATIONS

MBS Medical Ltd (for hearing aid audiologists). 129 Southdown Road, Harpenden, Hertfordshire AL5 1PU. *Tel:* 01582 767218

Music and Dyslexia Working Party. (1992) British Dyslexia Association, 98 London Road, Reading, Berkshire RG1 5AU

Musicians' Union Central London Branch. 60-62 Clapham Road, London SW9 0JJ. *Tel:* 0171-582 5566

Trayner Pinhole Glasses. Upton Noble, Shepton Mallet, Dorset BH4 6BB

CHAPTER 5

Musician versus Environment

Chairs and sloping floors
Travelling – cars, coaches and planes
Jet-lag and travel sickness
Inoculations
Late nights and early starts
Formal dress and heels
Touring kits
Room sharing and strange beds
Planning leisure on tour
Carrying cases
How not to get mugged

Chairs and sloping floors

Chairs are often designed with other things in mind than the people who will sit on them! Considerations such as cost of mass production, stackability, colour and other aesthetics seem to come first. They are often designed for lolling in, not for working in. School chairs, which one would have thought would be well designed for growing young backs, are particularly bad, and seem to find their way into most halls. Chairs are designed to fit the average person, and very few people are 'average'. They are also designed to fit in with the overall look of the stage or platform, to be seen as an even block of colour, with good and therefore speedy manoeuvrability by stage hands; they must, therefore, be basic and simple, which almost always means unadjustable. It also never occurs to anyone to design a matching footrest for the shorter members of the orchestra.

The backrest height and angle, the seat angle and the height from the floor are all critical and personal. Some people like to lean back, in which case their shoulder blades may catch on the backrest, yet this seating posture needs its support, or at least a lumbar support; others sit forward and thus have no need of a back or lumbar rest, but need good padding under the thighs to prevent the blood supply to the lower legs from being cut off. These dimensions vary enormously between one musician and the next, let alone their differences in playing style, even supposing they play the same instrument. The same, incidentally, goes for the height of the music stand, but that's another story.

What usually happens is that, at the start of a rehearsal, you think that you can put up with it, but, by about an hour later, you wish you hadn't. You are tired, your back aches, you become increasingly niggly and concentration fades. You take the coffee break, and then haven't time or opportunity to swap your chair, and you spend the last hour wishing you weren't there. All because of the chair. A fine attitude for artistic creation!

Most chairs slope front to back, whereas for playing, most Alexander teachers will recommend a flat or forward-tipping chair. Kneel chairs are fine at home and for desk work, but are often too fiercely sloped for playing most instruments (they also tire the knee joints and prevent pedalling), and you are very unlikely to find them in any concert hall except perhaps in Scandinavia.

Pianists with short arms, who sit on a normal chair, narrow or non-slippery piano stool, and who frequently play at the extremities of the keyboard, can suffer pain due to low back hypermobility. Their body will probably try to support them by growing stabilising arthritic spurs in later life, but a padded bench is by far the best option, allowing them to slide sideways without falling off, or playing with all their upper body-weight rolled on to one buttock.

Most cellists grab the piano stool when there is one available, because it's the only sort of support readily available that doesn't cut in behind the knees. The only other solution for a cellist, is to sit on the very front of the chair, which can be highly unstable, and there often isn't the room available to push your seat that far back.

It is worth remembering that the spine is not straight like a telegraph pole, but has gentle curves front to back. These should be maintained to act like a spring, and as a centre from which to move. The spine isn't equally flexible all the way up however, being more fixed at the pelvis, by the ribs in the upper back and where it joins the skull. This means that the neck and low back regions are more vulnerable, and have to compensate for wrong positioning of the more fixed areas. Look after them.

How can you help yourself? The answer is to make the horrible chair fit *you*. There are various options:

1. Tip the chair forward by putting piano leg-cups under the back feet.
2. Use a thin wedge-cushion, easily made or bought in back shops (Yellow pages) or from osteopathic or chiropractic supply centres. This will take up some of the slack, and is more discreet than piano leg-cups but more awkward to carry about.
3. In an emergency you can use a rolled or folded hand towel, but these are often gaudily coloured and so not suitable for the concert platform.
4. Perhaps best of all is bubble-wrap. It is light, cheap, can be rolled or folded to any shape (e.g. for an awkward chair or car sear, or for storage in your instrument case), and is easily obtainable from any garden centre. Then all you need is a couple of black drawstring shoe bags to disguise your wicked secret, and you can make the world fit you. Make sure, however, that it doesn't pop in a recording session!

Put your name indelibly on any such possession; they have a habit of staying on the platform and being forgotten, or going for a walk by themselves.

Provincial halls and theatres often have sloping stages. This is fine for a three-piece band who can arrange themselves centre stage, facing the audience. However, even in a small chamber orchestra, some unfortunates have to sit parallel with the front of the stage which, if it slopes, means that chairs, music stands and keyboards will be sloping too. This plays havoc with your posture, especially if you are already compensating for playing a one-sided instrument. If you use bubble-wrap, a chair-wedge or piano leg-cups, put them on the *downhill* side, and when you finish playing do some mirror imaging exercises (see Chapter 2).

Travelling

Car, train, coach and plane seats are also built for Mr Average and need the same treatment. *Make them fit you.* If you don't, inevitably you pay for it. Coaches vary so much in their internal facilities that you just have to find what suits you, and be a bit selfish about it, to arrive in the best playing condition. For instance, being travel sick, I prefer to sit in the very front and keep wide awake, so I can make a dive for the door if necessary. If you are open and straightforward about travel sickness, people understand, don't usually mind moving and don't hold it against you, but if you don't explain or negotiate a bit, they get understandably huffy. The bumpiest ride and smallest seats in coaches are usually over the front wheels, second or third row back. Unless your seat happens to fit you well, if you have back trouble or want to sleep, the best place is the back seat, where you can make a nest for yourself with bubble-wrap and a neck-cushion and stretch out flat on your back. The movement is less jarring there. The new seat-belt laws may soon prohibit this however and unfortunately, on orchestral coaches, that's usually where the big instruments are strapped down or the smokers or card players are to be found.

Planes can be a particular bugbear if you are over five foot six, as orchestras usually travel 'charter' to save costs. These planes are fitted with as many seats as possible, with minimum room for each passenger, let alone their precious instrument. Most people go for the window seat, but actually, because of the curve of the plane body, these seats are the smallest and draughtiest of all, and in any case you will probably be too bored to look out much at the clouds. If you can't wangle a seat by one of the emergency exits, where there is often slightly more leg-room, then go for an aisle seat. You can then get up and stroll around (without disturbing others) and stop yourself getting stiff and fixed in one position. Worst seats of all are the extra ones they put in at the very back; they haven't an adjustable backrest, air stewards and other people are constantly going past or standing in queues for the lavatories, bumping you and chattering loudly when you want to sleep. These seats should be avoided like the plague unless you are five foot nothing and deaf. Fortunately they usually put the cellos there.

If you tend to sleep mid-flight, then putting the seat right back, a blow-up neck-cushion and eye-shields may help. You should aim to fill the space between your head and shoulders and turn slightly on your side as you might in bed. On charter flights where it's not possible fully to recline the seat, I find my head lolls forward and I wake with terrible neck-ache. My only solution is to lean on the seat-tray and rest my head on the head-cushion of the seat in front, hoping its occupant keeps still. I find I can sleep quite well like this, but each to their own.

Jet-lag and travel sickness

Jet-lag is due to an upset of natural body-rhythms, combined with the stress of travel, strange 'plastic' airline meals at odd hours, and dehydration.

Natural body-rhythms are controlled by the chemical balance in the brain reacting to daylight, shutting down some body processes while you sleep and enhancing others. For example, during the day, you probably urinate every two to four hours, whereas at night it is normal to sleep right through or maybe get up once only. Travel across a lot of time zones upsets this, and can make you feel peculiar until it sorts itself out. Some people hate travelling east to west, but most find west to east worst. For every hour time change, allow a day to recover, i.e. five days from the east coast of the USA.

There are many techniques for altering your 'body-clock'. My favourite is to reset my wrist watch every two hours, telling myself firmly that the new time is correct, and running my meridians (see Chapter 15). I also sleep if I'm going east to west and try to arrive early morning and see the day through. West to east I don't sleep, and go to bed at the new, local bedtime whether I feel like it or not, and find that these methods seem to put my body-clock right faster.

On long-haul flights, although the air is changed every few minutes, this air is taken in at high altitude and is very dry. It is not usually rehydrated, which is why, together with the urinary upset discussed above, you become dehydrated without realising it. You should frequently sip water and avoid carbonated drinks and all alcohol and coffee (because they are diuretics and dehydrate you even more). The reason one feels so awful with a hangover is because of the dehydration it causes, and long-haul flights, because the air is so dry, become a minor version of the same symptom. Eat as lightly as possible, and eat according to the *new* country's time schedule. On your return eat as much fresh fruit, vegetables and soup as you can. (This is advice from an air stewardess.)

What does one do on a long-haul flight apart from two-handed chess, reading, eating, sleeping and trying to pretend the 300-plus other people aren't there? Overcome your natural shyness and reserve, walk about, and gently and sensitively talk to them. They are human too, probably as bored as you and often turn out to be very interesting people. I've made some great contacts that way.

Some people never grow out of **travel sickness.** The cause is conflicting sensory input between the balance mechanisms of the eyes and ears. It is made worse by sitting in a confined space (such as the back seat of a car), petrol or diesel fumes, by eating a rich meal or stimulants such as coffee just before starting out, by weaving in and out of traffic or in twisting, narrow lanes with high hedges, by a bumpy flight or sea crossing, poor visibility and stuffy, airless conditions. Proprietary drugs suppress the symptoms by calming the vagus nerve and with it the stomach, but since the vagus supplies so many other functions in the body, it is best to overcome the problem without medication if you can.

The conflicting sensory input to the brain causes the body to dump any overload, so don't give it one. Only eat lightly at least two hours before starting out, avoid all rich, fatty foods and stimulants, alcohol and coffee, and drink water, camomile or peppermint tea instead. One hour before you leave take homeopathic Nux vomica 6 (Borax 6 if you are flying and suspect air pockets, or a special travel sickness remedy made by Nelsons which also contains Cocculus 6 and other relevant homeopathic ingredients), and take with you a bottle of water containing four drops of Rescue Remedy. Some people are helped by sea-band cuffs, which put pressure on wrist acu-points. Keep as much fresh air on your face as you can, and sit up straight and breathe deeply (this stops your stomach being squashed). If you are going to vomit, give your driver as much notice as possible! When you have finished, sip the water and/or suck a homeopathic Arnica 6 tablet. Some people find it helpful to close their eyes (thus cutting out one sensory input) and 'allow' the vehicle, boat or plane to throw them about, rather than trying to fight and brace against the movement.

Inoculations

While on the subject of foreign travel, do realise that you don't have to fill your body with all the jabs going for tropical diseases. Travelling to South-East Asia, I rang the School of Tropical Medicine to find out what I might need and five different inoculations were suggested. Then I rang an uncle who is a British-trained doctor living out there, and he told me the up-to-date, on-the-spot situation which was quite different! In desperation I spoke to a homeopath, who arranged a special pack of the specific homeopathic tablets for all the diseases I had asked for and a few other relevant ones, and all I had to do was to remember to dissolve a few tiny tablets under my tongue at the prescribed intervals. I was the only one in the party who had not a day's sickness during the two months I was away, and no one asked to see a single inoculation certificate either. *Always remember you have a choice in the matter,* but mostly you are not told about it. *Ask.* If your doctor queries your choice, refer him/her to *Thorson's Encyclopedic Dictionary of Homeopathy.*

Late nights and early starts

People are divided into 'night owls' and 'larks', but touring catches both. Late concerts followed by a sponsor's reception and then an early start for the next venue, are all right when they occur singly, but when you get a week of it on tour, what can you do to remain functional throughout?

1. Negotiate to take turns going to receptions with another orchestral member.

2. Use your travel time to sleep or take naps – especially 'dead' time such as waiting to board a plane. Remember to tell someone to wake you, and make sure you are on the right plane!

3. Learn to cat-nap in broad daylight (maybe carry an eye-shield) or practise meditation – it's nearly as restful as sleep, some say more so. I shall never forget the sight of Szymon Goldberg on tour, putting a chair down in the middle of the noisy bandroom, immediately going to sleep on it for ten minutes then waking up fresh as a daisy to play/direct the entire *Four Seasons*. If you can't sleep or meditate, take a five-minute holiday (see Chapter 8).

4. Do lots of eye palming (see Chapter 4) and lying on the floor in the Alexander position (see below).

5. Learn meditation and t'ai chi.

6. Know your own 'feel-good' factors (see Chapter 8) and treat yourself.

7. Teach yourself to have an internal alarm clock. Just as you get a feeling when the 15 minute tea break is up in a rehearsal, your internal clock will wake you if you instruct it to. Last thing at night look at your alarm clock, set it for the wake-up time and say to yourself 'I have X hours sleep from now, and I will wake feeling fresh and well rested at Z o'clock.' Then go to sleep. Do this often enough and you will begin to wake just *before* the alarm goes off, providing you haven't taken a sleeping tablet, drunk a lot of alcohol or had your internal clock disrupted by jet-lag. Because you have woken naturally instead of being shocked out of the depths by your alarm or the hotel alarm, you will feel a lot better too.

Formal dress and heels

Men's bespoke tailors are well able and used to cutting a tails jacket to leave plenty of shoulder freedom and, although the initial outlay is high, two suits will last for years, and can be refaced in the worn spots or supplemented from good second-hand shops. It's useful to know who else in the profession takes the same size shirt, socks, jacket, trousers and shoes to save you when some such item is forgotten. It is also advisable to keep both a black and a white bow-tie and a respectably formal tie in the pocket of each jacket.

Most other problems with men's formal wear can be solved with a safety-pin, which will do up cuffs, top buttons and bow-ties. It will also rescue you from that worst of all men's fears – that of playing on stage with open flies, or a runaway zip. Safety-pins can be stored out of sight under lapels or in top pockets. Hotels often provide sewing kits, but a spare white-shirt or black-jacket button is always needed when there's no time to go and buy one.

Elegance versus practicality is always a dilemma for female musicians. The idea of black clothes is a hangover from the days when there were almost no women in orchestras, and those that there were had to blend invisibly with the men's dinner jackets or tails so as not distract the audience from their listening. We are still expected to look elegant, even in our 'working' clothes.

The demands of long black are: (a) crease resistance and wash'n'wear ability; (b) packability and minimum bulk; (c) absorbency, coolness and a reasonably flattering style without being too revealing; (d) to be warm and full enough in winter to accommodate thermal underwear or long-johns underneath, and not look like a sack of potatoes; (e) to be wide enough across the shoulders and still stay up when you play, wide enough in the skirt that you can sit with ease, and wide enough in the arms that you are not restricted in playing, especially when you have probably developed strong arm muscles for playing. Fashion ignores such needs.

Short black has much the same list of problems, but fortunately these days one is allowed to wear tailored slacks or long culottes. In these you can at least sit comfortably, with your legs a little apart for balance, without the men in the orchestra (and all the audience) looking up your skirt!

Unless you are absolutely stock size, the only solutions to such an exacting list and having reasonable 'working clothes' are to make your own (when?? I ask), find someone to make for you, or *always be on the look out,* whenever you go out of town or on tour, and pounce with no second thought when you find something that's right. I've even known people buy two identical dresses and put one away until the first is worn out.

At the same time as you buy your dress, if it is any colour other than black try to get some matching thread and fix some inside it somewhere for emergency repairs. I have a horrid memory of tripping on a loose hem at the foot of the stairs in the Concertgebouw and squashing a 1690 Grancino. Fortunately it was repairable but a lot more expensive than the cotton for the hem, and could have been utterly disastrous!

A problem particular to female violinists and violists is the twist in the spine caused by sitting to play. Unless short armed, or holding the instrument in such an extraordinary way that playing at the tip of the bow does not cause the heel of the bow to hit one's knees, you have to twist to the left and bow outside them, or splay them and bow between (unacceptable if you are wearing a short skirt; ungainly if you are wearing a long one). If you twist your knees left, when you finish playing or in rests, twist unobtrusively to the right, so you don't get fixed in a twisted position. This is a typical mirror image contra exercise. In doing this I twisted round and often got to know the people sitting behind me quite well!

Shoes are another bone of contention for women. 'Flatties' are practical and comfortable; 'heels' are elegant, but disastrous to balance and posture. The most ideal playing shoes would probably be patent leather flatties, because you don't have to carry polish around, but they are hard to find even in mid-range sizes. Heels of more than one inch throw your body-weight forward and, to compensate, you lock your knees back, arch your lower back or stick your bottom out. This then throws your shoulders back to balance the body, and your neck forward into the 'poked forward' head position, with all its knock-on effects (see Chapter 4). It also makes playing with freedom much harder and more tiring, as your centre of balance is now quite different.

If you insist on wearing heels, then you *must* do contra exercises and walk around barefoot or wear heelless 'Earth shoes' to compensate. Counter exercises for shortened Achilles tendons (that's what happens to you), are as follows:
1. Stand on a step with only your toes on it.
2. Now let your heels sink below the level of the step and feel the stretch at the back of your calf muscles. Do this three or four times slowly, don't bounce.

3. Now bend forward from the *hips* (not from the waist) and do some toe touching (or as near as you can get). Again, don't force or bounce, but gently, slowly, *s-t-r-e-t-c-h!*

4. Come down, sit on the step, and do some gentle neck exercises, then

5. Finish on the floor in the Alexander position, with a thin book under your head, your feet flat on the floor, knees bent pointing to the ceiling and slightly spread, and have a feeling of lengthening and widening the neck and shoulders. Don't push it there, *allow* it there.

As an interesting side note, wearing heels makes your neck muscles weak. Raised heels push your toes into your shoes hard against the front of the shoe, and this weakens the acupuncture meridian that controls your neck muscles. Try testing your neck muscles' strength with and without heels yourself and you will see what I mean.

Touring kits

Lists are useful things and can save lots of time and needless worry. I've concocted my own as skeleton lists which give me peace of mind and speed. They come under three headings: *Touring, House* and *Garden.* Their purpose is not only to be sure nothing vital is forgotten, that you'll worry about for the entire duration of the tour, but also to nudge you to get things done at the right time, so that there's a built in countdown to departure/lift-off like a pilot's check list. They were developed when free-lancing and doing shows and are equally usable by men who also have to cope with housekeeping. Keep them in your filing cabinet, *not in your suitcase* (where they would get messed up or lost), and never take them out of the house. When compiling lists, take into consideration that the only list worth making is one that is pruned of all fantasy, and gets completed.

The *touring list* is in several parts: clothes and vanity, instrument and spares, kitchen, medical, and odds and ends. There's also a list for shutting up the house before leaving it for more than a day, so I don't go away and leave the iron or cooker on and burn the place down, or rubbish under the sink to pong the place out. Put all knives in your suitcase not in your hand luggage as they are liable to be confiscated during the flight. Pack no aerosols or gas refills. Take no electrical gadgets or valuables except those you can put in your hand baggage.

Obviously a clothes' list varies according to whether you are going to a hot or cold country, but you can still write out the basics. You know how many changes of shirts, socks or underwear you need but *write them down*. Because they're obvious they are so easy to forget in a hurry, and then on tour you have to waste time buying what you already have a drawer full of at home! I've forgotten pyjamas more than once (but maybe you don't wear them anyway).

The vanity list will contain hair-dryer, hair things and shampoo, sponge-bag and make-up stuff/shaving tackle and adaptors, a universal bath plug, kitchen roll/wet wipes/loo roll/J-cloths. I have found it useful to collect tiny plastic 'free sample' bottles and film cases in which to put various creams and lotions instead of carrying heavy glass bottles about, but you have to be sure they won't leak with air pressure changes in flying; deodorants are the worst for this, so I always wrap them in a poly-bag separately. No pressurised hair sprays or shaving foam!

Instrument, spare parts and specialised repair kits are specific to you and your instrument. *Never* trust to luck or hope that someone else will have what you need. Life doesn't work like that. If you have any doubts about your instrument, ask your usual dealer/repairer if they can recommend someone in the country you are visiting. Your instrument's health is as important as your own on tour. A tropical tour may demand you take an inferior quality instrument to withstand being eaten by insects or falling to bits in the humidity.

The kitchen list should contain knife, fork, spoon and teaspoon, tin and bottle openers, a corkscrew, a mug, plastic bags (for shopping and storage) and a lidded (Tupperwear or similar) box (doubling as a plate). Although mostly available, take a travelling kettle or immersion heater, an iron plus adaptors, and spare batteries for your alarm clock or watch (unless you are going to South-East Asia, where they are cheaper). Washing powder, line and pegs are essential on a tour of more than four days, unless you are stationary and can afford hotel laundry service charges. Tea/coffee/herb tea bags, 'cup-a-soup' or soup cubes, Horlicks or what ever takes your fancy that is easily transportable and digestible when you get back to your room exhausted at night, are worth their weight in gold. Sometimes you can save goodies from airline meals that your fellow passengers don't want, like jam, juice, cheese or honey, provided the packet is still intact. Although it's nice to go to the bar with the crowd, sometimes a peaceful time alone in your room works wonders for morale, and the kitchen list means you can retire into your shell without the expense of room service.

Although the tour manager should carry a first-aid kit, I prefer to take a few bits of my own, like sun screen, ear-plugs and bubble-wrap or a blow-up pillow, hypoallergenic plasters, an ankle and a wrist support and a length of Tubigrip, herbal cough lozenges and witch hazel, and a homeopathic medley that's easily available. It contains:

Aconite 6 (first signs of feverish colds, stuffed up nose, chills, thirst, sudden muscle pain from chills, fright, fear of coming events);

Arnica 6 (bruises, any injury, accident, physical or mental tiredness, boils) or *Bach flower Rescue Remedy* which has a somewhat similar effect against accident or shock;

Arsen. Alb. 6 (mild food poisoning, non-persistent diarrhoea – especially from anxiety, vomiting and indigestion, running colds);

Gelsemium 6 (influenza and 'flu-like colds and sore nostrils, pre-exam/audition nerves);

Nux Vom. 6 (in. ligestion, over eating or drinking, non-persistent constipation, travel sickness);

Rhus Tox 6 (lumbago, sciatica, rheumatic pains, muscle over-use pains and ligament sprains, eye strain);

Hypercal cream or *Hypericum* and *Calendula* (external cuts and sores);

Pyrethrum liquid (bites and stings);

Cocculus 6 (if you are travel sick or have nausea, especially during pregnancy).

When you use these do not eat for 15 minutes before or after, and avoid eating/drinking or storing the pills near coffee (including decaffeinated), camphor (mothballs), peppermint (mint tea, sweets, toothpaste – use fennel, bicarbonate or salt instead), oil of cloves and mouthwashes, menthol and eucalyptus (muscle linament, Vick rubs, cough pastels and inhalants), cannabis or other strong smelling substances as they may interfere with the remedies' properties. A list of the extras I took to South-East Asia is in Chapter 6. Some people like to take Immodium with them against diarrhoea. I find it too drastic, and wouldn't dream of taking it merely as a precaution. Far better to eat sensibly (vegetarians survive better in hot climates), avoid contaminated sources of water, and use homeopathy if needed.

The odds-and-ends list contains: sun/rain hat, swimming costume, alarm clock, torch and batteries, camera and films, travellers cheques and money belt, relevant tourist information, paperbacks to ditch or swap, travel chess, cards, or whatever you can't bear to be without that makes you feel good and recharges you.

The *house* and *garden* lists get updated regularly. I make no apologies for including them, as being a musician is a way of life that needs all the de-stressors it can get. Why carry clogging information in your head and live in a muddle, when it can all be so easily handled? List writing doesn't mean the tasks on it are nailed to the floor for ever. At first I made the mistake of making horrendous, monolithic, dragon 'to do' lists and then beating myself up if I didn't complete them. I became totally 'in thrall' to them. That's *not* the idea. Only write lists you intend to complete. They are not a substitute for actually doing the job. You are in control, they don't control you. They are merely a list of options, a framework for keeping the clutter underfoot and clearing time for yourself. You can only fit so much into any one day before it impinges on the next and, when all's said and done, no doubt the universe is unfolding as it should!

In the house list are all the household chores: daily, weekly (like changing sheets), monthly (like dry goods and freezer checks), and quarterly and even yearly bills and standing order checks. It also contains fun nonsenses like making the mince pies and Christmas cake and lacing it for the freezer to cut down the Christmas rush; cleaning the cupboard under the stairs or the garage. There's also a 'wet day' section to inspire me to sort the filing cabinet or tool box, plan an exotic meal or ring friends in Australia, instead of moping about the weather. Shopping lists are a house rule – if you finish anything up, replace it or put it on the shopping list. The garden list is compiled from various gardening magazines as they apply to my patch, and is important to me because I love flowers. You may have your own year-round hobby list.

I've also found it useful to plan the week's menu and *then* go shopping, not the other way round. It's much cheaper, as there is little impulse buying. You are then in charge of planning delicious low-fat food (so also in charge of your weight). It's also a good idea to shop *after* a meal, not before. You are much more efficient and not so tempted to buy inessentials and rubbish.

I made up these lists in 'marginal time' (discussed later), threw the bits in a drawer and put them in order one Boxing Day when the world seemed very flat, and I have never regretted them. They are there for me to disregard at will, but I know if I use them, I can cope with the vagaries of life with minimum stress and the house won't fall down, and that leaves 'quality' time for family and friends, and for just loafing about and being me.

When I've made up the list for the day or week I then apply the 'Four Ds' – Do, Delay, Delegate or Ditch, and that which I do is then done according to my energy levels, and with a blithe heart, speedily and efficiently. I prioritise, which means the important jobs get done, and then I reward myself with a frivolous non-priority job. I try to do the one I have been procrastinating about by Monday night; otherwise I find I spend the whole week *not* doing it, and that's clutter I don't need in my head. The rest might be delayed until they become priority or delegated. It makes no sense to spend hours doing a job you hate or are slow or bad at. Resentment drains your energy and goes hand in hand with that killer, guilt. If you hate a recurring chore that takes you hours, find a professional who will do it in a few minutes. Work it out on a money or barter basis and keep to it strictly.

Think about it: if I charge £30 an hour for my work professionally, and it takes a couple of hours for me to type a single A4 sheet, making lots of mistakes and hating it the while, it has cost me £60, when a secretary will do it in 15 minutes and be glad of the odd extra £10. That way it has cost me £10 instead of £60 plus aggro, and in theory leaves me £50 with which to have fun or luxuriate for two hours. To do otherwise is a false economy and undervalues me.

In a large family chores can be split. They can be 'costed' by agreement of the whole family together, with the worst ones having the highest price. Chores are then haggled over or bid for, according to who needs time and who needs money. It removes the feeling of imposition, and works really well if the job judged by the entire family to be the best done is rewarded by a bonus to be spent entirely as the recipient wishes. No one then uses the house as a hotel, because they know it might be them cleaning up the mess next week!

Books by Shirley Conran and Peg Bracken are an amusing and thoroughly practical read on the subject. Typical is 'If it's loose pick it up; if it isn't, dust it; if it moves, feed it'.

Room sharing and strange beds

Fortunately MU rules require single hotel rooms for touring orchestras, but if you are going with a small group and paying for yourselves, you might share for cheapness' sake. If you are on your own, make the hotel room yours by re-arranging the furniture or the lighting (if its moveable) or the pillows – something that makes it different. If you share, do it together.

Providing neither of you snores, and you have similar sleeping habits, **sharing** presents no great problem, once you have dealt with initial shyness and embarrassment. The whole situation can only work by mutual agreement on house rules. These mean honesty about your needs – such as your need for ten minutes on the loo when there's only one and it's in the bathroom, or that you are a fresh air freak, or you require six cups of tea before you can crawl out of bed in the morning, or you sleep lightly and like to read between 3 am and 5 am and there's only one central light. If you come out with these personal peculiarities straight away, and also acknowledge it's as much their room as yours, then you can negotiate and compromise and the atmosphere stays sweet. You have, after all, a common aim: to be ready to play or travel at a specific time, which is usually not of your choosing. Find out what works for both and upsets both least. People assume others have the same speeds of getting ready as themselves. Wrong!

As a snorer I happily shared a room with someone who privately admitted to being deaf in one ear. When woken by my racket, it only required turning on to the good ear to shut out my snoring, and return to sleep. Surprisingly then, that was no problem, but we nearly came to grief because I am a 'last minute-er' – quick at getting ready once I start, but with no allowance for interruptions – and my room mate required four times as long. Yet when it came to seeking out cheap, good, back-street restaurants used by the locals, my room-mate was second to none. 'What is a friend? – just one with whom you dare to be yourself.'

Strange beds *can* be a problem, particularly if you have back pain. Hotel beds have improved vastly, but you still occasionally find a bed that is quite wrong for you, and good sleep is vital on tour.

If it's too soft, you can carry a folding, hard bed-board in the lid of your suitcase, but do invent a fail safe way of remembering to retrieve it from under your mattress before flying off to the next continent. Hard beds can be softened by putting a pillow under the knees if you lie on your back, or between them if you lie on your side. A folded towel under your waist will help that natural curve too.

The criterion to look for when you lie on your side on a bed, is that your spine and neck are in a straight line. Too soft a bed and your spine will be in a long curve, or you will roll into the soft hole (like all your predecessors in that bed), and then you will wake to start the day all crooked. Too hard and your body will sag between the shoulders and hips because the extra width of shoulder and hip girdles has not been absorbed by the springs. (This especially affects women who are more curvaceous.)

Some like duvets and hate blankets and vice versa. I take a duvet cover with me if I know I will get blankets, and put them in the duvet cover; if caught unawares, I untuck the blankets all round and kick out the bottom. Being tall, I hate having draughts down my sides and squashed feet. Conversely, an errant duvet can be anchored by the bed cover, or a sheet stolen from another bed, and tucked in firmly. *Don't suffer, ask for what you need to get a good night's sleep.*

Planning leisure on tour

Joe Public equates touring with holidays. You and I know differently; there is a limit to just how scintillating airports, coaches, concert hall back-stage areas and hotels can be.

Even assuming you are not too exhausted, there is precious little leisure time on tour, whereas an awful lot of time is forcibly wasted – long 'limbo' times spent sitting trapped in airports, planes, trains, coaches and boats. Instead of submitting to it all, being unutterably bored, shopping for overpriced stuff you don't really want, or eating, drinking or gambling, why not take charge of this time positively? You will find your energy is far less depleted. Here are some suggestions that need negligible or no forethought: personal stereo listening; learning useful phrases for your destination; instrument cleaning; origami; people watching; sketching; reading and crosswords; needlepoint, knitting, crochet; meditating or taking a mental holiday; letter and postcard writing; t'ai chi (if you can find a quiet corner); planning something, or learning something new for the fun of it.

Perhaps more important, is the rare actual 'free' time – taking into account that it's usually on a Sunday or saint's day when everything is shut, and that it's probably pouring with rain, or there's a local strike!

Decide who is congenial on the tour list before you go and divide the labour of gathering information between you. Then do the following:

1. Go to your local travel agent, look at tours going to that area and note the interesting places they visit.

2. Ring the tourist board (usually in central London) of the country you are visiting – it may be able to give you more details.

3. Pick out those places nearest the concert halls if you can. If not,

4. There may be useful bumph in the airport arrival lounge, so hunt around while you wait for the baggage.

5. On arrival at the hotel check: (a) where the good local shops are for the local specialities and whatever else you want to buy; (b) updated opening times of art galleries, museums etc. Ask *them* what's special/new in town; (c) go for a short walk with your 'congenial companion' and ask in local shops where *they* go to eat, and you will get good, cheap local food (this is why you studied relevant phrases in the local language).

6. *Before you set out, be absolutely sure you can get back in good time for the next band call, and tell a reliable person where you are going, so the tour management can rescue you if something goes wrong.* It's irresponsible not to.

7. Have FUN, and laugh lots – it's good diaphragm exercise!

Carrying cases

It used to be possible, when travelling with an orchestra, just to put your case outside your hotel room door and it would appear outside the next hotel room door. Now, because of stringent security checks, people must take personal responsibility for their luggage throughout a tour.

Probably the people who have least trouble carrying weights naturally are those who have no neck problems and carry the lot on their heads. Europeans just don't do that. Apart from the fact that it's exhausting carrying cases, there are very real dangers which get worse as you get more tired and tense during the tour. These are exacerbated if (a) you already have back problems; (b) you play a one-sided instrument which probably means your spine isn't as straight as it might be anyway; (c) you have hernia problems; (d) you are out in the sticks, a jumbo jet landed just before your arrival, and free trolleys are nowhere to be seen.

If you can, use a case or box with wheels attached for all heavy instruments and amplifiers etc. Spend time when buying it to find one that doesn't require you to stoop to use the wheels; most readily available makes seem best suited to short people. I also found it a good idea to contact the manufacturer and buy a spare set of wheels as they tend to get ripped off by baggage handling. Another solution is a lightweight foldable trolley. The only time these are a nuisance is when they won't fit in the overhead compartment on a plane. For your back's sake, where you can, take a backpack and several small cases rather than one large one, but remember to count them as it's so easy to forget one.

Wheels on heavy instruments are a good idea provided the instrument is adequately protected with foam or bubble-wrap against bumps and vibration. Straps to carry instruments over one shoulder are helpful, provided you swap shoulders regularly, and/or you have the strap across the body, not just dragging the one 'favourite' carrying shoulder down. Failure to balance carrying time between the two sides of the body will eventually cause curvature of the spine and all the aches and pains that it is heir to. If you can afford it, a high-quality lightweight case pays for itself many times over. Many musicians playing smaller instruments use a backpack which takes music too. There are some specially designed ones.

Packing can make a huge difference to stress levels, especially if you often lose things. We'll assume you have your packing check list. The next best piece of advice I can give you is to pack similar items together in large zip-top plastic bags with a couple of spares for dirty washing and things still damp from last night's wash. This has the following advantages: (a) your case doesn't instantly turn into a dog's dinner and you can find things immediately, especially if you put the most used stuff on top, and shoes and the heaviest things in the bottom; (b) clean things don't get dirty or smelly and stay ironed; (c) if you squash the air out of each bag this acts as a form of semi-ironing; (d) repacking can be done in a jiffy as you haven't got to refold everything.

The cardinal rule for all carrying is a straight back. Put as much as you

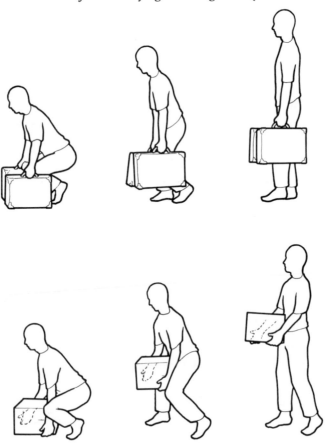

How to lift heavy instrument cases

can into a backpack. Put it on the table empty, fill it, and then pick it up from there, not from the floor. When you lift any case *bend your knees.* Then, if you have to bend more, stick your bottom out and bend from your hips not from your waist. Keeping the case as close as possible to you, the main lifting should be done by the longest, strongest muscles in your body that are built for the job, namely your thigh muscles, not your back (which should remain straight). The tiny muscles between the bones of the spine are *not* built for lifting. Remember we once walked horizontally and need-ed a flexible spine to be used like a cheetah to place hind foot in the hole which forefoot left, to get good forward leverage for speed. Your thigh muscles, in contrast, are built for strength, so use them. Each side lifts your entire weight off the ground every step you take.

Any one-sided pull made because you have one large suitcase will pull your spine over. It may then lock in that position and then you are *in trouble.* The only preventative available to you is to cut down the strain by swapping sides every 100 yards. Your hands will thank you, too.

If you have the misfortune to get a shooting pain as you bend forward to lift your case, drop the case and, supporting your back by putting your hands on your knees, gently straighten up and *immediately bend to the other side.* Do this before the muscles have had time to go into spasm. If you have torn muscle fibres you will be stiff as a board within half an hour so, as soon as you can, demand ice-cubes. While you are waiting for their arrival, take Arnica 6 (or Rescue Remedy) and Rhus. tox 6 tablets under your tongue or rubbed over the spot if you only have ointments. When the ice arrives, wrap it in a small towel or large hanky and get someone to rub the painful spot with it gently for 10 to 15 minutes. The recommended dose for homeopathic pills is two tablets per hour for the first six hours, then three times a day until better. Immediate treatment cuts down shock, spasm and swelling, and reduces injury to a minimum before protective bodily over-reaction sets in.

Queuing with your case is a bugbear. Don't try to lift it umpteen times as you inch forward. Gently push it in front of you with your foot if you can't get a trolley. Yes, it may damage the case, scuff it and make it dirty, but better that (and cheaper) than damaging you by too much stoop-ing and awkward lifting.

How not to get mugged

It's a curious fact that the people who are most frequently mugged are not frail, little old ladies, sexy blondes or the disabled, but young men who think they are not vulnerable. The others have more natural caution and a healthy distrust of strangers.

Musicians put themselves at risk in so many ways. They are particularly vulnerable because they work unsociable hours, often finishing very late at night when there's little public transport. Musicians travel to lots of strange cities and resorts, and stage doors tend to be down dark, narrow alleys, often in the less salubrious parts of town. They are sensitive people whose muscles are highly trained in a specific way which is not for combat. There are now a higher proportion of women and homosexuals in the arts as a whole than in most other professions, and that regrettably makes them more of a target for homophobic and drug-taking 'yobbos'.

As a 'Brit' in any foreign country you still stick out like a sore thumb. You may not be wearing Bermuda shorts, a pork-pie or bowler hat or speak with a plum in your mouth, but your clothes, stance, gait and manner still give you away, as though you had a label round your neck. Fortunately there are still many things you can do to look after yourself, even if you don't want to take a full self-defence course.

A film was taken at random of people walking down a street. It was then shown to a group of convicted muggers who were asked which ones they would pick to mug and why. They picked the ones who walked hunched over, walked in a daydream/daze, looked lost, uncoordinated or physically off-balance as the easy targets. That should tell us something. Be alert, know where you are going, walk tall and stride out with a purpose. *Expand your space mentally;* it's far less likely to be invaded. Then you are aware of what's going on all round you, just as you would be if you were playing chamber music. Dithering, map in hand, asks for unwelcome outside attention. Where possible, get very clear directions before stepping out into the street. Avoid putting yourself in any vulnerable state, such as by drinking too much. It affects your judgement, both of people and situations.

We all have self preservation instincts and intuition. If you feel something is wrong, or you are apprehensive in a place, trust that instinct, act on it and get out. Instinct is usually right. The worst you'll feel, acting on it, is mildly silly if you are wrong. If you are right it could save your life. Listen to it!

Reduce the risks by knowing where you are going and look as if you are eager to get there. Wear shoes which are comfortable and which allow you to run. The 'tap-tap' of high heels is a great give away, and a tight skirt will slow you down. Cover up skimpy clothes and evening gowns, even if it's boiling hot. Visible jewellery asks to be pinched. Hoods, sunglasses and open umbrellas restrict your all-round vision, and stereo headphones will prevent you from hearing an attacker creeping up behind. Long, dangling scarves are great for strangling people with.

Bags that go over your shoulder or under your coat with the fastening worn facing your body are not so glamorous, but far harder to steal. Bumbags are better than an open basket, but not much safer than a back pocket if they have a clip fastener. They have 'here it is' written all over them. It's odd that people assume that if *they* can't see their back pocket other people don't know it's there. Use a safety-pin to fix valuables in an inside pocket, not your bag – which you should be prepared to give up even if it does contain your Filofax. All irreplaceable documents should not need to be carried around all the time, and you should keep a list elsewhere of your passport, credit card and pin numbers (memorised, one hopes), together with a very recent photo of yourself and your blood group in case of accident. Never write your home address on a suitcase label – it advertises that your house is probably empty.

Don't reveal that you are living alone, or are going back to an empty building. Write down your address or room number rather than giving it out aloud in a public place or public phone; you never know who might be listening! Keep to well-lit, busy streets, even if it means walking the long way round. Avoid deserted places, lonely bus stops, derelict and dark buildings, waste ground, empty multi-storey car parks, bushes and alleys. If you have to go through an underpass or subway, take advantage of others going the same way and walk with them. Vary your daily route, and know where the pubs and garages with 'phones are. Unless the pavement is narrow, walk in the middle, facing the traffic to avoid kerb crawlers, bag-snatching bikers and people in dark doorways. The best thing if you regularly have to go through a dodgy area, is to arrange a lift-share with other members of the band. *Never* hitch-hike or accept unsolicited lifts, and beware of unknown self-appointed escorts. In late night trains or buses, sit near the conductor, guard or driver.

Investing in good, outside house security, such as infra-red lights or a porch light on a timer, is well worth the expense if your house is at all secluded, or the door is not lit by street lighting. If you are away for more than a day, get a neighbour to collect post and milk for you. Have a variable timer on an inside light. Apart from the security angle, such things are a nice welcome home. If you find the door tampered with, don't go in but get the police immediately.

Here are a few specific points with which to finish:
Cars. Make sure there's enough petrol in the car to see you there *and* home. Take a spare can and refill it on arrival, *not* when it's dark on your way home. If it's winter, take a newspaper for the windscreen and some WD40 for de-icing the plugs if it's cold and wet. Know the route or at least have the map easily accessible so you don't have to stop and ask a stranger. Keep enough change in the car for parking, or bus, train, tube and 'phone if you can't start the car. When you drive, lock all doors and windows. Take no hitch-hikers, even if female (could be a decoy), and don't stop to help if someone seems in trouble; go on to the next 'phone and call help for them. Don't stop for an accident either, unless you are properly qualified; you'll only clog up the road for emergency service vehicles.

When you arrive at the venue, park in a well-lit, frequently used, car park, in a place that's easy to get at, and safe when you return. If you can't find one immediately, go back in the rehearsal break, and move your car while it's still daylight and most shoppers have gone home. Keep a small torch in your coat pocket to check the car is empty before you get in, but don't use it to light your way to the car, because it advertises your presence and your poor night vision. If you have to stop on the way home or when it's dark, because you are falling asleep, or need the loo, stop at a pub or hotel with a well-lit forecourt, and walk in as if you owned the place. If challenged, explain your needs to the clerk on the desk.

When you arrive home, have your door keys ready, not in your pocket or bag where you might have to fumble for them. Get inside fast. You might think it worth investing in a AA or RAC membership, automatic garage doors, a car phone and learning how to change a wheel efficiently.

Cabs. Ask at the stage door for reliable minicab numbers. When you call ask for your driver's name. When the cab arrives, ask again to check the driver's name and the cab company name and then get in the back. Chat, but give away no personal details and ask to be dropped several doors away so you don't give away your address. Have cash ready, but get out first and pay through the driver's window. Again have your door keys ready and get inside the house fast. If you have an over-friendly cab driver, mentally note the cab name and number, have your money ready and, *pretending to be feeling horribly car sick,* ask to be set down as soon as you are in a well-lit, populated area.

Hotels. Don't ask for your room key by number loudly enough for everyone in the reception area to hear. Leave valuables in the hotel safe, but get a receipt for them. When in your room, lock the door and use the chain if there is one. Let no one in you haven't invited and don't recognise, or haven't checked with reception or your tour leader. Even if you are on the umpteenth floor, draw your curtains if there are other tall buildings about and you are doing something that might interest the owner of a telephoto lens. When you get in a hotel lift and you are unsure about the other occupant, check the buttons and make sure it's not set to go to the roof or basement unless you're actually going there. Stand near the door and look confidently at people as they get in. Don't let your posture have 'victim' written all over it.

Defence. Perhaps the most important thing is to know your own strengths. Are you best with your teeth, elbows, fingers in the eyes, a kick in the shins or crotch, or are you a very fast runner? Keys are a useful weapon – like a knuckle duster if threaded through between fingers. Attackers don't like noise so *yell,* call out to passers-by to get the police, throw a stone through a window or two to get attention. As a female, if you can, *run into a group of women.*

In an empty train *be disgusting.* Pick your nose and ears, scratch a lot. If you get groped on a very crowded train or lift, *grab the offending hand,* raise it aloft and ask in a loud voice who it belongs to. If the train is in a tunnel try to wait for the train to come out or to a station before pulling the cord. In a lift, *press all the buttons* to make it stop as soon as possible and, when the doors open, run into a populated area. *Never believe or trust your attacker. Don't bargain and, above all, don't agree to go anywhere else with him/her!*

You may think from the above that I am paranoid – no. It is unlikely that you will be attacked, despite what the media appear to say, but it's a good idea to know how to make it even less likely.

REFERENCES

1. **Bracken P.** (1963) *The I Hate to Housekeep Book,* Sphere
2. **Conran S.** (1975) *Superwoman;* (1977) *Superwoman in Action,* Penguin Books
3. **Conran S.** and **Sidney E.** (1979) *Future Woman,* Penguin Books
4. **Gaier H.** (1991) *Thorsons Encyclopedic Dictionary of Homeopathy,* Thorsons, Harper Collins
5. **Lamplugh D.** (1988) *Beating Agression,* Weidenfeld Paperbacks
6. **Lamplugh D.** (1989) *Survive Nine to Five,* Grapevine, Harper Collins
7. **Lockie A.** (1989) *The Family Guide to Homeopathy – The Safe Form of Medicine for the Future,* Hamish Hamilton, Penguin Books Ltd.
8. **Saunders H.** (1992) *Self-help Manual for Your Neck* (p32), The Saunders Group Inc. Chaska MN USA

ORGANIZATIONS

Osteopathic Supplies Ltd. 70 Belmont Road, Hereford HR2 7JW. *Tel:* 01432 263939

The Supply Centre, Anglo-European College of Chiropractic. 13-15 Parkwood Road, Bournemouth BH5 2DF. *Tel:* 01202 436236

Bed Boards. 3A Agincourt Street, Monmouth NP5 3DZ. *Tel:* 01600 6904 (and available at Osteopathic Supplies)

Nelsons Homeopathic Remedies. A. Nelson & Co, 5 Endeavour Way, Wimbledon, London SW19 9UH

Sea-band Ltd. Church Walk, Hinckley, Leicestershire LE10 1DW. *Tel:* 01455 251007/611092

CHAPTER 6

Food Matters

*Optimum diet and quality food; Weight
gain and loss; Re-education; Vitamins and
minerals; E numbers; What is good
digestion? Cholesterol; Acid and alkaline;
Ileocaecal Valve Syndrome (or IBS);
Allergies and food sensitivities; Addiction;
'A pill for every ill' and side-effects of
common drugs; More about homeopathy;
Selye, Lindlahr and naturopathy; Water;
Fasting and cleansing*

Optimum diet and quality food

For optimum nutrition, the intake of food and the ability to assimilate it must match output for repair and growth, heating and energy requirements. That sounds straightforward. It isn't. If you do manage to balance intake to need, your weight will remain stable, and you will be fit with plenty of energy. The doubt about it all has spawned an enormous industry in nutritional supplements, and the publication of thousands of cookery books. This is not the place for hard-and-fast rules, nor for treading on the toes of expert dieticians, just straightforward guidelines. What suits most musicians is a version of the Pritikin 'low fat, low protein, soups, salads and lots of composite carbohydrate' diet, with no 'empty' sugars like white sugar.

1. The younger you are, the more you are likely to grow, yet mother's milk only has a tiny percentage of protein, so as a grown adult you do not need much; probably not more than two to four ounces a day, and of course you can eat more. If we used the energy a toddler uses relative to his size, we would probably die of exhaustion!

2. Young digestive systems are less efficient than old, which is why food seems to go straight through children, and they are always hungry.

3. Older people eliminate less well and so tend to store toxins.

4. Large people can tolerate more toxicity than small people, before the system retaliates and you become ill.

5. Different ages and temperaments burn nutrients at different metabolic rates, even if these rates are only related to stress levels.

6. We digest better when calm, and certain specific chemical stresses drain body resources of water-soluble (and therefore not stored) vitamins and minerals. Generally, ideal proportions in a food intake should be four-fifths fruit and vegetables, to one-fifth fats, carbohydrates and protein. Most of this last fifth should be complex carbohydrates such as wholemeal bread, pasta, rice and other cereals, and potatoes.

7. As a general rule, the fresher a food is the better. Ask yourself how many miles it has had to travel, and where it has been. Food displayed outside in a busy street with heavy traffic will have a film

of petrochemicals all over it. Packaging, storage, processing, freezing and cooking all age food and deplete it of the life-giving forces of its vitamins and enzymes. Cutting up fresh food may speed cooking but also increases vitamin loss, oxydisation and rancidity. If you eat really fresh food, then large amounts of supplements are an efficient way of urinating away your money! If your digestive system works very poorly this is what happens to most of the goodness in your food too.

8. A musician's life uses more vitamins B and C than most other jobs. This is because high sugar, smoking and stress all use up B very, very fast. Junk food and all the long shelf-life processing, pasteurising, waxing, freeze-drying, tinning and freezing, not to mention rewarming and microwaving, remove most of the vitamin C, so these are the only two supplements I would recommend taking on tour.

9. If you can afford organic food, it may not look so beautiful, but you know it's reasonably fresh because without preservatives it would be rotten if it were old. It tastes better too, particularly and especially if you have grown it yourself.

10. Meat that is reared with compassion will be less stressed, therefore less tough and more tasty, but animals bred to be 'leaner than lean' hate the cold just as we do and given the choice may well prefer to live inside. If you buy 'outdoor reared' meat, therefore, you may have to cut off the fat and feed it to the birds in winter.

11. Fibre is not food. It is natural cellulose, which stimulates intestinal and bowel movement. This is essential, but doesn't actually feed you. It makes the contents of your intestine pass through faster, and therefore you don't absorb so much. That's why it's an efficient slimming food. You feel full up but don't actually absorb so much. Musicians need fibre because of the sedentary lifestyle our lower bodies lead, even if we are vigorously waving our arms about.

9. You are *not* what you *eat* but what you *assimilate*. If you could straighten out the entire 28 feet of tubing from mouth to anus you would see what I mean. If you assimilate well but don't use much, you store the goodies and put on weight. You eat because it's time to eat, not because you are really hungry. Your tummy rumbles because its been trained like Pavlov's dog to produce digestive juices in

response to the clock (instead of a bell).

10. For most people diets don't work. Even well-worked-out diets don't. In the long run you put it all back, because there is no re-education of our Pavlovian trained habits. As soon as you have lost the required pounds you go back to 'normal eating'. You are still addicted psychologically, and as anyone giving up smoking will know, your mind is much harder to retrain than the body's chemical need for nicotine.

Weight gain and loss

'"Yo-yo" crash dieting is known to increase the risk of heart disease and angina' (WDDTY 1995). Studies of weight loss have revealed that even after four years, the body will still be trying to return to its initial weight (British Medical Journal, March 1995 310:750). Meal replacements are dangerous too, in that they can lead to malnutrition and do nothing to encourage healthier eating habits. The story goes of a string quartet leader who loved his food and had three sizes of DJ and tails. When he was getting too fat for his largest size, he booked himself into Champneys for a month at vast expense, and lived on oranges until he could get into his smallest suits. This occurred about once a year. He never learned to say 'No' to food appropriately. Regrettably this is the story of most non-responsible dieting. For many POWs who were starved and deprived as part of their humiliation in the last war, the only remaining symptom years later is a preoccupation with food resulting in a fridge that's always stuffed full. The siege mentality remains. The same is true of people who are always dieting, but who cannot let go of the idea of 'victim' consciousness. The hardest part about being a food addict is that you can't totally abstain. The best you can do is supervise and control.

Most people are overweight rather than underweight, and there are plenty of charts available which correlate height, gender and weight. The anorexics amongst us need recognition and need medical help, but there are also others who are not anorexic but are underweight. What they need is help to assimilate the goodness better from what they do eat. You need a biochemist or an applied kinesiologist to sort out which vitamins, minerals and enzymes you are missing and which you need to boost assimilation. For most people it's all right to be about a stone under normal weight for your height, and while it's better in general to be under rather than over for your heart's sake, a stone either side of 'normal' is acceptable in a doctor's surgery.

Re-education

The question is 'How to deal with food addiction?' with all the food available, advertising and TV programmes. I have found the answer to be a change in attitude that is subtle and fundamental, and keeps you 'in charge' as opposed to being a victim, prey to whatever comes your way. You can also get herbal assistance. The hydroxycitric acid in tamarind (citrimax) is said to help, but you need professional advice on this before taking it. The first thing to do is to look at the real truth. Write down in a notebook everything that you eat for one week, including all the snacks. There's no point in lying, as you will only deceive yourself which defeats the exercise. The result will probably astonish you. It's even more effective if you put the same amount on one table and look at it. There should be no judgement, just observe that the table is carrying 'the facts' about your eating. You were responsible for putting that amount of food in your mouth and through your digestive system.

Next, write down when you eat what, including all the nibbles and 'little somethings', and whether you have your main meal before you need the main energy of the day or last thing at night. Notice if a stress pattern emerges, e.g. practising/chocolate biscuits, driving/peppermints, concerts/coffee and alcohol. Again no condemnation or self flagellation, just notice the connection. Finally, weigh yourself and decide on your goals – how much by when? Be gentle, sensible and realistic. Aim at about two pounds (one kilo) a week. A concurrent whole-body exercise programme helps.

With this knowledge there is the possibility and opportunity of being in control of it all because *you choose to*. It's not so much what you eat or when, but why. What is the fear that eating covers up? Be responsible for it and nurture it until it heals, and the embarassing scars get beyond being trophies of survival, to being of no consequence. Until you sort the fear out, you will be a yo-yo, and your body metabolism will always react with a siege mentality, storing all it can at every opportunity. I have put the following affirmations on tape and play them to myself at least once a day (preferably several times) and in any odd moment. You can easily do the same, and you don't need to play the whole tape every time. However, *the words must be your own* and have a 'zing' for you, to have any real, deep-down effect. Use the techniques to counteract any conditioning you want to throw off: influences and comments from other people, thoughts and feelings you have every day, and any unwanted rubbish that has been a part of your life until now. If you tell your brain something often enough it will believe it, even if it's not true. Using this fact, you can counteract all unwanted past influences with your tape. You will then have created a useful new habit because *you* decided what to tell your brain, rather than unthinkingly taking someone else's beliefs on board and letting them run your life. This is what is on my tape. Make your own!

Dear Inner Me,

Listen well please. I am painting a completely new picture of myself the way I want to be. This is the me I want you to create. Forget all the bad programming I gave you in the past, that you heard from others too. Use this new programming:

I am organised and in control of my life. I am a winner and I am going for it. I am inspired and inspiring. I am healthy, energetic, enthusiastic and full of joy and bounce. I like who I am and I believe in myself. I am in tune, on top and in touch. I have determination, drive, self-belief and zest. I am living the life I choose and I choose what's right for me.

Taking care of myself physically is important to me. I like keeping myself fit and feeling good. I value myself and am proud of myself. I eat beautiful food when I am hungry and don't when I'm not. I have no habits which control or influence me in any harmful or negative way. I always do what is best for me now and for my future. I am a lean machine that springs into life. I really enjoy breathing lots of clean, fresh air, and filling my lungs. I love the zest and energy it provides. I exercise regularly, keeping myself fit and healthy and I am enjoying a lifetime of energy and vitality. All my senses are clear and alive. Sight, hearing, sense of smell and taste, and even my sense of touch are all keener, sharper and more alive than ever before.

I feel safe with myself, even when I let go, at all times and in all situations. I am contented and satisfied, for all my needs are met, and I have no feeling of dissatisfaction in the pit of my stomach that needs to be filled full up with excess food, so now I am in touch with real hunger not false. Animals and plants have given themselves for me to be nourished, so to me food is a sacrament and I do not abuse it.

I plan my menus from low-fat and raw-food cook-books, to be delicious, nutritious, healthy and slimming, and then I shop for that, cook for that and enjoy that. The fresher the food, the less it's cooked and the more it's chewed, the better it is for me.

Each time I sit down to eat, I re-affirm my determination to achieve my goal. By eating properly and never giving in, I am reaching the weight I want to be, and my metabolism is working at optimum efficiency. I enjoy eating less and tasting and chewing more, so I digest better and feel fuller with less, whether I am alone or have company. I use a smaller plate, put less on my plate and less on my fork, so less goes on my waist, because that is what I want.

By ordering less in a restaurant and by serving myself smaller portions at home, I keep myself aware of the importance of staying with my goal, each and every day, until it is my healthy habit that I have created for myself. When I sit down to eat, at no time do I allow anyone else to influence, tempt or discourage me in any way. I do not let doubt show to be exploited, but am clear, direct, polite and firm. I eat to please *me* and I give no-one the right to hinder or control my success.

I am achieving my weight-loss goals for myself, my life, my future and my own well-being. I am never at any time tempted to take one bite more than I should, because I am strong, I am capable, I am in charge. I do not eat my meal in the room where all the food is stored, if I can eat elsewhere and so remove the tempting sight. There are never any leftovers or seconds to have to refuse because I immediately make them into a delicious nourishing soup to start another meal when I am ready.

Being in situations where a lot of food is put in front of me is not a problem for me now. I simply say 'No' to excess and 'Yes' to my success!

I enjoy sitting down to eat because each time I do, I conquer my past and I create a trimmer, happier, more self-confident future in front of me. When I sit down to eat I do not need someone else to remind me of my goal, or to keep me from eating something I should not, or from having 'just one more', because I'm doing it for me, because I take full responsibility for myself; no one else has to do it for me.

Controlling my weight and my appetite is easy for me now. I dislike gobbling, and missing all the subtle tastes and textures. I prefer smaller portions, smaller bites and a slower, healthier, more relaxed way of eating that gives me time to really taste and appreciate each mouthful. I have set my goals and I am staying with them. Nothing can stop me now, for I am ready to 'go out and fight dragons'. I have turned mealtime into 'delectable achievement time' and I am proud of myself!

In the above tape, there is no sense of 'should' or 'ought' or 'must' because I am deciding what I want, as you will if you make your own tape. There's no resentment or victim feeling, just a sense of creation. The format of the above affirmation is intentionally over-positive to counter-balance all the negative propaganda about without and within your head. The same format can be used to reprogramme worry, problem solving, victim consciousness and low self-esteem.

So how do I know what to eat, other than slavishly following recipe books? I use them for inspiration and to assist in avoiding impulse buying. This keeps bills down, especially if you eat what's in season, rather than buying out-of-season foods which you get sick of because you 'treat yourself' to them every week out of a misplaced sense of reward. You will only do that if you still think you are a victim. What you save you can invest in better-quality, organic food.

Vitamins and Minerals

The list that follows is useful to enable you to increase certain nutrients in your diet as part of a healing process, using the substances' natural sources rather than through supplements and vitamin pills. I hate taking pills and love eating fruit and vegetables. You may prefer to take pills and be sure that you are getting what you think you need and hang the expense, but you miss a lot of pleasure. Foods in italics have the highest content. The choice is yours.

Vitamins

A: Milk, butter, margarine, eggs, *fish oil,* carrots, yellow and dark-green fruit and vegetables, liver, tomato, cantaloupe melon. Deficiency causes night blindness, kidney stones, skin complaints.

B1 Thiamin: *Brewers yeast,* whole grains and brown rice, blackstrap molasses, organ meats (offal) and egg-yolk, soya bean, sunflower seeds. Deficiency can be caused by pregnancy, too many high-sugar foods, stress, alcohol, habitual antacids, and causes loss of mental alertness and depression, muscle weakness, respiratory problems, water retention and heart damage. **B2 Riboflavin (G):** Brewers yeast, whole grains, peas and beans, organ meats, blackstrap molasses, mushrooms, spinach. Deficiency causes tired, gritty, bloodshot eyes, cracks and sores round the mouth, dizziness, insomnia, slow learning, and is exacerbated by alcohol, tobacco and the contraceptive pill. **B3 Niacin:** Lean meat, poultry and fish, *brewers yeast,* peanuts, almonds, mushrooms, brown rice. **B5 Pantothenic acid** and **B6 Pyrodoxine:** as B3 plus wheatgerm, soya. Deficiency causes anemia, PMT, nettle rash, asthma. **B9 Folic acid:** Dark-green, leafy vegetables, organ meats, root vegetables, oysters, salmon, milk. Essential in pregnancy. **B12:** Organ meats, fish, pork, eggs, cheese, milk, lamb, bananas, kelp, peanuts. Deficiency causes sore tongue, nerve deterioration and tremors, menstrual problems and anemia. (Be aware of this if you are vegan.)

C: *Acerola cherry juice,* citrus family, *cabbage family,* chilli, melon, asparagus, rosehips, tomatoes, green peppers, strawberries, mango. Deficiency causes lassitude, muscle and joint pain, bleeding and infected gums, increased allergic sensitivity, irritability, decreased incidence of, or need for, colds and 'flu to help the body eliminate.

Bioflavanoids: Apricots, *citrus skin and pulp,* blackcurrants, broccoli, buckwheat, cherries, grapes, green peppers, *lemons,* tomatoes. Deficiency causes easy bruising and tiny skin haemorrhages.

D: *Cod-liver oil,* salmon, sardines, herring and kippers, milk, egg-yolk, organ meats, sardines, sprouted seeds, sunflower seeds, tuna. Deficiency causes rickets (bone softening and delayed ability to stand in children) and osteomalacia – similar in adults with bone pain, muscle spasm and weakness, and brittle bones.

E: Cold-pressed plant oils, *cod-liver oil,* eggs, parsley, peas, kale, *wheat germ,* organ meats, molasses, shrimps, soya, sweet potatoes, nuts and peanuts. Deficiency causes irritability, water retention, anaemia, lethargy and apathy, loss of libido, poor concentration and muscle weakness.

Be careful that your sources of vitamins A, D and E are not rancid.

Minerals

Calcium: Almonds, apricots, bananas, cabbage, cauliflower, cheese, dates, egg-yolks, figs, lemon rind, lettuce, milk, onions, parsnips, prunes, radishes, spinach, watercress, whole wheat. Deficiency causes tooth and gum decay and poor circulation.

Iron: Almonds, apples, apricots, asparagus, beetroot, carrots, dates, egg-yolks, figs, lettuce, leeks, all meats, peas, potato skins, prunes, raisins, radishes, spinach, tomatoes, walnuts, whole wheat. Deficiency causes anaemia, low vitality, poor disease resistance.

Magnesium: Almonds, bananas, beetroot, brewers yeast, whole barley, cabbage, chestnuts, coconut, corn-on-the-cob, dates, egg-yolks, figs, lettuce, lemons, milk, oats, oranges, peas, prunes, seafood, soya, tomatoes, walnuts. Deficiency causes acidosis, insomnia and nervous ailments.

Manganese: Almonds, whole barley, beetroot, chestnuts, citrus, egg-yolks, endive, kelp, mint, pineapple, walnuts, watercress. Deficiency causes hysteria and nerve problems, poor memory, and may be present in diabetes, muscle wasting and arthritis.

Phosphorus: Almonds, apples, asparagus, bananas, beans, brewers yeast, cabbage family, celery, cheese, cucumber, egg-yolks, canned fish, lettuce, milk, nuts, oats, prunes, radishes, soya, spinach, walnuts, watercress, whole wheat. Deficiency causes brain-fag, poor bone development, hair loss.

Potassium: Almonds, apricots, runner beans, cabbage, cauliflower, celery, coconut, figs, fish, grapefruit, lettuce, lemons, milk, molasses, oats, onions, oranges, parsnips, potato skins, soya, tomatoes, turnips, watercress. Deficiency causes constipation, liver disorders and skin eruptions.

Zinc: Beans, brewers yeast, canned fish, eggs, green-leaf vegetables, hard cheese, liver, meat, oysters, potatoes, rice, shellfish, wholemeal bread. Deficiency causes poor libido and sexual immaturity, poor appetite and sense of taste.

If your sodium or iodine levels are too high, you might like to avoid foods in the following groups:

Sodium (causing water retention and metabolite disturbance): Apples, asparagus, runner beans, beetroot, cabbage, carrots, cheese, coconut, cucumber, egg-yolks, endive, figs, fizzy drinks, leeks, lettuce, milk, oats, prunes, raisins, salted foods, sea salt, spinach, strawberries, turnips, watermelon. Deficiency causes indigestion and fermentation. Avoid too many foods containing sodium if you have high blood pressure or water retention.

Iodine (causing thyroid problems, weight loss, hyperactivity, irritability, finger- and toe-nail discolouration and malformation): Asparagus, artichokes, bananas, beetroot, cabbage, carrots, garlic, kelp, lettuce, onions, potato skins, seafood, strawberries, tomatoes, watercress. Deficiency causes goitre, obesity, and toxaemia and low vitality.

The above are but a tiny selection to show you how you can help yourself in this area. The reference section at the end of the chapter will give you further sources of information.

E Numbers

In 1984 a great press furore was whipped up about E numbers. Few knew what they stood for, and if an E number was mentioned on a label it was thought a food to be stringently avoided by purists. They were said to be signs of wicked producers' adulteration of food by the addition of synthetic, non-essential colourants and preservatives, emulsifiers and stabilisers, to prolong shelf-life and dupe the public into buying inferior quality food.

The truth is not quite like that. Many of the additives are natural substances used in kitchens for years, such as E100/turmeric, E101/vitamin B2, E120/cochineal, E150/caramel, E153/carbon black (i.e. burnt food!), E162/beetroot, E300/vitamin C. However, many others are coal-tar derivatives, or Azo dyes such as the notorious E102/tartrazine, a yellow colourant in orange squash that caused so many children to be hyperactive.

In general the numbers follow a numerical order according to their main function in the food trade. Many had been used for years but only came to public notice when labelling regulations forced them into the light of day. These labels also helpfully state ingredients in descending order by weight, so it's useful to see, in ham for example, whether the preservative is included before or after salt, or whether the main constituent is water rather than what you thought you were buying. Sometimes the name of the substance is on the label, sometimes only the number.

If you have food sensitivities you are probably already a label reader. If not, the following may give you some pointers towards foods to avoid in order to reduce your stress-levels from chemical pollutants when you are unable to buy fresh food. It is not an exhaustive list; get yourself *E For Additives* (see References).

Hyperactivity: 102, 104, 107, 110, 120, 122, 123, 124, 127, 128, 132, 133, 150, 151, 154, 155, 210, 211, 220, 249, 250, 251, 260, 320, 321

Asthma, lupus, digestive and endocrine disorders, circulation diseases, and rheumatoid arthritis: 102, 107, 110, 122, 123, 124, 127, 128, 131, 133, 134, 142, 151, 154, 210, 211, 212, 213, 214, 216, 217, 218, 220, 221, 222, 224, 226, 227, 230, 236, 239, 249, 250, 251, 252, 310, 311, 312, 320, 321, 322, 336, 385, 412, 413, 414, 421, 500, 503, 508, 621, 622, 623, 627, 631, 632, 635, 924, 925, 926

Skin irritation: 200, 210, 320, 321, 329, 336, 430, 431, 503, 508, 510, 622, 627, 632, 635, 924, 926

High blood pressure: 220, 320, 321, 336, 422, 514, 541, 622, 623, 635, 924, 925, 926

Low blood pressure: 306, 307, 308, 309, 336, 514, 621, 632, 635

Ulcers: 261, 326, 332, 336, 503, 510, 621, 622, 632, 635, 924

Fluid retention: 262, 290, 336, 510, 514, 541, 622, 632, 635

Candida: 230, 231, 232, 233, 236, 239, 263, 280, 281, 282, 283, 336, 503, 508, 610, 621, 622, 627, 631, 635, 924

What is good digestion?

Good digestion occurs when everything is properly broken down into its constituent parts, and what is needed is absorbed and the rest is removed. Biochemistry is complex. All you need to know is which bits of you digest which foods, and what are the most common things that go wrong.

So (a) the input must be good; (b) the 'machinery' must work; and (c) waste disposal must be efficient.

Input has already been discussed. The machinery consists of a muscular tube to push the contents through, with a series of sphincters (circular muscle constrictions) to divide up the different environments. The sphincters at each end (mouth and anus) are under voluntary control to stop the contents falling out, the rest are under the control of the vagus nerve which is strongly affected by your emotional state, working efficiently when you are calm and shutting everything down in emergencies, or under stress.

In the mouth (the first environment), food is well chewed to increase its surface area and sugar breakdown begins. You swallow, and the food passes down the gullet (passing through the diaphragm) and then goes through a sphincter into the stomach. This constriction is to stop backflow of the very strong stomach acids as the food is thoroughly stirred (the acidity stops sugar breakdown temporarily), to start to digest the proteins. The food then goes through another sphincter into the duodenum environment into which the gall-bladder empties a strong alkaline to break down fats, and the pancreas secretes insulin to continue sugar breakdown. The food continues on into the small intestine (all 24 feet of it), where most of the final digestion goes on and nutrients are absorbed through its enormous surface area. The remnants, and all the water and cellulose (fibre) empty into the large intestine via another sphincter-like constriction (the ileo-caecal valve, of which more later). In the large intestine, there are a series of sphincter-like constrictions to hold back the pressure as all the excess water is drawn off and some vitamin B is made, and you are left with the brownish mass you push out of your anus.

The main causes of things going wrong are mechanical and chemical.

1. *Mechanical:* (a) gobbling and poor chewing mean there's a reduced surface area for the juices to work on; (b) malfunction of the main sphincters (due to upset of the vagus nerve from compression, poisonous intake or stress) which mostly become lax, allowing leakage and back-flow (heartburn, 'gastro-oesophageal reflux' or hiatal hernia), or acid leak into the duodenum (and duodenal ulcers), or, lower down, toxicity (because by the time it's got to these lower sphincters, the 'food' is becoming putrid). If the muscular constrictions become too tight, and there is a pile-up

behind them because nothing gets through, digestion stops and you feel sick, distended and constipated.

2. *Chemical:* gobbling means food is in contact with digestive juices for a shortened time, so little breakdown occurs of sugars in the mouth, and of protein in the stomach, causing half-digested and toxic 'food'. If the gall-bladder fails, you can't digest fats and you get bilious attacks and eventually a form of jaundice. If the pancreas fails, or is exhausted, you will get sugar handling problems, mood swings and maybe adult diabetes. If the small intestine can't absorb properly you get malnutrition even though you eat well. Finally the large intestine may not work well because of lack of fibre and exercise to stimulate it, and you get bulges (diverticulitis), ulcers and ileo-caecal valve syndrome (or irritable bowel syndrome, see below), and haemorrhoids.

How can the musician prevent this sorry list of ills? By regular eating, i.e. an easily digested meal three hours before performing and a smaller one afterwards, with a high fruit and vegetable/low protein and fat ratio, making up the difference with whole grains and potatoes. The Hay diet is often recommended as being easier on the digestion, because it advocates not mixing carbohydrates (requiring alkaline digestion) with proteins (requiring acid digestion). This removes confusion, so the body does a better job with one environment while the other rests. You can also help yourself by not eating large, complex or rich meals when stressed, by chewing well and not sitting hunched up as you eat or bending about after eating. Exercising by walking helps things move along contentedly, rather than continually squashing the digestive tract by sitting all day.

Cholesterol

I'm often asked about cholesterol. Our bodies make a small essential amount. As a generalisation, fats are saturated and solid, or unsaturated and liquid at room temperature, unless they have already been heated. So if you cook with unsaturated fat, some of it becomes saturated and there are transfats that are part-way saturated and toxic. These have to be made harmless and excreted and so rob the body of otherwise useful fat. Far better to cook in completely saturated animal fats like butter used very sparingly (or half fat, half water) and make up your fat needs with cold-pressed plant oils when you can afford them.

What else robs the body besides long shelf-life and cooking? Water thrown away after boiling vegetables contains much of their water-soluble mineral content, so save it and make a nourishing, comforting and easily digested soup to have last thing at night. Some substances combine to become indigestible when taken in supplement capsule or pill form. The worst combination of these is vitamin E and iron, so take them at opposite ends of the day, or you waste your money. Antacids may cut down stomach acid too much, and you end up with half-digested protein that is toxic in the small intestine and has to be rendered harmless by a process which robs the body of further nutrients.

High-sugar diets, alcohol and smoking steal vitamin B and C to break down their toxins, so your body is robbed again. High-protein diets can lead to osteoporosis because, in metabolising the protein, a lot of calcium is lost. This occurs particularly in USA and Scandinavian countries where the most dairy products in the world are consumed (Clin Ortho Related Res, 152;35, 1980). Mucus from allergic reaction to dairy products coats the intestinal surfaces so that nutrient absorption is inhibited or lost. Finally, parasites are far more common than most people ever dream. Any mortician will tell you that 95% of the population have them, even in this supposedly hygenic western world, gathered from unwashed salad and undercooked meat and fish. Our large intestine is full of all sorts of flora – such as yeasts and bacteria, some benign, some not. Problems occur when the 'baddies' get the upper hand, aided and abetted by antibiotics which kill *all* flora and leave the field clear for the baddies to set up shop and give you candidiasis.

Acid and alkaline

According to Jo Schaffer (1992), if you have a tendency to diarrhoea, lots of internal gas, haemorrhoids and colitis it is likely that you eat too many foods which produce an over acidity in the colon. These foods make your liver over active, pancreas sluggish and your stomach also produces too much acid. All this is made worse by a stressful or anxious musician's life-style. You can help yourself by choosing foods that will help to calm down and normalise this reaction within. Other symptoms can be a tendency to colds, sniffles and breath holding, blood-sugar problems when you miss a meal, confusion and irritability, and cystitis.

The following produce the most **alkaline** colon environment. Chose from them:

Fruit: Apples, bananas, avocados, blackberries, raspberries, prunes, raisins, olives, dates, figs, dried peaches, persimmons, plums, pomegranates.

Vegetables: Peas, lentils, beans, potatoes, carrots, celery, spinach, cauliflower, artichokes, asparagus, Swiss chard, marrows, courgettes.

Starches and proteins all produce an **acid** environment in the colon, so keep these to a minimum. The following also produce a more acid ash (the remains in the colon after digestive breakdown)

Fruit: apricot, citrus fruits and melons.

Vegetables: lettuce, tomato family, cabbage family, beansprouts, beetroot, onion family.

Avoid these in large quantities. Balance with a selection from the alkaline ash list.

If you are the 'laidback' type who gets constipation, never gets a cold but has a smouldering temper, feels better if you don't eat, and can tolerate alcohol well, then you are too alkaline and should reverse the list above. The acidity/alkalinity of the foods by the time they reach the colon does not necessarily reflect their fresh acid or alkaline state, because by then they will have been the subject of the chemical reactions ocurring as part of normal digestion. People can change from one type to the other over the years, because of changes in hormone balance and life-style.

Ileocaecal valve syndrome (ICV)

Indigestion and bowel problems are very prevalant amongst musicians because of the stresses, strains and poor eating habits they inflict upon themselves as part of their life-style. The most frequent cause is ileocaecal valve syndrome (ICV), often known as IBS or irritable bowel syndrome. Let us look at the causes and what you can do to help yourself.

The ileocaecal valve is a supposedly one-way sphincter or circular muscular contraction between the large and small intestine. In the small intestine, the main goodness is drawn out of the food into the bloodstream. By the time the remains of the food has reached the large intestine, time spent in such a warm place has caused putrefaction to set in, and the 'food' is now more toxic than useful. In the large intestine it also becomes bacteria laden, hence the one-way valve ensuring a constant progression of intestinal contents in one direction only. Malfunction of the valve causes either spasticity, build-up and congestion, or flaccidity and back-flow. Both cause toxicity in the small intestine followed by a bizarre list of symptoms, including bloating, distension and flatulence; wandering pains; diarrhoea, constipation or alternating between the two; headaches, migraines or nausea; neck, shoulder and low-back pain; difficulty getting going in the morning, exhaustion and general malaise; sudden thirst, paleness and black rings round the eyes. It is known as the great mimic for good reason. The cause of malfunction is stress – mostly emotional and chemical, but occasionally physical or structural. Strong drugs of *all* types, spicy and strange foods, allergies and 'holiday tummy' may all set off the syndrome, and emotional stress keeps it going and often prevents it resetting itself naturally along with the other sphincter muscular constrictions described above.

To locate the ICV, draw an imaginary line from the tummy button to the outside top of the right hip. From the middle of this line go down one inch (2.5cm) diagonally towards the left knee. You are now right over the valve. Press in gently and test a previously strong indicator muscle (see Chapter 10). If it becomes weak, the Testee has the problem. Because the valve is very close to the appendix, manipulation by inexperienced hands is inadvisable and you should see an applied kinesiologist, chiropractor, osteopath or doctor. However you can help it considerably by doing the following:

1. Reduce stress levels by holding the ESR (emotional stress relief) points over the centre of each eye and half-way between the eyebrows and hair line, while the Testee thinks through whatever is stressing him/her three times. Stress is a prime cause of this syndrome, as the valve is controlled by the vagus nerve and a 'fight or flight' attitude.

2. Avoid all stimulants such as tea, coffee, alcohol and smoking, all of which increase stomach acid levels; avoid all raw, high-fibre foods, and cook all vegetables; increase intake of calcium and vitamin B complex. Re-introduce high-fibre foods slowly after 10 to14 days.

This area of your intestine needs to rest. Do not take purgatives. Have an enema if you are constipated.

3. Chew all foods very well and eat only when relaxed. If in doubt, don't eat for one meal, and avoid all foods that in the past have caused flatulence or acute reaction.

4. The following AK techniques may help (for a list of abbreviations, see the end of Chapter 10).

MP is on the top, front, inside left pelvic bone, a little below the level of the tummy button.

HP Acu-point pairs K-5 and Sp-2, K-7 and Lu 8, Lu-1 and S-23. K-5 is a thumb's width below and behind the inner ankle. Hold it with Sp-2 on the last joint of the big toe and on the side away from the other toes. K-7 is a hand's width above the inner ankle bone, and just to the back side of the shin bone. Hold it with Lu-8 on the extreme outside end of the right forearm bone under the base of the thumb. Lu-1 is below the outer end of the collar-bone about one inch (2.5cm) in from the shoulder joint. Hold it with S-23 one inch (2.5cm) out and two inches (5cm) up from the tummy button.

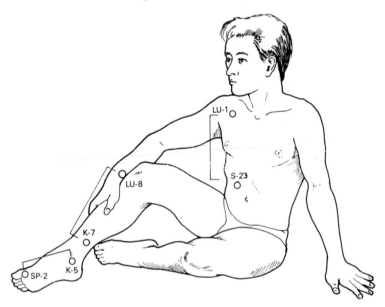

Acupoints for ileocaecal valve syndrome

5. Avoid tight-fitting clothes over the entire abdominal area and belts, especially those with large buckles.

6. Your GP may well suggest Gaviscon or Ranitidine, and finally surgery, but you shouldn't need them if you use these self-help ideas.

Allergies and food sensitivities

There is always something in the Press about athletes and drug abuse.

Occasionally pop musicians are mentioned, never classical. Why? Few people realise that drugs, whether medicinal or recreational, and alcohol are not the only things we put in our mouths which change performance. Even an antihistamine can have a drying reaction by removing natural lubrication, and should be avoided by wind players, brass players and singers until after the performance. Food sensitivity is not recognised in the same terms, yet it can have just as devastating an effect. Where that effect is a life-threatening allergy, it must of course be dealt with by a hospital. However the level of reaction can also be quite small, and can therefore be overlooked as an irritant or given a name like 'glue' ear or eczema and treated as an ear or skin complaint rather than a heightened sensitivity.

Allergies are an inborn intolerance by a particular body to what that body regards as a poison, or an inability to withstand or break down a harmful substance into a harmless substance. This causes the body to go into overdrive to rid itself of such 'foreign' substances. At worst the shock is dire, and anaphylactic shock leads to collapse and death. This is very rare. Mostly the body throws the substance out by turning it into a harmless or less irritant substance or gas. The main method of excretion is via the breath, then sweat and urine, and finally faeces in that descending order! Whatever is not water-soluble is stored in the body's fat deposits, or walled off in special cells so that it is no longer a nuisance. Unfortunately these fat-stored substances are released again when we diet to lose weight, because the body breaks down the fat stores for energy. This is why you feel so grotty, have headaches and want to break off the diet or fast – it's not because of real hunger, unless you are already anorexic.

Any food, be it the finest quality, fresh, raw, clean organic or whatever, which requires more energy from the body to assimilate it than it actually provides will cause a net deficit, and will cause an indicator muscle to become weak. The same is true of overdose of foods. This is why there is such lethargy after a huge Christmas lunch, transcending the normal animal need to rest quietly to digest. Food sensitivities are strongly suspect if you feel drowsy, lethargic, breathless, get headaches, itchy eyes or runny nose, or have mood changes and poor concentration after a meal, or at specific times in the day.

Ignore all the propaganda and advertising about a particular food or food supplement, and ask the body concerned (the Testee's body in front of you), 'Is this good and strengthening to eat today?' If a strong indicator muscle becomes weak the answer is 'NO'.

A lung irritant will give you lung spasm which is asthma or other breathing difficulties, a stomach irritant will give you a rash, eczema, hives or blisters, just as easily as a contact irritant. Other digestive defences are mucus, (ulcers are like internal skin boils) as in Crohn's disease and irritable bowel syndrome (ICV syndrome, see earlier). Excess mucus-like fluid can be stored in the sinuses (giving sinusitis) or in the ear ('glue' ear). Toxins can also be stored in joint spaces, causing inflammation and heat and changes in the joint membranes. The body starts to go into a self-destruct syndrome here. Typical of these syndromes is rheumatoid arthritis. Of course toxins are not the only causes of these problems, but they are the most common, and the mostly easily avoidable. Each of us has our own preferred disposal method from the body, and inborn weaknesses and predisposition. These are all normal reactions that have gone into over-reaction 'out of synchronisation with need'.

Almost anything can be taken in overdose, even vitamin tablets, so upsetting the finely tuned system of checks and balances. This is where reactions occur. Such sensitivities can be slight and temporary, or acquired following a drug taken for some other reason. Then they may become permanent. The body is alerted. Next time, in order to protect you better, it switches on the defence mechanism earlier, and there's your sensitivity. The problem with both allergens and sensitivities is that because the defence system is alerted and goes into attack mode, you get an initial quick 'high' from the attack substances released into the bloodstream, so you think the offending substance is doing you good. It isn't; you pay later. Coffee is a typical addictive and overdose substance which also unkindly 'binds to opiate-receptors in the body provoking a greater sensation of pain' (Nature, 1983; 301: 246-8). Let me tell you the tale of a cup of coffee, with milk and sugar, such as you might have for breakfast 'to get a good start to the day' before rushing off to a rehearsal.

Coffee contains many substances, with a predominant one, caffeine. This stimulates the adrenal (fight or flight) system, which stimulates the liver and the muscles to convert their stored glycogen into sugars and puts it into the bloodstream to give you the energy, ready to fight or run away. However, the two spoons of sucrose (sugar you put in the coffee), plus a little lactose (the milk sugar) have already started to get into the bloodstream through the membranes in the mouth, stomach and small intestine. The blood-sugar level therefore suddenly rises very fast, and you are hyperglycemic (too much sugar). Blood-sugar levels have to be kept within a narrow band, so the body notes what is going on, and, since you are not actually fighting or flighting, sets about controlling the unnecessary overload of sugar. Because it doesn't know when the sugar intake will stop (especially if there's a sticky bun about too), it overdoes the control a bit, pumping in lots of insulin. It uses up the body's stores of vitamin B to take the excess sugar out of the blood and turn it into glycogen for storage, or break it down and throw it out. By about one-and-a-half to two hours later you start to go into a blood sugar low because of the body's great efficiency in dealing with overload. You get brain-fag and feel tired and irritable (hypoglycemic – too little sugar) and it's time for the rehearsal break. You feel you need something to perk you up, so you have a cup of coffee with milk and two lumps, or a lump of milk chocolate, a biscuit or a Coke, and the whole yo-yo sequence starts again. Eventually, ones adrenal, insulin and vitamin B reserves are seriously depleted, the body can't cope any more and adult diabetes results. Far better to find a coffee substitute – decaffeinated or roasted grain if you can stand the taste – or drink/eat something else that contains a slow-release sugar such as the composite carbohydrates found in whole grains. This prevents sudden sugar overload. It doesn't mean never drink coffee, just be aware of your tolerence levels before you get tremors from the caffeine and diabetes from sugar sensitivity. (PS. The paper around the cigarette you smoked to calm the tremors also contains sugars and drains vitamins B and C amongst other things!)

Slight sensitivities can add up to a toxic level, even without the other sorts of mental and physical stress. This makes them very difficult to pin down. An example here are phenols which make you feel swimmy and unable to concentrate. A typical phenol is formaldehyde. Most of us only met this consciously as a preservative in the science lab at school, or at an art exhibition (Damian Hurst's 'Cow and Calf'). However it is an ingredient in paints, floor coverings, chipboard and wall insulation, furniture padding, plastics, Tupperwear-type food containers and cling-film, aerosols and detergents, all of which occur in new houses, theatres and concert halls, canteens and restaurants. It is also present in minute quantities in apples, cider, asparagus, avocado, cherries, coffee, honey, both cow's and goat's milk, mushrooms, pineapple and yeast. The situation is made worse by double glazing and central heating, which prevent the vapours escaping. All very confusing.

Testing and De-sensitisation

There is only one real way to pin this down – a fast in a formaldehyde-free zone which, given the list above, is hardly a practical solution. However, you might suspect the problem if you seem to react to an odd mixture of things. Maybe there's a common phenol. Go to an expert to be de-sensitised (see end of chapter) and start to perform and live again with a clear head! Otherwise, you can help yourself by not eating the foods above when you know you are near any new building or redecorating work, but other than turn down the gig, that's it.

A simpler problem occurs when a person is intolerant of everything in a family of foods. Typical here is coeliac's disease where there is an intolerance to gluten. Sufferers then avoid all grains except millet, although some can tolerate rice. Another common intolerance is the nightshade family (which includes potatoes, tomatoes, peppers and chillies, aubergines and tobacco!), or all the brassicas (cabbage, sprouts, spring greens, cauliflower and broccoli). Cow products upset a lot of people. Often goat's milk and cheese don't because the different constituent proportions more nearly match human milk. (Some even say that cow's milk is meant for baby calves not humans, so why drink it anyway? There are certainly many other and better ways of getting the calcium through whole grains and cabbage.) In this case all you have to do is to avoid that family

138

of foods as far as possible, or only have them when other stress levels are low.

The 'elimination diet' that is so much vaunted supposedly means living on lamb, courgettes and pears. Very boring! Like everything else it is a compromise diet. To most people these foods are hypoallergenic (they don't react), but they are a disaster to someone allergic to sheep products and lanolin. Do not try it except under proper supervision.

Provocative testing is done medically by injecting substances between the layers of the skin, and waiting to see if there is a skin reaction. That only has a low success rate because the skin may not be the area where that person reacts, or the concentration of the substance may not be correct to set off a reaction. However, you may get some results.

The other methods of provocative testing only tell you whether you are reacting against that substance *today*. They don't really differentiate between allergy and overload sensitivity, but merely tell you what you can't cope with today. Both methods use the meridians. Vega and Vol methods use the changing electrical resistance of the Acu-point being tested, and applied kinesiology tests an indicator muscle (see Chapter 10). However both methods narrow down the options enormously, speed up the search, and remove the need for the incredibly boring elimination diet. (The only other option is to go on a complete food fast, drinking water only, but this *must* be done with the guidance of a naturopath.) For the Vol and Vega methods you will need to see a practitioner. Muscle testing is described in this book and, done with common sense, will cause you no harm.

When you suffer an allergic reaction, you can help yourself by following these steps:

1. Make a note of all the foods in the suspect meal and start comparing reactions with other times there was a reaction and what was eaten then. If possible write down what was eaten in the last 24 hours.

2. For at least a week, collect and keep separately in the fridge a teaspoon of each suspect food or liquid.

3. Before breakfast, or when the Testee hasn't eaten for three or more hours, find a strong reliable indicator muscle (see Chapter 10). The Testee then chews a teaspoonful of a suspect food or holds a sip in the mouth as you test the indicator muscle again. If it has now

become weak, that substance should be removed from the diet for at least a month.

4. Where several substances are being tested, the mouth should be rinsed clean between each, or the substance removed and the Testee asked to swallow. This action resets the testing mechanism in the mouth.

5. The substance must be in the same state as it normally is when consumed i.e. cooked not raw, and without its peel if it is usually eaten that way. Cooking can change the chemistry, and peel may have preservatives, wax or insecticides on it. The same brand-name must also be used.

6. Where there is a choice of remedy, homeopathic pilules may be tested with this method, except that the remedy should not be placed in the mouth but put on the skin, preferably of the abdomen, or waved under the nose to smell if it is a liquid.

7. This type of testing only tells you about today. The Testee may react against a substance because today s/he has had an overdose from several sources (remember formaldehyde?). If you still find a reaction after a month's abstinence, the Testee probably always will react, and so should abstain from that food altogether or choose to face the consequences each time it is consumed. The choice is his/hers.

The one thing to realise about all of the above is that you almost always do have a choice in the matter. Where there is specific overdose but not overeating in general, then all you can do by yourself is experiment, beginning with only allowing yourself to eat a small amount once a week when unstressed and gradually increasing till overdose shows up as a reaction. Bear in mind that stress will make you less tolerant and foods do vary in the strengths of their constituents with the time of year, country of origin and brand-name.

Where actual allergy shows, in that you react this time and every time, there is still a choice. You can abstain or, if that's impossible because of your environment (as in reaction to petrochemicals or formaldehyde), you can either (a) suppress the unwanted reaction with antihistamines or steroids on prescription from your GP; (b) increase your tolerance by reducing general stress levels and reset the acupuncture meridian levels by a visit to an applied kinesiologist for the simple SET technique; (c) visit an acupuncturist; (d) use a homeopathic remedy specifically tailored to your needs by the Vega method; or (e) go to Southampton (see end of chapter) where that method is taught to doctors.

Addiction

Where the problem is overdose due to a long-lasting stress, as in alcoholism, coffee and smoking, then not only the chemical and physical sides of the triangle come into play, but the psychological too. It's comparitively easy to rid yourself of the chemical addiction by putting yourself in an environment where it's simply not available and 'dry out'. A week or ten days is often sufficient. But that doesn't handle the problem of why you became addicted in the first place. It will still be there when you return, to cause recidivism very quickly. Unless *you* can face what it is you fear or lack, and know that other resources exist to supply your need; unless *you* are responsible and take control yourself, no one else can help you, and you will not grow as a person into the freedom of being able to 'take it or leave it'. You will always be in thrall to your addiction, always reacting for or against it.

Part of making the decision and having the strength to 'move on' is knowing the disastrous long-term effects produced by your short-term gratification. Analyse and know clearly what the nature of the addictive 'enemy' actually is, what are its subtleties, strengths and weaknesses. Part of its insidious subtlety is thinking 'Well, I'll have just a weak one'. Fine if it's just one, once a year or on high days and holidays, but 'just one' once a day very quickly becomes 'just one more', and then there you are again, with all the old excuses, explaining an inability to abstain, still not looking at the cause, even though you have the best of intentions.

Another subtlety is thinking that one brand is the same strength as another, or that one can or pack is the same size as another. With alcohol, sparkling white wines and the new white ciders are part and parcel of having a good time, and are thought of as relatively innocuous. They are not. Many people think a 'single' drunk at home counts the same as a measure in a pub, when often it's nearer a double or treble because you don't want to seem stingy. There is no standard measure of wine. Weights and measures between take-home packs vary enormously and, after the first drink, who reads the small print anyway?

Two large, strong beers will put you over the permitted level for driving: know your limits although, obviously, drinking no beer at all is safest. Any alcohol causes a significant increase in injury incidence, even if it's just tripping over a step, because you were not attending to what you were doing. Even the College of Physicians admits that ten times as many young people die from alcohol-related accidents than from other causes. Low usage is a weekly consumption of less than 21 units for a man, and less than 14 for a woman. This means less than a pub double a day. Safe usage is said to be a little higher according to recent media information. Misuse is between 21-49 units for a man and 14-34 for a woman. That's a G&T and half a bottle of wine a day. Abuse is more than 50 units for a man and more than 35 for a woman.

Frequently people are shocked, when they are asked to keep a smoking or a drinking diary, to see just how much they do actually consume. If you doubt it, try it. Then you can look at the figures objectively and decide what you want to do about it before it becomes beyond your power to do anything. The figures given above are not dreamed up by me. They are well researched by Dr Marsha Morgan who specialises in the subject. There is a BAPAM helpline especially for musicians, but you can also find your local AA, Al-Anon and Drink-line in the 'phone book. You can also speak to your orchestral manager or fixer when on tour and ask that alternatives to alcohol and coffee are available in rehearsal breaks. It's just as easy to buy one sort of tea or coffee bag as another – the hot water is the same – and to buy fruit juice concentrate and add water (sparkling if you wish).

'A pill for every ill'

This is the modern interpretation of the Knidian ethic of attacking the disease rather than the person. (The other Greek philosophy was Hippocratic which treated the person not the disease, and this is what alternative and some complementary practitioners do.) Modern medicine has a view of health as healthy growth, with an absence of disease, rather than a state of growing healthier. GPs are specialists in general, everyday family medicine. They filter out people needing specialist care and refer them elsewhere, they prescribe drugs that need caution and give instuctions to you about their usage. They cope amazingly. They are in charge of a great many people, are bombarded with vast amounts of reading material, both about the latest treatments available and advertising blurbs from pharmaceutical companies. They are snowed under by the sheer volume of paperwork involved in running a practice. They are paid by the average time-slot and the number of patients on their register. All this means that they have to juggle enormous amounts of information, can only see you for a comparatively short time each visit, and don't often have time to tell you about all the possible side-effects of the drug(s) they are prescribing for you. The sheer volume of present-day drugs precludes even their encyclopaedic memories from recalling all the possible rarer and more obscure side-effects. This is where you can help yourself.

You can help the doctor by being very clear about what the symptoms are, when they occurred, and how long you have had them. It may help to make a note in your diary. You can also help by researching the problem yourself if it doesn't seem too serious.

1. Your local reference library may well have a copy of the *Merck Manual* which will give you a concise run-down on all aspects of the problem once you have a name for it, although you may need a medical dictionary too. Don't let it frighten you. Write down your questions and ask, but don't try to treat yourself without proper advice.

2. Your local chemist can often help you with OTC (Over The Counter) drugs so that you don't have to bother your GP and clog his/her waiting room. At least one big chain has a helpful series of booklets on some, but not all, common complaints, but beware – being part of their selling campaign, the leaflets are unlikely to tell you about the side-effects of any recommended drug. Of the turnover costs of making a pharmaceutical drug, 15% is for research and development, 27% goes on marketing. According to *What Doctors Don't Tell You* (WDDTY Vol.6 no.5), 87% of OTC advertising copy sent to your GP doesn't mention side-effects either.

3. For side-effects you can use a British National Formulary or Data Sheet Compendium. Again you may need the reference library's

medical dictionary as well. Better that than not knowing what's going on, and not knowing how and where to look. You can also subscribe to WDDTY which tells you all the latest papers on side-effects and has a very comprehensive list of subjects, but it tends also to mention the rarer complications which might scare you. Many OTC drugs of different brands contain the same 'active ingredient'. That's the one to research for side-effects. Occasionally it is the carrier cream or base that you might react to, so, just as with foods, take heed and start reading labels if you notice side-effect such as headaches, rashes or itching, vomiting or diarrhoea, swollen lips, tongue, face or hands etc. which seem to coincide with the start of use and have no other apparent cause, even if it is a supposedly harmless OTC drug. Don't forget, too, that some drugs taken for other conditions such as diabetes, or to lower cholesterol levels, will rob the body of nutrients – B vitamins in particular – and may therefore increase pain and lower energy levels (WDDTY Vol.6 no.3) or may mix unfavourably with other drugs to cause unwanted side-effects.

4. Never accept a substitute drug from your pharmacist without questioning the dosage with your doctor, and never 'phone for repeat prescriptions; it's too easy for the drug name to be misheard. Take the empty bottle with you to the chemist. Dispose of all old, unwanted drugs by returning them to the chemist, especially if they are past the 'sell by' date stamped on the label.

5. There is no drug invented that doesn't have a side-effect for someone. That doesn't mean that you should let your imagination run riot, or be paranoid and *assume* that you will react, but if you do, or if you have to keep having repeat prescriptions, check it. Then either ask your GP for an alternative or seek homeopathic or other alternative/complementary medicine advice, and don't forget that BAPAM has a help line. When your GP is prescribing, especially antibiotics and vaccines, *ask if the drug could affect you by blurring your vision, dulling your hearing, giving you a headache, give you tingling fingers or poor coordination, make you dizzy, depressed or affect your driving.* Drugs frequently prescribed to musicians include antibiotics, corticosteroids, beta-blockers, Prozac, non-steroidal anti-

inflammatory drugs (NSAIDs), all of which can have undesirable side-effects, specifically affecting you professionally. Don't assume that because your doctor has said nothing, that there's nothing to be said. Neither should you assume that if a doctor, no matter how eminent a specialist, says that nothing can be done to help you, or that you just have to accept and live with your problem, that there is no more to be said. It only means *that individual* doesn't know of anything else that could help you.

It may not have occured to you that foods can also have an effect on drugs (don't forget drugs were refined from plants originally). Supplements can also affect them. If you are consuming grapefruit, iron, liquorice, avocados, the cabbage family, or are on a very high-fibre diet, ask your doctor or practitioner if this will alter the efficacy or dosage of the drug being prescribed for you.

More about Homeopathy

To remind you, there are classical homeopaths, and doctor homeopaths who combine conventional or allopathic medicine with homeopathy. Homeopathic remedies are individualised to your personality; they are cheap, safe from side-effects, quick acting and don't interfere with other forms of medicine. When you open a remedy packet don't touch the tiny tablets/pillules with your fingers; shake out the dose into the lid and tip them into your mouth and under your tongue to be sucked until gone, not chewed.

Classical homeopaths treat with great expertise by using one remedy at a time, but as there is also no single remedy for any one condition, so there is no unnecessary medication, and you know which remedy is effective. However, those doctor homeopaths who mix-prescribe may, for example, give you Chamomile 30 with antibiotics. You can self-treat at low levels of potency such as 6x or 30x, which you can buy from an explanatory list in a health food shop and some chemists, but higher levels require great knowledge and experience because they are so much more complicated, precise and powerful.

For specific diseases Nosodes are sometimes used, which are very high dilution and succussion of tissues or secretions that give a well person apparently the same symptoms as the disease proper, but assist the body of an ill person to rid itself of the disease causing the symptoms. The body reacts to such remedies by sharpening up its immune response. If you are worried about the use of, and side-effects of, orthodox immunisation, or are likely to come into contact with potentially serious infections, consult your homeopath or one of the excellent books available (see References). When I travelled round S.E. Asia for two months, I found out which jabs I was supposed to have and then asked for the homeopathic equivalent and was given Cholera 30, Typhoid 30, Malaria 30, and Hepatitis 30. I was told to take one tablet each week for the first three weeks and then one per month. To me it was much more preferable than immunisation, but you may think differently.

Selye, Lindlahr and Naturopathy

In a way, everything I have put forward in this book is in line with the principles of Selye and Naturopathy, even if not specifically advocating these ideas. The philosophy aims to promote a whole, responsible, bright-eyed being with a spring in his/her step, who communicates his/her own special love of life (through music); to share a way of knowledge and choices about relevant adaptation, prevention, and self-restoration; to eliminate all possible obstructions and keep on an upward (or at least even) spiral towards strength, power, endurance, flexibility, agility, balance and awareness, to whatever is enobling, empowering and enriching.

In the 1930s at McGill University in Toronto, Hans Selye developed his ideas on the theory of 'Stress and Adaptation', by looking at the non-specific symptoms that people had in common, rather than at specific symptoms. He drew some interesting conclusions, which he called the General Adaptation Syndrome. The rationale is as follows: pollution, excesses and deficencies, infection, trauma, parasites, stress and heredity are all possible noxious influences which stimulate self-defence, elimination and self-healing as a survival mechanism at an unconscious alarm, or 'acute' stage. When this is unsuccessful there is sensory change and we feel discomfort and pain, as the body adapts or resists. If this is ignored and unresolved, it leads to decreased efficiency and functional loss which, together with other new acute problems, causes a chronic condition which quickly becomes a pathology due to exhaustion of reserves, adaptations and tolerances. Chronic fatigues are the hallmarks of the exhaustion stage. If they continue, eventually the body dies. Healing takes place from above down and from inside to out. These principles are behind osteopathic and chiropractic treatment with applied kinesiology.

Lindlahr was one of the great naturopaths of the early years of this century, who came before Selye and followed Hippocratic ideas. His method of treatment was to establish normal surroundings in accordance with nature's laws; economise on energy and vitality; build up the blood and immune system through good nutrition; promote elimination of waste and toxins; correct mechanical lesions; arouse an awareness and consciousness of personal responsibility. He did this through 'Nature Cure' (which is the forerunner of naturopathy) and taught that the primary cause of weakness and disease is disobedience to the laws of nature; he encouraged both study of these laws, and personal effort and self-help in assisting natural healing and cleansing by simple natural means which are in no way destructive to health and life, and are within the reach of everyone. By 'natural means' he meant air, light, water, mud baths, chi energy, exercises and massage, simple high-quality nutrition, relaxation, meditation, constructive thought, and spiritual nourishment. He was much in favour of toxic elimination and inner cleanliness, and of not suppressing the healing crisis but aiding it through wraps, poultices, homeopathy and herbalism. George Goodheart, one of the foremost thinking chiropractors and founder of applied kinesiology, clearly agrees with naturopathic ideas and has said that most infections are a failure of elimination, and that a coldpack to the stomach will increase antibody activity.

In Lindlahr's books, despite the old-fashioned language there is much plain common sense and scope for self-help, which could save the NHS a vast amount of money. These ideas are now carried out supposedly by health hydros, which vary from the 'lettuce leaf and carrot juice' variety to shrines to hedonism and to the 'exterior body beautiful' (when beauty should actually shine from within.) Few support Lindlahr's ideas about cold baths, packs and wraps, enemas, skin brushing, air baths and so on. Most are hotels with a gym, an exercise floor, a pool or two, a sauna, various massage, beauty and sports facilities, and an excellent cuisine with a bias towards salads and low fat foods. They are wonderful places to forget the world, rest and recuperate, but most are not really naturopathic any more. Regrettably in some, being seen to be wearing the 'right' clothes, which means the latest fashion sports wear, matters far more than your actual state of inner health.

Water

We all use water for drinking, bathing and keeping cool. Naturopaths also use it for packs, poultices, baths and douches to stimulate healing and circulation, and for a friction dry after a shower. If you are doing a fast (see below) it is comforting to sip water throughout the day as needed. We drink water for quenching thirst, to keep the body salts in balance, to detoxify the system and to counteract a dry mouth due to nervousness.

Not all the watery drinks we consume are giving us balance; tea and coffee, for example, are both actually dehydrating. Coffee stimulates the adrenals and bladder and bowel action via the sympathetic nervous system; alcohol and excessively sweet drinks have the same affect because water is used to break down and remove these substances from the body. You will also feel more thirsty if you eat a lot of meat, rancid foods, salted foods and tinned, packaged and preserved foods (unless they actually state that they are salt free).

There are other times when you need to take note of how much water you drink. Sudden thirst is a sign of ileocaecal valve malfunction. If the thirst persists, however, and you seem to be drinking a lot of fluids whenever you can, ask your doctor to do a glucose tolerance test. Such a thirst is the first sign of some forms of adult diabetes (which can be easily controlled).

How much water you should drink varies from expert to expert, and depends on both diet and environment. If you are a vegetarian or a vegan who eats large amounts of fruit, vegetables and salads, you may need very little extra. A confirmed carnivore or wine soak will need a lot more water to detoxify. Living and working in a dry, centrally-heated atmosphere will also considerably increase the amount you need, and some Americans recommend up to eight glasses a day. Flying, especially long-haul flights, causes dehydration, which is a definite contributory factor to jet lag.

What you drink depends on what is available. In general, bottled spring water is best, particularly if it is non-sparkling and has a low sodium content. Read the label – you will be surprised how the different brands vary enormously in the amount of sodium and other minerals they contain. Next best is filtered tap water. Do not drink a lot of distilled water. It may be pollutant free but, because it is mineral free also, it will leech *your* mineral reserves instead as it passes through the system.

When you buy bottled water anywhere outside the UK, make sure the bottle is either unopened, or opened in front of you. Unscrupulous vendors will refill old bottles from a local tap. The water may be harmless to them, as they are used to the flora and fauna it contains, but you are not and the water may give you diarrhoea. Similarly, be wary of ice-cubes and sorbets.

The American habit of having ice in drinks is not good for the digestion. It chills the stomach and reduces the flow of digestive juices. Similarly, do not drink a lot of water immediately after a heavy, rich meal (you will dilute the digestive juices), or after you have eaten a lot of rice (the rice will absorb yet more water, swell, and give you uncomfortable distension). Two hours later, when the food will have left the stomach, you can drink as much as you want.

Don't stop drinking water if you sweat excessively, get pre-menstrual bloating, or are incontinent. Drinking less won't stop the output, and will only make you even more toxic. Use other methods described elsewhere in this book, or talk to your GP.

Fasting and Cleansing

The general notion of **fasting** is either starving, or exclusively eating some food or other (as in a 'fruit' or 'brown rice' fast). 'To fast' actually means to go without eating, but does not imply starving, being a victim, or exclusive eating. Most people see it as starvation until they realise that they voluntarily fast for about 12 hours in 24 already, overnight. It is undoubtedly one of the cheapest and most potent of all natural remedies. True fasts are cold (not iced) spring water only (not distilled water, see above) and are useful as a cleansing and healing process only if they last more than four days. This is because it takes that long to empty the tract, lose time-related Pavlovian feelings of hunger and start self-cleansing (indicated by foul breath and body odour, a coated tongue and possible slight rise in temperature from all the fat-stored toxins and mucus). This is why you should take time out to do a fast, scheduling it in your diary or with your diary service. It is not money lost but ill health lost. Don't even think about fasting, however, if you are diabetic or have any sort of cardiac or malignancy problems.

A normal short fast is seen as seven days, and two short fasts of this length with a gap between are seen as more advantageous than prolonged fasting. During the first four days there may well be headaches, depression and insomnia, but after that energy returns and long walks are the best exercise (schedule absorbing things to do at main meal times during the first four days till food craving stops). A fast must be undertaken in a positive frame of mind. It is extremely unwise to undertake a fast for the first time without the advice and support of a naturopath, who will also make sure there are no contra-indications. However, once you have done one and know how you react, there is less need for outside monitoring.

Return to normal eating is via fruit juice, then whole fruit and finally vegetables and your normal food proportions. (The start of the fast should be prepared in the same way, only in reverse.) The cleansing process will be stopped when food is eaten again. Fasting has the added advantage of resetting your rate of metabolism and of putting you in touch with real rather than imagined hunger feelings in response to the clock, and giving you a clean, clear blood supply. Those who fast regularly see it as a rejuvenation. They do not do it as a means of weight loss although this happens temporarily too. The majority of those who fast for the first time are pleasantly surprised that the terrors of starvation exist only in the minds of people who have never tried it.

Before, during and after fasting, everything possible must be done to aid elimination and **cleansing.** However there's absolutely no reason why you should not do this at other times too with great benefit. The skin is the largest organ of the body. It breathes, and is able to absorb (as in aromatherapy), but is far more efficient at elimination. Apart from saunas, steam baths, bathing and the much cleaner showering, another less well-known method of cleansing the skin is an air bath and skin brush. You know how good it feels to kick your shoes off and walk barefoot after a long day wearing tight shoes and stockings? Well, for an air bath you need a private space where you can freely walk about naked to let the air get to your skin. Then take a soft, real bristle, long-handled bath-brush and brush your skin from top to toe. Always brush towards the heart, i.e. up the legs (foot to groin) and arms (hand to shoulder). At first it may seem a little scratchy, but as you remove old, dead cells and the microscopic detritis that collects there, your skin comes to life again and it becomes a pleasurable experience. You can also take a shower and rub yourself dry with your hands. This brings a wonderful glow, particularly if it was a cold shower, but most people take time before they have the courage to try that one.

Next, you need to clean your inner skin. The colon can be cleaned with enemas; again this should be done under a naturopathic or colonic expert's supervision till you have learned the proper procedure. A self-help method is to use Psyllium husks and abdominal massage, as carefully explained by Natural Flow (see References).

All these techniques require little equipment other than your attention, which means you can also take them on tour. They raise the body's own innate, natural healing ability and promote its optimum health, so that you can go on giving of your best as a professional musician into ripe old age. They are definitely Healthy Practice!

REFERENCES

1. **Airola P.** (1974) *How to Get Well,* Health Plus
2. **Berkow R.** and **Fletcher A.** eds. (1992) *The Merck Manual,* Merck and Co. Inc, New Jersey, USA
3. **Bounds S.** (1985) *Here's Health Guide to Fat-free Cooking,* Thorsons, Harper Collins
4. *British National Formulary* (updated yearly), British Medical Assn, and Royal Pharmaceutical Soc. of Gt Britain
5. **Davis D.** (1995) *Acid Reflux and Vocal Disorders,* (Performing Arts Medicine News, Autumn p36/7) BAPAM
6. **Goodheart G.** (1992) *Personal communication* (Brussels ICAK-E)
7. **Grant D.** (1982) *Food Combining for Health – a New Look at the Hay System,* Thorsons, Harper Collins.
8. **Gray R.** (1982) *The Colon Health Handbook,* Rockridge Pub. Co., Ca 94610, USA

9. **Hanssen M.** (1985) *E for Additives,* Thorsons, Harper Collins
10. **Kenton L.** (1984) *Raw Energy,* Century Publishing
11. **Kenton L.** (1985) *Ageless Ageing,* Century Arrow, London
12. **Lindlahr H.** (ed. Proby J.)(1975) *Natural Therapeutics, Philosophy, Practice and Dietetics,* C.W. Daniel Co. Ltd
13. **Lockie A.** (1989) *The Family Guide to Homeopathy,* Hamish Hamilton, Penguin.
14. **Maunder A.** (1986) *New Low Fat Recipes,* Foulsham.
15. **Mervyn L.** (1986) *Thorson's Complete Guide to Vitamins and Minerals,* Harper Collins.
16. **Montignac M.** (1996) *Eat Yourself Slim,* Montigac Publishing, UK
17. **Ostwald F., Baron B., Byl N., Wilson F.** (1994) *Performing Arts Medicine* (West J. Med 160:48-52)
18. **Polunin M.** (1997) *Healing Foods,* Dorling Kindersley
19. **Polunin M.** (1983) *Real Food, Fast Food,* Thorsons, Harper Collins
20. **Pritikin N.** (1980) *The Pritikin Programme for Diet and Exercise,* and *Diet for Runners,* Bantam
21. **Schaffer J.** (1992) Presentation (Brussels ICAK-E)
22. **Weight Watchers** (1972) *A Way of Life,* Hamlyn
23. **Yudkin J.** (1972) *Sweet and Dangerous – the Facts About Sugar,* Bantam Books

ORGANISATIONS

Allergy Testing – Phenols, Hydrocarbons and Food Sensitivities. The Centre for Complementary Medicine, 51 Bedford Pl, Southampton SO1 2DG. *Tel:* 01703 334752
British Naturopathic Association. Frazer Ho, 6 Netherhall Gdns, London NW3 5RR. *Tel:* 0171-435 7830
Natural Flow. Green Farm, Burwash Common, E. Sussex. *Tel:* 01435 882482
Citrimax. Nutri Centre. *Tel:* 0171-436 5122
WDDTY (What Doctors Don't Tell You). 4 Wallave Rd, London N1 2PG. Subscription magazine, handbooks and filo-fax guides

CHAPTER 7

Musicians versus emotions I

*Communication; Stage-fright; Helpful and
unhelpful language; Criticism, recordings
and perfectionism; Long- and short-term
self-help; Psycho-regulation; Visualisation
and Neuro-linguistic programming;
Behavioural barometer; Affirmations and
self-talk; Psychological reversal; Phobias;
Short-term stress remedies;
Burn-out and How to say 'No'*

Communication

This chapter looks at what you are trying to do, and what you are actually doing with your music. Learning to play a musical instrument is a bit like studying anatomy. There's so much information to absorb. Either you learn all about one part such as the arm and then do the next part, the leg, in which case you can easily lose sight of the body as a whole, or you learn about whole-body systems such as the blood flow or the nervous system, and then can't easily relate to what goes on in one specific part of the body such as the hand. In music you have an instrumental technique to make the machine you play make the sounds you want (a sort of 'whole-body' system) and then you make one part do specific things with the sounds to create communication. Ideally musicians use their music to honour and celebrate what they have to say. They carry the music within, needing no specific instrument. They *are* the music. All a bit high flown perhaps, but I think important to say.

There are some excellent books on sound interpretation (see References). As a performer I happen to agree more with Deryck Cooke than Anthony Storr. For me music is most definitely a language, and music up to the early years of this century fits with the natural rhythms and resonances of the woods and metals of the instrument, and the cavities, spaces and bones within the human body and is easily comprehensible, which is why chanting, choral singing and Bach (amongst others) are so satisfying. They actually enhance the body's energies and balance the acupuncture meridians. From Schoenberg onwards, with the break up of tonality, it's not just the intellectual effort that causes problems, the language is changed and the rhythms are often disruptive, and this is why these works are often so tiring to play and have less public appeal.

Style is a matter for your own research rather than what the editor or publisher has seen fit to print, and not relevant in this conversation on matters of health. Yet, just as you need gymnastic techniques, having decided what you want to say, you also need an expressive palate to give the music a sense of architecture and be reasonably true to the composer's wishes. Beyond that, the most important thing of all in my opinion, is *communication*. I shall never forget hearing Jacqueline du Pré playing the Debussy Cello Sonata utterly convincingly, and then being astonished to discover that she was not following the composer's dynamic markings at all! Was she wrong? I don't think so. She had made it her own, and was communicating *that* message superbly. Her technique 'happened' without thought and without creating any barrier. It was almost as if the instrument disappeared and there was just Jackie speaking. This is particularly evident in her recordings of the Elgar Concerto. It is also a tribute to William Pleeth's supremely inspired teaching. What stops the rest of us from reaching those heights? Since 'Fortune favours the Brave' it must be fear, or at least a terror of being wrong. At best this takes the form of making sure you are doing the 'right' bowing, fingering, tonguing, as well as the right notes, with the result that you get so engrossed in the minutiae that you don't see the whole, and are not able to glory in it, because it never gets put back together again. At worst it becomes a nearly impossible 'to do' list which is a predisposition to stage-fright.

Stage Fright

This can either creep up on a player, or hit one suddenly with a shock when it accompanies some other trauma. It is no respecter of age, ability, success or experience.

Capacity is a state of mind. The belief that you can't do something is often just a rationalisation for unwillingness to take risks. The sad thing is, that, while arguing for one's limitations, one tends to keep them! When you perform well communication is easy, because there is nothing between you, what you are saying, and the audience. When you are nervous, sometimes the hump can be got over by concentrating on the needs of the audience, rather than your own, on what they will get out of it rather than what you will. Until you can do this, 'playing the bits', or the solo part, grows in difficulty horrendously, and out of all proportion.

This is where some people resort to beta blockers, which block the effects of adrenalin on the body, but these drugs can precipitate asthma attacks and heart failure, nausea and diarrhoea, light-headedness and insomnia in susceptible people. Taking Prozac for the depression such fear causes, chops the top and bottom off all feeling, keeps you positively even, but can have similar side-effects and can also cause blurred vision. Either is better than alcohol which makes you clumsy. None of them solves any problems, they just shelve them. When musicians stop taking them, there is the problem again staring them in the face, with the added complication of side-effects to cope with. If you are driven to taking these drugs I strongly suggest you have psychological counselling at the same time. To have counselling doesn't mean you are 'off your chump'; it means you are being responsible and helping yourself with a temporary dysfunction.

'Psychoactive medications must be used judiciously with artists, keeping in mind that certain side-effects – drowsiness, dry mouth, insomnia, tremor – may interfere with high level performance', suggest Ostwald et al (1994). You may be prescribed beta blockers such as propranolol hydrochloride, amxiolytics such as alprazolam and diazepam or phenelzine sulphate if you are depressed as well. Look up their side-effects (in BNF, see References to Chapter 6) before taking them, so that you can discuss them with your doctor, and make an informed judgement for yourself.

When you take these drugs, what comes out is a conveyor belt of excellent tasks completed, not communication with emotion deep enough to get past the edge of the stage. Volume is not in question. Segovia or Julian Bream project enough to fill the Albert Hall without a microphone. It isn't that as people we are unfeeling and can't project. Far from it! Either personality and feeling get squashed because the player is shrunk to nothing with nerves, or the artist puts on such armour plating that the sound can't get out and blossom; or there *is* communication, and 'the medium is the message', but what communicates is fear in terms of the 'pearlies', split notes, wrong notes and quavery tone.

So many artists identify their Art with the Self. They talk about *what* they are, not *who* they are, and it's not so much that 'the show must go on', but that they *are* the show. They die a little every time they can't perform and only feel they really come alive when they do. This is unrealistic and obsessional, yet in a crowded profession many think that one has to be that way to get anywhere.

The skin is an excellent demarcation line in most people's understanding between 'us' and 'not us'; between the inside and outside environments. Most of our concern is with the outer and how to adapt ourselves to it but, in so doing, the inside environment is affected too. Out there are the instrument, music and audience; inside is just you and your five senses and all the logistics of running the particular bag of skin called you.

It's then, on stage, that you feel as though you are in a glass cage. Some people compensate by throwing themselves about, giving the audience a poor theatrical show instead of spell-binding, sublime music. Others 'do the expression marks' 150% so that the stupid audience 'gets it'. Others blame the audience for being hypercritical before they've even sat down. Yet the poor audience only paid good money to enjoy themselves. They *want* the artist to succeed, or they wouldn't have come.

Stage fright seems to be about 'them' (whoever 'they' are). Rarely is it about lack of courage. Actually it is about *you,* and the mental baggage you have heaped on your own back, with which you have shackled, poisoned and paralysed yourself. It is terrifying. A very real Black Hole. It is usually worst immediately before going on stage and in the first few minutes of performance, but there can be a long 'pre-burn' of panic and 'after-burn' of self-castigation, especially if you are the perfectionist most musicians are trained to be.

What are the causes? Often multiple and difficult to pin down, they tend to form a vortex of anxiety, and a vicious circle which drags you down to incapacity, and can even build into a phobia that rules your life, unless you have a means of stopping it in its tracks. The thoughts crowd in and absorb almost all your concentration, and you terrorise yourself. It amounts to Mental Malpractice. You think and feel so 'attacked' you can't give out, only defend, and go through the motions, longing for the blessed release when it is all over.

Stage fright can also be allied to family considerations and worries, as we shall see in the next chapter. It can also be a cover-up for not wanting to play. I was very struck by Andrew Evans' ideas when he asked (a) Which was the first artistic medium you used? (b) Which was the most successful? (c) Which is your favourite? (d) Which is your fantasy medium? (see references). They are not the same and may give food for thought.

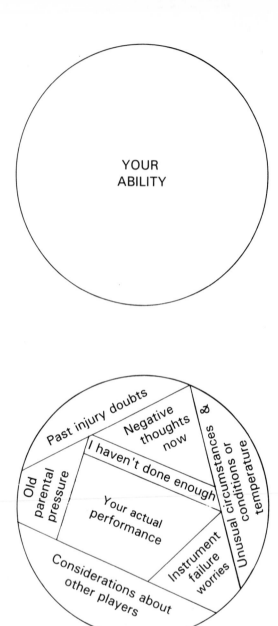

Ability v. actual performance

Nelson Mandela was quoted at the last European Quaker Peace Consultation as saying: 'Our deepest fear is not that we are inadequate. Our deepest fear is that we are powerful beyond measure. It is our light, not our darkness, that most frightens us. We ask ourselves, "Who am I to be brilliant, gorgeous, talented, fabulous?" Actually, who are you not to be? You are a child of God. Your 'playing small' doesn't serve the world. There is nothing enlightened about shrinking so that other people won't feel insecure around you. We are all meant to shine as children do. We are born to manifest the glory of God that is within us. It's not just in some of us, it's in everyone. And as we let our own light shine, we unconsciously give other people permission to do the same. As we are liberated from our own fear, our presence automatically liberates others.'

The opposite of love is not hate but fear and indifference, and 90% of fear is not justified by the facts or by what is actually happening. 'Love is letting go of fear' (Jampolsky). There is a natural excitement about performance, and there should be, but that's not real 'nerves'. A performance is a celebration of your ability and love of music, but it's often quite difficult to tell the difference between suppressed excitement, fear, hunger and sickness. They all happen in the stomach region, so we 'comfort eat' or starve ourselves, when what we actually feel is an emotionally heightened arousal state. If the arousal state is in proportion to the task to be performed we do well, but too much or too little and our performance suffers. This confusion of signals is always worst with a new task, and occurs because all the signals are carried by the sympathetic nervous system and one nerve in particular, the vagus.

There should be a balance between the sympathetic and parasympathetic systems, the level being set according to what you are doing. One of the two is always dominant. Highly strung perfectionists, living on the edge, are already set at high sympathetic levels, and it only takes a little to send them over the top. Laid-back, dozy people, who can't seem to get going, are set too low, and need a bomb under them or, at least, performance conditions before they do their best. They don't get stage fright – they need that extra stress.

Typically your tummy gurgles when you sit relaxed because it's a parasympathetic function. When sympathetic function is dominant because of stress, digestion is one of the first things to be shut down, and you get 'butterflies in your stomach' which is actually a slight ache from too much acid produced for the digestion that's no longer happening. Just like Pavlov's dog, you learn that certain things are dangerous and a habit of reaction is formed, so that eventually just thinking of playing 'that bit' to 'those people' causes the panic reaction. It is a normal survival technique which has become out of synchronisation with actual fact and actual need. You are too aroused. No one is actually going to kill you for not performing perfectly, are they? So you don't actually need to be ready to run away.

The original incident (the first time you did it 'wrong', perhaps due to a freak accident which is highly unlikely to occur again) becomes an assumption that you will *always* do it wrong. You are particularly vulnerable to such small mistakes when you are tired, have poor endurance, are not on top form physically, have high stress-levels for other reasons (e.g. at home) or for chemical reasons (mild overdose or sensitivity to some food), are suddenly faced with unexpected extras, lacks, or poorly timed criticism (whether justified or not).

Suddenly you doubt your ability; you become afraid of losing control; you remember that passage you haven't studied enough, worry you will forget it, lose your place; you think the audience are bored; the accompanist is late or makes a mistake; your shoulder-rest falls off; the music stand collapses; someone blocks your view. This causes dry mouth; short, shallow breathing; a racing heart; cold, sweaty hands; shaking; loss of feeling, seeing, hearing; or heightened awareness of other outside stimuli (like someone shuffling their feet); muscular tension and sickness, and your concentration goes to the winds. You *do* lose your place because your mind is wavering between the experience itself and the opinions you are forming about it all. The chatter of doom in your head is like a radio going full blast in your ears, telling you the worst *will* happen. You, poor victim, you believe it! You can't analyse anything any more, and so you go straight into paralysis like a rabbit caught in the headlights, and then the worst *does* happen. *Again.* And your self-esteem sinks another notch lower.

What can you do about it? The first thing is to realise that your reaction is absolutely normal, just a bit overcooked, and so are all the symptoms you feel, whether they are useful or not.

The second thing is to evaluate which aspects are the frightening trigger factors and what removable stresses there are in your life. Research has shown that musicians whose parents were professional musicians generally have a much harder time than those whose parents were interested non-professionals. There is expectation, covert persuasion, overt coercion and even persecution, with consequent anger and guilt resulting in either rebellion or failure, depending on the character of the child. There may also be social deprivation, if children have to spend hours practising indoors alone and not playing/socialising with their contemporaries (who will be their future audience/promoters/employers). Children of amateurs have high motivation, concentration and devotion, springing out of self-confidence in doing something of their own well. They are supported but not pushed mercilessly. Which were you? What spooks you?

The third is to defuse the old bogies, replace them with good successful experiences and keep away from new infectious ones. This is done by cleaning up practice methods, re-tuning the blaring radio in your head to another station with the help of 'self-talk' and visualisation, 'neuro-linguistic programming' and 'Inner Game' techniques, then facing the problem in a graded way with the help of a sympathetic colleague, as described below. Of course you can duck the issue and resort to beta blockers, but that only deals with the symptoms not the cause, and tends to make your playing flat and uninteresting.

Self-reliance comes from two things: a positive orientation towards your goal, and a reduction of inhibiting dependency patterns. Even genius is only fine observation, strengthened by fixity of purpose. You *can* recapture the excitement and wonder of a six year-old.

1. Collect information. Make a private list of all the times you had problems with 'nerves'. Look for recurring patterns and trigger factors. Evaluate them on a scale of 1 to 10 for scariness. If a specific thing happened, go back to the first time and write it down in all its gory detail. Use as colourful language as you like – no one else is going to see it and you can have the satisfaction of burning it later!

2. With muscle testing (see below) identify the words that have the most negative power over you.

3. With the scary situation that's coming up in the future, write down the best/worst/most likely outcome, and find solutions for each.

4. Listen to what you tell yourself, the names you call yourself when

161

something small goes wrong. Do you mutter 'Stupid idiot'? Worse? Much worse? Make a note of who first said that to you and who goes on saying it now. It's a known fact, that if you are told something often enough without investigating it, you will come to believe it, if not consciously then subconsciously, especially if you get agreement from others (look at Hitler, he persuaded a whole nation). You are being a little Hitler to yourself and you believe it. Then you act out what you tell yourself because the subconscious is programmed to do what you tell it; it doesn't know the difference between right and wrong, only your habit of thought. So if you tell your mind to be a stupid idiot, that's what it does!

Typically 'I can't/if only I could' is negative acceptance of this and clutters, blocks and confuses, turning self-assurance into self-doubt, crippling your best intentions and sabotaging ambition into mediocrity. These phrases hold you in a negative frame of mind and intensify the bad feelings you have about yourself. They are a negative 'self-talk' programme on the radio in your head. We will deal with that presently.

Having made your private horror lists, the first thing to learn is that *you* are in charge, in control, responsible. Remember Shakespeare said 'There is nothing either good or bad, but thinking makes it so'. *Stress isn't the problem, but how you react to it.* Living for approval is just another way of dying, yet this is what all artists do to a greater or lesser extent, unless they realise that you must play for *yourself* and then give that playing away by sharing your joy and love of what you do. There's nothing so catching as enthusiasm! 'Responsibility starts with the willingness to experience yourself as the cause in the matter. It is not burden, fault, praise, credit, shame or guilt; as all these include judgements and evaluations, they are not responsibility. Being responsible means being willing to deal with a situation from the point of view that you are the source of what you are, what you do and what you have. This point of view extends to include even what is done to you (and ultimately what another does to another). It is a context of Self as the source for the content and interpretation of what is, in your awareness.' (Erhard)

No one will ever breathe one breath for you, think one thought that is yours, or *ever* stand in your body, feel your fears, dream your dreams or cry your tears. We are born, live and leave this life entirely on our own.

That Self, and the divine spirit which drives it, are what we have to work with. No one else will ever live a single moment of our life for us. That we must do for ourselves. *That is responsibility.* So, decide now: are you going to be at the mercy of your feelings and fears, and let them run your life, or will you take charge? Be afraid and do 'it' anyway. This shows you who is in control, and that what you feared was the fear itself. Responsibility is the basis of our individual determination to accept life and to fulfil ourselves within it. For each possible course of action, consider (a) What does it cost me? (b) What does it buy me? (c) What are the possibilities I'm missing by taking this action?

People think there is 'something' that will make them happy, if only they could get hold of it. They have the patience to learn to play their instrument, but won't bother to learn how to operate themselves. They diminish themselves just in order to push away the chance of choice. People often say 'I couldn't help myself' when what they mean is 'I didn't help myself'. 'I can't' mostly means 'I won't'. Halfway is 'I won't yet/can't yet'. Actually, the saying 'the best place to look for a helping hand is the end of your arm!' is annoyingly true.

So, if 'they' make you nervous, you are acting like a victim and giving away your power. 'They' are not doing it, you are the one creating the pain. It takes two to make an argument, and if one side doesn't respond to the other, then there's no argument. You only act as a victim in this way because you don't see that you have a choice in the matter. You don't see that how you react is a learnt response, a habit that you can un-learn, an interpretation of the signs and symptoms that you can change, and that you can replace the reaction you don't want with one you do want.

By the way, if you look at all I have said and find you don't want to let go of old habits, that's all right too, but remember that then you have no moral right to complain about it all any more, because you have made a choice. Choice in itself has no goodness or badness, it's just a choice, as trivial as choosing between chocolate or vanilla. The power comes in what you do with the choice you make.

Helpful and Unhelpful Language

So, now the issue of responsibility is out of the way, what next? Examine how you talk to yourself, and also look at how you react to others' helpful suggestions. Are you a 'Yes, but' person? That 'but' ever so politely dismisses *everything* said before it, and means you haven't really listened to what was said to you. Get off your 'but' and replace it with 'and' and notice how it changes the communication. It *includes* both old and new ideas and now you have a choice and are open to learning. You can choose which later, so meanwhile *be coachable! live adventurously!* It's hard to move on when you dig your heels in.

Other judgmental words you might look at are 'right' and 'wrong'. How right, how wrong? It is more productive to break down the problem into small steps and then think in terms of goals that you update. Go for excellence and satisfaction, not perfection, because that's never obtainable, and you can't get it right unless you know what 'right' is for you. Give yourself clearer positive guidelines, not 'put-downs'. 'Right' is simply the next goal, until you know better or decide otherwise.

'Should' and 'ought' contain resentment and no personal responsibility. If you do something for any reason other than that you want to do it, then you are doing it to manipulate someone. Who? Incidentally that person does not have to be still alive, but they *are* alive in your head, and are probably the original source of the loud voice that's blaring at you on your internal radio. Don't get 'hardening of the oughteries', it shortens your life.

'Control' (of yourself, usefully interpreted as 'loving mindfulness') sometimes becomes equated with 'holding on', whether mentally or muscularly. It is then accompanied by lack of breathing or constipation, both of which are just resistances which come from fear. Fear that 'they', who are not to be trusted, will take over, or that you will not be able to cope or be responsible; or fear that, if you let go of what you have, there isn't any more for you. Often the word 'control' is misinterpreted as 'hold' giving the double message of 'stop/go'. This causes total confusion and disruption subconsciously, and gives a predisposition to mistakes, when 'control' should actually mean 'loving mindfulness of what is needed'. 'Control', when understood in the sense of 'hold' is therefore the opposite of spontaneity, intuition and joy at being here.

'Try harder' is the most useless request I know. It's actually physically impossible to carry out. Think about it for a minute. Then try to think about it, then try to do it. 'Try' is the last of the commonly used words which triggers stage fright. How does one succeed at trying to do something? It's either possible to do it, or not possible, that's all. Fritz Perls' statement 'trying fails, awareness cures' sums this up beautifully. Trying is hard work so that all one's energy is channelled into the effort, not into the success. It's the thinking about *you* and fear of *them* rather than communication, that causes the problem. Curiously when you try to succeed, you fail and when it's OK to fail you succeed. This same pressure and anxiety mechanism 'blanks out' things in an exam, that are remembered immediately the exam is over. The only real difference between humming a tune to yourself at home and singing it at the Albert Hall, is the opinion you have about the audience and the volume. In other words you need to distract your over-protective ego so that it doesn't interpret the situation as dangerous. That done, you simply go and do the job, trusting the practice you have done. You will then have X amount of success. The result will be excellent or will need more help – that's all there is to it, and without the ego terrorising it, the former is more likely. The secret is to separate the person from the deed.

From an acupuncture point of view, stress will cause one or more meridians to go into overload: you may show the symptoms on the opposite side of the body; or your normal positive, self-heal mechanisms may go into reverse and you do things that are bad for you, such as overdosing on alcohol, drugs or food that's not good for you (like a chocolate binge). That is called 'psychological reversal' (see below).

The triggers for this reversal can be subconscious, old and uncomfortable memories, and past physical injuries. Stage fright is a mental manifestation of this; the physical manifestations are poor speed, lack of stamina, muscle spasm, trembling, a thumping heart, sweating, inertia and breathing problems and panic signals of over-control and disorganised coordination. However, as musical performance isn't about winning a race or world records, the physical side seems less important than the awful emotional state people get into, until it gets so bad that playing is audibly affected. It can even get to a state where physical symptoms are worn like a badge which shows the person no longer has to be responsible, and then they give up playing. If you are willing to work at the techniques later in this chapter it won't get to that state, and you will establish for

165

yourself a firm foundation on which your self-belief can grow and your playing flourish.

Criticism, Recordings and Perfectionism

When it comes down to it, who is your sternest critic? The answer is always YOU. The self-critic you hear in your head. Your hands, ears and eyes are far more highly trained in observation than anyone in the average audience, and only you know your intentions about your performance until you've actually played. However your self-critic is at work evaluating and condemning long before that. If you can, silence it till you have finished, and then do a post mortem if necessary. At least that way your attention is undivided while you play, and can be usefully objective of the whole afterwards. There's a world of difference between saying 'I am a bad fiddle player' (personal brow-beating) and 'I played that badly', (i.e. but I do other things well). People who feel good about themselves produce good results. *Catch yourself doing something right.* Joy is not found in things, or 'out there': it is within *us*.

Remember that the self-critic certainly never acknowledges that you were doing your best! Would you be so merciless to anyone else? No. You would have compassion. The after-burn of re-living the mistake you made in a performance, and beating yourself up mentally for it all night, is cruelty, lack of compassion and forgiveness at its most destructive. The mind is capable of rehearsing and re-living the memory of self accusation, storing it up to add to the list of 'reasons' in the stage-fright catalogue. Don't be tempted to accuse. Acknowledge all the good bits that you played, *and* that you did your best, and get the good night's sleep you deserve. The you won't repeat the mistake the next time round out of sheer tiredness, crowning it with 'I told you so, see, it's the thin end of the wedge' when it happens again. If you are a tyrant to yourself, you will not tolerate comments from others, how ever well intentioned. Either you become defensive (you've already done the destruction job on yourself so don't need yet more), or you crumple. You can only do your best (particularly in ensemble playing) if you let others do their best too. It's almost always you *and* them and almost never you *or* them, yet we react as if it were.

Whether or not they have the right to do it, if someone criticises your playing, realise that:

1. It's only one opinion, not everyone's, and may be coloured by circumstances of which you are totally unaware, and which don't involve you. Unfortunately you were at hand as a whipping-boy, and what they say is more likely to be a reflection of their unresolved problems rather than yours.

2. Look at their motives. Is what they are communicating really about your work or a personal affront?

3. Consider how highly you value their opinion, not forgetting that help sometimes comes in curious disguises. Do they know what they are talking about?

4. Hear the critic out. Don't interrupt or think 'Yes but'. Be receptive to their ideas.

5. Acknowledge that that person isn't satisfied even if you are. Excuses are irrelevant, since they are talking about behaviour patterns not you. They are not being personal.

6. Don't blame the other person for *your* lack of understanding. Ask for more clarification. Ask what they *did* like, ask what's important to *them*.

7. If you can remain objective, the matter may resolve itself. You may even have helped them by providing an outlet for their pent-up problems.

8. Everyone is a potential winner, even you. Some people are disguised as losers, so don't let appearances fool you.

Gone are the days when Pepys described watching a man being hanged, drawn and quartered as entertainment, and then wrote about it in his diary! Most people view critics as people who think they are able to pronounce on what the music 'really means', without the need to ask the composer or the player who spent hours struggling alone, trying this way and that to improve the communication implicit in the notes, and laying bare their vulnerability.

Music critics in the media have a completely different view of life from you as a performer. They are not free publicity merchants. If they write for a paper, then that paper is their master, not the audience who heard you. They have deadlines and a limited number of words or column inches. This means they have to make invidious choices as to whose performance they cover. Even though you know they came to your concert you may still not get a mention. Sometimes there are so many performances on the same night that they go to the first half of one concert and the second half of the next. Don't assume, either, that they will talk much about your playing. They have to make it interesting reading to other people (who will not hear you unless you have a series or your concert is repeated), so they tend to show off their stylistic or musicological knowledge or compare your performance to Xxxx's.

However *they are human* and, even if they have good intentions, can make mistakes. They also want to help people if they can, so a new, young player or a world première will be encouraged before a more established player. They tend to be less polite the older one gets, until one is world famous, when they tend to gush again. Even when they have written about you with brilliant and fulsome praise, if some amazing news story happens that requires all available column inches, your bit gets ditched. Nobody will tell you it's not your fault, and it may not be theirs either.

If you are exceedingly lucky the ditched review might get into a later edition. It's just rather unfortunate that your reputation is in such hands, particularly when looking for music club bookings. Realistically or otherwise, unless a quote from a critic is vital to your publicity, try not to take too much notice.

Be honest, how many critics do you read other than your own? By the same token, judge by audience reaction today, not tomorrow's paper. The audience is whom you play to, and whom you have to persuade to come and hear you again, not a critic, who is perhaps better with his word-processor than a musical instrument. If you are consistently offered work despite your critics, then recognise what a lot of approval that actually implies.

Recordings have a lot to answer for. Your own home recordings are guaranteed to turn you into a perfectionist if you aren't one already, and then you start to hate how you play if you aren't careful. Professional recording releases are inevitably fossilised or at least deep frozen until you do the next version years later. They are like photographs, leaving no room for growth, the mood of the day, local acoustics and audience reaction. Despite this, for years, invidious comparisons between recordings of performances were made into radio programmes. Reproduction is so good on

CDs now, that the people buying them get used to every nuance of the playing (forgetting how much editing is done) and then are surprised when they go to a live performance and find the artist has the 'audacity' to be human and play the piece slightly differently. Kreisler became neurotic about it, and thought the audience sat and waited for a wrong note. Being a soloist is a very lonely life and it's easy to get things out of balance. Don't fall into the same trap.

Long- and Short-term Help

So, having put criticism in perspective, how can you help yourself both in the long term and immediately before a concert? How can you debug the system, let go and play like the dream you had when you first picked up your instrument?

For **long-term help** you might try the following:
1. Clean up your practice methods (see Chapter 3 on memory).
2. Study how to match arousal state to task (psycho-regulation, see below).
3. Remove as many of the other stresses in your life as you can, like poor posture, poor diet, work overload, visual and aural stresses etc., as well as family and personal difficulties.
4. Use the private lists you made when trying to deal with stage fright, and tackle the problems with the techniques explained later in this chapter: psychological reversal, behavioural barometer, visualisation, goal balancing, neuro-linguistic programming (NLP), and self-talk. See them as an opportunity for growth towards joyful playing and direct communication.
5. Decide you don't always have to feel bad like this. Go for it. Buy, read and use *The Inner Game of Music* to distract your ego, *The Secrets of Musical Confidence* which gives you the musician/psychologist's view, *What to Say When You Talk to Yourself'* which deals with the voice in your head and inspires you to take control, *Dynamics of the Singing Voice* which speaks for itself and is translatable to any instrument and *Frogs into Princes* for communication problem solving. These books are all easily readable,

contain extremely valuable information and go into these techniques in much more detail than I have space for here. Book details are to be found under **References** at the end of this chapter. Such a reading programme will build an internal support system which will become permanent if you want it to.

In the **short term,** you should abstain from all stimulants for at least six hours before playing, and try one of the short-term stress remedies detailed below. These remedies are just that; short term. Use them when there is mild, short-lasting stress only, or as a top-up that can easily be done in a quiet band room or green room, just before performance.

Breathing: Learning deep breathing is really only a matter of remembering to do it, since it was the first thing you ever did, the day you were born. Your brain can't function without a good supply of oxygen, so don't deprive it in its hour of need when you are performing! If you have never thought much about breathing, then do this exercise and notice the results.

1. Sit hunched up, head down, shoulders forward and up by your ears, breastbone sunk in, stomach squashed and diaphragm tight. Now, keeping this position, take as deep a breath as you can and see how long you can make a continuous sound as you breathe out.

2. Sit up on the edge of your chair so your knees are lower than your hips, shoulders back and down, arms loose, head up so your neck is reasonably vertical, lift your ribs out of your pelvis, and from there breathe in by pushing out your tummy; next breathe in more by filling your chest and pushing out your rib cage sideways; now breathe in more still by expanding the upper chest area upwards. This should all be done in one smooth movement from one area to the next. Now, before you levitate with all that air, make the sound again and see how long you can keep it going this time, by gradually letting the chest sink, the ribs deflate and the stomach push in. It should last much longer.

3. Don't be surprised if after a few breaths like this you feel slightly light headed. Your brain hasn't had so much oxygen in years! What does this tell you? Good posture = good oxygen intake = good brain function and calmness (because you were too preoccupied to be nervous). There is a lot of controversy as to whether or not it

matters if you breathe in through your nose and out through your nose, or out through your mouth. There are various schools of Yoga and each have their own rules on the subject, and about how long 'in' breaths versus 'out' should be. Circular breathing is interesting too, and involves controlling different bits of the breathing mechanism to be able to breathe out continuously to produce a very long phrase, but is not a really useful thing to try to do as first aid for stress.

4. If the above exercise causes you to hyperventilate temporarily (breathing hard, deep and fast with no gaps between breaths, and you can't stop), don't worry. Breathe into a paper bag. Re-breathing your own air will increase the carbon dioxide levels in your blood, and bring things quickly back to normal. Stop when you are in control again.

Stress-induced asthma is relieved, and breath control is helped, by breathing through a straw. Pollution and allergy-induced asthma may need medical help. Although smoking calms you temporarily with narcotics, it also poisons you by changing the gases in your blood and acidifying it, so the red cells won't give up their oxygen to your brain cells; it also contracts blood vessels so the brain gets starved, and the tars clog up the very delicate, one-cell-thick oxygen/carbon dioxide exchange mechanism in your lungs, leading to yet more oxygen starvation. Outwardly it makes your oxygen-starved skin coarse and lined, your breath smells, and your clothes and instrument stink to a non-smoker. You can smell the stale smoke as soon as the instrument case is opened. Smoking addiction is usually more social and psychological than narcotic, because you feel that you are 'at least doing something to counteract your nerves'. Well, it only deals with the symptoms like all other drugs and the long-term side-effects are known to be horrendous. You are the only one who can decide to be responsible enough to make the choice to look at and treat the causes, stop the need for it and give your brain the oxygen it needs for the best chance to perform well.

Centering: This is a simple technique which integrates your disparate energies and concentrates the mind and strength in one direction. Use it in the green room immediately before you go on.

1. Sit comfortably in a flat seated chair if possible, feet flat on the

floor, back and neck easily straight (not like a ramrod).

2. Place your hands on your knees and breathe deeply – some people find this enough and stop here.

3. Go into your innermost being and remind it that it is safe, housed, fed and watered.

4. Send a feeling of love out to all the people who have given up time to come and hear you play, and invite them into your space.

5. When you have done this for a couple of minutes, go out and play to your best friends out there. Don't play *at* them so much as *with* them. Share. Even out there you are still safe, housed, fed and watered, and now you are among friends.

Inner Game on the job: You have to exercise continual creativity with this way of handling your critical self, in the areas of awareness, will and trust. For pre-performance nerves you can remind yourself about what are your goals in music, clarify why you took it up, and what you love about it, to distract yourself, get away from the fright hype and get back true reality. Challenge yourself to recognise the opportunities that Inner Game methods offer you and be responsive to them. Examples of these are (1) During rehearsal, practise getting used to distractions with the help of an accomplice. Let them have fun trying to distract you, frighten you or make you giggle, by dropping things, coughing or sneezing loudly, or mimicking any other 'disaster' that comes to mind; (2) When it comes to the performance, concentrate on the emotions of the music; (3) Trust your practice; (4) Play as though you were your mentor/idol/role model; (5) Find something in the audience, other than a face, to hold your attention and play to. These ideas are wonderful in allowing you time and space to get back on top of that destructive critic in your head.

Rescue Remedy: This is a stress-specific combination of five Bach flower remedies, which works on the emotions and has much the same use as Arnica. Discovered in the last century by Dr Bach, a very sensitive Oxfordshire GP, there are 38 single flower essences at homeopathic dilution, preserved in brandy. You can either take two drops neat under your tongue, or put four drops in a tumbler of water and sip it slowly just prior to performance. Each essence has its own positive and negative emotion upon which it works, and you can also use the essences to change unwanted emotions behind an unwanted habit. They come with a clearly labelled chart or booklet, are absolutely safe for amateur and children's use, and can be bought in any health food shop. I've kept some Rescue Remedy in my instrument case or handbag for years. Some examples of more specific Bach flower remedies are **Cerato** for lack of confidence in someone always seeking advice; **Elm** for feelings of temporary inadequacy; **Rock rose** for extreme fear and panic; **Mimulus** for fear of known things, shyness and timidity; **Gentian** for discouragement leading to self doubt. If you are teetotal and are worried about the brandy content, the power in these remedies can be transferred by a radionics practitioner to spring water, which will then have the same effect.

Psycho-regulation

This is a Russian technique, explained to me by Professor Vladimir Ilyn, sometime Deputy Minister for Health in the USSR. It is basically positive medical sports psychology translated into musical terms. It entails observing the uniquely personal signs that occur when you perform to your optimum. This is when your breathing rate, blood pressure, and psychological arousal state best fit the performance required. In international competitions, millions may be watching/hearing you represent your country, and you will need the right level of confidence, courage and aggression, endurance and sensory awareness to win, not to mention playing like an angel! It's also useful for playing in public to a normal sized audience.

You know when your playing hits a purple patch! When you are totally inspired and in a Zen-like state, *your instrument seems to play you* rather than vice versa.

1. *Immediately* you finish, get out a stop-watch and ask someone to count your breathing rate, while you count your pulse for one minute by putting three fingers on the thumb side of the inside of your wrist, just below the wrist crease. (To recreate that state at a later date you may have to run round the block – not for nothing do they say that a three hour rehearsal is like a three hour rugby match!)

2. Observe your state of mind. Are you calm, excited, fearful, angry, exultant, aggressive? Find one word that encapsulates that feeling. What ever it is that you felt, *that* is the state of mind specific to you and needs to be recreated to play as well next time.

3. Make a note, when you felt inspired, of what you were thinking about and where in your body did you feel it? Remember and recreate that too.

4. Make a positive habit out of your findings. They harness your natural optimum state by *emphasising what works consciously*. It is your zenith when compared to the nadir of being either bored to death or scared to death (as most viola players are when surviving a ballet season of *Giselle!*).

The Russians combine these techniques with visualisation very successfully. They also take note of biorhythms too, so that where possible, they choose to play on days when the natural ebb and flow of body energy is at its most auspicious, and avoid 'critical' and 'low' energy days. Having many time-zones within the country they are also used to acclimatising themselves well before performing.

Visualisation

There are various areas in which this is particularly useful. You can either just close your eyes, or you can go into a meditative state. To do this:

1. Sit or lie still and breathe deeply with your eyes closed. (NB you are not going to sleep, so you may prefer to sit.)

2. Imagine yourself sitting outside in the shadow of a large cloud. Watch the cloud dissolve slowly as it passes over, and relax bit by bit as you feel the sun's warmth sinking into each part of your body, starting at your toes and going gradually, gradually upwards until you are basking in its gentle, golden light.

3. Take yourself to a favourite, secret place and do your chosen visualisation (see below) or just enjoy the luminous silence – there's so little of it in a musician's life.

4. When you have finished, remind yourself where you are, before you open your eyes and smile.

Useful visualisations: (a) Go through in your mind, and be absolutely clear about every single detail of a specific piece of music you intend to play, so that the signals from brain to hands are absolutely precise. Any bits that are foggy will show up in your performance, so clear them out now. A good memory aid, it can be hard work first time round, so don't be too discouraged, persevere until all is clear.

(b) Some people find it extremely helpful to picture their most admired performer, and while keeping that image in mind, play (without instrument) as though they were that person, with all the skills, sound and brilliance of that person. Later, keeping the image, play with instrument, matching everything to your role-model, perhaps still with eyes closed, but not lying on the floor!

(c) Get under the skin of a specific animal that has the characteristics you wish to emphasise in the piece you wish to play. *Be* a growling tiger (fur, whiskers and all), a flower or a tree, a bird or a snake. It adds immediacy to your playing (Haydn quartets played as a caricature, for example, can be hilarious and very witty). Ensemble playing suddenly becomes easy if you all create similar characterisation. You inspire each other with a common conception and aim.

(d) Become very clear in you mind as to the picture (rather than the written dynamics) the composer had in his mind, as, for instance, in Vivaldi's *Four Seasons.*

(e) Use visualisation to prepare you for playing in new, unusual or difficult circumstances. See the room/hall, see who will be there, give them interested, happy faces. Play about, and imagine the worst that can happen, embellish it till you make it so grotesquely awful that it becomes funny. Next make it the absolute best that can happen until it's unbelievably wonderful in a way that's special to you. Then visualise it being so easy and enjoyable that you look forward to it. (This technique works well with NLP reframing to which it has similarities, but I recommend reading *Frogs into Princes,* or doing a course and using their 'anchoring' techniques.)

(f) If you feel pressed for time and space, visualise yourself as 10 feet tall and 4 feet wide, then stretch your skin to fit both front and back, and head to toes; then expand the muscles, tissues, organs and bones. Now you have room inside to think things out, be flexible, look at several choices, or room to be just you. (Thank you Meribeth Bunch for that one!)

(g) You can use visualisation to plan your 'Golden Future'. Think, if you could wave a wand, and with money, time and energy no object, where would you be and what would you be doing? When you have that, put it five years hence and plan backwards making clear all the steps to getting there. So, where must you have reached in three years, one year, one month? Then even what you do today is in line with your ideals, and gives you a lightness and sense of purpose that can transcend something like stage fright in a single leap by putting present worries firmly in their insignificant little place.

(g) If you are into chakras, visualise each one from the lowest to the highest, staying with each one until it is crystal clear in your mind, and full of light. Then start at the heart and integrate the whole of you in concentric rings of radiant energy spreading outwards – heart chakra – shoulders and hips – elbows, knees and crown – hands, feet and interpersonal chakra above the head.

Visualisation increases in value the more you do it. Do it at least daily, until you feel you have got all you can out of it, want to change it or want to move on. All the above ideas get you away from 'them' and victim status into *being in charge, and being the cause of how you are, and how you will be.* The techniques are great fun, wonderfully inspirational, playfully serendipitous and irresponsibly responsible. And YOU are doing it. It's also a wonderful **Five Minute Holiday** (see Chapter 8).

Behavioural barometer

This is a list of ordinary words and associated words that people find disturbing. People generally react to negative words, but occasionally to the positive counterpart too. To use this technique you need to know two things. Firstly, how to muscle test (see Chapter 9) and secondly, the location of the 'Emotional stress release' (ESR) points. They are found on your forehead, over the centre of each eye and midway between the eyebrow and the hair line (or where the hairline used to be). You will need a friend to help.

1. On the list on p178, test the words in capitals in the right-hand column, top to bottom, by saying them out loud with a strong indicator muscle tested by your friend. When the strong muscle goes weak, that is the section of the list to work at.

2. Test the negative words in that section. Again, the strong muscle will go weak on the words needing help.

3. Your friend now holds the points on you forehead lightly and says the word in as many different emotional ways as possible (crossly, pleadingly, smugly, sorrowfully etc.) and then uses rhetorical prompts like: *'When did you last feel XXX?' 'How does it feel to be XXX?' 'Who around you is XXX?' 'Who else is XXX?' 'What's it like to receive XXX?' 'What else makes you XXX?' 'Where in your body do you feel XXX?' 'Think of a time long ago when you felt XXX.' 'When was the first time you felt XXX?' 'Who was there?' 'What would you like to have said/not said, done/undone then that you didn't?' 'What would have made it all right then?' 'How about now?'* None of these questions need be answered out loud; it's an entirely private matter for you and no one else. The idea behind the prompts is to keep you thinking about the word (you won't want to because it's uncomfortable, and it has had such power over you, for such a long time.) You may get a bit emotional as you let go of the long-held grief it caused you, but it's worth it, you feel so much better afterwards and it has lost some, if not most, of its power over you.

4. When you run out of questions, check for reactions with the positive counterpart in the opposite column, and, if need be, deal with it by repeating steps 1 to 3 above.

5. You've finished when none of the words weaken your muscles any more.

6. You can also use this technique to de-stress a future event, together with Visualisation.

ACCEPTANCE
Choosing to, Approachable
Optimistic, Acceptable
Adaptable, Worthy
Deserving, Open

WILLING
Receptive, Adequate
Prepared, Answerable
Encouraging, Refreshed
Invigorated, Aware

INTEREST
Fascinated, Tuned in
Needed, Welcomed
Understanding, Appreciated
Essential, Caring

ENTHUSIASM
Amused, Jubilant
Admirable, Attractive
Delighted, Elated
Alive, Trusting

ASSURANCE
Motivated, Daring
Protected, Bold
Brave, Considered
Affectionate, Proud

EQUALITY
Lucky, Cooperative
Involved, Purposeful
Reliable, Concerned
Sincere, Productive

ATTUNEMENT
In tune with, Congruent
In balance, Creative
Perceptive, Appreciative
Tender, Gentle

ONENESS
Quiet, Safe
Calm, At peace
Unified, Completed
Fulfilled, At-one-ment

ANTAGONISM
Attacked, Bothered
Questioned, Burdened
Annoyed, Indignant
Opposing, Inadequate

ANGER
Incensed, Furious
Over-wrought, Fuming
Seething, Fiery
Belligerent, Hysterical

RESENTMENT
Hurt, Embarrassed
Wounded, Used/Abused
Unappreciated, Rejected
Dumb, Offended

HOSTILITY
Trapped, Picked upon
Put upon, Frustrated
Deprived, Sarcastic
Vindictive, Withholding

FEAR OF LOSS
Let down, Not heard
Bitter, Disappointed
Threatened, Overlooked
Frightened, Unwelcome

GRIEF & GUILT
Betrayed, Conquered
Discouraged, Unacceptable
Self-punishing, Despondent
Defeated, Ruined

INDIFFERENCE
Pessimistic, Immobilised
Rigid, Numb
Stagnant, Unfeeling
Destructive, Disconnected

SEPARATION
Uncared for, Unloved
Unacceptable, Unloveable
Unimportant, Melancholy
Morbid, Deserted, Loveless

Affirmations and self-talk

Affirmations are a bit like the lines my grandparents used to have to write for misdemeanours at school. To a lively mind they are exceedingly boring. You decide upon some undesirable aspect or habit of behaviour e.g. 'I always try to fit in one more thing, which means I'm always being late for appointments'. Rewrite this in the positive – 'I always leave the house in plenty of time and enjoy arriving with time to spare, to look at the music.' The idea is then to write this out in first, second and third person singular at least 20 times a day.

You can imagine how many people would stick to that, let alone believe it will change them! However, attaching the affirmation to a ditty helps. I hummed the ditty in my head and the words came without effort. I attached 'I am /always in the /right place at the /right /time, suc/cessfully en/gaged in the /right activi/ty' to Clementine. I was never late through my own fault again, and it calmed me down when I was stuck in traffic. From someone who used to get detention after detention at school for lateness, I suddenly realised how rude it was to assume my doings were more important than everyone else's, and I developed a reputation for reliability. This meant that on the odd occasion I was late, no one turned a hair. I just apologised quietly later and never got 'het up' about punctuality again.

Shad Helmstetter's self-talk is a similar technique. It is used to countermand the negative programme on the 'radio in your head'. Instead of repeating one affirmation endlessly, you put together a series of positive thoughts around all the different aspect of the troublesome behaviour you want to change, then read them on to a tape. Play it night and morning and whenever else you can, like when driving or washing up. I found it very useful for weight loss (see Chapter 6), but it could be used to great effect for low self-esteem, stage fright or practically any other ill that you wish to change.

Psychological reversal

Failure to sort out and handle problems is sometimes due to self-sabotage. The pattern shows up when, using muscle testing (see Chapter 9), the

179

indicator muscle goes weak when a musician states a positive goal which s/he says s/he desires to achieve, and when a failure or negative aspect of the same goal is imagined the indicator muscle stays strong. (If both positive and negative aspects test weak then either it is the wrong goal, or there is too much stress around the subject as a whole which must be cleared out first with the behavioural barometer or similar technique.)

These psychologically reversed people are individuals who respond poorly to suggestions of help and, where there *is* improvement, tend to dismiss it or pass over it quickly, and get back to dwelling on the negative aspects. Psychological reversal can be very specific. Muscle testing may react normally strong to the idea of playing but reverse and test weak when a specific aspect of playing or specific piece of music is mentioned. A typical example might be that right hand technique to a string player tests strong but long, slow notes 'ponticello' causes a reversal. The cause can be a physical, mental or personal upset, and is usually related to something that that movement, idea or person represents, and often involves self-judgement in the light of it.

Saying firmly 'I profoundly and deeply accept myself with all my problems and shortcomings' will return the muscle test to normal, but shows up a lack of self-acceptance. Acupressure points SI-1 or SI-3 will sort this out. SI-1 is found on the outside of the little finger nail bed, and SI-3 is on the outside of the little finger side of the palm crease that appears when you make a fist. No needles are required, so you can relax! Tap these points three times a second while saying the positive aspects of the goal at least ten times out loud. (These Acu-points come from AK Manuals.) A dose of Rescue Remedy on completion won't come amiss (see above).

Phobias

A phobia is an irrational fear which can be directed at almost any aspect of normal life. Your reaction is unrealistic and out of all proportion to the actual danger. Body energies go haywire and your total attention is taken away from musical communication, and given entirely to avoidance of the feared object or task, be it stage fright, flying, lifts, playing in a place where something awful once happened, specific colours, positions of the moon, stars, walking under ladders, whistling in theatre or whatever. Often a phobia will severely limit your life outside music as well.

First you need to clear any psychological reversal (see above). Failure to do so may mean failure to clear the phobia.

1. Using muscle testing (see Chapter 9) test with the general statement 'I want to have a good life' and 'I want to be miserable' which should give strong and weak tests respectively. Then test with 'I want to get rid of my fear (e.g. stage fright)' and 'I want to keep my fear (stage fright)'. Again these should react to testing logically. If not then use psychological reversal on them.

2. Next, evaluate the fear level on a scale of one to ten, with one reading as 'I am perfectly calm and relaxed with this fear', and ten as 'I can't bear it and must escape because I'm in total panic'. The degrees in between pro rata. Take into account that it may be OK to *talk* about 'it' but not *do* 'it', or *be near* 'it'.

3. While you think about, or confront, the phobia have someone test an indicator muscle and it will go weak. Now touch Acu-point CV-12 (which is half way between the tummy button and the lower end of your breastbone), while you think of the phobia again, and if the indicator muscle now goes strong, tap Acu-points St-1 (under the cheek bone under the centre of each eye) and St-45 (on the outer edge of the nail of the second toe). Tap them together about 30 times while you keep thinking about or confronting the problem. (These are AK Acu-points.)

4. If stage 3 above is ineffective, repeat the process, touching the end of the last rib in your lower back, instead of CV-12. If it weakens the indicator muscle, strengthen it by tapping Acu-points K-1 (on the heel end of the crease on the underside of your forefoot) and K-27 (in the dip below the collarbone where it joins the breastbone), at the same time as thinking of or confronting the phobia.

5. Confront the phobia and re-assess on the one to ten scale. If the rating is above two, repeat the process. On retesting, the indicator muscle should now test strong, as you think about or confront the phobia.

6. Now put it to the test again while you think about/confront 'it' again, but this time hum a tune, count out loud, and then finally do

it with eyes open and eyes shut. If either of the first two causes a weak indicator muscle, touch CV-12 and tap the points again. For weakness with eyes open, tap the back of the head at the very top of the neck, and for weakness with eyes closed, tap the centre of the forehead, thinking/confronting the while during each Acu-point tapping. These last two tapping points integrate right/left brain and front/back brain. Stress levels should be down to one or two by now.

Although many of these ideas can be used on tour as well as at home, the band room or green room is not the best place, because it is too public, too stressed a place and too late. Find a quiet hotel room or other private place with plenty of time to spare. They are powerful techniques which may need recovery and integration time.

For short-term help with a phobia, try *Breathing, Centrering, Inner Game* and *Rescue Remedy* techniques, all discussed under **Short-term stress remedies** earlier in this chapter.

Burn-out and How to Say 'No'

This is a recognisable over-stressed state, and may need medical help. Your GP will know all about it because it occurs so frequently in the medical profession! It definitely needs REST, and the signs and symptoms are: tiredness, yet poor sleep; listlessness and irritability; raised blood-pressure or depression; a feeling of being driven yet being utterly drained with no time for yourself; no interest in doing the things that you normally love doing; and a shut-down of any will to give out to other people, other than as duty. Often all this is accompanied by poor feeding habits; over-reliance on stimulants, calmatives, or other over-the-counter drugs; and poor general health with irritating coughs or colds that just won't go.

Burn-out is indicative of a one-sided lifestyle. Too much stress, work, travel, performing, and not enough playing, recreation and feeding the soul/spirit with other interests. There *is* life outside music, but because you work unsocial hours, you rarely meet anyone who isn't in the music business.

The only way to deal with it is to take the long-term view. Decide how many weeks holiday you deserve in a year and then how many years since you had a really restorative holiday, add them together and jolly well take

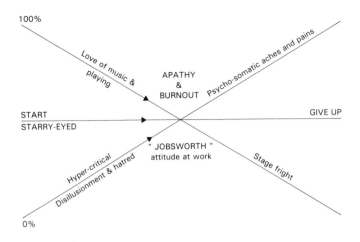

100%

Love of music & playing

APATHY
&
BURNOUT

Psycho-somatic aches and pains

START
STARRY-EYED

GIVE UP

"JOBSWORTH"
attitude at work

Stage fright

Hyper-critical

Disillusionment & hatred

0%

Joyful expectation to burnout

that holiday, going where you are really well looked after; stop the over-the-counter drugs, coffee and alcohol; eat well and, above all, rest. It will be hard at first, because it's so unusual for you.

'But what about my dates/contacts/fixers?' I hear you cry! If you broke your arm and couldn't play, or suddenly *had* to go to Australia, what would you do? Tell them when you will be back, so do the same now. This is a similar crisis: recognise it as such. Your body already has! It has tried to attract your attention by posting signals in the form of all those symptoms you feel. If you don't listen now, eventually it will shut down completely and *make* you listen.

If you are in any doubt, talk to your GP. It's no good earning all that money if you have no energy left to enjoy it with, or are too ill to enjoy the rest of your life. Burn-out ignored makes everyone round you miserable too, as you become more and more difficult to live with, even though you think you are doing your best for the family. It often leads to strokes, heart attacks and unforced accidents that can easily be lethal, because you are just 'not with it', are too tired to recognise it and make mistakes. *These mistakes are your body forcing you to stop.*

Learn to say 'No'. Energy and self-esteem are not inexhaustible. They are more like an emotional bank balance. You have to put something in before you can draw it out. Don't overdraw too often, or your body manager will foreclose the account. The very least you can do is to find out what your 'Feel Good Factors' are (see Chapter 8) and make sure you take regular doses.

'How do I say no?', you ask
1. Fixers want a good band with minimum hassle. If you have to turn in a job after accepting it, with most fixers it works best to be straightforward. They are just as good as you at smelling rats! Ask who they would like you to get, who they have already asked, and offer to do the 'phoning yourself. In the long run it's cheaper in energy and financial expenditure, even if there are still theatre rules about paying deputies an extra 25% fee.
2. Have a good spread of freelance work rather than only one sort. The regular orchestras have their free time written into the contract but you won't have that, and have to be firm if you are to make time off for yourself. If you don't you will pay in poor health.
3. Some people save 10% of everything they earn so that in seven years, with compound interest, this will be enough to take a sabbatical year off. Think about it! A year's paid holiday!
4. Think about this too – empowerment is about letting go so that others can get going.

REFERENCES
1. **Andrews E.** (1991) *Muscle Management,* Thorsons, Harper Collins
2. **Bandler R.** and **Grinder J.** (1979) *Frogs into Princes,* Real People Press, Moab, Utah, USA
3. **Bartley, W.** (1978) *Werner Erhard: the Transformation of a Man,* Potter, NY, USA
4. **Bunch M.** (1995) *Dynamics of the Singing Voice,* 3rd Ed. Springer Verlag
5. **Cooke D.** (1964) *The Language of Music,* Oxford Paperbacks, OUP
6. **Diamond J.** (1981) *The Life Energy in Music,* Archaens Press, NY, USA
7. **Evans A.** (1994) *The Secrets of Musical Confidence,* Thorsons, Harper Collins
8. **Green B.** and **Gallwey T.** (1986) *The Inner Game of Music,* Pan Original

9. **Hay L.** (1982) *Love yourself, Heal Your Life Workbook,* Eden Grove Edition, Airlift Book Co.

10. **Helmstetter S.** (1982) *What to Say When You Talk to Yourself,* Pocket Books, NY, USA

11. **Jampolsky, L.** *Healing the addictive mind,* Celestial Arts, Berkeley, California

12. **Ostwald P., Baron B., Byl N.,** and **Wilson F.** (1994) *Performing Arts Medicine* (West J Med 160:48-52)

13. **Salzer F.** (1962) *Structural Hearing in Music,* Vol 1&2, Dover Pub. Inc

14. **Storr** (1992) *Music and the Mind,* Flamingo, Harper Collins.

ORGANISATIONS

Arts Psychology Consultants, 29 Argyll Mans, Hammersmith Rd, London W14 8QQ. *Tel:* 0171-602 2707

CHAPTER 8

Musicians versus Emotions II

Other people 1 and 2; 101st Messiah;
Personal relationships; Blame;
Time and emotion study;
Being tired all the time; Pick-me-ups;
Negotiating; Practising;
Psychosomatic aches and pains;
Feel-good factors.

Other people 1

The heart of music is about relationships between spaces, just like quantum physics or chaos theory. It is also about adventure and entertainment. Yet to listen to many professional musicians it is about pain, drudgery and boredom. Why?

We were so starry eyed when we began, were probably the best in school, maybe in music college too, and then we get out into the real, wide world, and suddenly we are a very small minnow in a shark-infested pool, and no-one has taught us how to cope. 'Eat or be eaten' is how it feels. You or me, not you *and* me. We have to learn a sort of stainless-steel professionalism, and 'cold porridge' correctness about our playing. Praise stops, help stops, and individuality is suppressed in dress and manner as well as playing. We find there are many more 'bosses' to pacify or please instead of just one teacher, who is no longer there to support us.

Teachers usually learn psychology and social skills as part of their teacher training. No such training is given to orchestral players, section leaders or conductors, yet the situation has many similarities to sitting in class at school. There is even less team spirit. Players mentally continue with the conductor in the same child/parent relationship that they had with their teacher. The corners are knocked off by hard experience in the orchestral jungle, and occasional bullying is not unknown either. Blandness is encouraged, as it makes for malleability. Conductors like compliability and tend to use the orchestra as blocks of sound rather than as groups of people. Musicians become production line workers for dot translation, working for the boss from an instruction manual on the music stand. Improvisation and composition are frowned on as disruptive. No wonder synthesisers are used so often! According to Andrew Evans' research, creativity, artistic work and communication are the three most preferred job-values in musicians, yet it is precisely these values that are squashed, and the least preferred job-value of routine predictability the most encouraged.

We are taught to be good at music listening, but not at people listening. Your instrument is a surrogate voice and you are not taught how to communicate outside it or without it. No section leader is instructed in being a team leader, in pastoral care, or how to motivate his team and build its self-esteem. There is no section aim, visualisation, plan, aware-ness of opportunity or feed-back of positive ideas.

Instead there is often muttering behind hands, rather than talking openly to the person who can actually solve the problem. There's a lot of petty niggling amongst cliques, or between desk partners. These constitute the little things that cause the marriage of desk-sharing to break down, like hogging the stand, too-early (or too-late) page turning, exasperating remarks no one else can hear, and very cruel undermining of confidence. The way to destroy a player is not to pull his playing to bits, but subtly to suggest he plays out of tune, or spread a rumour to that effect.

Orchestral manners sometimes leave a lot to be desired. It used to be that one learned how to behave as a youngster in a provincial orchestra. It isn't 'dog eat dog'. The most obvious rules are:

1. Never take music home between rehearsal and concert. If it is forgotten, it means your desk partner can't play either.

2. Never draw attention to/point at the perpetrator of a wrong or 'spare' note. Even worse, glare at someone else when you have played one. They are also doing their best.

3. Never turn round and stare at the players behind you. Playing on the front desk is cosy. It is much harder to play on the back desk, where you can hear no-one but yourself, are frequently deafened by the brass behind and have to play 'on sight' and trust and un-nervingly far 'behind the beat'.

4. Do say 'Good morning'. Do thank your desk partner at the end, who has spent all day marking the part and turning the pages for you, before you rush off home.

5. Don't bring 'home problems' to work. It can upset the whole section. Keep calm, however uncomfortable you are and, when you can, go to someone who can do something about it, rather than 'dumping' your problems (as though your desk partner were your councillor), or whining continuously.

6. As far as possible without surrender, keep on good terms with everyone. It's a good form of prevention.

These 'orchestral manners' apply even if the orchestra is permanently attached to a touring opera or ballet company, for there the orchestra becomes a substitute home, particularly if home life is uncomfortable due to poor relationhips.

All too often, in most orchestras the only trouble-shooting there is becomes compromise not real communication. This leaves a taste of resentment behind to fester till the next explosion. There is no knowledge of how to inspire both 'sides' to have a common aim to work for. You are in the midst of people and yet you feel alone. You can't talk because you are rehearsing, and the more you focus on the situation, the lonelier you get, and the more you want to break out or escape. People feel so held down, and feel that all responsibility is usurped; no wonder they behave badly on tour and set fire to hotel lifts or behave like soccer hooligans.

It would be interesting to see what would happen if all one section did an exchange with another orchestra. Or perhaps they could organise a party, wear green shirts, take their families by charter to Paris to go grape picking or to Disneyworld. How would it be if they played inter-section or inter-orchestra chess, Trivial Pursuit, cricket, or some other game by way of building team spirit and thinking positively about each other? This would be an interesting contrast to many players usual behaviour – running out of the building as fast as possible after rehearsal, and pretending they don't know each other behind their newspapers on the tube because they aren't used to real communication, are shy, or think they may divulge something that could be used against them later. Musicians rarely have any idea what the other members of the orchestra are interested in, or what other abilities they have outside music. They remain strangers who meet every day.

Businesses train their managers and personnel departments. Orchestras don't. Yet they are 'in business'. Odd. Who trains conductors? At least they are not all like the martinets and tyrannical Toscaninis of yesteryear. In his day Beecham was loved for what he did *not* say as much as for what he waggishly did. He said 'I just get the best players and let them play. After a very long experience I have discovered that the only way to have a really living and vital performance is not to rehearse it. Everyone will be listening hard to the music and that makes a great tension. I assure you it affects the public in that way too. When you rehearse a work, let the orchestra play it to you. Any mistakes they know about as well as I do, so we play it through again; then they know it. And I know what they are going to do. (Learn it from the orchestra and then you can make suggestions.) . . .*They don't know what I am going to do* . . . so that at the performance everyone is on his toes, and we get a fine performance.' Would that other conductors had his trust! Orchestral musicians loved him for it, and he could make them play well even when they were exhausted. Those conductors who tour, have now learned not to over-rehearse and expect a concert performance at all rehearsals (as Sargent did until bravely told otherwise). According to conductor Ben Zander, interviewd on BBC Radio 3: 'Conductors should only speak to what's best in people, and trust they are giving their all. He is only powerful because he has the ability to make others powerful and flourish.' Would that all conductors thought so! However it is still supposed to be a mark of superiority to have the last word; to be able to pick out the tiniest flaw in an otherwise perfect performance, to withhold praise in case it would be taken advantage of. The bias is so often negative. Conductors can be 'energy vampires' – if their energy is low they will draw on yours, or force you to submit to their low energy-levels, and you end the rehearsal feeling like a wet rag.

Together with management, orchestral life is still a hierarchy built on fear. True discernment is not about finding flaws but catching true creation; about catching people doing things right, and inspiring more out of people not less.

There's the idea that familiarity breeds contempt. Only if you let it, since it takes two to agree to this situation. Thank goodness we are over the idea that the use of first names shows lack of respect. But we are not much further on. We still go around with the idea that second violins and violas are 'Untouchables', and brass are 'Loud Old Contemptibles' who have to resort to black humour to survive, and a hundred and one other similar clichés. Sectionist behaviour!

When does the back desk of violas ever get to suggest the programme, or the bass section decide where they sit? At present they almost have to be a board member to decide such (and some have made it too!). Why not arrange a programme around works that show off a particular section's abilities, and enlighten the 'supporters' club' members in the audience (especially those who play instruments of that section who might feel inclined to sponsor it in some way)? Does the management know the non-musical talents lurking as a hidden resource amongst their players, things in which the whole orchestra might take a pride? Perhaps someone is quietly brilliant at, and loves doing, DIY, languages, low-fat cookery, music copying or filing, yoga, tai chi or a team sport. I wonder how many players know what makes their orchestra unique.

Other people 2

The other problem with being a professional musician is that others aren't. They have no idea what's involved, or of the gulf between professionalism and amateurism. It's summed up in the frequent questions asked in refined, dulcet tones after a particularly fine performance by you, 'And what do you do for a living?' Or on an out-of-town gig they want the kudos of your company, but say 'We would so love you to come back to our house after rehearsal for tea' – usually just that and a biscuit or two, when you need a square meal to last you until you get home after midnight! Or 'We put the heating on for you' – only just now, and it's a freezing cold church that would take a fortnight to heat to room temperature! Again, 'I do so envy you going on tour to all those wonderful places' – as if you ever had time to be a tourist on holiday when you work abroad, and 'Why can't you put your instrument in the hold with all the other luggage?' or 'Why don't you do your own DIY, it's easy enough for you at home all day?' You even have to watch the sweetest cleaning ladies, who invariably replace your violin case so carefully upside down, after industriously cleaning underneath it. Last trains and buses are often ridiculously early, and there's often only a pub, a chip shop, an Indian or a Chinese open when you need to eat, particularly in New Towns. And if you are allergic to mono-sodium glutamate, have a stomach or duodenal ulcer, or are trying to lose weight, that makes eating appropriately even more difficult. 'Ho Hum!'

101st 'Messiah'

I choose this title because this oratorio is the most frequently performed choral work that you may be booked to play, but it applies to anything repetitious. In these circumstances, perhaps the most annoying thing a musician has to face is being told, by a professional conductor, how to play his instrument when he has spent a lifetime studying it, or being shouted at by an amateur conductor in a piece you can almost play by heart.

There are various points to consider here. On the principle that without understanding you condemn, and with it you don't, think on the following:

1. You have to have a very large ego to want 100-plus musicians to do everything exactly your way, and sometimes it needs defending by attacking lesser mortals (i.e the musicians themselves).

2. The conductor has to sell himself, and has managed to get himself paid to have opinions; you as a musician haven't and aren't. You are paid to make the right noise in the right place, nothing more. Invent your own fun.

3. Few conductors have the time/inclination/ability to be able to play all the instruments in the orchestra as well as you play your own special one, nor do they have coaching in personal communication skills.

4. With 'foreign' conductors, they are used to foreign ways of working and poor orchestral sight-reading ability. They may also have some 'unwritten' rules and assumptions on orchestral behaviour about which you know nothing. Explain quietly and kindly in private later.

5. The balance they hear in front of the orchestra is different from the balance you hear from your seat in the middle of it all, which is something they forget. Also, being bombarded constantly by sound, they might already be a little deaf through aural nerve fatigue without being aware of it, or if they are aware, feel that admitting to such a defect would be suicide. Don't rub it in!

6. The reason conductors live longer than most of us is that, by and large, they choose what music they conduct, whereas orchestral players have to put up with, and have no choice, in what's on the programme. Hate it or not, they have to play it, or turn down the entire date.

Amateur conductors are occasionally skilful, but for the most part don't know what they don't know. You only appear on their 'big day'.

1. Mostly they are choral conductors who know you can make or break it for them. They are nervous of you, but won't show it, and prefer attack to defence.

2. They may be used to shouting at the choir because of distance and choir chattiness, or a different and dead rehearsal room. They may also think that the longer their baton the more authority they have.

3. Your high standard suddenly makes them aware of all that still has to be improved for the performance tonight, yet the poor conductor can't wear out the choir, and, because he rehearsed piecemeal, he may have forgotten (a) that the piece is actually too long to do more than the arias and a few 'corners' in a three hour rehearsal; (b) the choir may not be full membership strength until tonight; (c) the choir hasn't sung this piece with this orchestra before *or* (d) is singing for the first time with new seating and new acoustics and an audience they think is critical.

4. The conductor is probably a pianist or organist with a little singing experience, and is therefore justifiably terrified of making an utter fool of himself because of something he says or does. If he feels his whole next year's appointment may be on the line, he's going to be very nervous and probably will forget important things like down-beats.

5. He may have been rehearsing it 'wrong' with the choir for months and probably can't cope with 'changes on the day'. Don't disillusion him. Leave him in blissful ignorance *this* time!

6. There are 'corners' in every piece that *we* know about that aren't obvious from the piano score that he's probably using, let alone collating the lettering and page numbers. *Messiah* is no exception. Have pity on him and help him *quietly and privately*. He will be grateful to you for life, will book you next year and probably seek your advice beforehand next time too.

7. It's not always entirely the conductor's fault. I remember an occasion when there were three desks of firsts and two desks of seconds, a cello and only two single violas booked for the Fauré Requiem with full choir. No-one checked the full score or told the fixer! I don't need to give the game away by explaining further!

8. Have you ever tried standing and waving your arms about above shoulder height for three hours at a stretch?

When you play something you know backwards many times in a season you can get bored. Play it eight shows a week for a year, and you will find you will go through the boredom barrier, and don't even notice it anymore if you are truly efficient. I found, much to my surprise, I still loved the music for *Jesus Christ Superstar* after a year, and I got through some reading material too!

Coping with boredom is many faceted. The worst thing you can do is show how bored you are, that will get you nothing and certainly no respect. Use the time for training and observation, but don't advertise that either (see 3 below).

1. Leave your worries behind and use it as a sort of meditation.
2. Observe others' technique and see what you can learn. You can observe a lot by interested watching.
3. Take one aspect of technique and use the show to work at it thoroughly (e.g. breathing, refingering not using one finger, bowing, finding other ways of producing the effects required etc). Keep it within the bounds of musical decency that you are paid for!
4. Plan your future, Christmas, the next DIY, the garden or whatever.
5. With amateur conductors and choral societies you never know what's going to fall to bits, so watch out! Concentrate on how you can enhance the day for them to make it particularly special. It doesn't have to be a big gesture. A genuinely appreciative comment in the right ear, or constructive criticism (about something immediately remediable), can work wonders for their self esteem. You may not get thanked, but you will feel good about yourself, instead of spending the day wishing you hadn't taken the job on. Climb into their shoes instead of tripping up on your own big feet. Use the time productively and you will receive more than your pay cheque. Boredom is *your* problem, not theirs. *Messiah* number 101 is an opportunity for 101 new ideas, and they don't all have to be yours originally, you just have to spot them. HOPE = Helping Other People Excel. You never know, they might be better next year!

Because non-musicians neither know or understand your needs and lifestyle, you have to be able to explain things *very patiently* and double check all arrangements (unless you have a tour manager). You have to be able to be assertive, and to be able to negotiate when you least feel like it. To them it's an unimportant and pernickety extra, to you it's your bread and butter. You have to be able to organise your diary and your tax as well as run the family, unless you have an 'ever-loving' who does it all for you.

Relationships

The last main problem with being a musician is that while you happily spend most of your time with musicians, two of you in the family often doesn't work well for long. Frequently you both need emotional support at the same time, so someone has to take a back seat. If you are to avoid it always being the same person, you must both be very aware or resentments will quickly build up. One solution might be for one of you to do a regular orchestral job while the other freelances. This means there is some stability about the place, and the emotional highs and lows are better spread.

As well as only meeting other musicians most of the time, we live in a curiously false social situation with so many acquaintances, and few actual real friends. In an orchestra there may be 100-plus people whom you see daily, but can't talk to because you are rehearsing. In the breaks there's the dash to the one and only loo or the coffee scrum, and then they're off like lightning at the end of the rehearsal or concert because of trains to catch, or a gig to cram in elsewhere, and you've not had a chance to communicate any of the nitty-gritty of life or find out about them, to understand them. It's a bit like window shopping after hours and can lead to all sorts of unreal fantasies you are wrongly 'sure' about. Often too, there are astonishing things you could have shared and helped each other with, which you don't discover until years later.

Besides the peculiarities of the musician's job, there is all the baggage that each partner brings to the relationship – all the unwritten rules of the profession which are out of place in a domestic partnership. Typical of such 'rules' are:

Don't show affection/anger/sadness.

Never admit you are wrong/anxious/frightened.

Sex is dirty/a status symbol, or the only way to make up/show love.

We come with parental commandments like 'Be perfect', 'Please me', 'Hurry up', 'Be strong', 'Try hard', and these run our lives, and are particularly increased by being a musician. Long after we have left home, they are so embedded in our minds we still have to follow the injunctions as if our life depended on them. (Originally, as a tiny child it might have done, but now?? I doubt it. Yet how come this child's strategy was never revised? It is such a habit of thought, that we don't want to change – because it's unknown territory and that's even more dangerous: 'better the devil you know. . .' What you don't see is that now you are cheating yourself as an adult. Rebelling against these commandments will no longer hurt your parent; failing to rebel may be crippling you.)

You may find it helpful to modify the commands as follows:

instead of 'Be perfect' try 'Go for excellence'

'Please me' Be considerate to all, *including* yourself

'Hurry up' Forward planning and delegation

Procrastination Courage now

'Be strong' Consolidate

'Try hard' Persistence

Judging yourself by superhuman standards is another way of mistreating yourself, and a good excuse for giving up. Don't judge, accept yourself warts and all, and move on from there. Life lies in letting go and giving up your chains and your grievances, and taking command of what you want, rather than remaining hooked on your childhood. Getting rid of old habits and poor ways of thinking takes a lot of perseverance. It's not enough to want to change, you have to want to want to change, and to want to change even when you don't want to. Learn to talk to yourself, to explain and reassure yourself. When the child in you is up to mischief, there is usually a time when you can stop and discuss it and say 'No', at the moment when things could go either way. You have the power to stop yourself, and sometimes you won't. Don't glory in lapses, just jump back on track. It's the job that's never started that takes the longest to finish. Procrastination is 'the thief of Time'; it's also self-sabotage and slow suicide. 'What stops you is what runs you.'

This is no place to be a psychologist/therapist, but there are helpful books: *Families and how to survive them, Parent/Leader effectiveness training, Getting things done,* and *Don't do, delegate* are some helpful ones which I have come across (see References). May I also remind you of the ideas suggested in Chapter 5 about family chores and forward planning (remember Shirley Conran's books?) so that the house runs itself and all the extra and unnecessary stresses are removed. If you want to sort your-

197

self out further I would recommend Landmark Education seminars and Breathwork courses (details in the Reference section), or counselling and psychiatric help, but they can be long term. One reason such analysis sometimes takes so long is the refusal of many people to realise that, at bottom, change is up to them. We are all accustomed to or even dependent on someone else to give us a kind word, but we have so many kind words available to give to ourselves if only we would use them, instead of berating ourselves yet again.

When you are on tour, a major energy drainer can be worrying about the family at home. A large phone bill is a small price to pay at such times, and reassurance is worth diamonds in sharing intimate thoughts, off-loading stress to someone who understands, and keeping partners from straying.

It is very difficult in a family with freelance musicians to have quality time together. If the family is to stay together, give *family time* the same recognition and status as work and block it out in the diary in the same way. Make it something you specially like doing together, even if it's only Sunday lunch! Quality time together acts as a sort of reliable glue, a place to sort things out, celebrate and console each other over the so very important minutiae of life that cause so many partnerships to fall apart.

When there is a family tragedy, don't expect to carry on, work it off, or hope it will go away. It's well worth seeking help – Cruse were wonderful when my husband died. They helped me get things into proportion and keep them there. The service is free, they will come to your home or arrange for you to join a group, and you will find them in the phone book. In your own time you *will* be able to let go of what you no longer have, and fill your own need. It doesn't diminish what you had together. There are also Relate and Samaritans, both wonderful lifelines and only a phone call away.

Blame

People vary as to whom they attribute praise and blame. There is an interesting bias in favour of the self, i.e. if something goes right, then I did it; if something goes wrong then it's either someone else's fault or the circumstances prevailing. Over and above this there is also a gender-based bias. If something goes wrong in a relationship between a man and a woman, men are usually more aggressive and therefore likely not to blame themselves but to blame either the woman or a third party. Women tend to be more submissive and will blame themselves first. If the partnership itself is threatened, however, then blame will be attributed strategically. Being aware of this tendency in western society helps to reduce stress-levels. (Don't assume the same in other societies, where values may be different.)

Time and Emotion Study

Men tend to regard women as generally rather unstable emotionally because their hormonal cycle is more obvious. Interestingly, women think that both genders are equally responsible for their actions.

Hormonal cycles are not the only ones which affect us. As sensitive people, musicians are more than usually aware of what affects them beyond the obvious day and night rhythms of waking and sleeping. Short-term, within the 24 hours, there is the meridian cycle, where two-hour energy surges pass round the 12 meridians. The acupuncture meridian and nervous systems operate in complementary fashion and each meridian has an associated emotion. These need not be of great concern to musicians except where a pain always follows a specific emotion, or occurs at a specific time of day, or they are short of sleep because they always wake at a specific time of night and then cannot go back to sleep for a couple of hours. An example of this might be waking with breathing difficulties between 3 a.m. and 5 a.m. This is the lung meridian time, and some acupuncturists feel that asthma attacks are best treated then.

Peak energy times for meridians are:

a.m.		p.m.	
1 – 3	liver	1 – 3	small intestine
3 – 5	lungs	3 – 5	bladder
5 – 7	large intestine	5 – 7	kidney
7 – 9	stomach	7 – 9	pericardium/sex organs
9 – 11	spleen/pancreas	9 – 11	triple warmer
11 – 1pm	heart	11 – 1am	gall bladder

The next most important cycle which affects us are the Biorhythms. These chart the fluctuating energy on the physical, emotional and intellectual cycles. Charts to calculate these cycles can be bought in New Age shops. All three cycles are calculated from your birth date and have plus and minus energy-level phases, with critical days where the cycle changes. The most important days to beware of in each cycle are these critical days, because our expectations are still with the previous part of the cycle and we therefore under- or over-estimate our reactions. Where two or more critical days from different cycles coincide, great care should be taken. You will be unreliable on such days, in many subtle, and not-so-subtle, ways.

The physical cycle is 23 days long. Days 2-11 are peak energy time when you will feel most endurance and strength. This is a time to put in the hours of practice. Critical days are 1 and 12, when you may be accident prone. Ebb days are 13-23, when you should plan to rest, recuperate and reduce physical activity wherever possible.

The emotional or sensitive cycle seems to be in harmony with the lunar month, as it lasts 28 days. Days 2-14 are harmonious days where you enjoy social relationships more, and feel more positive about life. Days 1 and 15 are critical, when both men and women are less emotionally stable. Days 16-28 are times when you will be more negative and moody in outlook.

The intellectual cycle lasts 33 days. Days 2-16 are creative, when judgement and perception are at their keenest. Days 1 and 17 are critical days when judgement is prone to error, and days 18-33 are days when your thinking is below par and decisions, new projects, new pieces or studies are best avoided, or postponed to days 2-16 next time round.

Monthly or astrological rhythms are well known and need no description here, but longer rhythms are worth noting. SADs (seasonally affective disorders) affect many people. If you find that between the end of January and March you feel rather less enthusiastic about life than in the summer months this is normal, and is to do with nutritional levels, cold weather and a lowered immune system. However, if your mood conspicuously changes with light-levels as well as with the weather (you feel awful from the day the clocks go back until they go forward again, have a tendency to leave lights on in the house overnight by mistake, and all you want to do is sleep or growl at everyone) then you may have a heightened reaction to low light-levels.

The great pianist Sviatoslav Richter had this problem. He was well known for practising all hours in the summer, but hardly wanted to get out of bed in the winter. Musicians spend a lot of time back stage in low light-levels, and you might be helped by investing in special daylight bulbs (available from specialist chemists and, possibly, even on prescription) and practising in front of them for a couple of hours each day. These bulbs help because the particular light quality they emit stimulates the pineal gland, and this affects energy levels. If you can afford it, escape to somewhere warm and sunny in January, or go skiing – the reflected light off the snow is just as good.

To recognise that someone is grouchy *not* because they are reacting to you or to other people but because of low light-levels removes all blame from the situation, helps you to understand and should thereby reduce your stress-levels also. SADs are not the only reason for tiredness, however.

Being Tired all the Time

One of the most disruptive and difficult things in any family is tiredness. There are 101 reasons for feeling 'tired all the time' (TATT). Some are trivial and easily handled as soon as recognised, others are signs of something more serious. All are important because they build up, and yet they are so often ignored. TATT is one of the most frequent reasons for a visit to a GP and the cause is often difficult to pin down without a lot of questions.

If you feel TATT, go through the following check-list and see what fits you. You're not being a hypochondriac, you are doing good preventative medicine. However, don't run away with the idea that you have got *everything!* or even the worst ones on the list. If in any doubt talk to your GP. Don't suffer in silence – your family is probably also suffering because of your tiredness. Tiredness isn't necessarily old age creeping up on you. You can be tired because of physical problems, internal or external chemistry, systemic, psychological or idiopathic causes.

Physical problems are the most obvious: too much travel and jet lag, overwork, practising, teaching and rehearsals; late-night gigs, insomnia or sleep deprivation if there's a new baby in the family; obesity and pregnancy plus holding up a heavy instrument (like constant weight-carrying); post operative recuperation, prolonged pain, arthritis in all its various forms; the long-term effects of any of these are exhausting. Neurological disorganisation and poor coordination also waste enormous amounts of energy.

Internal chemistry problems causing chronic tiredness are almost all gut problems, frequently from irregular eating and hunger. They include hepatitis and liver cirrhosis from long-term alcoholism; gall bladder and fat absorbtion problems; ileocaecal valve syndrome (ICV/IBS), with its attendant chronic diarrhoea and/or constipation, metabolite and malabsorbtion problems (also often due to stress-related peptic ulcers); and we shouldn't forget parasites from strange foods on tour. Tiredness can also be a sign of kidney malfunction, hormone imbalance, fat intolerance and diabetes. Blood and oxygen imbalances can also lower energy-levels. They include conditions like anaemia, heart or vascular problems, or restricted breathing due to chronic obstruction of the airways from emphysema after years of smoking or asthma.

External chemistry causes you to feel tired mostly as a side-effect or reaction to various drugs (especially chemotherapy), allergies or food sensitivities. Airborne phenols like formaldehyde are in so many building and furnishing materials and paints (see Chapter 6); heavy metals such as lead lurk in water from piping in old buildings (like theatres); your own old tooth fillings may even be leaking mercury because you haven't had time or given priority to going to the dentist.

Systemic infections mean the whole of you is under par. Best known of these are post-viral syndromes (myalgic encephalomyelitis – ME – and its variants). Rheumatic and glandular fevers in the young, and polymyalgia and other forms of arthritis in the old, are very tiring and weakening too. Candida, a yeast infection which proliferates when beneficial flora as well as the baddies are cleared out of the gut by antibiotics, can be an exhausting nuisance. Hormone imbalances are the cause of premenstrual tension and menopausal neuroses because they also affect the whole of you and drag you down, and cancers and leukemias and their treatments drain the energy out of you.

If you are 'dog tired' every night, maybe you growled all day! Nothing was ever achieved without enthusiasm, and there is no task that doesn't become difficult and tiring when you do it with reluctance, or when suffering the frustration of trying to perform your best when unable to through sheer fatigue. The *psychological* reasons for feeling constant exhaustion include depression, resentment, procrastination, grief, low self-esteem, isolation, loneliness and anxiety, a feeling of being helpless and hopeless, prolonged stress and long-term unemployment or unexpected redundancy, marital problems, worry, poor appetite, anorexia nervosa or bulimia, and alcoholism (causing depletion of the body's vitamin B stores which leads to unnecessary worry, irritability and poor stress tolerance).

Pick-me-ups

The above is by no means a complete list of reasons for TATT, but does include most common causes. If your GP has given you a clean bill of health and you still feel tired, yet want to take charge and do something about it, then I recommend improving the positive side of your life. Put something back into your energy bank and get the sluggish system going by:

1. Improving your diet and exercise (see Chapters 6 and 15).
2. 'Power nap': take a short sleep in your break instead of yet more coffee.
3. Do something new and special every day for a month – it doesn't have to be large or important, expensive or time consuming, or even serious (and it can also be any of these).
4. Keep a diary every night of all the good things that happened that day whether expected or not. Friendships should also be kept in a constant state of good repair – for your sake as well as theirs.
5. Know your own 'feel-good factors' and use them (see below).
6. You see and find what you look for, so start looking for the good side of life. Miracles happen to people who are ready for them. 'The greatest march begins with a single step.' There are opportunities for magical moments every day of our lives; we need only to creep out from beneath the self-imposed stones under which we lurk (because we think they protect us), and come out and blink and smile in the sunshine.

Negotiating

Music is your life and therefore your business; if you are not naturally business-like you will learn a lot about thinking in a business-like way from business books. You sell yourself by your playing to audience, colleagues, conductors and fixers, and you negotiate.

Negotiating is not reserved for international conferences, it is something you do everyday. The person you negotiate with most is yourself, only after that come your family and work. Not realising this, many musicians think it as a 'no-go' area. We are not used to haggling in this country as a general rule. The most people ever do is to take faulty goods back to a shop, and that rather apologetically. 'Negotiating is definitely to be avoided, because "they" always win!' Rubbish! So much misunderstanding is implied in the above. Remember, if you always agree with 'the other side', one of you is not necessary. See a dispute as the beginning of negotiation. Here are some suggestions that will clear up the fear eventually, if not immediately.

Ten Rules for Negotiation:
1. Understanding is not the same as agreeing or condoning, but it will prevent condemning.
2. People are always certain that what they most fear, the other side is bound to know, and will definitely use against them. Negotiating should not be an 'I win – you lose' situation, it is an 'I win – you win' situation.
3. Their tolerance depends on their stress-level more than on yours.
4. Only complain to someone who can actually do something about the problem. Don't 'dump' on the nearest passer-by or underlings who are more bound by rules than the top people. It's also common sense to listen to the people closest to the problem, and not gossips and third parties.
5. Plan what you will say with *key words,* so you stay focused. Keep your statements simple and keep your entire communication under 30 seconds long. *Smile* when you talk, as it makes a big difference (you can even hear a difference on the 'phone).
6. Do more listening than talking, even when you are complaining,

and, no matter how upset you are, if your adversary feels you understand *his* point, then he will listen to *you,* not before. Avoid a showdown. Before you can stand in another person's shoes you have to take off your own.

7. Sell the sizzle not the sausage. List the benefits (low cost, handy size, wonderful taste, enticing sound, delicious smell etc.) not what pig's guts they come from. You will be more successful when you stop trying to get what you want, and start helping others get what *they* want. Reinterpret what you want in their terms.

8. When you want someone else to do an unpleasant job, enrol them into helping you decide what's to be done, and thank them for volunteering (they usually do).

9. Praise first, then criticise, then say what you want. It can't be heard the other way round. Mollify before modify, but remember: most people compromise too soon when they bargain.

10. Clarify, show, tell; explain the possibility, the opportunity, the action. There's no such thing as an unrealistic goal, only an unrealistic time-span. 'Misfortunes are mainly miscalculations.'

You will find the *One Minute Manager* series of booklets helpful in both home and business life, as well as Mark McCormack's ideas, but they will need a certain amount of translation into musical terms. If you find it hard to get to the point when you are nervous, Milo Frank's *How to get your point across in 30 seconds or less* is a brilliant booklet.

Listen properly as you negotiate. There are many sorts of listening besides Chinese Whispers or sitting back and letting the music 'transport you away from it all'. I've listed here seven other types:

1. Not listening. You are present, but are actually rehearsing very hard what *you* are going to say, in case you forget an important point.

2. Passive listening. You sit there, nod and grunt in the right places and let them 'run out of steam'. You contribute nothing and there's no real communication.

3. Active listening (I). Every two minutes you break in, either to (a) make a one-sentence summary of what you think they have said, or (b) keep them to the point. You end with 'Thank you, in summary I understand that. . .' They then feel understood, relaxed, and ready to listen to you.

4. Active listening (II). You listen for points of common ground, needs to meet, and plus points to be joyful about. This is a form of giving.

5. Aggressive listening. You size up your partner for pointers which will help you to sell your ideas to them. This is like taking from them.

6. 10% 'ask', 90% 'listen and learn'. This is 'Being on Receive'.

7. You listen like a chamber music player, take over what you receive and hand it on enriched with your love. This is creating together.

Which do you do most of? Which of the seven is actually most appropriate to your aims?

Practising

Non-musicians often can see no difference between a professional's need to practise and the thump-thump of a maladjusted ghetto-blaster, so for the perennial complaints about noise, it's advisable to know the local decibel laws and keep strictly to the rules.

Practising is often a bone of contention in musicians' families. It is a very individual thing. Some need to do lots ('to run in order to keep still'); others only need to keep supple or retrain their 'banana fingers' after a holiday. Some stretch themselves by learning new repertoire out of interest, others feel they 'practise on the job', and have no further interest, never going to concerts they are not paid to attend. The hours you practise also depend on the natural physical attributes you have, and the demands of the instrument you play.

Most musicians choose their home with a view to practice and neighbour toleration. This works until your nice neighbours move away and new, objectionable ones move in. Although you have prior occupancy, beware of 'change of use' clauses; you need to know the law on the subject of noise in general and the local bye-laws in particular. As a general rule, practising is allowed between 8 a.m. and 11 p.m., but most people don't start that early or go on that late unless pushed. Even so, you can run into trouble with awkward neighbours' ghetto-blasters or complaints to the council about you. However unjustified it might be, once a complaint has been received the council has to investigate and can make your life a misery. I know of one case where foreclosure of a piano school was threatened, and the wrangling went on for six harrowing months, even though the musician had put in double glazing at her own expense before moving in. The complaint was entirely malicious, but it was only proved to be so when the council people finally came with a decibel meter and measured the noise outside the windows, while she pounded away on her grand piano inside. The noise from the local traffic was found far to exceed what could be heard of her playing through the double glazing! Meanwhile she had lost work and nearly had a nervous breakdown.

Get used to practising with the windows shut. It makes a fresh-air break all the sweeter. Churches are another solution if space or noise is a problem. Vicars often are glad of a little extra in the plate and someone reliable keeping an eye on the place, but don't forget how cold church buildings can be in winter! Beware of practising in a room with an echo. While it may temporarily boost your ego, it's a snare and a delusion. Shock is the only way to describe what it is like to play on the outside of the back desks in the Barbican, Royal Festival Hall or the Reading Hexagon. You hear no-one but yourself and the sound is pathetically small because the acoustics are dead. Thespian acoustics rarely suit players' needs for feedback and good orchestral section playing.

Hotels are a different matter. Other guests have as much right to quiet as you during the day, even though they dance in the disco downstairs half the night. They have paid for peace and quiet and are probably on holiday, while you are on a working tour. Fortunately, soundproofing is often better in new hotels than in new houses but, even so, you have to be more considerate or risk being thrown out, because the premises are not yours.

If there are complaints, there's often somewhere 'below stairs' like the laundry where you can practise, but you may have to compete with machinery and cross a palm or two with local currency. Don't do what the percussionist did when I was on one particular tour with Ballet Rambert. She moved her kits from the pit into the ladies' lavatory because the dancers were rehearsing on stage. The lavatory was nice and roomy and tiled throughout; can you imagine the din? The rest of us fled! On 'Tomorrow's World' they have recently examined a trumpet mute with waist electronics pack and ear pieces. To an outsider there is no sound, but the player hears himself as normal. Marvellous!

Usually by the time you are on tour, your main repetitive work has been done. Make use of peace for mental work, and visualisation for clarity and memory. People have been known to learn a whole concerto on a train, with a cardboard keyboard, but that's unusual. Silent practice with your instrument is less useful to string players than wind because of the accuracy needed in finger placing for good intonation. Practice mutes are a last resort; they dampen the sound so much that it's not really good for the instrument, but then you can't really practise a stringed instrument under a duvet or in a cupboard!

There are days when you ought to practise, but it's the last thing you want to do. The following plan might help you to open the instrument case:

1. Decide what the resentful 'child within you' really wants to do and give it ten minutes only, now. *Time it.* 'Opportunity knocks but once, temptation *leans* on the door bell!'

2. Decide on some practice goals – technical, musical etc.

3. Set the ring timer for a further ten minutes and work hard at some small aspect, rather than playing through, so you have a feeling of accomplishing something. 'Ideas don't work unless we do!' People who produce results feel good about themselves, and go for more.

4. If, after ten minutes practice you still can't bear it, STOP. You won't do any good and are wasting your time. Do what you want to do with a clear conscience and *enjoy* it, don't mess that up too by spending the time 'not' practising and beating yourself up about it. Know when to reset your goals and when to reprimand. 'Can't do' is a training problem, so reset the goals; 'Won't do' is an attitude problem and deserves a reprimand but remember, only positive consequences encourage good performance. The secret of change is to focus all your energy not on fighting the old but on building the new.

5. If you are so pressed that you have a marathon ahead, use the ring timer for the following timetable: (a) work flat out for 50 minutes; (b) rest flat out on the floor for ten; (c) as (a); (d) take half an hour off and do something completely different. Repeat (a) to (c) followed by a one-hour meal break. As a string player it is possible to do four

cycles of real concentration like this in a day – occasionally. Push it more and you will suffer next day. As a brass player it would probably finish you, so don't even try.

Your neighbours won't thank you for many marathon days like this, but during the week they will probably be out at work anyway. Be aware they may be on shift work and use that knowledge to mutual advantage and consideration. It takes discipline to work this hard, but it pays huge dividends. Some find it helpful to do the first session (a) above as a scale and exercise session, the second session (c) as a study session, a short sight-reading session or specific technique session, and the remaining sessions for repertoire. (NB, if you opt for sight-reading, avoid the temptation to sight-read what you are about to study, because you don't want to start with mistakes you will have to iron out later.) The ten-minute rest slot is for thinking and analysing the previous 50 minutes. Use the *One minute manager* PRICE system:

> *P*inpoint areas to work on
> *R*ecord current performance
> *I*nvolve all types of strategy
> *C*oach by observing performance and consequences
> *E*valuate present and future strategy.

According to the *Way of the Peaceful Warrior,* an expert trains the physical body with the purpose of winning. The master dedicates his training to life. Don't persist in gloating over a few physical skills and then become depressed if the physical training doesn't go so well one day. If one area isn't going well it's still an opportunity to train others. On some of your weakest physical days you can learn most about your mind, or the mind of the composer.

It makes sense to end with something you play well, not only as a reward, but also to re-establish just how well you play in your subconscious mind. You do need determination, but that does not mean you should force yourself. Forcing is not treating yourself with respect. Change doesn't have to be imposed from above; real growth comes from within. Work with yourself, even if you do occasionally need gentle persuasion. We are not our behaviour, but the person who manages our behaviour. When you end a reprimand with praise for the things you caught yourself doing right, you will think about your behaviour, not the parent figure that's 'telling you off'. Useful feedback is 'the breakfast of champions'.

Psychosomatic Aches and Pains

If you say someone has a psychosomatic pain, the immediate reaction of most people is the assumption that the pain is imagined and unreal and that the sufferer must be a bit neurotic. Not so. The pain is very real, and the person perfectly normal. What the word actually means is 'psycho' (mind) plus 'soma' (body). In other words, what your mind won't/hasn't resolved, your body will try to save you from. It's part of the survival mechanism with which you were born. Even physical tension stemming from mental stress is 'psycho-somatic'. Your muscles are tense because you are in a constant, mentally unresolved fight/flight situation.

There are two techniques which are worth trying even if you don't think your pain is psychosomatic. The worst you will do is merely lessen the pain; you won't make it worse, and you might lose it.

The first technique recognises that any pain is a call for help. It is your body's way of getting your attention. So thank it and give it attention.
1. Sit quietly, breathe deeply, close your eyes and focus on the pain, allowing it to be there. Rest your hands lightly on your forehead.
2. Describe out loud the pain's (a) precise position; (b) size (2 by 3 ins, or 3 by 7cm); (c) shape (round, oblong); (d) density (soft, hard, like steel, wood, rubber, misty, woolly); (e) its edges (rind, carapace or shell-like, hairy, melting); (f) its movement (shooting, spinning, pulsating); (g) its colour (green, red, grey, brown etc.). Sometimes it's helpful to have a friend ask for the descriptions ('How is it now?') while you look at it in your mind's eye.
3. Keep breathing and observing and 'being with' the pain for 30 seconds.
4. The suggestions in brackets are to help your imagination. Repeat steps 1 to 3 describing each aspect of the pain as it changes, as though you were seeing it for the first time, continuing until it contracts to nothing or spreads out and evaporates.
5. If it returns later, notice what the trigger factor was and deal with it.

The second method is to use the metaphysical causation connection already described under posture in Chapter 2, and originated by Louise Hay. Weave relevant affirmations into your self-talk tape (see Chapters 6 and 7) along with the Bach Flower remedy that most nearly fits the problem. In her book *Heal your Body* Louise Hay describes the unresolved, negative mental programming behind every ailment. The book is arranged alphabetically, from abscesses and back-pain, constipation, headaches, haemorrhoids and hands to ulcers and varicose veins, giving you both the negative thought and the affirmation to counteract it. Here is a typical example:

Backpain: *probable cause* = Lack of support. UPPER BACK: lack of emotional support, holding back love; LOWER BACK: lack of financial support. Fear of money. *New thought pattern:* Life itself supports me. I trust the Universe. I freely give love and trust.

What you thought about then has made you what you are now. What you think about now governs your future. Think on it! I take some of Louise Hay's more obscure examples with a pinch of salt but, by and large, there is usually a definite connection, and who's to say you think/react as I do? At any rate, I'd far rather try these ideas (which can only have beneficial side-effects) before I opt for drugs or surgery, both of which have the inevitable unpleasant side-effects.

While on the subject of psychsomatic aches and pains, it is important to recognise that there are definite attitudes which predispose one to noticing pain. This is known as 'illness mentality'. The person concerned takes little or no responsibility for how they are; there is a tendency to become institutionalised, in that insignificant activities are carried out to an unjustifiably rigid timetable; ills and hurts are rehearsed, even exaggerated; there is an investment in remaining unfit because it generates special attention; there is no initiative, and effort in any sphere is minimal; there is a tendency to live in the past with a negative attitude to the future, and the present seems to be about endlessly waiting for something to happen over which the person has no control. A 'wellness mentality', is the reverse of this. The person is willing to take responsibility and live within normal tolerances and knows when to say 'no'; is individualistic, has initiative and radiates energy and well-being. This person can give as well as receive, does thing at the appropriate time, lives zestfully in the moment, and is optimistic about the future.

Feel-good Factors

If you are too busy to have a laugh, you are too busy. Sometimes the best action is 'masterly inaction'! It is vitally important that you recognise the main stressors and energy drainers in your life. Where possible, keep these down to one or two a week, and aim to resolve as many as you can, rather than compound them by procrastinating. I had a rule that I'd do the worst thing of the week by Monday night if I could, but life doesn't always work like that in a freelance world. Invent a rule which works for you.

Strive always for excellence, never perfection. Check your diary, your extra-curricular activities, reading list, TV watching etc., and *axe everything that doesn't give you a feeling of accomplishment, satisfaction, or is ennobling, empowering or energising.* Remember Do, Delay, Delegate or Ditch!

Being aware of your own achievements is not egotism, egocentricity or big-headedness. You can't start to feel good about yourself unless you have a daily sense of accomplishment, a recognition of your joys and successes, however small they might appear to the outside world. It's up to us to give ourselves recognition. For some people, finding things that help them feel good about themselves is a real challenge: it's as if they wore blinkers which shut out all the bright and joyous things. Perhaps there are hidden pay-offs for them in continuing to suffer. Take a look at yourself. It's so imperative to know what makes you feel good, *really* good – on top of the world – light and free – full of bounding joy and energy. When you've identified something to which you can give a name, *write it down.* Now remember what you were doing the last time you felt this, even if it is so long ago you were a child, and *write it down.* What makes you feel utterly relaxed, soft and dreamy? *Write it down.* Now remember a time you were like this. What else were you doing? *Write it down.* Do you like massage (see Chapter 14), aromatherapy with scented oils such as lavender, jacuzzis, candle light, scents, what? *Write it down.* If you don't know clearly what you like best, how can you ask for it, how can any one give it to you, or you give it to yourself? Go for it! *Who* was there, *What* was the feeling, weather temperature, consistency, colour, lighting, taste, sounds, scents, *Why* was it so special, *When* did time or timing matter, *Where* were you, inside/outside, on the ground, flying, *How* did you do it, what was your attitude/mood/method?

Really get in touch with your sense of pleasure, so that you know what makes you glow, what recharges you, wakes you up or relaxes you positively and restores your self-esteem, encourages, empowers and ennobles you, and wipes away all the hurt and buffeting you receive.

What are the treats in your life? I suspect they are far too few. If you rely on others to produce them, they will definitely be too few. What would you like to have which you can give to yourself; something which is yours, to share if you wish, but *only* if you wish?

We all love praise, but have you noticed how quickly the glow from a compliment fades? Indeed we often help it on its way with denial. When we compliment ourselves, the glow stays. Make a list of your achievements, not only the academic or musical ones, but *all of them.*

Doing what makes you feel good about yourself is not just self-indulgence but the opposite. It doesn't mean gratifying an isolated part of you, it means satisfying your whole self, and this also includes any feelings for, and ties and responsibilities to, others. Self-indulgence means satisfying only the smallest part of you, and that only temporarily. No one wants the fruits of someone else's self-denial. Self-denial is the worst kind of self-indulgence.

Write all those good things down somewhere. It's so easy to forget them in the hurly-burly of daily life, and at least 50% of the population don't think they deserve to feel good. You may think *they* are being ridiculous, but what about you? When was the last time you spoiled yourself silly? You can use the list you have just made to give yourself a **five-minute holiday**, right now, by closing your eyes, taking yourself to one of the events you have just written down, and drinking deep in what you find there. Once you know your 'feel-good factors' you can take them anywhere in the world with you; they cost nothing and you can't be robbed of them. You can change them at any time, and add to them at will as you find new joys. You can even take a five-minute holiday in **marginal time** while you wait for the pot to boil, the bus to come, the fixer to ring back. There are no 'ordinary moments', they are unopened possibilities, extraordinary moments full of potential.

Keeping an **'Interest' book** every night of all the good expected and unexpected things that happen each day has two benefits. It calms the mind before you sleep and puts you in a relaxed, positive mood. It is also enjoyable reading to look back and live off the invested interest a little, so the world doesn't seem such a bad place after all.

I also keep an **'Inspiration' scrapbook** to browse through or open at random. It is full of all the articles, books, sayings I have come across that have inspired me over the years. It is so easy to forget wise words, and often I have re-read something in the light of my current situation and learned from it or gained some clarity. 'Great dreams are never fulfilled, always transcended.'

You may think it relaxing to read a 'Whodunit' but I suspect, after you have tried my ideas and found the benefits, you'll want to collect more ideas of your own, because you are investing in what's good *about* you and *for* you!

When you finally settle down to sleep, give yourself that extra TLC (Tender Loving Care) by asking each bit of you if it is entirely comfortable exactly where it is. Would it prefer to be slightly more this way or that, bent or straight, more curled up or tucked in? Start at your toes and work up to your head, by which time you will probably be asleep. Good night!

REFERENCES

1. **Atkins H.** and **Newman A.** (1995) *Beecham Stories,* Warner Books.
2. **Arnould-Taylor** (1981) *Aromatherapy for the Whole Person,* A-T Education
3. **Black R.** (1989) *Getting Things Done,* Michael Joseph. Penguin
4. **Blanchard K.** and others (1983-86) *The One Minute Manager Series,* Fontana, Harper Collins
5. **Bourke H.** (1990) *The Sleep Management Plan,* Harper Collins
6. **Evans A.** (1994) *The Secrets of Musical Confidence,* Thorsons, Harper Collins
7. **Frank M.** (1986) *How to Get Your Point Across in 30 Seconds or Less,* Corgi Books
8. **Gardiner D.** and **Beatty G.** (1988) *Never Be Tired Again,* Rawson Perenial, Harper and Row
9. **Gordon T.** (1980) *Leader Effectiveness Training, Parent Effectiveness Training,* Wyden, Bantam
10. **Hay L.** (1976) *Heal Your Body – The Mental Causes for Physical*

Illness, and the Metaphysical Way to Overcome Them, 425 East 51st St NY 10022

11. **Jenks J.** and **Kelly J.** (1985) Don't Do, Delegate, Kogan Page Ltd.

12. **Lindenfield G.** (1986) *Assert Yourself. How to Reprogramme Your Mind for Positive Action,* Thorsons, Harper Collins

13. . **McCormack** (1984) *What They Don't Teach You at Harvard Business School,* Fontana, Harper Collins

14. **Millman D.** (1984) *The Way of the Peaceful Warrior,* Kramer, Tiburon, Canada

15. . **Orlick T.** (1986) *Coach's Training Manual to Psyching for Sport,* Leisure Press, Illinois USA

16. **Proto L.** (1988) *Take Charge of Your Life – How Not to be a Victim,* Thorsons, Harper Collins.

17. **Skynner R.** and **Cleese J.** (1989) *Families and How to Survive Them,* Mandarin, Octopus.

ORGANISATIONS

Breathwork and Workshops by Distinctions. Perceptions UK Ltd, Sunninghill, Berks SL5 7BH. *Tel:* 01252 540930 *fax:* 01344 26176

Churchill Centre. 22 Montague St, London W1H 1TB *Tel:* 0171-402 9475. (Classes in Remedial Massage)

Landmark Education. 23 Gosfield St, London W1P 8EA. *Tel:* 0171-580 1997 *fax:* 0171-637 3194

CHAPTER 9

The Physical Nitty-Gritty

How the arm works down to the fingers;
Agonists, antagonists, synergists and
stabilisers; Sway, tension, balance and
muscle-tone; Ligaments; Proprioception;
Normal range of movement; Arm supplies;
Nerve impingement and other common
conditions; The Sciatic Nerve; Arthritis

This and the succeeding chapters are about the purely physical side of playing, and go into detail, muscle by muscle. Some muscles are used by all musicians, some by specific instrumentalists only, and some are postural. If you feel daunted by testing them, don't worry. Work on the points suggested. These can only help or, if not needed, have no adverse effect.

How the arm works – down to the fingers

The shoulder girdle is suspended round the upper body torso and is basically made up of the clavicles and the scapulae. The two collar bones (clavicles) sit either side of the top of the breast bone (sternum), and the other end of each collar bone joins the shoulder blade (scapula) above the shoulder joint. Underneath this, the upper arm bone (humerus) sits snugly in the cavity at the narrow outer end of the shoulder blade.

The shoulder joint is unusual in that it is a 'ball and socket' joint like the hip, but the socket part is about the size of the bowl of a teaspoon, and even more shallow, so the muscles that cross this joint have to hold the upper arm bone in the cup at the end of the shoulder blade. This gives the joint tremendous flexibility, but at the expense of stability. It is therefore far more likely to dislocate than the hip joint, which has a much deeper socket and strong ligaments to hold it together. The two shoulder blades don't actually meet behind, or they'd grate over the knobs of the spine that stick out at the back. They are held against the back by muscles, so that they can slide in and out over the back, allowing you to expand and contract the ribs with breathing, or to move out as you raise your arms above horizontal.

The upper arm has one bone, the forearm has two. The bone on the little finger side of the forearm (ulna) is the larger and makes a hinge joint with the upper arm, forming the elbow. The bone on the thumb side of the forearm (radius) has a wider end at the wrist, and a swivel head just below the elbow, and that allows you to turn the whole forearm and hand palm up or palm down. The wrist is made up of a lot of small bones (carpals) that slide over one another allowing some degree of movement in any direction. The palm and ball of the thumb contain five separate bones (metacarpals) and then each finger has three bones (phalanges) except the thumb which has two, with little hinge joints between them. The base of

218

the thumb has a joint shaped like a saddle which allows it an almost circular movement, and also to oppose the other fingers to make a pincer grip.

Conveniently the muscles which have similar function have mostly been sited together on the bones of the shoulder and arm. The following description of the main muscles will give you an idea of how the upper limb works and the various bits are moved about. It is by no means an exhaustive list!

The muscles that raise the shoulders are found on the top of the shoulders and are called *levator scapulae* and *upper trapezius*. The upper-arm raisers are attached to the shoulder tip and the upper arm and are the *deltoids* and *supraspinatus*. The arm lowerers are assisted by gravity and mainly constitute the *latissimus dorsi* which are big muscles running almost from the hips at the back, to the top front of the upper arm. The muscles that pull your arms across the chest are the *pectorals*, (running from the upper chest to the upper arm) and *coracobrachialis*, (which runs from just inside the shoulder joint to the upper arm). The *rhomboids* live at the back between the shoulder blades and pull them together, assisted by the *middle trapezius* which runs from the spine in the upper back to the shoulder tips.

The muscles on the front of the upper arm bend the elbow *(Biceps, Brachialis* and *Brachioradiali)* and the elbow straightener (the *Triceps*) is found on the back of the upper arm. If you stand with your elbows at your side, arms bent and palms facing in, the muscles that will pull your hand further in and flex the fingers are attached on the inside of the elbow – *Flexor carpi radialis* and *ulnaris* and *Flexor digitorum superficialis*. Pain on the inside of the elbow is often called 'golfer's elbow'. Still with your elbows at your sides, arms bent, the muscles that pull the hand back are the *Extensor carpi radialis* and *ulnaris,* and they are attached to the outside of the elbow. Pain on the outside of the elbow is usually called 'tennis elbow', but may be due to spasm in your *anconeus* muscle which is both a stabiliser and straightener of the elbow. There are also shorter muscles within the hand which add strength, bend and straighten the fingers and thumb and move them into opposition to one another for pinching and holding things. The sideways movement of the fingers is done by muscles between the fingers called the *interossei* (those on the palm bring the fingers together, while those on the back of the hand ones spread them out), and the arch of the hand is made by the *lumbricals* which are also on the palm.

Turning the forearm and hand palm up is done by the *supinator* which works by twisting the thumb side of the forearm out (and therefore it lives mostly on the outside of the elbow), while turning the palm down is done by the *pronator* which is found on the inside of the elbow. So you see it's all very logical really, and there's no need to be frightened by all the long Latin names. If you feel muscular pain and tiredness in these places, you will find how you can help your muscles recover by looking in Chapters 12 and 13.

Agonists, Antagonists, Synergists and Stabilisers

Muscles never work entirely on their own, always at least in pairs and sometimes in groups. This is because the main function of a muscle (the **agonist**), is contraction in straight lines along the direction of the ratchet system of its fibres (see Chapter 2). It therefore needs another muscle (acting as an **antagonist**), to pull in the opposite direction to undo the first contraction. Actually it's not even as simple as that, because at any one time not all the fibres of a muscle are working. The fibres take it in turns. This is why you sway slightly when you stand, and why when very tired, tipsy or otherwise drugged, there is poor communication between muscle fibres clogged with waste products, and you sway more and even stagger about, or have poor coordination in your playing. One of the reasons for the excess movement that some players exhibit, is an unconscious attempt to overcome this, egged on by the idea that they are so 'moved' by the music.

Agonists and antagonists complement and balance each other, and this is best illustrated by what happens when you jump. Take off is effected by contraction of the muscles that straighten the bent legs to push against the ground, but landing involves taking up the slack and reaction to gravity so that the shock of landing is minimised. Similarly when you bend your elbow, your front upper arm muscles contract, but they could not do so if the muscles at the back of the upper arm didn't let go and allow themselves to be stretched: if bending and straightening the elbow joint slowly as you might do with a trombone slide or bow stroke requires constant re-adjustment by the muscles to one another and to gravity, think what's required in a fast passage!

This is where the synergists and stabilisers come in. **Synergists** are ordinary muscles that are near by, whose fibres might run in a slightly different direction, but which have a similar pulling function to the main one you are using. They add strength and give respite when the main muscle is damaged or over-tired. (They can therefore also complicate recovery.) **Stabilisers** are the muscles which hold the whole joint in a specific place while you use other muscles to bend the joint, e.g. they might hold your arm, elbow and wrist so you can reach the instrument with your fingers. They are just as important, subconsciously, in coordination as the muscles you use consciously, but you only become aware of their importance when they don't work. They are another reason for testing all the main muscles in the arm when something goes wrong with one part. We are not just a bag of bits, but a coordinated whole, and those who say that playing your instrument goes from the feet up are not talking airy-fairy guff. In the end, moving one small part of you enough involves the rest of you too. But then nor do you have to throw yourself all over the stage unecessarily in order to play, unless you wish to. The opposite is also true, that constantly held muscles due to stress and tension (whether realised or not), will inhibit far more than just those tight muscles. This is why good habits and stress-reduction techniques from the start are essential, and why Alexander and Feldenkrais teachers flourish.

Sway, Tension, Balance and Muscle Tone

Ideally there should be a **balance** between power and coordination, relaxation and stress, and between the desirable and the possible. Your ability to resolve these apparent opposites has a direct bearing on the length of your career. Control should mean mastery, not rigidity. There should be appropriate **muscle tone** for the task, given the exterior conditions at that specific time, and this means neither floppiness nor tension (which, to quote an Alexander teacher, causes 'severe spinal damage at 0 miles per hour!'). Nor should that same tone persist beyond the task for which it was needed; when you finish the task you should be able to let go.

Tension is sometimes used to express and keep the feeling of deep emotion that the instrument itself cannot by its very nature express. An example might be a crescendo on a harpsichord or piano where the note fades immediately it is struck, or because of constraints of ancient or baroque styles.

Sway is mainly a more modern phenomenon. Sometimes it is due to legitimate follow-through from a particularly large, powerful movement (as witnessed, for instance, in Jacqueline du Pré's playing); but more often it is just theatre, to which I have no objection if it does not interfere with, or become more important than, the musical communication. Constant jigging about, that could by no stretch of imagination be called choreography, is another matter. There are also those who use body-sway to move their arms rather than arm movements. I shall not forget the sight of two well-known violinists playing the Bach Double Concerto, where one swayed forwards and backwards and the other side to side, nor of a violist who appeared first one side then the other of two stable soloists playing Mozart's Sinfonia Concertante! One became distinctly queasy.

Both excessive tension and sway are indicators of inappropriate body use. You can help yourself by taking Alexander or Feldenkrais lessons.

Ligaments

Ligaments are extremely strong fibres which bind joints together and which are usually bluish-white. They are almost completely inelastic and, having less blood supply than muscles, take longer to heal once torn. Muscles are bone movers and are the most elastic, then come the less elastic tendons that are made from the muscle fibre (sheaths that cover the muscle like a sausage skin, and attach it to the bone covering), and finally the ligaments, which are the least elastic and bind the bones of a joint together to provide stability, and stop it wobbling sideways. Occasionally it is difficult to categorise precisely what's what because their functions tend to merge (as for instance the tiny structures between the side fins (transverse processes) of the bones of the lower spine, which are given different categories in different anatomy books). Once a ligament has stretched it will remain stretched, and can be the cause of dislocation because the joint has too much play and the bones can flop about and easily slip out of place.

Proprioception

Within almost all joints, and certainly within the big joints like the shoulder, elbow and hip (and within the muscles too), there are specialised nerve endings called proprioceptors that measure tension, stretch and pressure and give the brain feedback as to exactly where that part of your anatomy is in space, and where it is in relation to other parts of your body. They also tell you if a muscle or joint is about to go beyond its normal range of movement, warning you of possible impending damage. Proprioceptors also have a good kinaesthetic or physical memory stored at the other end of the nerve cells in the brain, helping you to learn new physical techniques, and protecting you by remembering the position you were in during previous injury.

Normal Ranges of Movement (ROM)

The normal ranges of movement are the normal extent to which you should be able to move, and at the end of which there is still an elastic feel. Because the figures I give are average, there will be those who can move further or not so far. What matters is that both sides should move equally, as this gives the figure that is normal for you. Taking the shoulder in an arc from the side and up to the head (abduction) is 180°. It should go across your chest or behind your back (adduction) 45°, and should go forward and up to the head (flexion) 90° and back (extension) 45°. It should turn in (internal rotation) 55° and out (external rotation) 40° to 45°. There's a quick test you can do to see if your movements are equal both sides. Taking one arm up over your shoulder and the other behind your back, try to touch fingers. Then bring one arm across your chest and see how far it will go over your shoulder. Repeat both the tests the other way round. In both cases, you will probably find it easier one way than the other, whereas they should be equal. It may help you to see how you use each arm and shoulder joint differently, and the restrictions that causes.

The elbow should bend from straight 135°-150°. It will not go 180° because your upper arm muscles are in the way, and the bigger your biceps the less you can flex the elbow. That is what is known as being muscle bound, a problem many body builders have. The elbow will extend about 5° beyond straight, often more in women than men. You should be able to turn the forearm palm down and palm up 90° both ways, and there might be slight sideways play of a degree or two. However violinists and violists would do well to remember that the left hand is at its limit of turn in normal playing position. Playing an instrument that is too large, when combined with a short little finger, will cause enormous stress on that finger, the wrist and the elbow. To minimise such stress, the whole arm should be brought across the chest first, and the index finger twisted away, rather than the little finger pulled forward, in order to get the hand parallel to the fingerboard.

The wrist will bend forward 80° and back 70°. Children can often move much further, but this is because the bones are not fully hardened yet (see Chapter 2). It will also move 30° towards the little finger side and 20° to the thumb side. The base of the fingers will flex 90° to 100° and extend anywhere between 30° to 45° according to Hoppenfeld, but I find it's often not much more than 5° in many Caucasians, and much more in most Asians. The last joint of the fingers will flex 80° to 90° if you hold the finger on the hand side of the joint, and the fingers will separate from each other by about 20°. The thumb will move sideways across the palm to the base of the little finger and out to the side about an equal amount, 45° to 50°. It will move away from the palm forwards about 70°. The last joint of the thumb will flex 90° and extend beyond straight 20°, but this varies enormously with use. Just occasionally there is an anatomical anomaly in the flexor tendons of the hand which means that the ring and little finger have less movement. Schumann tried to cope with this problem with a machine which effectively ended his pianistic career. String players and guitarists have the most problems here, when trying to play double stops in first position, which characteristically causes forearm pain. Depending on the degree of tendinous interconnection, stretching exercises over years may or may not help, and refingering may be the only solution.

All these measurements of joint flexibility are average, but remember your use of your joints is not average, particularly if you play a one-sided instrument. It is the continual stress on them that causes problems.

While we are discussing range of movement it seems appropriate to mention that the neck bends as a series of joints. In a normal adult it bends forward so that you can touch you chin to chest, backward so you can look directly at the ceiling, tilts or laterally flexes 45° towards each shoulder, and twists or rotates till your chin is over the top of each shoulder. If yours doesn't, don't force it, but do make a note of the differences and ask yourself if it has anything to do with how you play your instrument. It's quite possible you have found some of these details tedious, but they are very reassuring things to know when you do develop a problem, and want to get back to normal.

Arm Supplies

The blood and nerve supply to the arm are reasonably straightforward and we needn't concern ourselves with them in detail. But it is helpful to know just where they can become squashed or stretched, what happens if they are, and what you can do to prevent it happening or help recovery.
First a few simple rules:
1. Everything needs a blood and nerve supply before it will work.
2. Conveniently, large nerves and blood vessels tend to travel together through the shoulder and upper arm, at least until they have to branch off to go to a specific area.
3. The higher up in the neck the nerve supply comes out of the spine, the nearer to the neck the area supplied. It follows that the supply to the shoulder blades comes out near the top, and that to the fingers near the bottom of the neck, where it joins the torso.
4. Blood vessels and nerves are softer than muscles, tendons, ligaments and bones, so they can be stretched or squashed by any of these. Good posture is essential and ensures proper spacing of these structures, giving plenty of room.
5. Unequal, one-sided or over development of specific muscles can alter posture drastically.
6. Where there is friction, swelling develops, and that causes even more friction because there is less room still, so you must find a way

to stop the swelling and break the vicious circle.

All of the above means that there are certain places that need care. Where the soft nerves and blood vessels pass (a) close to a bone or a joint, (b) through a narrow space, (c) under or through a well-developed group of muscles, or (d) where large muscles cross each other, nerves and blood vessels are at risk. The structures which are supplied by them further down the arm then get starved of blood, go flaccid, or cause muscle imbalance and spasm. To a lesser extent the structures above a compression like this become engorged, but because there is often a double drainage system it's less of a problem.

Nerve Impingement and other Common Conditions

Squashing or stretching a blood vessel or a nerve causes malfunction, sometimes at the impingement site, and usually beyond that point. Subsequent common symptoms are weakness, pins and needles, coldness and a white colour; or redness, swelling, pain and spasm. The symptoms can be made better or worse by usage and are often worst at night.

Since specific areas of the arm and hand are served by specific nerves and blood vessels, it's useful to know what does what. Unfortunately, nerve impingement problems are often compound i.e. a 'double crush' syndrome. Two places are compressed, neither of which singly is bad enough to cause a problem, but together they do. Pain can also refer from one place to another; the cause is in one place, but the pain or weakness is felt in another place served by the same nerve, causing a non-specific or vague aching. Typical of this is a weakness in the hand which may be due to a neck, a shoulder, an elbow, a wrist or even a local muscle problem. This means that although you only apparently have a hand problem, you need to check the whole arm, and maybe even shoulder and neck, before you find the solution. Simple, first-stage checking, you can do yourself or with the help of a colleague. For the second stage you may need to go to a chiropractor, an osteopath or your GP for tests and an X-ray in case you have a common anatomical anomaly such as an extra rib in your lower neck. Ideally your first-stage self-help and prevention techniques will stop the problem in its tracks and prevent spread.

Posture of the head and neck doesn't only make a difference to singers. I've already described the many structures the neck contains, and yet it has to be so flexible. We mistreat it by clamping it round an instrument or poking it forward instead of lifting the instrument to our lips. The eight nerves that come out between its seven vertebrae can be easily squashed or stretched by bony misalignments and bad posture. Having got out of the spine, the nerves then have to pass through the deep neck muscles, so there they can be affected by a stiff neck or muscle spasm.

Next, in the upper chest area above the collar bone, large blood vessels join the nerves as they go toward the arm. They can be squashed by the collar bones, ribs and outer ends of the shoulder blades. The causes are: (a) bad posture because you bring your shoulders forward (round shoulders); (b) letting the chest sink in and down, collapsing and decreasing the space available dramatically (typical in double-bassists, guitarists, viola players and harpists in the left shoulder area, or in flautists and horn players in the right); (c) raising the collar bone so high by using the neck auxiliary breathing muscles and over developing the chest muscles, that the first rib pushes up against the collar bone, squashing what's in between. A combination of the three occurs with a wrongly fitted shoulder-rest, which jams the whole area. The above postures can cause weak arm and hand muscles, a weak *latissimus dorsi* (and consequent back or elbow problems), and trigger points and tension in *pectoralis minor*. The congenital anomaly, an extra rib, usually only starts to cause problems after the age of 40 when general posture deteriorates, then it may squash the nerve that supplies the little-finger side of the hand. The same nerve is squashed in players of heavy instruments who frequently use a shoulder strap for carrying.

All of these problems are all called 'thoracic outlet syndrome' (TOS) and *posture is the key to all of them*. You can test for TOS by feeling the wrist pulse on a normally placed straight arm, then reproducing the poor posture. Retest the pulse, which will be weaker or disappear if the poor posture is causing the problem (the pulse will reappear when good posture is restored), or will remain unchanged if it's not. The best you can do for yourself is to work to improve head, neck, upper back and chest posture. You may need a chiropractor or osteopath to put things right. Do some stretching and/or swimming backstroke (see Chapter 15), strengthen the upper back muscles (see Chapters 12 and 14) and then see an Alexander teacher to learn how to maintain correct posture as you play.

Don't forget that gall bladder problems, lung tumours and cervical disc problems can also refer pain to the shoulder, upper arm and neck. If you have shoulder/neck pain and also have difficulty digesting a fatty meal, if you smoke, or have had a whiplash or other neck injury, talk to your GP, osteopath or chiropractor before you work on self-help remedies. If, on the other hand you have just painted two ceilings in the middle of playing the Ring cycle, don't be surprised if you have pain!

Remember also that added stress can alter posture for the worse. Necks are the meeting place between the logical brain which gives commands with 'must', 'ought' and 'should' in them, and the emotional body which sometimes says 'Don't want to', or 'I'm frightened'. There being no compromise between these two opinions pulling in opposite directions, all the poor neck can do is hang on for dear life, or become transfixed with indecisive terror while you end up with neck problems.

Next, just before they enter the arm pit, the nerves and blood vessels have to pass under *pectoralis minor* muscle (it binds a knob on the outer front of the shoulder blade down onto the ribs). If the area immediately under the outer end of the collar bone, and just inside the shoulder joint is tender, and goes on being tender as you work down towards the nipple, look up *pectoralis minor* in Chapter 12. It may need stretching to release the structures underneath. It tends to be worse in violinists and violists on the left because of the shoulder-rest position.

As a musician, it's always worth routinely checking all the muscles around the shoulder joint if you suspect any infection or inflammation in any part of the arm, because the body drains out toxins in the upper chest area. This is particularly important if you are a woman, as the area tends to become congested with premenstrual water retention, and swelling could be a source of understandable but incorrect worry about breast lumps. The shoulder muscles work together very much as a coordinated unit, and a problem in one muscle upsets all the others, eventually causing problems such as frozen shoulder which could stop you playing for six to eighteen months or more. Keeping that area in a good state with a few minutes' daily work is definitely a good investment.

Now if we move down to the elbow, the nerves and blood vessels have here spread out to go to specific areas. In broad terms, the hand is divided into two main areas for two motor nerves. The thumb, index and middle finger are served by the median nerve, and the ring and little finger by the ulnar nerve. Let's look at where they can become impinged, remembering that everyone's anatomy is slightly variable.

In front of the elbow the median nerve goes under or through the pronator muscle, so spasm here when you turn your forearm palm down, will squash the nerve, and cause hand symptoms. This problem can be compounded by a fibrous extension of the biceps tendon. Here the symptoms in the hand are made worse when you bend your elbow, contracting the biceps and crushing the nerve underneath.

About two inches below the elbow crease, the nerve passes under a tough arc of fibre which is part of the muscles that flex the fingers. This arc can bind the forearm tightly, especially if the finger strength is highly developed through playing and gripping, as in guitar or bass. Since the nerve then has to pass between the two forearm bones, any tightness in the connecting fibres (or even from a tight wristwatch strap) will adversely affect it. Finally the nerve has to pass through the carpal tunnel (a small space between the wrist bones).

The carpals are the wrist bones. They are bound together by a tough ligamentous band on the inside of the wrist and palm base called the *flexor retinaculum*. Eight muscle tendons, blood vessels and the median nerve go through the tunnel underneath. It has very little spare room. Tendons have outer coverings which swell with overuse and friction. When this happens, there is even less space and more friction, so the softest structure, the poor old nerve, gets squashed, and the fingers don't work well, or become weak. If you put pressure on the base of the palm about half an inch above the wrist crease and it causes worse symptoms, then this is where you must work, rather than with the fingers (see Chapter 15). Pain from entrapment here can also spread or refer right back up the arm.

The median nerve can also become irritated by too wide a stretch of the hand as might be found in the left hand of a 12-string guitarist, or wide stretches of more than a tenth on a keyboard instrument. Other causes of swelling in this area occur with fluid retention, pregnancy and vitamin B6 deficiency. This is why more women than men have this problem, compounded by the fact that they often have slender wrists in the first place. Carpal tunnel help is in Chapter 15.

The ring and little finger are supplied by the ulnar nerve which has fewer danger spots than the median. Everyone's heard of the 'funny bone'. This is where the nerve passes through a small channel in the ulna on the back inside of the elbow. The ligament that holds it in place occasionally becomes calcified like a bone and compresses it, giving you half-hand pins and needles if you lean on it, have broken your elbow, or do a lot of work at the tip of the bow, constantly locking and unlocking the elbow. The left elbow of string players and right elbow of a piccolo player are also particularly vulnerable due to constant maximal flexion. It is worth checking the *flexor carpi ulnaris* (FCU) and also *flexor digitorum profundus* muscles which surround the elbow (Chapter 13), for hypertension (Chapter 15) because the nerve passes between the two heads of FCU and could be compressed. You can help yourself here by wearing a skateboarder's elbow guard; cellists can use higher and thumb positions, upper strings keep to lower positions and piccolo players practise on the flute, all of which will lessen the degree of elbow flexion and consequent ulnar nerve stretch. You can lessen inflammation with an ice pack round the elbow, for ten minutes at a time before and after playing.

The only other place the ulnar nerve becomes commonly affected is as it goes into the heel of the hand on the little-finger side. It fortunately doesn't go through the Carpal Tunnel, but does pass close by the smallest bone in the wrist, the pea shaped *pisiform,* and can get squashed in the tunnel of Guyon, between the pisiform and the small hook-like part of the next wrist bone, the *hammate.* Falling on your hand, slamming it against drums or swing doors are the most common cause of this problem, with symptoms of weakness and tingling in ring and little fingers.

The *radial nerve,* not so far mentioned, can become entrapped too, but much more rarely, and may need specialist care. Compression in the armpit usually only occurs if you use crutches, unless you hold the arm very tightly in to the side when playing the horn, bassoon or piccolo. Any impingement here will affect the triceps, anconeus and supinator muscles. This makes straightening the elbow and turning the forearm palm up difficult, but because the radial nerve also supplies the extensors of the wrist, fingers and thumb, it causes 'wrist-drop' and over-curled fingers if the compression is above the elbow, but no wrist-drop if it is below. Radial nerve compression at the wrist merely causes loss of sensation on the back of the hand and ball of the thumb.

The *brachioradialis* muscle (or its fibrous extension) is the most frequent cause of compression at the elbow. This muscle is often hypertense – more frequently in men, who develop it more and who anatomically often find it harder than women to straighten the elbow a full 180°. Impingement here gives pain or numbness in the outer part of the forearm, and in the wrist below the thumb. Violent straightening of the arm, as in a *ff* down bow or percussion stroke, may trap the nerve in the muscle convulsion, and lifting the middle finger with the arms straight will be painful.

While we are on the subject of hand problems, the thumb tendon and a branch of the radial nerve can sometimes becomes stretched or inflamed (De Quervain's disease) as it passes over the end of the forearm bone (radius). Test for this by making a fist with the thumb tucked inside the fingers, then bend the wrist towards the little finger. (Someone with the lovely name of Finkelstein invented this test!) Inflammation will cause a sharp pain at the wrist below the thumb, and in the forearm, but if it's just nerve compression, there may be tingling or numbness in the back of the thumb and index finger. The problem occurs in the right thumb of string players, especially playing at the heel of the bow, in pianists doing a lot of arpeggio practice, in harpists at the top of the instrument and in percussionists and trumpeters. The only help you can give here is to put ice cubes wrapped in a handkerchief over the painful area for ten minutes at a time before and after playing, and experiment with your wrist position as you play so that (a) it's not under strain, and (b) it does not cause scissoring of the nerve as it passes between two tendons about 2 ins (5cm) back up the forearm, where many people wear their watch strap. Having said all the above, it is also very common for the joint at the base of the thumb to become arthritic. Compressing the bone at the base of the thumb with your other thumb will give discomfort and pain if you then flex and bend the wrist in the normal way. Unfortunately there's nothing further you can do about it yourself, but a physiotherapist or acupuncturist might help with pain control.

The Sciatic Nerve

Since several instruments are commonly played when standing, it's important to mention the sciatic nerve. The longest nerve in the body, it leaves the spine in the low back and goes all the way down to the toes. It can cause pain *anywhere* along its length, depending upon which fibres are compressed or stretched. There is one place you can get at it – where it passes through the *piriformis* muscle. This muscle is a pelvic stabiliser which lives underneath the buttock muscles. Again people vary, since in 92% cent of the population the sciatic nerve goes under it, in 7.2% it goes through it and, for the remaining few, the nerve fibres go over it or only through the top few muscle fibres. Spasm of this muscle can therefore give you buttock, thigh, calf and even foot pain. Turn to the notes in Chapter 13 to test and work on it, but if you have no success do go to see a chiropractor, osteopath or doctor, as pain in these areas can have other causes which may need their help.

Arthritis

This is a condition that regularly strikes musicians. The term is a 'catch all' meaning joint inflammation. There are many sorts of arthritis, from rheumatoid to gout and osteo-arthritis or degenerative joint disease (DJD), and most need X-rays and blood tests for definitive diagnosis. However, there are things you can do to help yourself.

Probably the most painful arthritis is rheumatoid, because it is an auto-immune disease that affects the lining of *any* joint, and usually both sides of the body. The inflammation comes and goes and movement makes it worse when the disease is in its active stages. It can strike at any age, there appears to be an inherited tendency, it causes great destruction of the affected joints, with considerable deformity and pain, and the highest incidence occurs in this country. It probably means the end of your career as a performer but not as a teacher or composer. All you can do is lessen its effects. Other sorts of arthritis such as DJD (see above) are less damaging to small joints, and tend to appear only in places that have been damaged or grossly over-used. This means that only one side of the body is usually affected, although it can cause havoc in the spine, and that its onset tends to be in later life. There are inherited forms of this too.

Where the affected joint is the one that carries the weight of your instrument while you play, be inventive. Change the angle slightly to prevent fatigue, or think of a completely different way to carry the weight, like some sort of sling or post. There are various inventions available (see Chapter 2). If you are overweight it will obviously put great strain on weight-bearing joints such as the hips, so the first thing to do is make sure you lose what excess weight you can.

Allergy testing, and eating organically to keep toxin levels down, are often extremely worthwhile, as this helps to prevent the build-up of irritating sediment in the joints, sediment which seems to cause inflammatory flare-ups. Many people find that the same foods which give them migraine, asthma or eczema will also cause more arthritic pain. Typically these are: dairy products, red meats and animal fats, red wine (can be any alcohol), dark red fruits and vegetables, rhubarb, citrus fruits and wine vinegars, added sugars, tea, coffee, cocoa and chocolate. This is because the digestive break-down of these foods produces prostaglandin 2, a substance which appears to increase the sensitivity and inflammation of the nerve endings that sense pain. Prostaglandins 1, 3 and 4 are produced from break-down of plant and fish oils and do not have this effect. Aspirin works by inhibiting *all* prostaglandins (so you lose the effects of prostaglandins 1, 3 and 4 too), and is bad for peptic ulcers. Knowing this allows you to make a choice about what you eat to help yourself. A naturopath might well even suggest a fast to clear the system (and lose a bit of weight), but don't do this alone without proper advice. Keeping mental stress-levels down helps, as stress seems to acidify the body and cause flare-ups too.

To help yourself, therefore, I suggest you try the alkaline diet (see Chapter 6) and increase your intake of B, C and E vitamins with zinc and primrose oil. Some people find wearing a copper bracelet helps. Medically a daily dose of half an aspirin is often prescribed, but ask your doctor first as there may be complications. Ideally you should visit a homeopath for a proper consultation, to get help specific to you, but meanwhile Arnica 6, Aconite 6 and Rhus tox 6 will probably help and will do no harm.

In the non-inflammatory stages of the disease, gentle exercise might help the stiffness, but stop if the pain gets worse. A simple exercise is to try and move the joint about as if it were a giant pencil, and write the letters of the alphabet in as large capital or lower-case letters as you can with that joint alone. This moves the joint in all possible directions and is far less boring than 50 circles this way and 50 that way. You can even write rude words to vent your frustration! You might also find it easier to do this letting the joint hang so that gravity takes its weight.

Your doctor, chiropractor or osteopath might well suggest a wax bath for arthritic hands. You can make an approximation of this for many joints with two warm hot water bottles each wrapped in a towel, and use an oily hand cream, or olive oil with a little Rhus tox 6 added if you have it in liquid form. Anoint the affected joint and put it between the bottles. It helps you regain some movement and lessen stiffness, but never use this when the joint is already hot and inflamed as you will simply make the pain worse. If in doubt, compare the temperature of the arthritic joint with other similar joints, and if it feels even slightly warmer, don't use this technique.

By all means go to your chiropractor or osteopath to help straighten out the rest of you, and work on muscle spasm and mobility, but very painful arthritic joints should not be manipulated. Acupuncture may well afford you some pain relief, but again this is not a self-help matter.

For severe arthritis there are many aids and products available – your local chemist may have a catalogue. These will reduce the stress on the joint during normal daily usage, and save you for playing a bit. Gadgets include levers and jar wrenches, large handles to utensils, and car power steering and you might consider having the action of your instrument made lighter, with a lower bridge and softer strings. Obviously avoid typing, carrying, and small muscle dexterity-type jobs where possible.

REFERENCES
1. **Hoppenfeld S.** (1976) *Physical Examination of the Spine and Extremities,* Appleton-Century-Crofts, Prentice-Hall, NY, USA
2. **Sobel D.** and **Klein A.** (1996) *Arthritis: What exercises really work,* Robinson Publishing Ltd.
3. **Walther D.** (1989) *ICAK-E Presentation and Applied Kinesiology Vols.1&2,* Systems DC Pueblo, Colorado.

CHAPTER 10

Testing what's wrong

*Introduction to the concept of muscle
testing; How to test muscles;
Assessing the problem; Which muscle?
The pitfalls to avoid; Indicator muscles;
Abbreviations.*

Introduction to the concept
of muscle testing

Pain and muscle tension are the principal reasons for you to be reading this and ensuing chapters. Pain is most often suffered in the left hand by string and guitar players, in the right hand by woodwind and keyboard players, in the fingertips by pianists, in the forearms by string and keyboard players, and in the upper arm and shoulders by all who hold up an instrument or use a bow. Wide finger stretches may also cause problems for pianists, violists and cellists, bass, guitar and bassoon players. As well as using these techniques, consider the possibility that the cause of your pain may be a fault in your instrumental technique.

The methods presented in the ensuing chapters are both preventative and restorative. They are about muscle management for musicians. This is where you find out if you are an instrumentalist first or a musician first. The techniques aim to catch stresses, strains and potential weaknesses before they become serious problems and before accidents happen. They often work when nothing else will, and are especially good when there is still a remaining hesitancy in performance following the best of modern medicine and physiotherapy. The methods are safe and do not conflict with conventional medicine or instrumental practice and, despite their apparent simplicity, have been welcomed by those medics who have had the courage to try them. You need no specialist knowledge, just a willing pair of hands.

The techniques were developed almost 30 years ago by an American chiropractor, George Goodheart, from techniques and lore drawn from chiropractic, osteopathy, cranial work, dentistry, homeopathy, herbalism, nutrition, acupuncture and conventional medicine. He formulated the International College of Applied Kinesiologists (ICAK), which continues research and correlation between disciplines. An associate of his, John Thie DC, made the basic technique available to a wider readership through his book *Touch for Health*. I make no claims of originality other than its translation into musical terms.

Muscle testing is a form of functional neurology. It deals with the quality of reaction within level five (or possibly four) on the medical model scale, which means the muscle reaction is potentially normal and is not grossly weakened as it might be after a complete tear or surgery. There are over 50 reasons why muscles become 'weak'. They can be roughly divided into a triangle of mental, physical and chemical causes. Few problems have only one cause; the other two sides of the triangle are almost always affected to some degree. With self-help, once you have found the right relief points to work on, the effect is instantaneous and very pleasantly surprising. It's very exciting to feel the strength return and know that you have done it yourself.

The relief points are often not at the site of pain, but nevertheless speed the healing process; they can be used before and after playing and even in the green room between appearances on stage. I have covered the most common relief points and a few advanced techniques, which together will deal with 80% of the niggling sort of problems that musicians encounter. The other 20% are way beyond the scope of this book, and for these you will need to see an applied kinesiologist approved by ICAK. Don't be dismayed: what you *can* do is easy, fun and safe, and will work wonders in most cases.

The subject of discussion here is why muscles 'switch off' just when they are needed, and how old injuries can inhibit present performance (especially in the areas of accuracy, speed of reaction and coordination), even though you are not thinking consciously of the old injury. The assumption is that you are basically healthy. You may want an outline of how you can get that extra coordination needed for really clean playing, or to find out about food sensitivities and vitamin deficiencies, as well as to understand better the causes of muscles feeling 'weak, wobbly and unsure'. If we take a single example: muscle pain leads to mental stress, which impinges on clear thinking. Fuzzy, negative thinking, causes 'holding back' in a difficult passage, then worrying about it and having 'butterflies in your stomach'. This means poor digestion and causes poor assimilation of vitamins and minerals, and toxicity in the system from half-digested foods. Such chemical stress leads eventually to clogging of muscle fibres with waste products, and muscle starvation, which means they function poorly and fatigue easily. Poor response is disappointing and leads to 'trying too hard' (or too long), and this is when accidents and injuries occur causing yet more pain. You are now part of a downward spiral which compounds itself as it goes.

Only when the whole body-machine is working perfectly can smooth improvement be hoped for in terms of good coordination, injury avoidance and the confidence to reach for success and full potential. With all these in place, the performer has the chance to satisfy his/her hunger for a really fine performance of pure musical communication.

How do you do it? First you have to realise that there is no such thing as a reachable state of 'perfect health' where you can stay. *Health is a continuous process,* not an event. Optimum health is all you can aim for in a world where conditions are changing all the time. The body is in a constant state of repair and renewal. All you can do is find out what it needs, given the conditions in which it exists right now, and do your best to provide that. The best way to find out is to ask the body itself by muscle testing.

How to test muscles

N.B. Without reading this section most carefully, you will fail to get results.

Unfortunately you can not remove a muscle, test it and replace it like a spare part in a car! You will need two people to test muscles (I will assume that you are the Tester, testing an injured musician – the Testee). Nor can you ever really test one muscle at a time. There are bound to be other muscles helping, because there is almost always a back-up system of synergistic muscles. All you can do is make sure that the one muscle you think you are testing is the one doing the main work, and that the synergists are put at a disadvantage by your positioning before testing. Frequently, if the main muscle is weak, the Testee will twist to try to use one of these synergists, so *precision positioning by you as Tester is essential* to get the right muscle. Sloppy testing gets sloppy, unreliable results. Be precise in following the illustrations about positioning the Testee's limbs.

As often as possible I have given an alternative test position for each muscle so that you can either use the most comfortable one, or test both to make sure your findings are correct. Do not test each muscle more than twice in close succession, or you will cause fatigue causing the muscle to seem weak when it actually isn't.

There are two types of muscle action important to the musician: (a) *Action* – as when you leap off the ground, or push or lift (the brain is used because *you decide* to leap, push or lift) and (b) *Reaction* – such as when your muscles take up the shock when you land after your jump, play a keyboard staccato or a bowed spiccato (using the spinal reflex pathway, which is instinctive).

The test position for both is the same; it's a matter of who initiates the test, the Tester (you) or the Testee (the injured party). Either action or reaction can be upset, so both need to be tested. To test an *action,* place the limb accurately and ask your Testee to push first then, one second later, you push in the opposite direction to overcome the Testee's push. This can become a contest; do not let that happen. You are only testing quality, not strength. To test *reaction,* place the limb accurately and ask the Testee to hold the position (often against gravity). Wait one to two seconds and then push against the hold. The Testee *reacts* instinctively to hold the limb in place.

Realise that this way of testing is not quite the same as the type of testing that is taught in hospitals and medical schools (although it does come under their definition of Grade 5 testing). Here we are *not* testing for gross strength or range of movement. Nor is it competitive testing, nor is there a right or left-handedness about it. You are testing too lightly for any of these to make any difference. You are simply asking if the muscle 'switches on' when you ask it to, by testing it.

You are looking for *quality* of reaction not quantity. The test is done within a two to three second time-frame, and between a half to a two- inch depth of travel as you push, not more. As you push, ask yourself 'How does it feel?' Is the reaction immediate, spongy, jagged, painful? Anything other than an immediate lock against the Tester's light pressure counts as weak.

In other words you test slowly and lightly, but deliberately and not too deep. Using the same pressure each time, it's almost as if you were listening for the response. If you are testing the many fibres of a large muscle, you then vary the starting angle slightly, but not the depth of testing. Beginners may find a little difficulty for the first few minutes, but as musicians we are used to varying our touch, and it's quite easy to attune yourself to the 'feel' of your Testee's reaction. The more people you test the better you get, and the better you become at teaching others to test you.

Always compare right and left, not because they will be different (although your Testee will try to tell you they are), but because they should be the same. Also, don't forget that a muscle must have a stable base to push against or the whole body will twist to give support, and that then gives you no idea what you are testing. Support varies according to whether your Testee is standing, sitting or lying, because gravity and support change relative to body position. When you find a weak muscle, note it down, and go on to find any others. Then look and see if they have MPs or HPs (see below) in common. Treat those first and retest, because they may clear up the whole problem. Finally, when you have finished your treatment on the muscle, retest and make sure it is strong when in a playing position. If it's not, refix it in that position, or as near it as possible.

Assessing the Problem

How do you know which muscle to test? First assess the problem by getting answers to the following questions. Write down the answers. They will be useful reference points later, give useful clues about where to look (what muscle or muscle group performs the action which causes the pain), and so how to solve the problem. Ask the questions again after working on the points twice a day for a week, and you will be surprised at the change in the answers.

1. Where is the pain? Does it feel deep or surface?
2. Does it have a defined size or border or is it vaguely in an undefined area (often a referred pain)? Does it move about or stay in one place?
3. What kind of a pain is it? Shooting, stabbing, radiating (often muscular or structural cause)? Searing, burning (often a chemical cause)? Throbbing, pounding (often to do with circulation)? An ache and stiffness (often a chronic or residual problem rather than acute)?
4. What caused it and when does it happen now? (Be precise about the body position of the Testee when it happens; it may be necessary to test the muscle when playing.)
5. What makes it worse and what relieves it? Does it hurt without movement?

6. What precisely does it stop the Testee doing?

7. Is it getting better or worse? Suddenly or gradually?

8. How long has it existed? Has it happened before, or has something like it happened before?

9. Has there been an operation with scar tissue there or near by?

10. What type of warm-up/warm down and stretching exercises are done? You may need to invent some relevant exercises (see Rehabilitation Ladders in Chapter 15).

11. What are the flexibility and range of movement like on both sides of the body using this muscle(s)?

12. Is the Testee over practised or over performed?

13. Is adequate endurance practice done? Is the Testee used to playing the whole work through with all its repeats and movements as in a performance?

14. Are the muscles generally used equally on both sides of the body, or does playing this specific instrument use one limb much more, or even exclude others from movement?

15. On a scale of 0 to ten, if 0 equals no pain and ten equals the worst pain imaginable, how bad is it now? At its best/at its worst? Give a score out of ten and make a careful note of it, because it is hard to remember how bad a pain was when it's gone.

Which Muscle?

Now find the muscles to test by consulting Fig.2 and identifying which muscles most nearly approximate the same area as the pain. Don't forget that there may be several layers of muscles with fibres going in different directions. List them. Look up the information for each specific muscle. Test each muscle by copying the positioning in the accompanying illustration as closely as possible. The position given offers you access as close as possible to the two ends of the muscle, while at the same time putting other muscles with a similar action at a disadvantage. If the muscle is strong, reacts immediately and easily and does not cause more pain, then test the others around it that have a similar action. Also test the ones that have the opposite action, which could also be the cause of pain now. Remember, when a muscle is switched off and slack (to protect it from

241

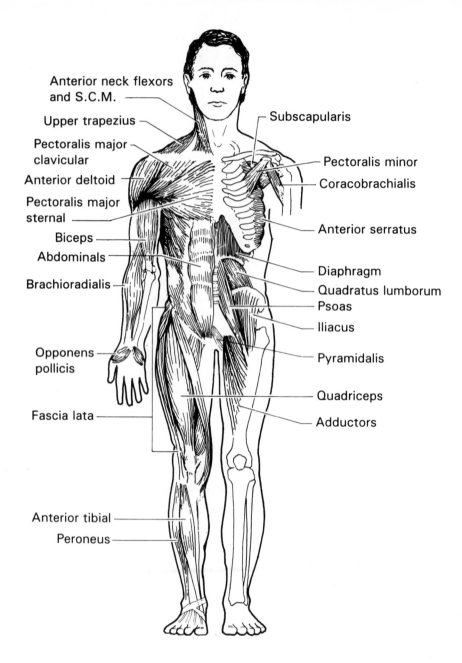

Anterior neck flexors
and S.C.M.

Upper trapezius

Pectoralis major
clavicular

Anterior deltoid

Pectoralis major
sternal

Biceps

Abdominals

Brachioradialis

Opponens
pollicis

Fascia lata

Anterior tibial

Peroneus

Subscapularis

Pectoralis minor

Coracobrachialis

Anterior serratus

Diaphragm

Quadratus lumborum

Psoas

Iliacus

Pyramidalis

Quadriceps

Adductors

The muscles of the body (front)

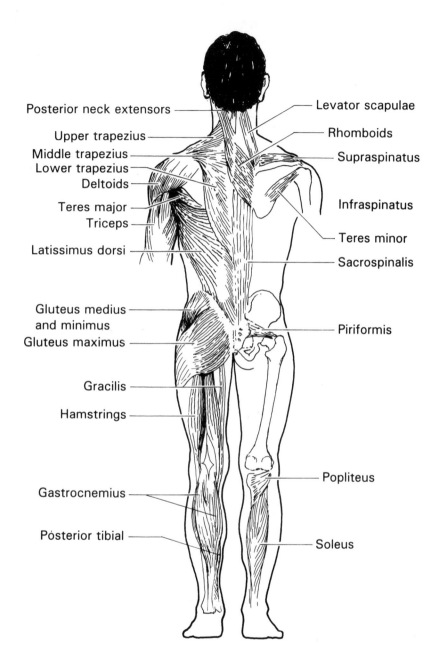

Posterior neck extensors

Upper trapezius

Middle trapezius

Lower trapezius

Deltoids

Teres major

Triceps

Latissimus dorsi

Gluteus medius
and minimus

Gluteus maximus

Gracilis

Hamstrings

Gastrocnemius

Posterior tibial

Levator scapulae

Rhomboids

Supraspinatus

Infraspinatus

Teres minor

Sacrospinalis

Piriformis

Popliteus

Soleus

The muscles of the body (back)

trauma) it causes imbalance with its opposite number (its antagonist). That muscle now has to take up the slack and may therefore have gone into spasm. The reverse can also happen, *viz.* a muscle may be cramping through overwork and congestion with uncleared waste products, and can't relax. Its opposite number then can't contract and may be weak through no fault of its own. It has to work at half strength and, naturally, it complains by being painful.

It is also worth testing the same muscle on the opposite side of the body (i.e. test both right and left *latissimus dorsi*). Also test muscles with a similar action anti-gravity (i.e. abdominals and *sacrospinalis*). The presence of pain does not mean that you should not test, although of course you proceed with caution, rest between tests, and don't test repeatedly. Often the pain will disappear if the Tester or Testee touches the relief points at the same time as the muscle is being tested. If this occurs, it means that the points are active and need working on, because they are directly related to the problem.

Strengthen the muscles according to the relief points on the relevant page. **Massage points** (MP) are shown as solid dots. Approach with caution. They can feel anything from 'a bit bruised' to 'hit-the-roof' tender. Do these points twice daily for 30 seconds, until they are no longer sore. More than that will simply fatigue the points. However, be aware that lightly brushing the skin won't help at all, and will actually make the muscle weaker, so work on them as deeply as pain will allow. *Never massage over any broken skin,* as you will only rub in infection. **Hold points** (HP) are shown as open circles. Hold them for at least 30 seconds, lightly enough to just stretch the skin. You may even feel a pulse; if you do, wait until it is slow and even. You do not need to have an acupuncturist's pinpoint accuracy on the acu-points, three finger pads over the area will do, until you feel you can narrow it down to one. However, do not worry either if you feel nothing: just wait for a couple of minutes anyway, you can do no harm. Continue until all the muscle points that are needed are done. [*NB* When you hold points, make sure you hold the same hand as foot (i.e. right hand and right foot). Do not mix them.]

To see whether a muscle needs MP or HP first, have the Testee place his/her hands over each of the points in turn while you retest the muscle (not forgetting to rest between tests). Work most on the points that strengthen the weak muscle best.

Now reassess the pain level (out of ten) and retest, but do not try out the muscle in full action yet. Be content with immediate pain reduction and greater strength; healing takes time, so let it settle and, if necessary, work on it again tomorrow. If there is still a problem then go to the section on advanced techniques in Chapter 14. If there is no pain then the muscle may be gently used. Waiting is a good idea because a muscle doesn't work by itself; the whole body has to rebalance itself in the light of the new found strength (as any dancer will tell you). *NB* Pain is there as a warning and should *never* be 'worked through'. That only stores up trouble for later.

Use the relief points given for each muscle as a preventative measure to keep you fit longer. Use them also as part of the 'warm down' routine after a practice session to help the body clear away the excess waste products of your work in the muscles. This will pay handsome dividends in reduced stiffness and aches, as well as improving posture, balance, muscle strength and general physical fitness.

If, after trying even the extra points in the advanced techniques, there is still a high level of pain, then you should go to see a doctor, chiropractor or osteopath. The muscle may have been more damaged than you realise. *Safety first! These techniques do not replace injury treatment,* they are simple aids to rehabilitation, injury prevention and muscle improvement.

The Pitfalls to Avoid

'What happens if I do it wrong?' Very little. If you mistakenly weaken a strong muscle by mistreating the points, the body will quickly put it right. The worst you can do, if you follow the directions above, is to cause bruising by massaging too hard, and some people bruise very easily. Avoidable pitfalls occur in two areas. The seven most common *Tester faults* are:
1. Poor positioning of Tester or Testee. Both must be as comfortable as possible. An awkward or unbalanced Tester can't do a good test. Think about your position and hand-holds before picking up the limb to be tested. Don't have more than one joint between your testing hand and the muscle you intend to test, because then you will be testing joints, not muscles. Above all do not put your stabilising

hand on, or squeeze, the muscle you are attempting to test!

2. Too heavy, too long or too deep testing, and too many repetitions, will tire a muscle already under stress. Be clear about what you are doing and feeling and do it efficiently. *Twice is enough* without a rest period in between.

3. Making the Testee hold the test position for a long time, whilst you make up your mind how to test, leads to needless fatigue and poor results. Work it out first, then test.

4. Squeezing the part of the limb you are holding will cause pain, and the muscle will weaken as a reaction. Watch out for rings and bangles digging in also.

5. You test the wrong muscle, or your own muscle is weak and your Testee acts as a surrogate for you (see Chapter 15 for this).

6. Your testing is not objective. Because you *so* want to find the weak muscle they all test weak, or you *so* want a muscle to be strong that your will-power alters the test result. If you suspect either might be happening, get someone else to check you, or deliberately think about something else as you test.

7. Asking the Testee to 'try to hold' or 'try it again' instead of just saying 'hold' or 'hold up/down/in/out' as appropriate. Asking someone to try implies that they may not succeed. It is a mixed message and confuses the brain by asking for effort, but not asking for success in a specific action. The muscle will invariably test weak, and the harder you try, the weaker it will be, no matter how much energy and effort is expended *(Teachers, please note!)*.

The most common *Testee faults* are:

1. The Testee will use a synergist to help. This is unconscious cheating. The first priority of a human being is survival. Knowing at an unconscious level that the muscle is weak, the Testee will 'survive' by using other muscles to do the job, by moving or twisting slightly, or bending another part of the body to use the synergist back-up system provided by nature. Watch out for this. Other muscle 'recruiting' can be quite subtle. In particular be careful when the Testee starts to learn the test position. He/she will helpfully hold the limb up, but of course it will be in the best strongest position and not the best test position, so *it is important that the Tester places the limb*

not the Testee.

2. The Testee will hold his/her breath while you test. This can change the result of the test. If in doubt, make him/her talk as you test.

3. The Testee will hook one limb or joint round another or round the edge of the testing table to give support. Unhook the limb and retest.

4. The Testee will forget to concentrate. Too often they will say 'I do not understand what you want me to do'. They mean they instinctively know they can't do it, so they don't understand physically. Frequently too they will lift the head to see what you are doing, or close the eyes to concentrate better. Do not allow this as results can be altered. Physically show them what is wanted by patting the part and say 'Push/hold here'. That also gets round any confusion over left and right.

5. Subconsciously the Testee knows what will strengthen their body and will frequently instinctively place their hands over the relief points for that muscle. Watch especially for crossing the hands on the chest or putting them behind the head. Remove them to either side of the body and not touching it, then retest.

6. Most people can't wait to get back to normal playing, but just occasionally the Testee may be so worried about a muscle that they 'quit' on the test. Show the test first on the opposite (strong) side of the body, then go back and test the first muscle while you make them talk about something else like 'What are you doing for the holidays?' This problem is rare and usually means either that they have no incentive to get back to playing or are more damaged than you realise. If this does happen, look at Chapter 6 on communication.

As you can see from the above lists, it pays to be a bit pernickety at first, until you get the hang of it. Ideally find someone who can already muscle test to show you, or go to a 'Touch for Health' class. Above all *don't* dive in and test without first asking permission. You risk a charge of common assault! Make sure too, that there is no known reason why you should not test muscles, such as a pinned joint, plate or replacement hip or other such problem. Do not assume such things will be obvious; they won't be, so always ask.

Indicator muscles

Just as you have been testing a weak muscle to see if it is now strong, you can also *test a muscle known to be strong and use it as an indicator* of what causes the Testee's body to go weak. This is useful in testing for food sensitivity (Chapter 6) and emotional upset (Chapter 7). In these cases it matters not which muscle is used, provided it is strong first. All you are looking for in this case, is a change in strength as a direct result of contact with the substance, or thought of the emotive thing or situation. The only time a strong muscle will not respond normally like this is when it is hypertense (see Chapter 15). Remove the hypertense state and it will act as an indicator again.

The muscles in succeeding chapters are arranged in groups according to location and action, and the relevance of each muscle to the musician is explained, with instructions and illustrations on how to position the Testee and in which direction the testing should be done. This is followed by the relief points to work on, specific to that muscle, together with dietary and allergy advice, and finally emotional connections for use with affirmations (see Chapter 6).

Abbreviations

To assist you to understand the information given in the following chapters, you may find it useful to photocopy the following list and use it as a bookmark for quick reference.

TP – test position

A – antagonist muscle (having the opposite action to the main muscle being tested), which may need work on it as well.

M – Chinese acupuncture meridian.

MP – massage points. These are areas of neuro-lymphatic congestion, which may feel puffy and engorged. Go carefully. They may just feel a little tender as if slightly bruised, or 'hit-the-ceiling' tender! Their tenderness will lessen with regular deep massage, but longer than 30 seconds at a go will only cause overload, and is counter-productive. In locating these points I often mention ribs and rib spaces. The collar-bone sits directly on top of the first rib in the front so count it as though it were such. Rib spaces are the dips between the ribs.

HP – holding points. These are acupuncture or neuro-vascular points, which should only be lightly held, perhaps with a slight skin stretch, but never massaged, unless specifically directed. You may or may not feel a pulse. If you do, wait until it is slow and even.

N – nutrition. Mostly it is suggested that you increase intake of the food source rather than take pills. This avoids most possibility of overdose.

S – possible allergy or hypersensitivity indicating substances to avoid until the problem is solved.

E – emotionally relevant words for making an affirmation. These are not the only likely causative emotions, but the most likely. Together with most of the nutritional suggestions, they have been researched by John Barton DC. The fact that there are many repetitions only goes to show how destructive these negative emotions are. More than one pair may be relevant.

BF – Bach Flower remedies. Those given are the main ones for the relevant meridian given, but not the only ones that can be used for the prevailing negative emotion.

TL – therapy localisation point, or touch point. Touching this point while you test an otherwise strong indicator muscle (SIM), will cause it to weaken and become a weak indicator muscle (WIM), if there is a problem of *whatever kind* at that point. It does not indicate specifically what is wrong.

Where any of this information is omitted under the instructions for a particular muscle, either it has not been researched, is unknown to the author, or is not thought suitable for self-help treatment. It is worth repeating that *if you are not sure about your testing, work on the relevant MP and HP points anyway.* You will do no harm.

REFERENCES
(as for Chapters 14 and 15)

CHAPTER 11

Muscles of the face, neck and jaw

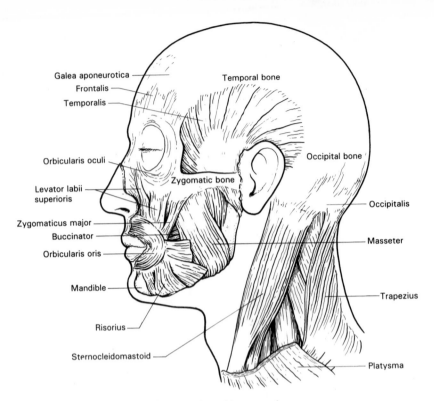

Face, neck and jaw muscles

Muscles of the face, neck and jaw

In this chapter we examine how to test and assist the muscles of facial expression, the cheek and jaw, and the neck. We shall not deal with all the muscles of the face, but the important ones for musicians. The information available on these muscles is not as full as for the muscles of the rest of the body, as less research has been done on their connection with acupuncture meridians, massage points and nutrition. Many of them are also so small that strengthening techniques are limited to working on the muscle itself (see Chapter 15). Against that, they are being exercised every time we speak, so they are strong for their size. This means that the main tendency of these muscles is to cramp through over-use rather than to be weak. They can also, with the exception of the neck and jaw muscles, be tested by yourself alone.

When testing, pull the appropriate 'face' and observe yourself in the mirror to see if both sides are contracting equally. If not, work on the longer muscle to shorten it by pushing the two ends together, and on the shorter one to stretch it by pulling the two ends of that muscle apart till they are balanced. Do the holding points where given; construct affirmations round the relevant emotions mentioned, and work also on all the other nearby muscles. Then observe how you play and whether that upsets the muscle balance, the habits of your embouchure, or whether other unnecessary tensions might have crept in. It's possible you may even need a jaw adjustment from an applied kinesiologist rather than a dentist. The face muscles are not affected by the position of your head and neck in a way you can work on yourself, because the cranial nerves which supply them leave the brain stem via the skull, not the spine.

The consequence of this is that any misalignments and torsions on the skull bones, through which these muscles have to pass, affects their function, together with that of ears, eyes, nose, throat, and tongue. Such problems might occur following a bang to the head, heavy dental work and plates, bridges or false teeth, or be due to embouchure changes. The therapist you then need is a cranial osteopath or kinesiologist, who may be able to help you considerably, even before possible referral to an ENT specialist (to whom your doctor may send you).

Muscles of facial expression
Muscles which raise the mouth/upper lip (*Levator anguli oris, Levator labii superioris*)
Muscles which straighten the lips (*Risoris, Zygomaticus*)
Sphincter (*Orbicularis oris*)
Muscles which lower the mouth/lower lip and tense the neck skin (*Mentalis, Depressor anguli oris, Depressor labii inferior* and *Platysma*)

Levator anguli oris. This muscle is found one each side, on the upper lip just on the nose side of the corner of the mouth. When both are used together they form part of the embouchure, particularly in brass playing.

TP Draw one side of the angle of the upper lip as if to smile on one side, and show one canine tooth. Look for matched contraction each side.

Can also be tested by TL.
A Depressor anguli oris.

Risoris. This muscle is found one each side, at the corners of the mouth in a straight line with the lips, and is important to oboists, bassoonists, flautists and brass players.

TP Draw the angle of the mouth back towards the earlobe.
M Stomach.
HP S-41 and SI-5. S-41 is found on the top of the foot in the centre of the ankle crease. Hold it with SI-5 which is on the little finger side of the wrist, at the end of the forearm bone.
E Nervous/restful or upset/calm.
BF Willow.

Zygomaticus. This muscle, one each side, runs between the corners of the mouth and the cheek bone. It is important to all wind and brass players and anyone who likes smiling! Malfunction can cause speech difficulties and tender cheeks. It may also be an indicator of jaw-joint problems.

TP Draw the angle of the mouth upward and outward as in smiling.
E Nervous/restful or upset/calm.
BF Willow.

Orbicularis oris. This is the circular muscle found all around the lips. It is used in whistling, and (in part or entirety) in all wind and brass playing. Because of its meridian association, weakness is often associated with flatulence and tight abdominal muscles. It can also indicate jaw-joint problems.

TP Close lips and protrude them as for whistling or sucking a straw.
A All muscles that open the mouth wide.
M Small intestine.
HP SI-3 and GB-41. SI-3 is on the back of the hand, halfway between knuckles and wrist and between ring and little finger. Hold this with GB-41 which is similarly placed between the base of the fourth and fifth toes and the ankle crease on the top of the foot.
E Confused/confident or withholding/cooperative.
BF Star of Bethlehem.

Depressor anguli oris. This muscle is found between the corners of the mouth and the chin, and is used by brass players to make lower notes, in conjunction with the muscles that drop the jaw a little.

TP Draw the angles of the mouth down.

A Levator anguli oris (which raises and protrudes upper lip.)

Mentalis. This muscle is found between the lower lip and chin. It is most used by flautists. Weakness is sometimes associated with haemorrhoids because of the meridian association.

TP Contract chin skin against the jaw and protrude lower lip.

M Large intestine.

HP LI-11 and S-36. LI-11 is found on the outside of the elbow (thumb side) about 2 inches(5cm.) from the point of the elbow, and just below the elbow crease. Hold it with S-36, which is below the knee about 2 inches(5cm.) out on the fibula (little shin-bone), in a little dip.

N Magnesium.

E Unwilling/willing, separated/united.

BF Pine.

Platysma. This muscle is found under the skin over the front neck area and is contracted in conjunction with the use of *Depressor labii inferioris,* which draws the angles of the mouth down. It is mostly used as part of the general contraction required to reach enough pressure for the highest notes in brass playing. Weakness often occurs at the same time as a dry, itchy throat or 'frog in the throat', neck pain, frontal headaches, whiplash and jaw-joint problems.

TP Draw angles of the mouth down and tense the neck skin.

M Stomach

HP As Risoris

N Calcium

E Confused/confident, overbearing/submissive, grief for others/companionship.

BF Willow.

Muscles of the Cheek and Jaw
    Buccinator
    Pterygoids
    Masseter
    Temporalis

Buccinator. This muscle is found on each cheek and runs between the jaws and the angle of the mouth. It is vital to all brass and wind playing, particularly in so-called 'circular breathing'. Weakness causes biting the cheek, speech problems, jaw-joint problems and 'hat-band' headaches.

    TP Press the cheeks firmly against the side teeth, and pull back the angle of the mouth.

    N Vitamin B complex.

    E Self-centred/kind, unobservant/observant.

    S Foam rubber.

Pterygoids. These small, very strong muscles are vital to the jaw joint. They are most easily found at the very back of the mouth each side, behind the wisdom teeth. This means they are vital to jaw alignment and embouchure of all sorts. Weakness causes clicking jaw, malocclusion and toothache, neck pain, cranial faults, and runny nose. The inside muscle clenches the teeth, the outside muscle protrudes the lower jaw and both are involved in chewing.

    TP Protrude lower jaw.

    TL Inside mouth pointing directly back behind molar teeth.

    M Stomach and Liver.

    HP As Risoris.

    N Vitamin B, potassium, orange peel.

    E Confused/confident, imposed on/accepted, nervous/restful, unwilling/willing, empty/fulfilled, irresponsible/responsible, restless/calm.

    BF Willow and agrimony.

Masseter. This muscle is found on the outside of the cheek between the cheek bones and the angle of the jaw. Malfunction causes jaw-joint problems and difficulty chewing and holding the mouth piece of a clarinet or saxophone. Concurrently the incisor teeth may be painful.

TP Bite firmly. You can feel the contraction easily by placing your fingers over the muscle near the back of the lower jaw.

M Pericardium (Cx).

HP Cx-9 and Lv-1. Cx-9 is at the end of the middle finger pad, on the side nearest the index finger. Hold it with Lv-9, which is on the big toe near the corner of the nailbed on the side nearest the other toes.

N Vitamin B3, magnesium, Brazil nuts, garlic, parsley.

E Unworthy/worthy, confused/confident, unfulfilled/fulfilled, useless/useful, unwilling/willing.

BF holly.

Temporalis. This muscle is found in a fan shape above and behind the ear, and it runs down to the jaw, which it both closes and retracts. This means it is used greatly by all wind players for embouchure. It is involved in all jaw-joint problems and can cause temporal headaches and cranial faults.

M Heart and Lung.

HP H-9 and Lv-1. H-9 is on the nailbed of the little finger. Hold it with Lv-1 which is on the corner of the nailbed of the big toe, on the side nearest the other toes.

N Vitamins E and B6.

E Nervous/restful, unwilling/willing, depressed/cheerful, confused/confident, bitter/forgiving.

BF Hornbeam and water violet.

Muscles of the neck

Neck flexors *(Sterno-cleido mastoid* and *scalenes)*
Neck extensors *(Semispinalis* and *splenius)*

Sterno-cleido mastoid (SCM). The SCM and scalenes together are called the 'neck flexors'. The SCM is the bar-shaped muscle which runs from just below and behind your ears, to the middle two ends of your collar bones. It becomes very prominent when you turn your head against resistance, or lift your head against gravity when you are lying down. It is strongly assisted by the *Scalenes* through which the nerves for the arm pass on their way from the spine. The scalenes are found at a deeper level and

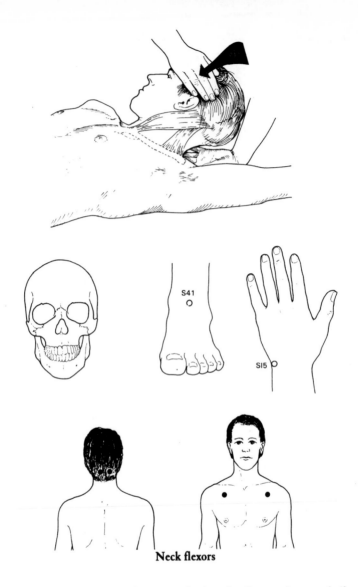

Neck flexors

further back than SCM, and are attached to the first and second ribs. Apart from pulling the head and neck forward, these muscles are used as auxiliary breathing muscles when there are breathing problems (as in asthma, when the normal breathing muscles are in spasm) or when you need to breathe very deeply. They account for the high-chested and forward head position of many wind and string players, because they can become over-

258

developed or over-contracted through poor breathing habits or from holding a violin or viola too tightly. This causes neck pain, headaches, shoulder pain and collar-bone pain. There may also be tinnitus, vertigo or visual problems, heartburn and constipation or diarrhoea. They are badly
affected by any allergy or mental or physical stress, by a 'crick in the neck'
from sleeping on strange/wrong pillows, or any kind of whiplash injury
from even minor traffic accidents. These are hazards for any freelance
player who drives a lot. Pain can also be 'referred' to the neck from digestive or other internal organ malfunction. One very surprising cause of
neck-muscle weakness is over-tight shoes, where the toes are pressed hard
against the front of the shoe, or from high-heeled shoes, which have the
same effect as far as the toes are concerned. Other symptoms might
include slowness, tiredness, possible low blood-sugar, easy bruising and
cold hands.

TP Lie face up with the chin tucked in and the hands above the
shoulders. The head is raised and pressure is placed on the forehead
to push it back to the table. To test one side at a time, lift and turn
the head 45°. Pressure is then applied to the uppermost temple to
push the head directly back to the table. Watch that the Testee does
not try to turn or twist the chin, to change the angle, to recruit other
muscles. When pressing down, the Tester's other hand is placed
under the head, not touching it, but to break the fall if the muscle is
weak, rather than banging the head down on the table. Extreme
weakness means the Testee will be unable to hold the head up at all.
To isolate the scalenes, turn the head 10° only, and test with pressure
from the little finger side of the Tester's hand on the forehead above
the eye, straight back to the table (and not in line with the 10° turn).
Watch that the Testee doesn't try to turn the head further to recruit
extra SCM strength. If these muscles are weak, also test the pectorals
and trapezius.

A Neck extensors.

M Stomach.

MP (1) The second space down from the collar bone between the
ribs, in line with the nipples. (2) Either side of the spine at the very
top of the neck (C2 lamina).

HP (1) On the side of the jaw directly under the outer corner of the eye. (2) Acu-points S-41 and SI-5. S-41 is on the top of the foot at the centre of the ankle crease. Hold it at the same time as SI-5 which is on the side of the wrist, on the bump at the end of the forearm bone and below the little finger.

N Since these muscles seem to have associations with the drainage system for the head and sinuses, it is important to check for airborne or food sensitivities or allergies if there is constant muscle weakness. Eating seafood which contains iodine will help, but for general congestion problems all the B vitamins are needed, especially B3 and B6. Yoghurt may help, but otherwise cut down on all dairy products to lessen mucus formation generally. Increase non-dairy sources of calcium, magnesium, manganese and zinc; vitamin E face-cream spread over the area is said to help.

S Mung bean sprouts and cinnamon.

E Unwilling/willing, irritated/tranquil, hard/adaptable, confused/confident, rebellious/accepting, defeated/successful, nervous/restful, insecure/secure.

BF Willow.

Semispinalis and Splenius. These muscles are the neck extensors which hold the head up and back against gravity, and are the upper part of the complicated system of cross-hatching of muscles which supports the entire spine at the back. *Semispinalis* and *splenius* contract when you look up at the ceiling over your head. In holding up the head, which is the heaviest

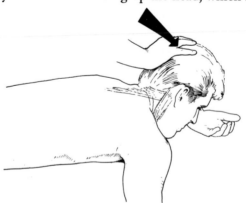

Neck extensors

260

part of your body and furthest from the ground, muscles in this group have to fight gravity and tire easily when you are constantly looking down at a keyboard or holding a stringed instrument. They cramp when holding up the head for a highly held wind or brass instrument, particularly in brass-band parades. Good coordination between all the neck muscles is vital to your sense of balance, because they govern how you hold your head.

TP The Testee lies face down with both arms above the head. The head is then raised off the table, and pressure is put on the back of the head to push it back down to the table. To test one side at a time, turn the head towards the side to be tested and put pressure on the head above the ear to push the head to the table. Watch for sideways bending to recruit other muscles and, as with the neck flexors, it is kinder to place your hand between the head and table. Other muscles to check if this is weak: Pectoralis major clavicular (PMC) and Upper trapezius.

A Neck flexors.

M Stomach.

MP As for neck flexors.

HP As for neck flexors.

N As for neck flexors.

S Bay leaves.

E and BF As for neck flexors.

CHAPTER 12

Muscles of the shoulder, upper arm and elbow

Muscles of the shoulder, upper arm and elbow

The muscles in this chapter and the next are probably the most important in the book to musicians as a whole, and string and keyboard players in particular.

Muscles of the Shoulder

Muscles which raise the shoulders *(Upper trapezius* and *Levator scapulae)*

Muscles which rotate the shoulders *(Subscapularis, Infraspinatus, Teres major* and *Teres minor)*

Muscles which draw the shoulders down *(Lower trapezius)*

(Latissimus dorsi also performs this function. See under back muscles)

Muscles which draw the shoulders back and together *(Rhomboids* and *Middle trapezius)*

Upper trapezius. This muscle is the upper division of the big, kite-shaped muscle on the back. It is attached from the nape of the neck and all the neck vertebrae, out to the shoulder tip, and is attached to the shoulder-blades behind, and the outer end of the collar-bone, and gives the slant to the top of the shoulder. It raises the shoulder girdle and bends the neck to one side, while turning the head to the other side. Right and left work against each other to hold the head centrally between the shoulders. By far the most common problems occur when the shoulders are raised because of stress. The pull of the upper trapezius on the back of the skull affects the balance of ear, eye and hand in relation to the body, and constricts some of the blood supply to the head, leading to blurred vision or ear problems and making it hard to think clearly. It is also often developed one sidedly through holding upper stringed instruments and flute, or always carrying the instrument case or handbag in one hand or on one shoulder. Weakness both sides causes a hunched upper back and forward head position (as often occurs post-menopausally in women). This causes upper back pain and neck pain as the trapezius tries to compensate and hold the head up.

TP The Testee sits and tilts the head to bring the back of the ear

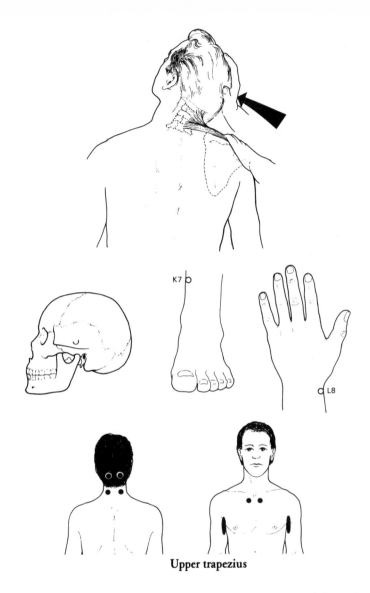

K7

L8

Upper trapezius

towards the shoulder. Pressure is put on the shoulder and the side of the head to prise them apart. Other muscles to test if there is weakness: *levator scapulae,* neck flexors and extensors, *rhomboids* and *pectorals.*

A The trapezius on the other shoulder.

MP (1) The top three inches of the front of the upper arm in the groove between the muscles. (2) Up against the skull at the top of the neck. (3) Between the second and third ribs next to the breastbone. (4) One inch either side of the most prominent bone at the base of the neck on the back.

M Kidney.

HP (1) Half-way between the corner of the eye and the top of the ear. (2) Acu-points K-7 and L-8. K-7 can be located by measuring a spot one hand's width above the ankle bone on the inside of the shin. Hold it at the same time as L-8 which is on the very end of the forearm bone under the thumb.

N Increase intake of foods rich in vitamins A and B, calcium and iron. Abstain from caffeinated drinks and foods containing oxalic acid, such as rhubarb, purple fruits and chocolate.

S Some grains and cooking oils, soya products and pineapple.

E Unwilling/willing, insecure/secure, doubtful/certain, guilty/innocent, irresponsible/responsible, irritable/agreeable.

BF Scleranthus.

Levator scapulae. This muscle runs from the top four bones in the neck to the top inner corner of the shoulder-blade. It lifts the shoulder-blade and draws it towards the spine. It reacts badly to stress, being part of the 'shoulders-up-by-your-ears' syndrome, and causes headaches, stiff neck and sore shoulders. When it is very weak the shoulder-blade can't be drawn in towards the spine, so the *upper trapezius* has to take over and creates pain at the top of the shoulder. Persistent weakness may need a chiropractic or osteopathic adjustment of the neck.

TP The Testee is seated. The elbow is fully bent and pulled down till it is touching the top of the hip, slightly back from the centre. Hold the top of the shoulder down towards the hip, whilst pulling the elbow away out to the side. This position removes as much recruitment of upper trapezius and rhomboids as possible. Other muscles to test if it's weak: *rhomboids, trapezius, latissimus dorsi, pectoralis major clavicular* and neck muscles.

A *Trapezius* and neck extensors.

MP (1) In the corner, just under where the collar-bone and

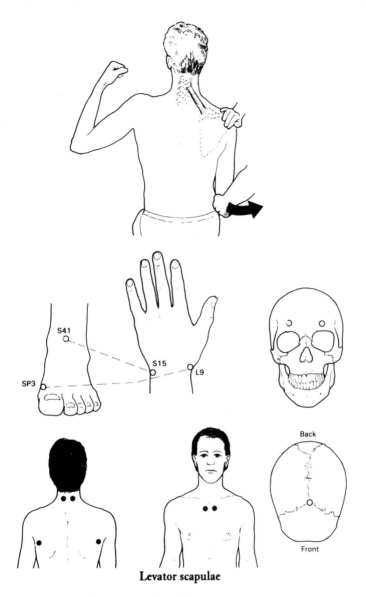

Levator scapulae

breastbone meet. (2) Either side of the most prominent vertebra at the base of the back of the neck. (3) On the outer border of the shoulder-blade, level with the armpit, when the arms are by the sides.

M Stomach or lung.

HP (1) Above the centre of each eye, half way between the eyebrows and normal hairline (2) Anterior fontanel – the spot one thumb's width back from the vertex of the head. (3) Acu-points S-41 and SI-5. S-41 is on top of the foot in the centre of the ankle crease. Hold it together with SI-5 which is on the little finger side of the wrist at the end of the forearm bone. Alternatively use L-9 and Sp-3. L-9 is at the base of the thumb on the outside of the wrist crease. Hold it together with Sp-3 which is on the heel side of the big joint at the base of the big toe.

N This muscle becomes weak if there is acid disturbance in the stomach. Avoid eating when stressed, and chew food very well. Avoid sugary foods as snacks just before a meal, and increase vitamin B intake.

S Sawdust and wood pulp products.

E confused/confident, left out/included, unwilling/willing, irritated/tranquil, nervous/restful, haughty/meek, restless/calm, intolerant/understanding.

BF Willow or mimulus.

Subscapularis. The name of this muscle means 'under the shoulder-blade' which is where it is. The nearest you can get to it is to feel the lower inner edge of the shoulder-blade where it is attached. The other end is attached to the upper arm just below the shoulder joint. It pulls the upper arm in and down, when it is raised above the shoulder, and allows the shoulder blade to glide over the ribcage. It also helps to hold the upper arm in the shoulder joint. Symptoms that can be associated with its weakness are difficulty in raising the arm, difficulty combing your hair, easy dislocation in very loose-jointed people (as musicians often are), shoulder or chest pain and palpitations, bleeding gums, dizziness, low blood-sugar, cold shivers and itchy, runny nose, tender shins and hiatal hernia. It is involved in the 'down bow' stroke of all string players, and especially 'cellists.

TP (1) The Testee sits, raises the arm to 90° out to the side, and the elbow is bent to 90°, so that the forearm hangs down. The Tester stands behind the Testee and stabilises the shoulder, while pushing the wrist straight forward and up. (2) The Testee lies face down with the arm out to the side 90°, and hanging off the edge of the

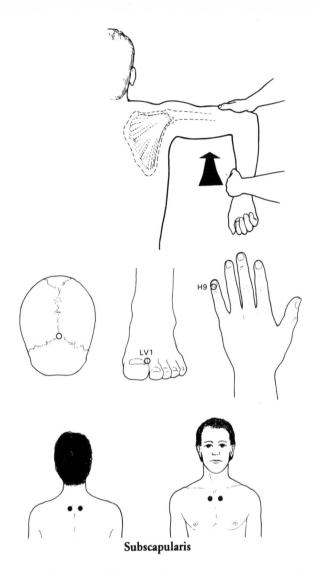

Subscapularis

table at the elbow. Stabilise the elbow as you push the wrist away
from the feet.

A *Infraspinatus.*

MP (1) Between the second and third rib next to the breastbone.

(2) Between the second and third ribs either side of the spine.

M Heart.

HP (1) Anterior fontanel, a spot one thumb's width back from the vertex of the head. (2) Acu-points Lv-1 and H-9. Lv-1 is found on the inside of the nailbed of the big toe. Hold it together with H-9 which is on the nailbed of the little finger.

N Increase intake of calcium and vitamins E and B complex.

E Nervous/restful, irresponsible/responsible, unwilling/willing, confused/confident, unfulfilled/fulfilled, repulsive/acceptable, upset/calm.

BF Hornbeam.

Infraspinatus. This muscle is found on the back of the shoulder-blade beneath its horizontal ridge. Like *subscapularis* it is one of the four muscles which hold the upper arm into the shoulder joint. Very often it shares a common tendon with *teres minor*, to which it has a similar action. It is most active when the arm is raised above horizontal. It is partly used to hold the arm up. With *coracobrachialis*, it is used in order to produce the correct playing position for the upper strings and harp. It acts as an antagonist partner to *subscapularis* in the right arm for all string players. Weakness may manifest as elbow, wrist and shoulder difficulties. Hyperactivity, irritability, and digestive disturbance often accompany weakness in this muscle, and because of its meridian association, it seems to be an indicator of thymus and thyroid function. When these are not on top form there may be hyper-activity and irritability, weight change, unwarranted or uncontrolled crying, sweating, getting out of breath, cold, chapped hands, redness around the eyes, dizziness, or a sluggish feeling that makes it hard to get out of bed in the morning.

TP The Testee sits with arm raised to 90° and the elbow bent at 90° with the forearm vertical. Pressure is put on the back of the wrist to rotate the upper arm forward and downward towards the feet (and even beyond). If the shoulder-blade moves, do the test lying down where the Testee's weight will prevent it from moving. Watch for any attempt to move the arm in or out to recruit other muscles because of weakness. Other muscles to test if weak: *teres minor, supraspinatus, upper* and *middle trapezius,* and *rhomboids.*

A *Supraspinatus.*

MP (1) Between the fifth and sixth ribs near the breastbone on the right chest wall. (2) Just above the lowest ribs on either side of the

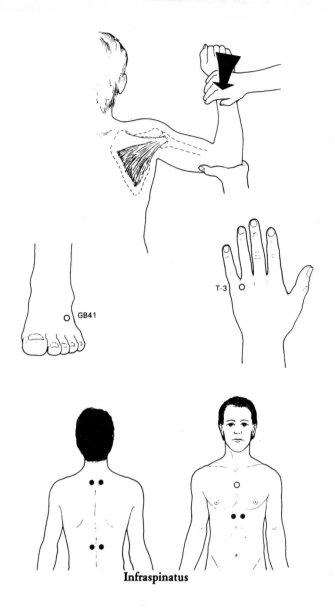

Infraspinatus

spine. (3) Either side of the spine between the second and third ribs.
M Triple warmer.
HP The Angle of Louis, which is the ridge found about three finger widths down from the top of the breastbone. 2. Acu-points GB-41 and Tw-3: GB-41 is found on the top of the foot, about halfway

between the ankle crease and the base of the fourth and fifth toes. Hold this with Tw-3 which is in a similar position on the back of the hand.

N Vitamin B complex and calcium. This muscle also responds to foods high in natural iodine such as seafoods and seaweed. Poppyseed and tarragon are also beneficial. Avoid cheese, bananas and oats and, if taking vitamin A for some other reason, check that you haven't overdone it (see Chapters 6 and 15).

S Soy products, cabbage and all peas and beans, and cedar products.

E Unwilling/willing, grouchy/agreeable, unjust/just, confused/confident, defensive/listening.

BF Mustard.

Teres minor. This muscle runs from halfway up the outer edge of the shoulder-blade to the back of the arm. It draws the upper arm in towards the body, and turns the arm outward at the same time. It is often joined by a common tendon to *infraspinatus,* and has a similar action. It also opposes *subscapularis* and is one of the muscles which holds the upper arm into the shoulder joint. It is most used by pianists playing at the extreme ends of the keyboard, and by the 'underhand' method of bowing used by some bass players. Weakness can cause, or add to, shoulder, elbow and wrist problems, and can refer pain to the pelvic bones on which you sit. Its meridian connection with the Triple Warmer and thyroid mean that weakness may be accompanied by overwrought crying.

TP The Testee sits with arms by the side and elbow bent at 90°, palm in. Support and stabilise the elbow against the body whilst pushing the back of the wrist across the body. Make sure there is no twisting to use other muscles such as *triceps.* Other muscles to test, if weak: *infraspinatus, trapezius* and *rhomboids.*

A *Subscapularis.*

MP (1) Between the second and third ribs next to the breastbone. (2) Between the second and third ribs on the back, next to the spine and level with the top of the shoulder-blades.

M Triple Warmer

HP (1) Just in the hair-line halfway between the corner of the eye and where the top of the ear meets the head. (2) In the dip above

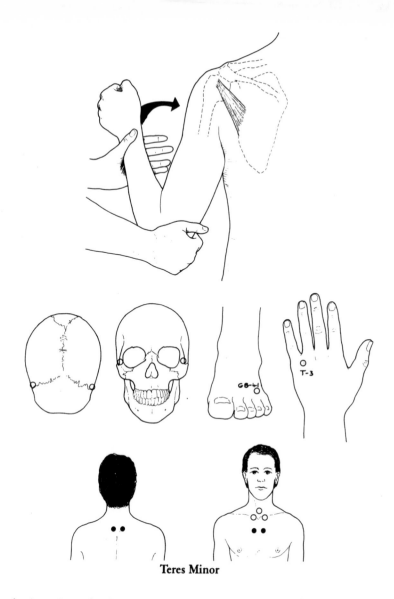

Teres Minor

the junction of collar-bones and breastbone. (3) Acu-points GB-41 and Tw-3. GB-41 is found on the top of the foot, half-way between the base of the fourth toe and the ankle. Hold it at the same time as Tw-3 which is on the back of the hand half-way between the base of the ring finger and the wrist.

N This muscle can also be an indicator of thyroid function,

therefore foods containing organic iodine, such as sea food and seaweed, help. Use honey rather than sugar, and eat millet.
E Unwilling/willing, unworthy/worthy, confused/confident, lack of respect/ respected.
BF Mustard.

Teres major. This muscle runs from the bottom corner of the shoulder-

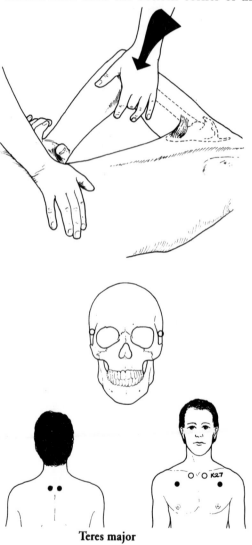

Teres major

274

blade to the top front of the arm, so it draws the arm in to the body, rotates the arm inward and pulls it back slightly behind the body, near the shoulder-blade. It is most often used by women doing up their bra strap behind their back, and by bassoonists to position the lower hand, where it may cramp if the finger spread is too great, or the instrument is held too tightly. It is also very important in 'frozen shoulder' syndromes. It may be the cause of shoulder-blade pain.

TP (1) The Testee sits and places a fist on the back of the pelvis while pushing the elbow backwards. The shoulder is stabilised, while the elbow is pushed forward by the Tester. (2) The Testee lies face down and the arm is bent back to place a closed fist on the back of the pelvis. Pressure is placed on the elbow to push it to the floor, while stabilising the opposite shoulder to prevent body rock. Take care not to overpower the Testee. Other muscles to test, if weak: *middle trapezius* and *rhomboids*.

A *Teres minor.*

MP & **HP** As for *teres minor.*

N As for *teres minor.* If food seems tasteless, add foods containing zinc and vitamin E to the diet rather than more salt.

E Confused/confident, separated/united.

BF As for *teres minor.*

Middle and *lower trapezius.* There are also two lower divisions of the kite-shaped trapezius muscle found on the back. The middle division runs from the top five vertebrae of the back, out to the ridge in the middle of each shoulder-blade. It holds the shoulder-blade in to the centre of the body and turns its outer end down. The lower division runs from the next six vertebrae down the back, out to the ridge in the middle of the shoulder-blade, so that it rotates it, draws it in or stabilises it, also keeping the mid-spine upright. These muscles are often involved in shoulder and arm problems in general, but most particularly in one-sided use and mid-back problems, as they will be stretched differently with unevenly developed shoulders in upper strings. This pulls the spine out of alignment, causes a round-shouldered posture and caved-in upper chest. This complaint is frequently suffered ·by many musicians (especially upper strings, oboe, and any small manual keyboard player such as harpsichord), and anyone who has to sit for

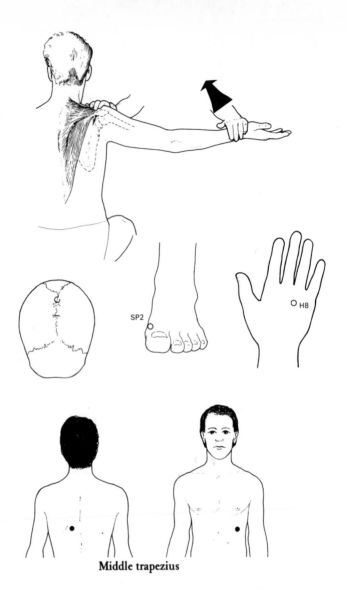

SP2

H8

Middle trapezius

hours on a chair with a sloping back seat. Weakness in these muscles is associated with poor spleen function, sore throats and hearing loss, anaemia and other blood disorders, headache or ache behind the eyes.

TP *Middle trapezius* The Testee sits and raises the arm 90° to the side and level with the floor, and with palm up. The shoulder is stabilised while the upper-arm is pushed forward. *Lower trapezius*

(1) The Testee sits with the arm raised to the side another 45°
beyond horizontal, with palm in towards the head. The Tester
stands behind the Testee, stabilises the shoulder and pushes the
upper arm forward. (2) The Testee is lying face down with arm
raised to 45° away from the head, palm in, and the Tester stabilises
the opposite hip while pushing the upper arm to the floor. In all
cases, the upper-arm is being used as a lever via the shoulder-blade,
to test the muscle. Other muscles to test if either division is weak:
anterior serratus, pectoralis major clavicular (PMC), upper trapezius
and *levator scapulae.*

A All three pectorals and *latissimus dorsi.*

MP (1) Between the seventh and eighth ribs on the left, just below the
level of the end of the breastbone (or for women, just under the bra
cup wire). (2) On the back, on the left side of the spine between the
seventh and eighth ribs, level with the bottom of the shoulder-blades.

M Spleen.

HP (1) At the mid-line of the head, directly above the back of the
ears. (2) Acu-points Sp-2 and H-8. Sp-2 is found on the inside
of the foot, on the nail side of the joint at the base of the big toe.
Hold it together with H-8, which is on the palm of the hand,
on the crease below the little and ring fingers, between the palm
bones.

N Buckwheat and foods high in vitamin C and calcium.

E Nervous/restful, hating/affectionate, unwilling/willing,
tongue-tied/expressive.

BF Mimulus.

Rhomboids (major and minor). These muscles are short, powerful and so
close together that they help each other. They join the inner edge of the
shoulder-blade to the spine in the upper back, and draw the shoulder-
blades together. They also help counterbalance the weight of any instrument held in front of the body, keeping the player upright by stabilising the
back of the shoulder girdle, together with the *trapezius.* They help the posture of a pianist playing at both outer ends of the keyboard at once. Most
problems occur with one-sided development (as in upper strings), having
the effect of pulling the upper spine to one side chronically, causing one

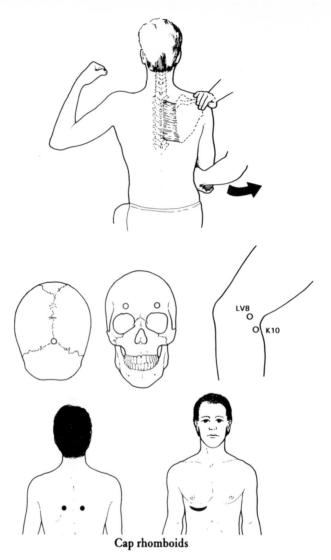

Cap rhomboids

rhomboid to be flaccid and weak, and the other one to be tense and in spasm. Weakness generally causes pain between the shoulder-blades, and a sore lower neck. Other symptoms may include water retention, cold hands and feet.

TP The Testee sits, bends the elbow maximally so that the hand is at the shoulder *not* on the chest wall (the other arm being raised above the shoulder to prevent recruitment). The shoulder is

278

stabilised and the upper arm pulled away from the body to the side. Watch that the shoulders are level. If the rhomboid is weak, the shoulder-blade will pull away from the spine as you test. Other muscles to test, if weak: the other rhomboid, *upper trapezius, levator scapulae, anterior deltoid, latissimus dorsi* and the pectorals.

A Pectorals.

MP (1) Between the fifth and sixth rib spaces on the chest wall, one rib space down from the nipple. (2) Between the fifth and sixth rib space next to the spine. Authorities vary as to whether left or both sides need working on – if both are tender, do both.

M Liver.

HP (1) Anterior fontanel – a spot one thumb's width back from the vertex of the head. (2) Frontal eminencies – above the centre of each eye between the eyebrow and the hairline. (3) Acu-points Lv-8 and K-10. Lv-8 is found in between the lower, inner end of the thighbone, and the hamstring tendon near the inner knee crease. K-10 is almost next door, at the innermost end of the knee crease when the knee is bent.

N The association of this muscle is with the liver and stomach, so avoid fizzy drinks, all forms of caffeine, and all foods that are rich, fatty or fried. Increase intake of foods high in vitamins A, B, kelp and zinc, garlic and parsley.

E Confused/confident, fearful/courageous, unwilling/willing, squeamish/settled, nervous/restful, unsociable/sociable, frustrated/satisfied, obligated/willing, unsupportive/supportive.

BF Agrimony.

Muscles of the Upper Arm

Muscles which raise the upper arm *(Supraspinatus* and *Deltoids)*
Muscles which draw the upper arms forward and together *(the three Pectorals* and *Coracobrachialis)*

Supraspinatus. This is the last of the four muscles which hold the upper arm into the shoulder joint. It is found above the horizontal bar on the shoulder-blade, and therefore only has a mechanically weak lifting action on the arm from hanging by the side to about 15° away from the body. Any

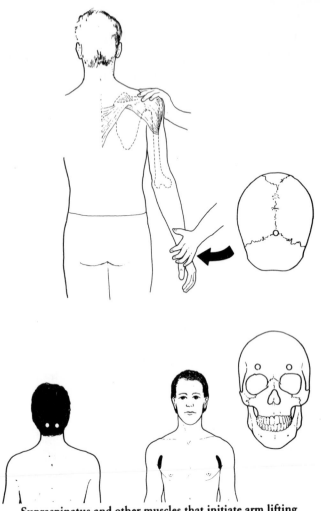

Supraspinatus and other muscles that initiate arm lifting

lifting of the arm beyond 15° is done by the *deltoid* group. It has no special significance on its own to musicians, other than prevention of dislocation. However, weakness causes shoulder pains. Because of its meridian association, hard mental work, driving and emotional stress seem to fatigue it. It is also often weak in children who are slow learners.

TP The Testee sits with head turned away from the muscle being tested to inactivate the *trapezius* as far as possible. The straight arm is taken out to the side and forward about 15°, palm in and thumb forward. Pressure is put on the back of the wrist to push the arm back to the groin. Watch that the shoulder is not raised, nor the spine twisted to recruit other muscles. Other muscles to test, if weak: *deltoids, upper trapezius,* and the pectorals.

A *Teres major* and *coracobrachialis.*

MP (1) Under the outer end of the collar-bone, just inside the shoulder joint and down along the chest wall for about four inches (10cm.). (2) As high as you can right up under the skull at the top of the neck, either side of the spine.

M Central.

HP Anterior fontanel and frontal eminencies together: that is, one thumb's width back from the vertex of the head, with the two points over the centre of each eye, half-way between eyebrows and hairline.

N Foods high in lecithin such as soya products. Avoid high-fat, high-sugar foods, and over-the-counter drugs containing adrenaline and cortisol, unless prescribed by a doctor.

E Confused/confident, unsuccessful/successful, difficult/easy.

Deltoids, middle, anterior and *posterior.* The *deltoids* are the group of muscles which join the upper arm to the shoulder like a hinge. They spread all the way round the point of the shoulder like epaulettes. They are extremely strong, and because they wrap around the arm, they lift the arm forward *(anterior deltoid),* sideways *(middle deltoid)* and backwards *(posterior deltoid).* This means that the front and back divisions work against each other when swinging the arms, but together as a group for side lifts. In all instrumental playing these muscles are used actively to raise the arms, or passively as upper-arm stabilisers to allow lateral forearm movement. Typical signs of weakness are an inability to place your hand in your back pocket; shoulder or upper arm pain when you sleep or lie on it; or a rolling, unbalanced gait because there is no counter-balancing arm swing as you walk. Because of meridian associations, weakness may be accompanied by chronic colon malfunction and pains, myopia and light-sensitivity, arthritis or itchy palms.

TP The Testee sits or stands with the arm raised 90° to the side and with the elbow bent 90° so the forearm is horizontal. Take care

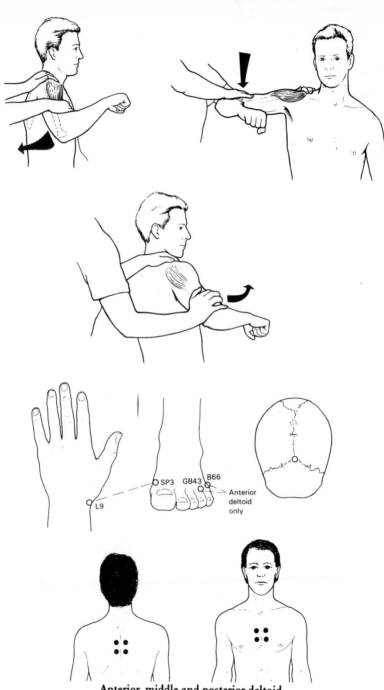

SP3 GB43 B66
L9 Anterior deltoid only

Anterior, middle and posterior deltoid

282

when stabilising the shoulder. Hold it firmly near the neck, or stabilise the opposite shoulder, to avoid touching the muscle being tested and to stop body rotation. To test *Middle deltoid*, the shoulder is stabilised and the elbow is pushed straight in towards the body. To test the *Anterior deltoid*, the upper arm is brought forward five degrees and the forearm is raised another 5°. The Tester stabilises the shoulder joint while pulling the upper arm back and slightly down. To test the *Posterior deltoid*, the upper arm is now retracted 5° and the forearm lowered 5°, the shoulder stabilised and pressure is applied to bring the upper arm forward and slightly down.

MP (1) Between the third, fourth and fifth ribs either side of the breastbone. (2) In between the shoulder-blades against the spine (between third to fifth ribs).

M Lung.

HP (1) Anterior fontanel, found one thumb's width back from the vertex of the head. (2) Acu-points Sp-3 and L-9. Sp-3 is on the heel side of the big joint at the base of the big toe. Hold it at the same time as L-9 which is on the outside of the wrist crease at the base of the thumb. You may also try (3) Acu-points B-66 and GB-43. B-66 is on the outside of the foot at the base of the little toe. Hold it together with GB-43, which is next door at the base of the fourth toe.

N Vitamins A, B1, B6 magnesium, potassium, zinc, calcium, lecithin, figs and mushrooms, cayenne, garlic and parsley.

S Cotton.

E Unwilling/willing, shy/bold, nervous/restful, useless/useful, unsociable/sociable, incapable/capable, unresponsive/responsive, unfulfilled/fulfilled, confused/confident, hopeless/trusting, forsaken/accepted.

BF Water violet.

The Pectorals: PMC, PMS and P.Minor. These muscles are all found on the front of the chest in a fan shape, just under the collar bone. They all bring the shoulder forward to a round-shouldered position when they are contracted. Spasm frequently occurs when holding a violin or viola too tightly against the upper chest.

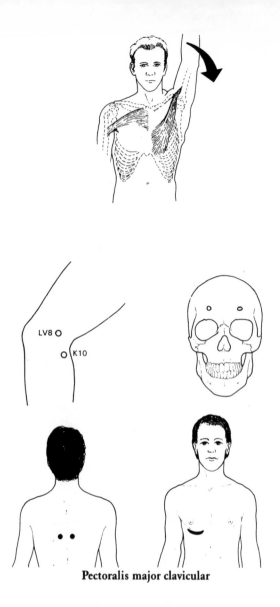

Pectoralis major clavicular

Pectoralis major clavicular (PMC) runs from the upper part of the breast-bone and the collar-bone, across the armpit, to the upper arm. It pulls the arm inwards and up towards the opposite ear.

Pectoralis major sternal (PMS) runs from the breastbone below PMC and joins it on the upper arm. It pulls the arm in and down. The right PMC

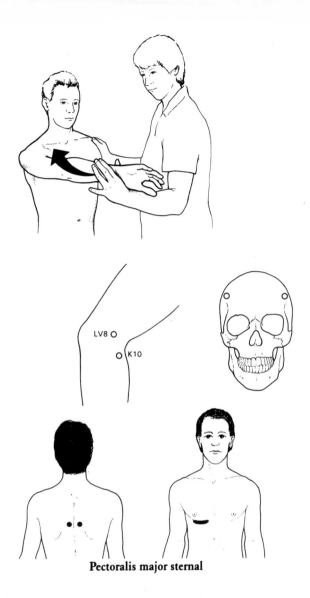

LV8

K10

Pectoralis major sternal

and PMS are therefore some of the main muscles used in moving the upper arm in bowing by all string players, but particularly upper strings, and for crossing arms in all keyboard instruments.

Pectoralis minor runs under PMC and PMS in the opposite direction and joins a small extension of the shoulder-blade, found just under the collar-

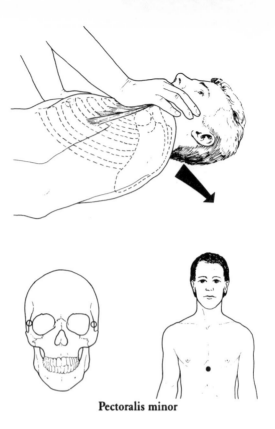

Pectoralis minor

bone, to the upper ribcage. Because it is a deep muscle, the nerves and blood vessels to the arm, and the main body lymph drainage systems, are often affected by its malfunction. A sure sign of congestion is if you often wake with your arms above your head. This is your body's way of trying to clear the problem, but it can also cause shoulder-joint pain. Because it is attached to the ribs, this muscle is also one of the extra breathing muscles, used when there is a breathing problem such as asthma, or when a sharp, hard intake of breath is required of a wind or brass player in a very long musical phrase.

All the pectorals are used to stabilise the shoulder and hold up the upper arms, which hold up all wind and brass instruments. Be aware, also, that although pain in this area may be due to muscle tension, it could also be due to heart or lung problems. If you are in any doubt, go and see your GP; better safe than sorry!

TP *PMC, PMS* Testee sits or stands, the straight arm is raised 90° to the front, so that it is horizontal, and then the arm is turned so that the palm faces outwards and the thumb points to the floor. The other shoulder is stabilised. For *PMC* the Tester pushes the arm down and out; for *PMS* the arm is pushed up and out. *P. Minor* The shoulder is pulled forward and the straight arm is held across the body towards the opposite knee. The opposite shoulder is stabilised, while the straight arm is pulled out and up towards the shoulder being tested. Alternatively, the Testee lies face up with the shoulder raised up off the table and down towards the hip. The opposite shoulder is stabilised while the Tester pushes the front of the shoulder back down to the table, making sure the direction of push comes as if from the opposite hip. Other muscles to test if weak: *Middle trapezius, latissimus dorsi.*

P. Minor At the lowest end of the breastbone, in the upturned V where it joins the ribs. There are no points on the back.

A *Rhomboids* and *trapezius.*

MP *PMC, PMS* (1) Under the left nipple between the fifth and sixth ribs on the chest wall. (2) Either side of the spine at the level of the fifth and sixth ribs, level with half-way down the shoulder-blade.

M *PMC* Stomach; *PMS* Liver.

HP *PMC* (1) Frontal eminences over the centre of each eye, and midway between the eyebrows and the hair line. (2) Acu-points S-41 and SI-5. S-41 is on the top middle front of the ankle in a small dip. Hold it with SI-5 which is on the side of the wrist below the little finger, on the end of the forearm bone (ulnar nerve).

PMS (1) In the hairline above the outer corner of each eye. (2) Acu-points Lv-8 and K-10. Lv-8 is in the dip on the inside of the knee joint between the extreme end of the thigh-bone and the hamstring tendon. Hold it with K-10 which is almost nextdoor at the inside end of the knee crease, when the knee is bent.

P. Minor On the temple about 1 inch back from the outer corner of the eye.

N *PMC* This muscle reacts very badly to an upset stomach and mental stress. Don't eat when upset and don't drink caffeinated tea, coffee and coke. Avoid sugar, the digestion of which will drain the body's store of B vitamins, so much needed to combat mental stress. Replace it with 'slow release' carbohydrates such as whole grains. Increase intake of all foods that contain vitamin B, garlic and parsley. Avoid any food or drug that gives you a skin rash.

PMS Long lasting headaches and photo phobia, spots in front of the eyes and 'liverishness' all contribute to a weak PMS, so avoid fatty and fried foods, fizzy drinks, caffeinated tea and coffee and alcohol. Eating liver and foods high in vitamins A, B6, B12, and E, zinc, apple cider vinegar and rosehip syrup will help.

P. Minor Foods rich in vitamin B complex, especially B3 and B6, lecithin, zinc and cayenne.

E *PMC* Unwilling/willing, sour/agreeable, confused/confident, abandoned/included, nervous/restful, unappreciated/appreciated.
BF Willow.

PMS Confused/confident, unloved/loved, abandoned/included.
BF Agrimony.

P. Minor Unwilling/willing, fearful/courageous, intolerant/understanding, wrong/understood, nervous/restful, irritated/tranquil, unsuccessful/successful.

Coracobrachialis. This muscle shares the same extension of the shoulder-blade under the collar-bone as *pectoralis minor.* It runs from there to the front of the upper arm, so it draws the upper arm up and in. It comes into play when (a) holding up the right arm near the violin or viola to play pizzicato; or (b) to bow (at the heel of the bow, or in *spiccato*) on the lower strings of violin or viola or the upper cello strings; (c) in playing and tuning the top notes on a harp; (d) holding up a smaller brass instrument. Weakness will cause shoulder pains, difficulty in putting the hand behind the head or combing the hair, and heaviness in the arms during eating, because the arms feel weak and tired. It is associated with insomnia, mouth sores, chronic cough and exertion asthma.

TP The Testee sits, with elbow maximally bent and drawn in across the chest, the hand on top of the shoulder, or beyond it with the palm facing backwards. Support the back of the shoulder as the upper arm is pushed out to the side.
A *Posterior deltoid.*

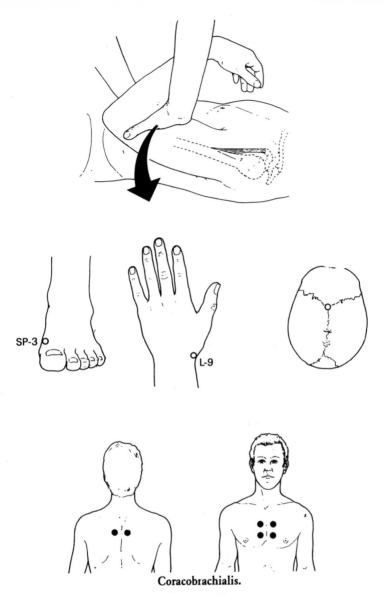

SP-3

L-9

Coracobrachialis.

MP (1) Between the third and fourth ribs, next to the breastbone.
(2) Between the fourth and fifth ribs, either side of the spine
between the shoulder-blades.
M Lung.
HP (1) Anterior fontanel – one thumb's width back from the vertex

of the head. (2) Acu-points Sp-3 and L-9. Sp-3 is on the heel side of the large joint at the base of the big toe. Hold it with L-9, which is at the base of the thumb, at the end of the wrist crease.

N Take plenty of vitamin C, also B3, lecithin, magnesium and manganese.

E Unwilling/willing, disorganised/organised, confused/confident, not needed/needed, upset/calm, nervous/peaceful, forlorn/hopeful.

BF Water violet.

Muscles of the Elbow

Muscles which bend the elbow *(Biceps Brachii, Brachialis* and *Brachioradialis)*

Muscles which straighten the elbow *(Triceps* and *Anconeus)*

Biceps brachii, Brachialis and Brachioradialis. Biceps b. and *Brachialis* are both found on the front of the upper arm and have a similar action. *Biceps b.* runs across two joints, the shoulder and elbow, attaching on the shoulder-blade end with its long tendon and the upper arm with its short tendon and at the other end to the forearm on the thumb side (radius). *Brachialis* runs from the upper arm to the forearm on the little-finger side (ulna). Both flex the elbow and, although not terribly well arranged mechanically for lifting, they have extra strength to make up for any inefficiency. As elbow flexors (together with *brachioradialis)* the uses to which musicians put them are obvious. However, over-practising any one action repeatedly can tire these muscles and/or give you shoulder and elbow problems.

Brachioradialis is attached to the upper arm lower down than the other two, and then runs down the forearm almost to the wrist on the thumb side. This means that it increases the strength of the other upper arm muscles greatly. It is particularly active when quick bursts of energy are required (e.g. a fortissimo up-bow) although it normally only comes into play when you are lifting more than four pounds (two kilos). It can also assist *supinator* and *pronator teres* turning the forearm palm up or palm down. Weakness will make it hard to put your hands up behind your back. There may also be a skin rash on the back of the forearm, or itchy, scaly elbows.

TP For all three, the Testee sits with the arm bent at 60° to 80°,

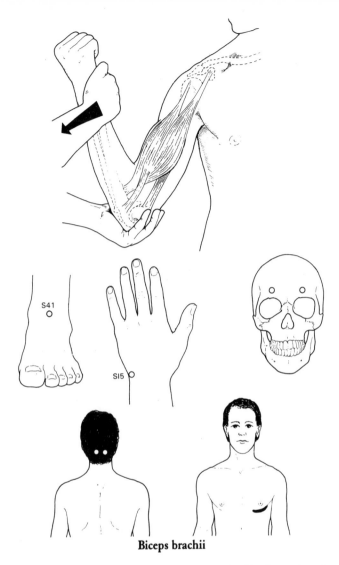

Biceps brachii

elbow in to the side. For *biceps b.* and *brachialis,* the palm should face the shoulder, and for *brachioradialis* it should be facing inward. In all three, the elbow is supported while pressure is put on the forearm to straighten the elbow. Other muscles to test, if weak: *rhomboids, teres major* and *minor, PMC, latissimus dorsi.*

A *Triceps* and *anconeus.*

MP (1) Between the fourth and fifth ribs three inches either side of

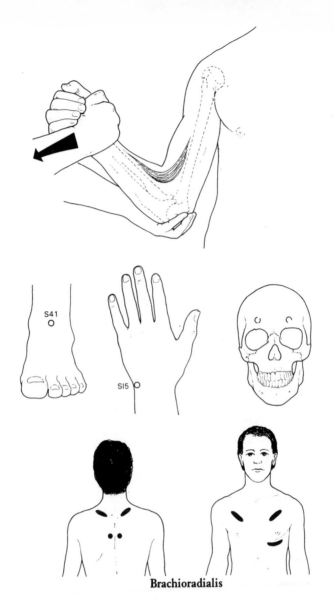

Brachioradialis

the breastbone. (2) Over the entire area of the pectoral muscles. (3) Either side of the very top of the spine, where it meets the skull. (4) Between the fifth and sixth ribs, either side of the spine – level with the middle of the shoulder-blades. (5) Above the central ridge of the shoulder-blade. Not all of these areas may be tender; work on those that are.

M Stomach.

HP (1) Frontal eminences – over the centre of each eye, and half-way between the eyebrows and hairline. (2) Acu-points S-41 and SI-5. S-41 is found on the top of the foot, at the centre of the ankle crease. Hold it with SI-5 which is found at the end of the forearm bone on the little finger side of the wrist.

N These muscles are associated with stomach and intestinal disorders and gluten sensitivity, so go carefully in what you eat. Chew everything very well and avoid any food that makes you feel flushed, and all foods to which you are sensitive, especially white flour and white sugar. Increase intake of foods containing vitamin B complex, zinc, magnesium, iron, potassium and calcium.

S Onions, polyester and foam rubber.

E Self-centred/kind, reclusive/sociable, nervous/peaceful, forsaken/accepted, indignant/empathetic, apprehensive/secure, confused/confident, pressured/desirable, irritated/tranquil, defeated/success, forced/helpful, nauseated/comfortable.

BF Willow.

Triceps brachii and *anconeus.* These muscles are on the back of the upper arm, and work together to straighten the elbow.

Triceps has three heads, two on the upper arm and the long head which goes to the shoulder-blade. The other end is attached to the back of the elbow (ulna).

Anconeus is much smaller and crosses on the outside of the elbow joint, but acts like a fourth division of *triceps,* while stabilising the joint. Because they work against the *biceps* group they are in use as the antagonist 'other half' of many of the same occupations for musicians, especially in bowing, in holding the upper arm so that the forearm and hands are appropriately placed for playing. Weakness of both can cause elbow and shoulder problems, and *triceps* is often blamed for tennis and golfer's elbow. In such situations it is always worth checking *latissimus dorsi,* as weakness there causes *triceps* to overwork. Pain in the back of the arm can also be referred from

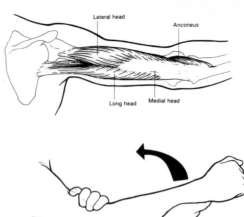

the neck or wrist.

TP (1) These muscles are tested together as their action is similar. The Testee is seated, and the arm extended behind the shoulder. The front of the elbow and upper arm is supported while the forearm is pushed to bend the elbow. (2) The Testee is seated, the elbow slightly flexed. The elbow is supported underneath, while pressure is applied to the back of the wrist to flex the elbow more. Other muscles to test, if weak: *levator scapulae, rhomboids* and *latissimus dorsi.*

A *Biceps* group.

MP (1) Between the seventh and eighth ribs on the left, more central than directly below the nipple. (2) Either side of the spine, between the seventh and eighth ribs, level with the bottom of the shoulder-blades.

M Spleen/Pancreas.

HP (1) On the head just above and behind the ears. (2) Acu-points Sp-2 and H-8. Sp-2 is found on the side of the foot at the nail end of the large joint at the base of the big toe. Hold it with H-8, which is on the palm of the hand in the crease just below the base of the ring finger.

N Avoid sweets and refined sugars. Eat foods high in vitamin A,

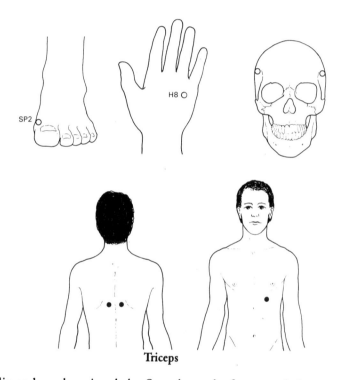

SP2

H8 ○

Triceps

garlic and parsley, zinc, kelp. Strawberry-leaf tea may help.
S Aduki beans, buckwheat, citrus fruits.
E Nervous/peaceful or restful, sorrowful/joyful, pity/grateful, hard/adaptable, confused/confident, helpless/powerful, unwilling/willing, distressed/content, arrogant/listening, futile/assured
BF Mimulus.

CHAPTER 13

Muscles of the forearm, wrist and hand

Muscles of the forearm, wrist and hand

Muscle names explained

The muscles in this chapter look long and complicated. They are not. Do you remember the rule that all the flexors (or joint benders) are attached on or near the inside of the elbow, and all the extensors (or joint straighteners) are attached on or near the outside of the elbow?

Muscle names also tell you what they do. *Palmaris* means 'of the palm', so there's a long muscle that bends the palm. *Supinator* turns the palm up, the *pronators* turn the hand palm down. *Carpi* means 'of the wrist' so there's a muscle for each forearm bone that bends or straightens the wrist. *Pollicis* means 'of the thumb', *indices* means 'of the index finger', and *digitorum* means of the (other) fingers, so you'll never guess what *digiti minimi* means! Some of the smallest muscles have the longest names. *Superficialis* means near the surface, and as they bother to mention that, it seems reasonable to assume there must be a deep one, and there is, the *profundis*. If they bother to say *longus* there must be a *brevis*. Other odd words like *quadratus* describe the shape of the muscle (four sided), or where it is found: *radialis*/on the radius. Simple! This description and demystification is in this chapter because these are less well-known muscles than those in the previous chapter. Yet they are some of the most important of all to all musicians, who may well be put off by long Latin names and give up instead of reading on, learning useful information and helping themselves.

Forearm muscles

> *Supinator*
> *Pronator Teres* and *Quadratus*
> *Palmaris Longus*
> *Flexor carpi* (*radialis* and *ulnaris*)
> *Extensor carpi radialis* (*longus* and *brevis*) and *Extensor ulnaris*

Supinator. This muscle turns the forearm from palm down to palm up. It is located at the elbow joint on the outside, like an extensor. It mostly lies between the upper-arm bone and the forearm bone on the thumb side, but a little slip goes to the other forearm bone too. This muscle is particularly

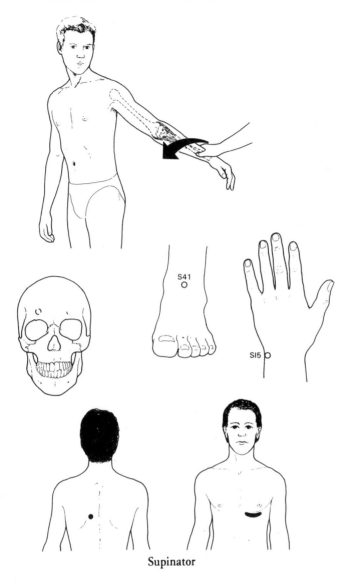

Supinator

used in the right arm by flautists, in the underhand method of bowing used by some bass players, by all upper-string players in the left arm, and in both arms by harmonica players. Spasm can also cause nerve entrapment and referred pain to wrist and shoulder.

TP (1) The Testee sits or stands with the elbow bent and hand palm up. The upper arm is stabilised and the forearm is twisted into

pronation (palm down). However the *biceps* group is very active.
(2) Extend the straight arm behind the body, palm down. Stabilise
the upper arm and twist the forearm palm up. Here the *biceps* group
is elongated and at a disadvantage. Watch for twisting the upper arm
sideways. (3) The Testee bends the elbow and places it over the
same shoulder, palm back. The elbow is stabilised and the forearm
twisted palm front. Do this test gently or *biceps* will come into action
and cramp. Other muscles to test, if weak: *triceps, biceps brachii*.
A *Pronator teres.*
MP (1) Between the fifth and sixth ribs on the left under the breast,
near the breastbone. (2) Between the sixth and seventh ribs either
side of the spine, one rib-space higher than the bottom of the
shoulder-blades.
M Stomach and Small intestine
HP (1) Frontal eminences, which are above the centre of each eye
and between the eyebrows and the hairline. (2) Acu-points S-41 and
SI-4. S-41 is on the top of the foot in the centre of the ankle crease.
Hold it with SI-4, which is on the little-finger side of the wrist at the
end of the forearm bone.
N Eat extra foods that contain vitamin B comlex and B2. May also
need vitamins A, E, garlic and parsley.
E Nervous/restful, compelled/eager
BF Willow and Star of Bethlehem.

Pronator teres and quadratus. These are both muscles which turn the forearm bones so that the palm faces down towards the feet when the elbow is
bent, or behind you if the arm is straight. *P. teres* is at the elbow and crosses the elbow joint on the inside (so it joins the *flexor* group). It twists the
swivel head of the radius against the ulna so the two forearm bones cross.
P. quadratus has a similar though limited effect at the wrist. To twist as far
as possible, both are needed. These muscles are used in most string playing when bowing, particularly at the tip, in pianists playing at extremes of
the keyboard, and in the bassoonist's and guitarist's right forearm and
hand. They can also be involved in carpal tunnel syndrome, because
P. quadratus passes directly over the inside of the wrist. Any cramp will
restrict the space underneath, and can cause referred pain to the elbow and

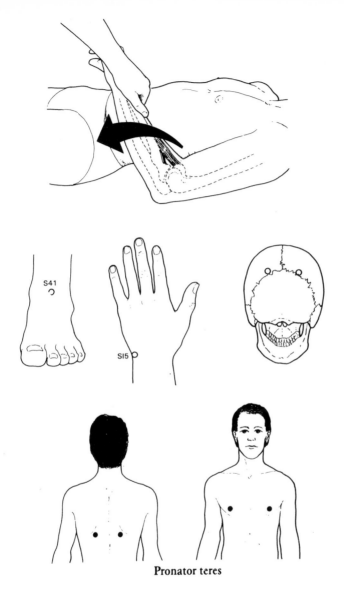

Pronator teres

shoulder as well as wrist. Weak *pronators* can also cause difficulty opening doors and jars, picking up a full cup, and itchy, swollen palms and fingers. They can also cause pain which is often mistaken for tennis or golfer's elbow.

TP The Testee sits or stands. The elbow is bent less than 90° and the palm turned towards the feet. The upper arm is stabilised and the forearm twisted to turn the palm up, away from the feet. To isolate *P. quadratus,* bend the elbow maximally and turn the palm away from the body. The elbow is stabilised and the forearm twisted to face the shoulder. Other muscle to test, if weak: *Brachioradialis.*

A *Supinator.*

MP (1) Between the fourth and fifth ribs behind the nipples, *gently!* (2) Between the eighth and ninth ribs on the back, just below the bottom of the shoulder-blades.

M Stomach.

HP (1) On the back of the head 2.5 inches (4cm) diagonally up and out at 45° from the centre of the top of the neck. (2) Acu-points as for *supinator.*

N There is a meridian association with stomach function here and both respond well to vitamins B2 and B6, with B complex and E. Slippery elm is said to help.

E Unwilling/willing, unaccepted/accepted, nervous/restful, disappointed/satisfied, confused/confident, insecure/secure.

BF Willow.

Palmaris longus, Flexor carpi radialis and *ulnaris.* These are all muscles which bend the wrist, and are all attached to the common flexor tendon on the inside of the elbow. *Palmaris longus* pulls the palm straight to the elbow

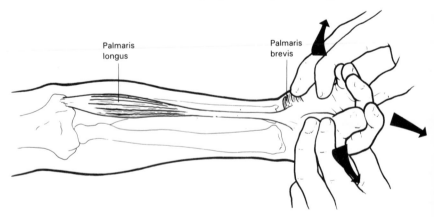

Palmaris longus and brevis

and also crosses the elbow joint, helping to bend that too. Because it is attached to the fibrous band across the inside wrist (the *flexor retinaculum*), it can be involved in Carpal Tunnel syndrome causing pins and needles in the thumb and index finger. *Flexor carpi radialis* flexes the wrist but to the thumb side, by attaching to the index and middle finger bases, and thus pulling on the wrist on one side only. *Flexor carpi ulnaris* pulls on the other side only, because it is attached to the two wrist bones under and including the base of the little finger. All these movements are used in almost all instrumental playing at some time or other as part of wrist flexibility. Weakness leads to weak wrist grasp, wrist, forearm and elbow pain, carpal tunnel and tunnel of Guyon problems, and can be mistaken for golfer's elbow. There is a possible meridian link with diabetes.

TP *Palmaris longus* Testee sits with bent elbow and wrist and cupped palm. The back of the hand is supported with the Tester's thumbs, as the Tester opens and flattens the Testee's palm.

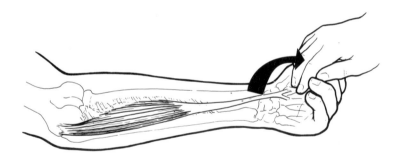

Flexor carpi radialis

Flexor carpi radialis The forearm is supported while the pressure is put on the thumb side of the palm towards straightening the wrist towards the little finger side.

Flexor carpi ulnaris The position is reversed. Pressure is put on the little-finger side of the palm to straighten the wrist towards the thumb side. Other muscles to test, if weak: *supinator, opponens pollicis.*

A Extensors of the wrist.

M *Flexor carpi radialis* Spleen; *Flexor carpi ulnaris* Heart.

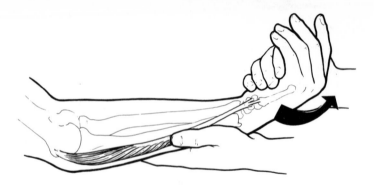

Flexor carpi ulmaris

HP *F.c.radialis* Acu-points are Sp-2 and H-8. Sp-2 is on the nail end of the big joint at the base of the big toe, on the side of the foot. Hold it with H-8, which is on the palm of the hand in the crease under the ring finger.

F.c.ulnaris Acu-points are H-9 and Lv-1. H-9 is on the nailbed of the little finger. Hold it with Lv-1 which is on the inside nailbed of the big toe.

N Vitamin B complex and slippery elm.

E Unwilling/willing, empty/fulfilled, unaccepted/accepted, nervous/restful.

BF Mimulus and hornbeam.

Extensor carpi radialis (longus and *brevis),* and *Extensor carpi ulnaris.* These muscles work as a group to bend the wrist straight back, or singly to bend it back one side only. The *longus* and *brevis* of *extensor carpi radialis* (ECR)

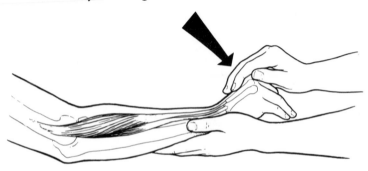

Extensor carpi radialis

lie side by side and can really be considered as one. They run from the outside of the elbow (the extensor tendon that inflames to become tennis elbow), across the forearm to the knuckles of the index and middle fingers.

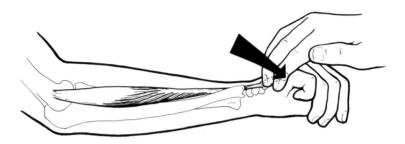

Extensor carpi ulnaris

Extensor carpi ulnaris (ECU) starts in the same place but, as the name implies, stays on the same ulnar side and goes to the knuckle of the little finger. These muscles between them are responsible for the arch of the hand and the ability to move the hand sideways when the forearm is still. They are used in all sorts of bowing techniques in string playing, and reaching and extension in fingering techniques in almost all playing. As a consequence, too much extended and sideways stretching during playing can cause forearm and wrist pains, and tennis elbow, though you never touch a racquet! Because of its meridian association, there may also be itchy skin under the hair, and dizziness if you stand suddenly.

TP The Testee sits with arm extended almost straight on a table, and the wrist extended. The wrist is supported underneath, while pressure is applied to the back of all the knuckles to push the hand to the table. This tests all the extensors together. To test *ECR* alone, the index and middle fingers should be raised highest with a deviation of the hand towards the thumb. Pressure is applied to their knuckles only. To test *ECU* alone, the little finger side of the hand is raised highest and the hand is deviated to the little finger side. Pressure is applied to the back of the little finger knuckle only. Other muscles to test, if weak: *supinator, pronator teres, latissimus dorsi, triceps* and *anconeus.*

A Flexors of the hand.

305

MP Along the back of the forearm from the outside of the elbow to the knuckles.

M Pericardium (Cx.) and Small Intestines, Spleen and Stomach.

HP Cx-9 and Lv-1. Cx-9 is at the end of the middle finger pad on the side nearest the index finger. Hold it with Lv-1 which is on the corner of the nailbed of the big toe, that's nearest the other toes.

N Vitamins A, B5, B6, B complex, E, potassium/iodine, lecithin, cayenne, mustard seed and greens, alfalfa, apricot, banana, nettles and slippery elm, brown rice.

E Unwilling or obligated/willing, frustrated/satisfied, confused/confident, tongue-tied/expressive, nervous/peaceful, unappreciated/appreciated, deceived/truthful, difficult/easy, upset or restless/calm, concerned/trusting.

BF Holly, Star of Bethlehem, Mimulus and Willow.

Long hand muscles

Flexor digitorum (superficialis and *profundis)*
Extensor indices, Extensor digitorum and *Extensor digiti minimi*
Flexor pollicis longus (and *brevis*)
Extensor pollicis longus (and *brevis*)
Abductor pollicis longus (and *brevis*)

It may seem surprising that the strongest muscles of the hand are not located on the hand itself. This is for practical reasons. Large muscle bulk would fill up the palm-space available, and long muscles exert better leverage and so are stronger. The forearm is an obvious place to park them. There are, of course, lots of muscles on the hand, but they are mainly used for light and fine movement and speed, not movements requiring strength of grasp.

Flexor digitorum superficialis and *Flexor digitorum profundis*. These muscles both flex the fingers. *Flexor digitorum superficialis* (FDS) flexes the middle bone and *Flexor digitorum profundis* (FDP) flexes the last bone. Just occasionally, the tendons or nerve supply of one becomes inflamed or squashed by muscle bulk and then the joint it supplies won't work. Weakness of *FDS* decreases grip strength and interferes with finger function, so that the middle bone is flexed but the last one is straight or even

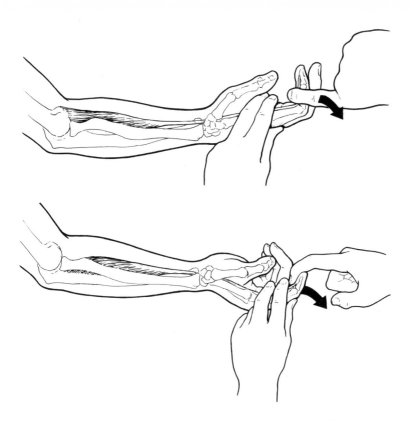

Flexor digitorum superficialis and Flexor digitorum profundis

bent backwards. Weakness of *FDP* means difficulty in flexing the last joint of the finger, which will affect any precision movement, especially intonation and balancing tone on a piano. If finger weakness is not affected by gentle pressure on the base of the palm, half an inch above the wrist crease, then there is no carpal tunnel problem (see Chapter 15). The tendons of both can become subject to nodules on the palm of the hand in both trigger finger and Dupuytren's contracture, which shorten the tendons. Smoothness of finger action is affected, and the palm gradually closes; correction is possible with very delicate surgery. The ring and little fingers of men aged about 40 are most commonly affected. Because of its meridian associations, there may be digestive disorder, nausea and headaches; alcohol or sugar handling difficulty; feeling irritable, or cold and hating draughts; varicose veins, sore gums and easy bruising.

TP *FDS* The Testee is seated, the elbow slightly bent and the knuckle firmly held while the next joint is flexed. Pressure is applied to the middle bone of each finger in turn to straighten it. You can't always isolate the action of the little finger.

FDP Test position is the same but now the middle bone of the finger is held firmly, the last joint flexed, and pressure is put on the finger pad to straighten the finger. Other muscles to test, if weak: *interossei, palmaris longus.*

A Finger extensors.

MP (1) Massage the muscles from inside the elbow to the wrist. (2) Between the seventh and eighth ribs on the left side of the ribcage in the soft cartilage. (3) Either side of the spine, level with the bottom of the shoulder blade.

M Heart.

HP Acu-points H-9 and Lv-1. H-9 is found on the nailbed of the little finger. Hold it with Lv-1 which is on the inside of the nailbed of the big toe.

N Vitamin B6, B12, E, lecithin, potassium/iodine, calcium, alfalfa, banana, nettle, slippery elm, cayenne, strawberry leaf tea, apple cider vinegar, liquorice.

S Turmeric.

E Nervous/peaceful, restless/calm, defeated/successful, unwilling/willing, not needed/needed, confused/confident, sour/agreeable, hungry/full, incapable/understandable, unloved/loved, speechless/communicative, grief for others/fellow feeling, unconcerned/caring, revolting/attractive, undesireable/pleasant.

BF Hornbeam.

Extensor indices, Extensor digitorum and *Extensor digiti minimi.* These muscles all straighten bent fingers. The last two are so close together they almost work as one, except that we can extend each finger separately. They run from the common extensor tendon on the outside of the elbow to the tips of the fingers. There is an extra muscle for greater strength going to the index finger *(extensor indices – EI)* which joins from the forearm near the wrist. These muscles are involved everytime we pick up the fingers in

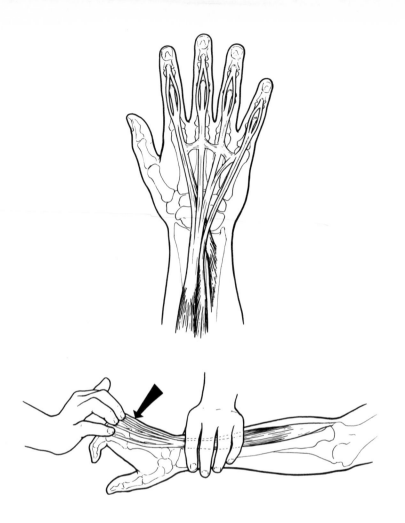

Extensor indices/digitorum and extensor digiti minimi

any kind of fingering work on any musical instrument.

    TP The Testee's wrist is stabilised, and the knuckles are arched back. Pressure is put on the back of each knuckle in turn to flex it.

    MP as for *ECR* and *ECU* (see above)

    M as for *ECR* and *ECU* (see above)

    HP as for *ECR* and *ECU* (see above)

    N as for *ECR* and *ECU* (see above)

    E as for *ECR* and *ECU* (see above)

The Long Thumb Muscles

Once again, these main *longus* muscles are not on the hand but on the forearm, to gain extra strength through longer leverage. They are backed up by smaller, local *brevis* muscles, which are found on the hand. In each case the *longus* muscle goes the furthest distance i.e. crosses the furthest joint, and *brevis* crosses the nearest. Harpists and guitarists tend to use the last joint to play, so the *longus* muscles are vital. Some schools of brass playing bend the fingers more from the knuckles, so for them, *brevis* muscles are more important. Keyboard players use both.

Flexor pollicis longus (FPL) runs mainly from the forearm, but there is a small, strong connection which crosses the elbow joint. It then goes under

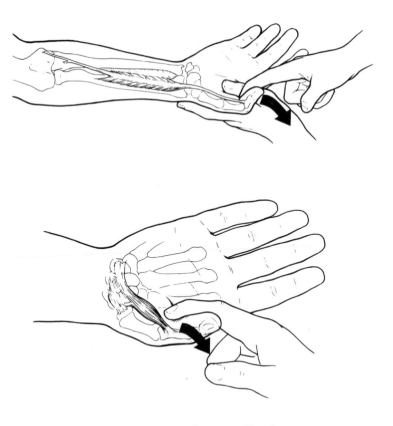

Flexor pollicis longus and brevis

the wrist fibres through the Carpal Tunnel to the base of the last bone of the thumb. *Flexor pollicis brevis* (FPB) runs underneath it and connects the base of the thumb to the strong fibres that cross the inside of the wrist. Surprisingly *FPL* is not affected by carpal tunnel syndrome, because although its tendon runs through the carpal tunnel, its nerve supply doesn't. *FPB is* affected, because although the muscle is beyond the tunnel, its nerve supply goes through it – a definitive test. Both *FPL* and *FPB* bend the thumb towards the elbow, and away from the back of the hand. Cramp can occur if you hold your instrument tightly for too long, or do too many exercises that pass the thumb under the other fingers on a keyboard instrument. Weakness will make holding a full cup difficult, and there will be poor fine control of grip, and a sore or 'bent back' thumb. Because of the meridian association, there may be a tendency to irritability and low-grade systemic infections.

TP *FPL* Hold the base and first joint of the thumb while the Testee bends the last joint. Pressure is put on the pad of the last bone to straighten the thumb.

FPB Hold the base of the thumb only. The Testee bends the thumb enough for it to lie straight, alongside the base of the index finger. The ball of the thumb is stabilised and pressure is put on the second bone to move it away from the index finger. Other muscles to test if *FPB* weak: *adductor pollicis* and *opponens pollicis*.

A *Extensor pollicis* group.

MP (1) Behind the areola on the chest wall *(go gently!)* (2) Immediately under the point of the bottom of the shoulder blade.

M Stomach

HP (1) Frontal eminences – over the centre of each eye, half-way between the eyebrows and hairline. (2) Acu-points S-41 and SI-5. S-41 is on the top middle front of the foot in a small dip in the centre of the ankle crease. Hold it with SI-5 which is on the little finger side of the wrist, on the end of the forearm bone.

N Vitamin B6, B complex, beetroot, brown rice, aloe vera juice, calcium, apple cider vinegar, cayenne, garlic, parsley.

E Unwilling/willing, stubborn/yielding, defensive/listening, nervous/restful, disorganised/organised, proud/humble.

BF Willow.

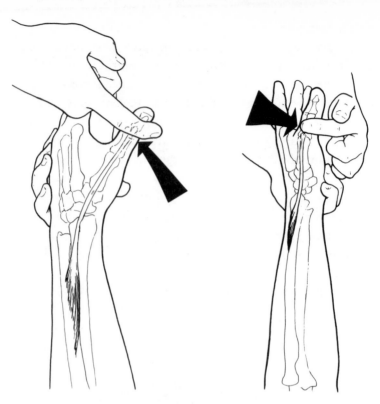

Extensor pollicis longus and brevis

Extensor pollicis longus and *brevis*. These two muscles work together to straighten the thumb. They both start on the forearm; *extensor pollicis longus* (EPL) on the thumb side, and *extensor pollicis brevis* (EPB) on the little finger side. As usual *longus* goes to the end of the thumb whereas *brevis* doesn't. Both muscles are also attached to the membranes which connect the two forearm bones, and so will be badly affected if either is misaligned, as can happen with an over pronated forearm (as in some schools of string playing, or poor hand position in flute and guitar playing). Abnormal protrusion of either forearm bone will cause irritation to tendons that pass over them. Typical problems might cause tenosynovitis, tenderness, inflammation and swelling, all of which could be prevented by better positioning during playing.

TP The thumb is extended in line with the wrist and forearm. For *EPL,* the base of the thumb is held either side and pressure is put on the nail to bend the last joint. For *EPB,* the little finger side of the hand is held while pressure is put on the back of the thumb to bend the joint at the base of the thumb. Other muscles to test, if weak: *abductor pollicis longus.*

A Thumb flexors and opposers.

MP Massage down the inner forearm towards the thumb.

M Pericardium (Cx).

HP Cx-9 and Lv-1. Cx-9 is at the end of the middle finger pad, on the index finger side. Hold it with Lv-1 which is on the nailbed of the big toe, on the corner nearest the other toes.

N Vitamin E

E Confused/confident, deceiving/truth.

BF Holly.

Abductor pollicis longus. If the hand is palm up, the *abductor pollicis longus*

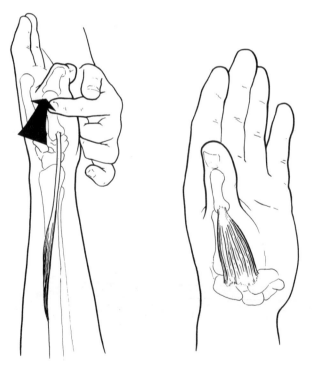

Abductor pollicis longus and brevis

313

(APL) muscle moves the thumb away from the palm and the floor (whereas the extensors move it away from crossing the palm out to the side, and keep it the same distance from the floor). Its main use to musicians is as an antagonist to both the *flexor* and *opponens* groups of muscles. Since it crosses the wrist joints on the thumb side, it also assists *extensor carpi radialis* in bending the wrist laterally. *Abductor pollicis brevis* (APB) assists *APL* and is rarely weak except where there are multiple allergies or wrist fracture, both of which are beyond the scope of this book. There may be accompanying rectal irritation.

TP The little finger side of the wrist is stabilised, the thumb moved away from the palm to about 70° from the plane of the other fingers. Pressure is placed on the side of the lower of the two thumb bones next to the base of the thumb, to push it back to the index finger. Other muscles to test, if weak: *extensor carpi radialis longus* and *brevis*.

A *Adductor* and *opponens* muscles of the thumb.

MP Massage from half-way down the thumb-side of the forearm to the middle joint of the thumb.

M Triple warmer.

HP TW-3 and GB-41. TW-3 is on the back of the hand, halfway between the base of the ring finger and the wrist, on the little finger side of the bone. Hold it with GB-41 which is on the top of the foot, half way between the base of the fourth toe and the ankle.

N Zinc, lecithin.

E Concerned/trust, self-centred/kind, disrespect/respect.

BF Mustard.

Intrinsic hand muscles

Adductor pollicis and *Opponens pollicis*
Abductor digiti minimi, Flexor digiti minimi and *Opponens digiti minimi*
Interossei (*dorsal* and *palmar*)
Lumbricals

These are the little muscles on the palm and back of the hand. Great care should be taken when testing them, not only because they are small and therefore easily overpowered, but also your livelihood depends on them. In testing them, the tendency is to use a group of the strongest muscles of both hands to test one poor little muscle. This is where its vital to *remember that you are testing for quality of reaction, NOT GROSS STRENGTH.* This applies particularly when testing single fingers, especially the little finger. Don't cause more problems for yourself like Schumann.

I know of no musician who hasn't complained about his/her little finger at some time or other. So often it has to reach further, or is at a disadvantage because of leverage distance, quite apart from the fact that it is the smallest finger. Those who have a large discrepancy between finger lengths definitely do have a greater coordination problem than those with 'square' hands. The fifth finger is blessed with its own set of muscles and this helps, but the tendency is to damage it by over-training or over-compensation. This upsets the balance of the hand, and even upsets wrist or elbow at the extremes. (If you look for it in other books, the little finger may be listed as *digiti quinti* for obvious reasons.)

Adductor Pollicis and Opponens Pollicis. These muscles bring the thumb towards the palm, and bring the thumb inwards in opposition to the little finger. Both run from the base of the thumb at the level of the webbing, *adductor pollicis (AP)* going to the middle of the palm bones, and *opponens pollicis* (OP) going to the *flexor retinaculum* – the band of tough cartilage that covers the carpal tunnel. They work closely with *flexor pollicis brevis* (see above). All these thumb muscles are vital to smooth scale playing on keyboard instruments, because with weakness, the only other way to pass the thumb under the fingers is to lift and pronate the wrist to bring the fingers into a more vertical position, which makes for a bumpy legato, and general lack of control due to differing finger lengths.

AP and *OP* are also vital to changing position in the left hand of string and guitar players, for holding most wind instruments, all drum sticks etc. in percussion, and even for holding a pencil to mark your music! Little more is known specifically about symptoms associated with weakness of these muscles other than toxic headaches. However, being able to test specifically which one is weak is useful in diagnosis of Carpal Tunnel Syndrome which frequently afflicts musicians. Chronic tension in these muscles may

315

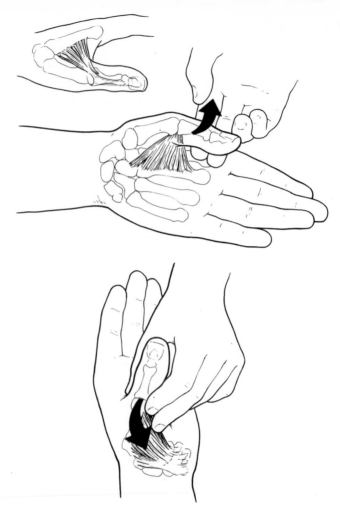

Adductor pollicis and opponens pollicis

often lead eventually to arthritis.

TP For *AP* the straight thumb lies on top of the index finger and palm (whereas with *FPB* it lies next to the index), and with *OP* the ball of the thumb lies across the palm. In all cases, the little finger side of the palm is stabilised. To test *AP* tuck two fingers between thumb and the base of the index finger, and pull the thumb away from the palm towards the inner elbow. To test *OP,* the ball of the thumb is pulled out sideways to flatten the palm. Other muscles to test, if weak: all the other thumb muscles, *longus* and *brevis*.

A All the thumb extensors.

MP (1) Under the front of the pelvic bones (above the very tops of the legs and more centrally than the groin) (2) On the back of the top of the pelvis in between the two dimple marks either side of the base of the spine.

M Stomach.

HP (1) The frontal eminences – over the centre of each eye, half-way between the eyebrows and hairline. (2) Acu-points S-41 and SI-5. S-41 is on the top middle of the ankle crease in a small dip. Hold it with SI-5 which is just below the little finger side of the wrist, on the end of the forearm bone.

E Unwilling/willing, restless/calm, revolting/attractive.

BF Willow.

Abductor digiti minimi, Flexor digiti minimi and *Opponens digiti minimi.* The first of these muscles *abductor digiti minimi* (ADM) moves the little finger from lying next to the ring finger out to the side. It runs from the forearm bone on the same side to the outside of the bone nearest the palm. Next to it is *flexor digiti minimi* (FDM). This muscle is further round on the palm, and runs from the wrist to the same bone at the base of the little finger. Further round still, and even shorter, is the very important *Opponens digiti minimi* (ODM), which runs from the wrist bones to the base of the little finger, still on the palm. This is the muscle which allows you to touch thumb and little finger, tip to tip. It may also be weakened by Guyon tunnel syndrome, where its nerve is squashed between two wrist bones (see Chapter 14).

TP *ADM* The straight little finger is moved away from the ring finger in the same plane. Support the rest of the hand and put pressure on the outside of the finger to push it towards the ring finger.

FDM The straight little finger is flexed from the knuckle. The rest of the hand is supported, and pressure is put on the palmar surface of the base of the little finger.

ODM The straight little finger is flexed towards the base of the thumb. The rest of the hand is supported, and pressure is put on the

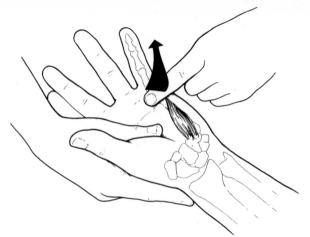

Opponens digiti minimi

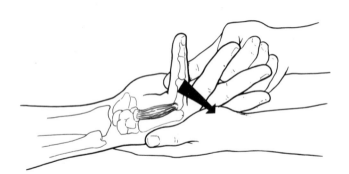

Flexor digiti minimi

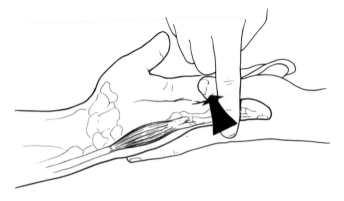

Abductor digiti minimi

318

palm under the little finger to flatten the hand. Other muscles to test, if weak: Other *digiti minimi* muscles, finger flexors and extensors, supinators and pronators for which it may be compensating.

A *Extensor digiti minimi, palmar interossei.*

MP as short thumb muscles

HP as short thumb muscles.

N Vitamins B6, B12, B complex, magnesium, lecithin.

E Nervous/peaceful, not needed/needed, unwilling/willing, frustrated/satisfied.

BF Willow.

Interossei. There are two sets of *interossei:* the *palmar* (on the palm) which bring the fingers together, and the *dorsal* (on the back of the hand) which

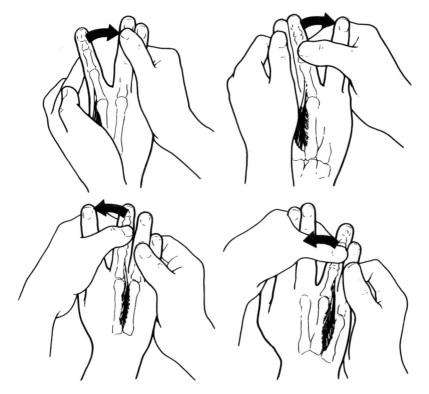

Dorsal interossei

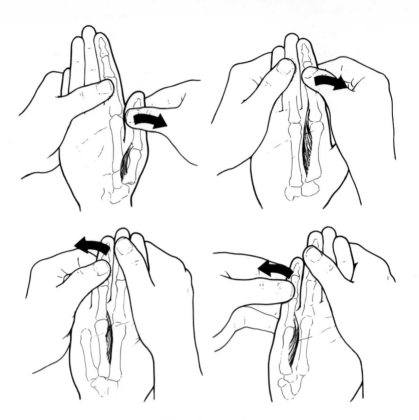

Palmar interossei

spread them. You can see them on the palm if you flatten your hand and hold the fingers close together, or on the back of your hand if you spread your fingers. They are the little bumps between the bones near the base of the fingers. In musicians they are likely to be well developed. Weakness may cause hand pain and poor coordination. Because of meridian association there may also be sciatica, and poor dental health.

TP *Palmar Interossei*. Hold the thumb and fingers straight and close together. To test, pull each finger away from the next.
Dorsal Interossei. Spread the fingers, keeping them straight and in line with the palm. Test them by pushing each pair together.
A The other *interossei*.
M Tripple Warmer and Spleen.
HP TW-3 and GB-41. TW-3 is on the back of the hand, half-way

between the base of the ring finger and the wrist crease on the little finger side of the bone. Hold it with GB-41 which is on the top of the foot, halfway between the base of the fourth toe and the ankle.

N Vitamin B6, iron, lecithin, garlic and parsley, thyme and marjoram, apricot, apple cider vinegar, asparagus, cabbage, grapes, citrus fruits, figs, soya and yogurt.

S Potatoes and foods containing zinc.

E Unwilling/willing, defensive/listening, concerned/trust.

BF Mustard and Mimulus.

Lumbricales. These muscles are used to bend straight fingers at the knuckle by flexing the joint at the knuckle, whilst extending the last joint of the fingers, as when holding a piece of paper or a fan of cards between the flat pads of the fingers and thumb. They run from the tendons of *flexor digitorum* to the base of each finger just beyond the webbing. With marked weakness it's very difficult to hold a book or paper in one hand. This results in a claw hand deformity, such that the finger with the weak muscle will not flex in all joints completely if the palm is flat, giving pain at the

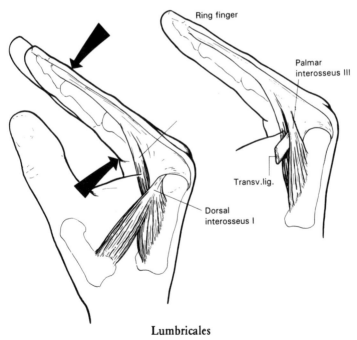

Lumbricales

base of the fingers. These muscles are specifically used in heavy brass playing by the three middle fingers.

TP This requires two tests because of its double action. With straight fingers bent only at the knuckle, pressure is simultaneously put on the palmar surface of the bone next to the palm to straighten the knuckle, and also on the nailbed of the same finger to bend the last joint.

A Finger extensors and *flexor digitorum profundus*.

MP Massage between the bones of the hand from the wrist to the fingers.

M Spleen.

HP Sp-2 and H-8. Sp-2 is on the nail end of the big joint, at the base of the big toe, on the side of the foot. Hold it with H-8 which is on the palm of the hand on the first crease below the base of the ring finger.

N Vitamin B3, cayenne

E Unwilling/willing, unaccepted/accepted.

BF Mimulus.

CHAPTER 14

Muscles of the abdomen, back and other postural muscles

Muscles of the abdomen, back and other postural muscles

Torso muscles
Serratus Anterior
Abdominals
Diaphragm

Serratus anterior. This muscle is serrated (hence its name), as it fits between the ribs on the side of the chest wall. It holds the shoulder-blade on to the rib cage, and weakness creates difficulty in raising the arm both to the side and to the front. At the same time the shoulder-blade 'wings' out at the back. It is used in bowing in all stringed instruments, turning pages when seated at a keyboard instrument, and playing in the upper registers of the harp where raising the shoulder would upset the position of the harp resting on the shoulder. Weakness will also cause bursitis, unequal chest expansion, upper backache, pain at the bottom corner of the shoulder-blade and armpit, or pain when reaching across to the opposite side. Because of its association with the lung meridian, it is often weak in wind and brass players when under stress.

TP The Testee sits and raises a straight arm 45° above horizontal and 45° to the side, with the thumb up and palm in. The lower tip of the shoulder-blade is stabilised while pressure is put on the forearm to push it to the floor. Other muscles to test, if weak: *diaphragm* and *levator scapulae*.

A *Anterior deltoid, coracobrachialis, rhomboids.*

MP (1) Between the third, fourth and fifth ribs, either side of the breastbone. (2) Between the third, fourth and fifth ribs, next to the spine and level with the top down to the middle of the shoulder-blade.

M Lung.

HP (1) Anterior Fontanel – one thumb's width back from the vertex of the head. (2) Acu-points L-9 and Sp-3. L-9 is at the end of the wrist crease, at the base of the thumb. Hold it with Sp-3 which is on

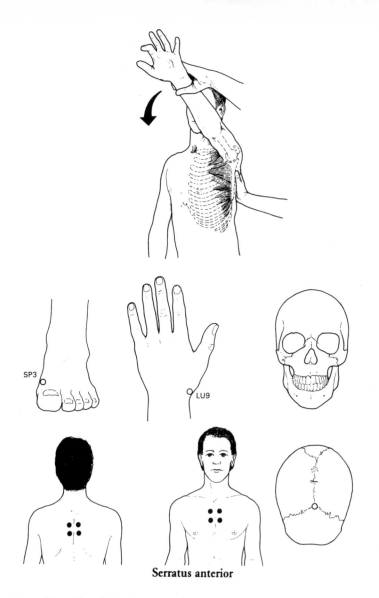

Serratus anterior

the ankle side of the big joint at the base of the big toe.

N Lots of fresh air and avoid smoky, dirty or mouldy atmospheres. Avoid all dairy products as these are mucus forming. Increase intake of foods high in vitamins A, B complex and C, kelp, alfalfa, ginger, apple cider vinegar, garlic, parsley, maple syrup, chamomile.

E Nervous/restful, discontented/contented, depressed/expressive, confused/confident, futile/assured, unwilling/willing, grief/fellow feeling, scared/courageous, useless/useful, haughty/meek, smug/compassionate.

BF Water violet.

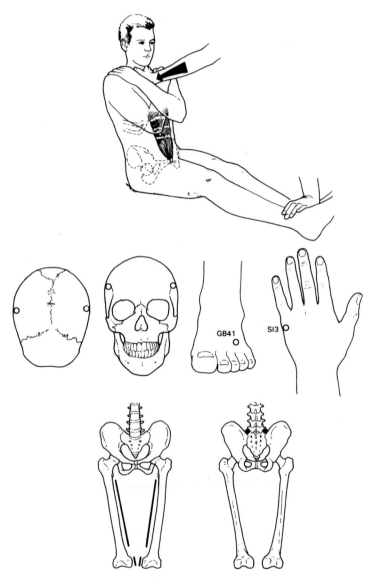

Rectus abdominus

Abdominals. There are many parts to this group muscle. *Rectus abdominis* runs straight up the front in a series of bands from pelvis to ribs, and is involved in breathing control. Either side there are the *transverse abdominis* and *oblique abdominis* which are involved in holding the slightly twisted posture when playing a one-sided instrument; anchoring them all at the bottom is *pyramidalis,* which I will ignore except to say that it is involved in counter-balancing the pull of the back muscles against gravity. The abdominal muscles protect the soft abdominal contents, which are vulnerable between ribs and pelvis in the front, but protected behind by the ribs which reach down lower, and the spine. A flabby belly or distended 'stomach' area is a sure sign of flaccidity. Abdominal muscle weakness is the most usual cause of back pain, because the back muscles have to take up their chronic slackness and so go into spasm. The lower abdominals are also particularly subject to herniation in men, through a natural developmental anatomical weakness, and this can be exacerbated by lifting heavy instruments or poor technique in brass playing. Pain may occur in the groin and pubic area, on top of the hips and lower ribs at the side, on twisting the upper torso, or there may be difficulty in breathing deeply when side bending. Bladder infections may occur concurrently.

TP All Abdominals. The Testee sits leaning back slightly, with legs straight out in front, head up and arms crossed to the shoulders. The legs are stabilised, while pressure is put on (a) the mid-chest or crossed arms to push the Testee straight backwards; (b) the same position but with pressure on the right shoulder directly backwards; (c) the same position again but with pressure on the left shoulder directly backwards. For (d) the Testee now twists so that one shoulder is pointing forward, and pressure is put on the forward shoulder to push it directly backwards; (e) the same as (d) but the other shoulder forward. The degree of backward lean in the starting position determines at what level on the abdominal wall the muscles are being tested, although of course they are all working to some degree all the time. To test the lowest level, test with the least backward lean. Other muscles to test, if weak: *psoas, sacrospinalis, latissimus dorsi.*

A *Sacrospinalis, quadratus lumborum, latissimus dorsi.*

MP (1) The inside of the thighs in a broad band stretching from the

groin to the knee. The lower part helps *rectus a.* and *pyrimidalis* most, and the upper part *transverse a.* and *oblique a.* (2) The most prominent knobs at the back top of the pelvis either side of the spine (PSIS).
M Small intestine.
HP (1) Three inches (8cm) above the ear, at the widest part of the head. (2) Spread your fingers out either side of a line running from the centre front to the back of the skull, and as the Testee breaths in and pushes the head upwards, gently pull the spread fingers outwards as though to widen the head between the ears. Do this five times. It assists the normal motion of the skull during breathing. (3) Acu-points SI-3 and GB-41. SI-3 is on the side of the hand mid-way between the base of the little finger and the end of the wrist crease.
N Arnica. Foods rich in vitamins B complex, E, kelp, lecithin, calcium and zinc; avocado, cucumber, raisins, radish will help. Avoid spicy food, caffeine, alcohol, sugar, white rice and white flour.
S White flour, celery, cinnamon, sugar intolerance.
E Nervous/restful, in vain/useful, unsuccessful/successful, confused/confident, resentful/appreciative, unwilling/willing, hopeless and helpless/trusting and powerful, hard/adaptable, rebellious/accepting, discontent/content, frustrated/able.
BF Star of Bethlehem.

Diaphragm. The *diaphragm* is one of the rare, almost horizontal muscles in the body. It divides the torso into two parts, the upper part containing the heart and lungs and the lower containing the liver, spleen, stomach and other digestive organs. It is attached to the inside of the lower ribs on the front, sides and back and has large centrally placed holes in front of the spine, through which pass the main blood vessels and the gullet, and some smaller holes for nerves and other vessels. Being a muscle, its natural elasticity is occasionally lost. Over-elasticity can cause digestive problems, such as heartburn and hernia, due to laxity or constriction of the passage to the stomach. It is the main muscle of breathing, its contraction altering the pressure around and within the lungs to draw air in, and it also helps to hold the breath in and control its release in a long musical phrase. Most breathing out is done by gravity, but can be assisted by the diaphragm pushing up and decreasing the available lung space. Obviously good function is essential to all wind and brass players and singers. The most frequent misuse occurs in other instrumentalists however, particularly players of upper strings and keyboards who have a bad habit of holding many muscles in tension including the diaphragm (and therefore the breath) in anxiety states.

TP Inaccessability makes this muscle difficult to test without a spirometer which is usually only available in hospitals. However in the interests of simplicity, a fairly good indication of normal function is the ability to hold a good breath in for 40 seconds without releasing it. Any wind, brass player or singer should beat this easily. It might be helpful to note your own 'normal ability' in seconds, and compare it with your ability when stressed. There is the further possibility of gently pushing three fingers up under the bottom of the breastbone whilst testing an indicator muscle (see Chapter 9). This will only indicate that the diaphragm is weak, in a general way. Some control of today's all-too-prevalent asthmatic spasm can be achieved by learning to breathe through a straw, but oboe players who do this habitually as they play are occasionally subject to sharply painful air leaks into the space outside the lungs and this needs immediate medical attention. Other signs of weakness include hiccough, pain in the lower rib cage, and pain on deep breathing. Because of its meridian association there may also be accompanying sciatica. Other muscles to test, if weak: abdominals, *upper trapezius,* pectoral muscles, *teres minor* and *psoas.*

A Abdominal muscles.

MP (1) The whole length of the breastbone. (2) On the right-hand side of the spine, level with two inches below the lowest part of the shoulder-blade.

M Lung.

HP (1) Anterior fontanel – one thumb's width back from the vertex of the head. (2) Acu-points L-9 and Sp-3. L-9 is on the end of the wrist crease at the base of the thumb. Hold it with Sp-3 which is on the inside of the foot, on the heel side of the large joint at the base of the big toe. Holding these acu-points can increase the length of time you are able to hold your breath by half as long again!

N It goes without saying that smoking reduces lung capacity. It constricts the blood supply, as well as clogging the airways and causing spasm of the delicate and very fine lung tissues. 90% of the smoking habit is psychological dependency rather than drug dependency, so it's much easier to give it up if you reduce the panic, stress and psychological need. Increase intake of foods high in vitamins B3, C and E.

E Unwilling/willing, not needed/needed, tongue tied/expressive, confused/confident, barrier/clear, undesirable/pleasant.

BF Water violet.

Back muscles

> *Latissimus dorsi*
> *Errector spinae*

Latissimus dorsi. This is one of the more easily visible large back muscles, and often works together with *lower trapezius* (see previous chapter). It is joined to the pelvis, middle and lower spine by a strong sheet of cartilaginous tissue. This wide muscle narrows down to a single very strong tendon which catches the bottom tip of the shoulder-blade as it passes, and twists round on itself as it goes under the armpit, to attach to the front of the upper arm. Its action is to twist the arm inwards, and to hold it and the shoulder-blade close against the body. Its nerve supply comes from the upper back. Where the lower back is unable to support the body due to low-back nerve injury (with consequent incapacity of the normal walking muscles), this muscle can take over and assist walking by pulling on each hip alternately, because of its large expanse across the lower back. It is used by upper string players in the upper half of the bow on all down-bow strokes, especially at the tip of the bow. Weakness causes shoulder and low-back pain and elbow pains (which can be mistaken for tendinitis or tennis elbow), due to forced over-use of synergistic muscles. Because of its meridian association there is often an accompanying sugar intolerance. There may be a raised shoulder on the weak side and flatulence shortly after eating, dizziness or tiredness.

TP The straight arm is held to the side and turned palm out, with

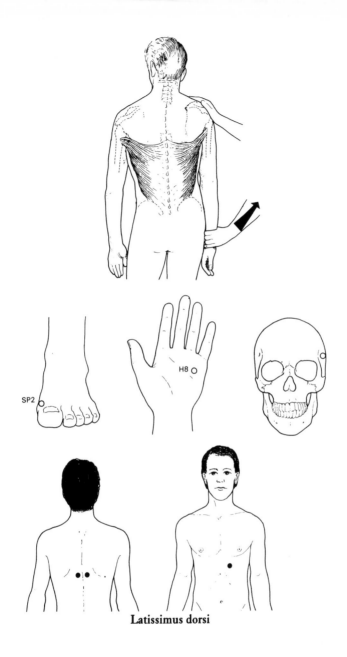

Latissimus dorsi

the thumb facing backwards. Stabilise the shoulder, and be sure the elbow is locked straight as you pull the forearm away from the body to the side and 45° to the front. Some women can overstraighten the arm, some men can't completely straighten it. This is of no consequence as long as it is held as straight as possible, with the feeling of holding the *elbow* in, not the wrist. The most common fault in testing this muscle is to let the Testee bend the elbow. Other muscles to test, if weak: *upper trapezius, PMC, triceps.*

A *Posterior deltoid* and *trapezius.*

MP (1) Between the seventh and eighth ribs on the right side of the ribcage two inches (5cm) below the nipple and an inch towards the breastbone. (2) Between the seventh and eighth ribs either side of the spine and level with the bottom of the shoulder-blade.

M Spleen.

HP (1) Either side of the head at about one inch (2.5cm) above and back of the ear. (2) Acu-points Sp-2 and H-8. Sp-2 is on the outside edge, just nail side of the big joint, base of the big toe. Hold it with H-8 which is on the palm crease, under the ring finger.

N A consistently weak *latissimus dorsi* may indicate sugar handling difficulty whether hyper-insulinism, diabetes or low blood-sugar. Avoid all quick-release 'empty calorie' sugars such as sucrose and glucose like the plague! Be aware that these occur in all sorts of disguises in processed, packaged and tinned foods, in most soups, smoked meats, hams, sausages, bacon and salamis as well as bottled concentrates or reconstituted juices, pies, sweets, cakes and biscuits. Learn to read labels! Keep your blood-sugar supply constant by eating slow-release carbohydrates such as whole grains, and avoid all stimulants such as tea, coffee, cola and alcohol as they raise blood-sugar levels too fast. Increase intake of foods containing Vitamins A and B complex, lecithin.

E Unwilling/willing, bitter/ forgiveness, unaccepted/accepted.

BF Mimulus.

Erector spinae (Sacrospinalis). This muscle has two names because it is a composite muscle, combining most of the complicated structural support of the back against gravity. It joins ribs to spine, ribs to other ribs and ultimately the pelvis to the spine, neck and back of the head. Despite common ideas, it is rarely weak but very frequently in spasm, which is the cause of the pain felt. 90% of back pain is due to weak, stretched and flaccid

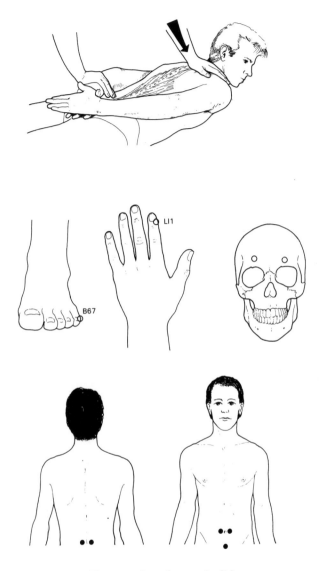

Erector spinae (sacrospinalis)

abdominal muscles which the *erector spinae* have to counterbalance. Its main function is to bend the spine backwards when both sides contract, or to assist side-bending when only one side contracts. True weakness of *erector s.* causes many areas of pain and disfunction, arthritis, referred pain, shoulder and elbow problems due to compensation, spinal curvature ('C' curves and 'S' curves), sciatica, pain and tingling in the legs and feet. It is also noticeable that emotional feelings of lack of support (whether in the family or professionally) certainly add to back pain and may compound problems due to seating, prolonged standing, practising for hours or playing a one-sided instrument – notably the double bass, a heavy viola or bass trombone. Other typical back problems are caused by poor lifting techniques where, because the person tends to bend from the waist instead of the hips, the tiny muscles between the bones of the back take the strain, instead of the thigh muscles which are built for the job. If there is a 'back' problem read Chapter 5, to learn how to adapt chairs, beds and concert platforms to fit you, and, if female, how to counteract wearing high heels. Bladder infections, and prostate problems due to meridian association, are less common causes of *erector s.* malfunction. To help this always wear cotton underwear, and follow the dietary advice below.

TP The Testee lies face down and clasps hands over the back of the pelvis. Both shoulders are then lifted off the table. The Testee then looks over and raises one shoulder. The hands are stabilised on the pelvis and pressure is put on the raised shoulder to push it back to the table. Swap head turn and shoulder to test the other side. Other muscles to test, if weak: *latissimus dorsi, quadratus lumborum, psoas, gluteus maximus, tibials* and *peroni.*

A All abdominal muscles.

MP (1) One inch (2.5cm) either side of the tummy button, and over the middle of the pubic bone – *rub the bone, don't squash the bladder!* (2) Either side of the spine, 2 inches (5cm) below the lowest ribs.

M Bladder.

HP (1) The frontal eminences – over the centre of each eye and half-way between the eyebrows and hairline. (2) Acu-points B-67 and L-11. B-67 is on the nailbed of the little toe. Hold it at the same time as L-11 which is on the thumb side of the nailbed of the index finger.

N Increase intake of foods containing vitamins A, C ,E and calcium. With bladder problems drink camomile tea and barley water (water in which barley has been boiled, not squash or fruit juice!), eat melon, pumpkin seeds and garlic. If you have to take antibiotics for some reason, watch out for rashes, nausea, depression, diarrhoea and headaches, and when the course of antibiotics is finished eat lots of live yoghurt.

S Caffeine, chocolate, rhubarb and purple fruits, spicy foods.

E Frustration/peace, unsupported/supported, not needed/needed, unhelpful/helpful.

BF Impatiens.

Lumbar muscles
Psoas and *Iliacus*
Quadratus lumborum

Most of the muscles which follow, in this and the remaining two sections, are not directly connected with playing a specific musical instrument. They are included because they are vital for posture, are jeopardised by a musician's lifestyle, and can be the foundation cause of compensatory tensions in muscles used in playing.

Psoas and *Iliacus*. *Psoas* connects the inside of the lower spine to the top of the thigh-bone, running across the edge of the pelvis as it does so. It is a hip flexor, and on it depends the low back curvature. When weak it causes 'sway back'. Feet that splay like Alice's fish footman and won't walk 'Indian file' are often compensating for 'sway back' by dropping the arches to cause 'flat feet'.

Iliacus connects the inside of the pelvic rim either side of the spine to the top of the thigh bone. Its tendon melds with *psoas*. Both *psoas* and *iliacus* can be the cause of low-back pain, burning leg pains, spasms and sciatica, skin irritations and digestive upsets. If you frequently suffer from constipation or diarrhoea, turn to Chapter 6 on Ileocaecal valve syndrome (IBS) correction. Weakness and spasm also appear to have an effect on general coordination.

TP *Psoas* The Testee lies flat on his/her back. One straight leg is raised 45° up and 45° out, with the foot turned out.
The opposite hip is stabilised to prevent rock, while pressure is

335

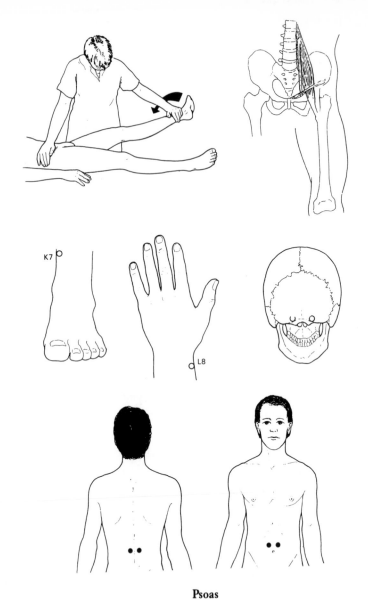

Psoas

applied to the lower leg to push it down and out. Do not put
pressure over the knee joint.

Iliacus works very closely with *psoas* and shares its tendon; it is tested the

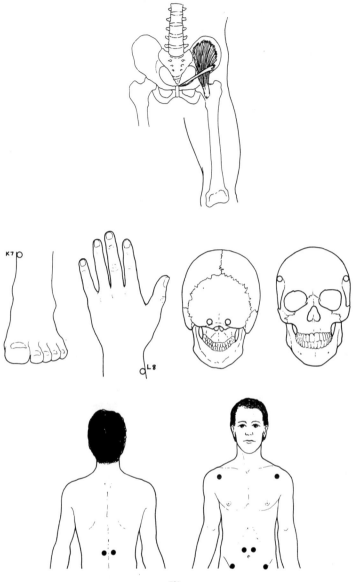

Iliacus

same way, but the leg is lifted up 60° to 70°. Other muscles to test, if weak: *TFL, gluteals, erector spinae (sacrospinalis)*.

    A *Gracilis, pyramidalis, TFL* and *sartorius*.

    MP One inch (2.5cm) out and up from the tummy button. (2) On

the mid-back at the level of the last ribs, either side of the spine
(3) Inside the front, side edge of the pelvic bones (4) In the dip on
the front of the shoulder joint.

M Kidney.

HP (1) Find the little bump on the skull over the valley at the top of
the neck. Go diagonally up and out one inch (2.5cm) (2) Acu-points
K-7 and L-8. K-7 is three finger widths up, and one back from the
inner ankle bone. Hold it with L-8 which is on the side of the
forearm, three finger widths below the wrist crease, thumb side.

N These muscles are very badly affected by caffeine and
dehydration, so don't go and drink coffee or alcohol which are both
diuretics when working in a dry centrally heated studio! The same
applies to long-haul flying where there is a similar atmosphere.
Increase intake of foods high in vitamins A, B complex, E, zinc,
iron, kelp, Brazil nuts, cabbage, lecithin, molasses, cayenne.

E Unwilling/willing, unhelpful/helpful, confused/confident,
suppressed/encouraged, irritated/tranquil, failure/success,
nervous/restful, argumentative/agreeable, hard/adaptable,
embarrassed/ modest, frustrated/satisfied.

BF Scleranthus.

Quadratus Lumborum. This muscle is found either side of the lower back,
and joins the back of the pelvis to the lumbar spine and the lowest ribs. It
stabilises the lower back with the lowest fibres of *erector spinae
(sacrospinalis).* It helps the diaphragm with breathing by stabilising the
lowest ribs, and can either pull the pelvis up to the ribs, or pull the ribs
down to the pelvis during side bending. This muscle can be badly affected by hours in a badly fitting chair or car seat, when under stress. There
may be pelvic pain, shoulder-blade pain, and it is also blamed for back
pain, spasm (lumbago) and sciatica, when the problem is really caused by
lax abdominals. Because of its meridian association there may be bowel
upset and flatulence, ear-drainage problems, dry, irritated eyes and
anaemia.

TP The Testee lies face up, and holds the treatment table for upper
body stability. The legs are held together and swung out to the side.
The opposite hip is stabilised, as the legs are pushed back to the
mid-line of the table. Watch that there is no swivelling of the pelvis

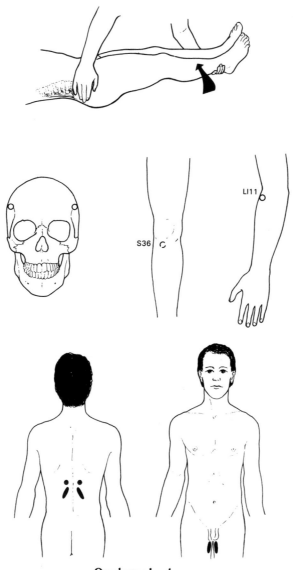

Quadratus lumborum

to bring other synergistic muscles into alignment. Other muscles to test, if weak: oblique abdominals, *erector spinae, psoas, iliacus*.

A Abdominals and the other *quadratus lumborum*.

MP (1) The top six inches (15cm) of the upper inner thigh. (2) The most prominent knobs on the back of the pelvis (PSIS). (3) The end

of the last rib, and between the last two ribs either side of the spine.
M Large intestine.
HP (1) Three inches (7.5cm) above the ear at the widest part of the
head. (2) Acu-points LI-11 and S-36. LI-11 is found at the end of
the elbow crease on the thumb side. Hold it with S-36 which is two
inches (5cm) outside the bump below the knee cap, on the front of
the shin.
N Increase intake of foods rich in vitamins A, B6, C and E, lecithin,
calcium, zinc, iron, garlic, arnica, yarrow, apple cider vinegar, alfalfa.
S Yeast, eggs, figs and olive oil, hypersensitivity to chlorinated water.
E Unwilling/willing, irresponsible/responsible, nervous/restful, grief
for self/fellow feeling, confused/confident, insignificant/important,
disappointed/satisfied, bored/enthusiastic, discontent/tranquil,
incapable/success, sour/agreeable, proud/humble.
BF Pine.

Pelvic and Thigh muscles
Piriformis
Gluteals
Quadriceps
Hamstrings
Tensor fascia lata
Adductors

Piriformis. This is one of the inner buttock muscles. It is a postural muscle, in that it helps support the transference of upper bodyweight through
to the thighs. The musician's interest in it is due to its variability. Under
stress, everyone 'holds on' with some part of their anatomy. Some clench
and grind their teeth, others' shoulders go up round their ears, others
clench their buttocks. The variability of *piriformis* is that the sciatic nerve
may go under, through all or part of it, or even over it. Any chronic tension
in this muscle will therefore compress the sciatic nerve nine times out of
ten, and ultimately causes excruciating sciatica. Since musicians *have* to
keep their arms free (and some are even aware of shoulder tension), *piriformis* tends to be the main tension victim. This muscle is employed when
you sit and spread your knees sideways, and so is particularly used by

340

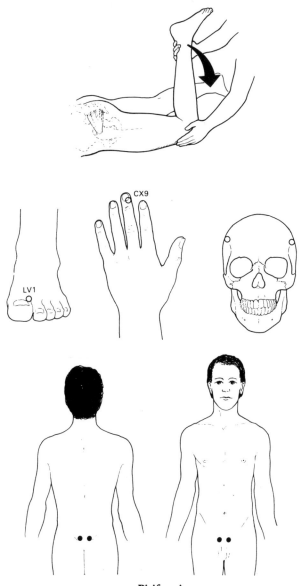

Piriformis

organists. However, most orchestral musicians sit knees apart, with their instrument or bow between their knees. This doesn't mean you should not sit like this – far from it – ask any Alexander teacher! What it does mean is that you need to be aware of excess tension and 'holding on' in this area.

Given ideal posture it should not be necessary, but one-sided instruments like the violin tend to foster tension on one side to get the knees out of the way of the bow. This also twists the pelvis and lumbar region chronically. Weakness will cause deep pelvic pain (especially during intercourse), turned-in foot and ankle pain.

TP (1) The Testee lies face down and the knee is flexed at 90°. The outside of the knee is stabilised and pressure is put on the inner ankle to pull the lower leg out to the side. (2) The Testee sits, knees bent at a right angle. The lower leg is taken across over the ankle of the other leg (not knee over knee), the knee is stabilised, and pressure is placed on the inner shin to push it out sideways. Other muscles to test, if weak: *gluteus maximus, TFL,* hamstrings and adductors.

A *Iliacus.*

MP (1) Top of the pubic bone. (2) The most prominent bumps on the top back of the pelvis (PSIS).

M Pericardium (Cx).

HP (1) Parietal eminence – three inches (7.5cm) above the top of the ear at the widest point of the head. (2) Acu-points Cx-9 and Lv-1. Cx-9 is the end of the middle finger on the side nearest the index finger.

N Foods rich in vitamins A, B complex and E, zinc and magnesium will help.

E Unwilling/willing, forsaken/accepted, weary/refreshed, nervous/restful, unmotivated/motivated, confused/confident, incapable/understandable, arrogant/listening, belligerent/agreeable.

BF Holly

Gluteals: gluteus maximus, gluteus medius and *gluteus minimus.* These are the buttock muscles.

Gluteus maximus is at the back and provides the mass of the bottom, shielding the pelvic bones from shock and compression when you sit;

Gluteus medius and *gluteus minimus* are round at the sides and provide the 'panniers'. They are large, strong muscles which connect the pelvis to the

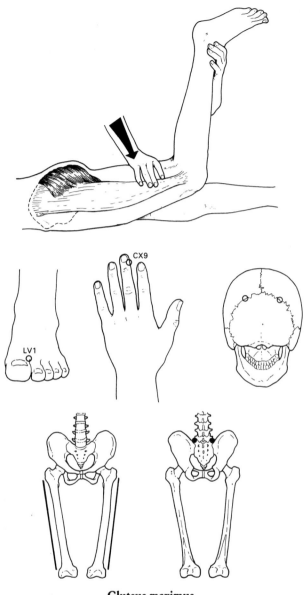

Gluteus maximus

legs, and prevent forward flop or excess sideways sway of the torso when you walk. They are part of the chain of muscles *erector spinae,* gluteals, hamstrings and calf muscles, which pull top-to-toe down the back of the

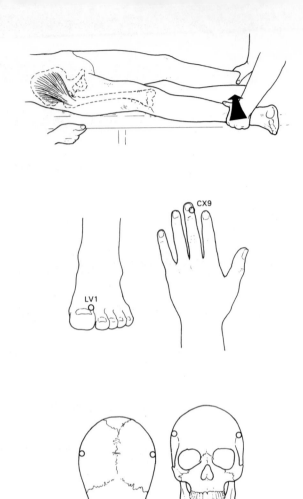

Gluteus medius

body to counteract the lack of bony support on the front of the body and keep it upright. If you play a heavy instrument (e.g. bass trombone or tuba) which has to be carried, these muscles have to counteract that as well. *G. maximus* is mainly used to stabilise the back and hips when going upstairs or running, *G. medius* and *minimus* are used to take the leg out to the side (as in organ playing) and stabilise the side of the pelvis and hips. These muscles can spasm if you tend to put most of your weight on one

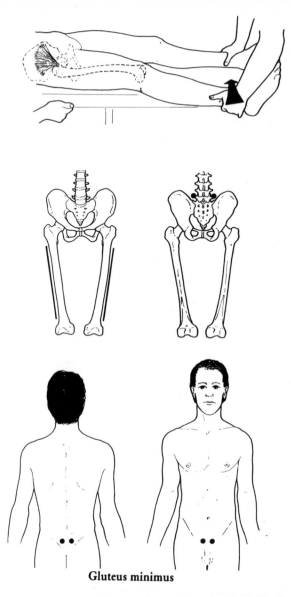

Gluteus minimus

leg when standing to play (particularly in upper strings and flute to counterbalance the instrument weight), when telephoning, waiting for a recording playback or doing household chores such as sweeping or washing up. Unless you switch sides frequently, unequal use of this sort torsions the entire pelvis and sets you up for uneven hip and shoulder heights, back and buttock pain! If there is constant weakness, meridian association may mean a glandular imbalance and depressed appetite.

TP *G. max.* (1) The Testee lies face up and resists a pull to lift the straight leg off the table. (2) The Testee lies face down with the knee bent at 90°, foot in the air. Raise the whole leg off the table. Pressure is put on the back of the thigh to press it back to the table, whilst stabilising the opposite side of the pelvis. Watch that there is no 'hip rolling' or change in knee flexion to recruit *quadratus lumborum* or hamstrings.

G med., G. min. (1) The Testee lies face up. The straight leg is taken out to the side with toe out 45° for *G. med.,* and toe straight up for *G. min.* Pressure is put on the lower leg to bring it back next to the other leg, while the other leg is stabilised. (Watch for hip twisting to recruit *tensor fascia lata*) (2) The Testee is side-lying. Lift the straight leg 45° for *G min.,* but back slightly, with a slight toe-out for *G med.* The hip is stabilised and pressure put on the lower leg to push it back to the other leg.

MP *G. max.* (1) The whole of the outside-front of the thigh.
(2) The most prominent bumps on the back of the pelvis (PSIS)
G med., G. min. (1) Upper edge of the front of the pubic bone.
(2) The most prominent bumps on the top back of the pelvis (PSIS).

HP *G. max.* Two inches (5m) behind the ear on an imaginary line extending from the corner of the eye through the top of the ear.
G. med., G. min Three inches (7.5cm) above the top of the ear at the widest part of the head.

M as for *piriformis*

HP as for *piriformis*

N Foods rich in vitamins B complex, E, kelp, lecithin, honey, calcium.

S Garlic.

E Unwilling/willing, undesireable/pleasant, confused/confident, guilty/innocent, insecure/secure, not listening/attentive, abhorrent/adoring, impatient/patient, concerned/trust, irritated/tranquil, obdurate/submissive, unhelpful/helpful, hungry/fulfilled, forsaken/accepted.

BF Holly.

In the muscles which follow, *quadriceps* bring the knee forward; hamstrings take it back. *Tensor fasciae lata* (as well as the gluteals discussed above) take the leg out to the side, adductors bring the legs together.

Quadriceps. This is a group of four muscles which make up the front of the thigh. Their main function is to straighten the knee, but they also help *psoas* to flex the hips. The lower tendon contains the kneecap, which acts as a fulcrum to give extra strength. Quads., together with the shin and calf muscles, are mainly used in walking, but also in any form of pedalling (all keyboards, timps and harp), and in driving most vehicles. These are the muscles which should be used for lifting heavy cases, not the little interspinal muscles. Make them work by bending your knees, and then, keeping your back straight, take hold of the heavy weight. Lift by straightening your knees. Similarly, move a piano on its castors by bending your knees first. Lean your weight against the piano and push, with the strength coming from your thigh muscles, not your arms. Remember, the thigh muscles are well trained, each one singly lifts your entire weight every step you take! Weakness causes knee and thigh pain and fatigue climbing stairs; there may also be leg cramps.

   TP (1) The Testee sits on a table with legs dangling over the side, one leg is horizontal and straight. The Tester puts one hand under the knee of that leg to protect the hamstrings from the table edge, and pressure is put on the shin to bend the knee. (2) The Testee lies face up with one leg bent 80° and the shin just above horizontal. Support the lower leg under the ankle. Horizontal pressure is put on the thigh just above the knee, pushing straight towards the feet, straightening both knee and hip joint. Other muscles to test, if weak: *sartorius, TFL, psoas,* abdominals.
   A Hamstrings.
   MP (1) All along the underneath of the front of the ribcage.
   (2) Either side of the spine, level with the bottom of the shoulder-blade and three rib spaces below.
   M Small Intestine.
   HP (1) Parietal eminence – three inches (7.5cm) above the top of the ear, at the widest part of the head. (2) Acu-points SI-3 and GB-41. SI-3 is on the back of the hand, half-way between ring and little

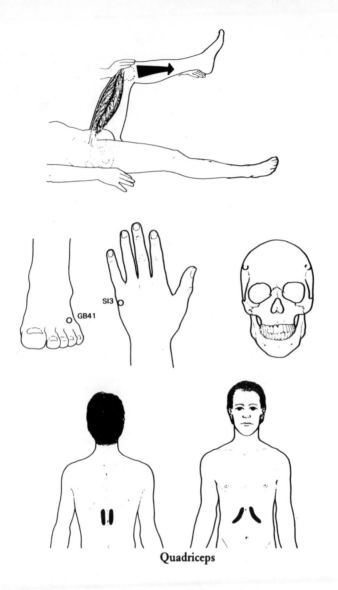

Quadriceps

fingers, knuckles and wrist. Hold this with GB-41 which is similarly placed on top of the foot, half-way between the base of the fourth and little toes, and the ankle crease.

N This muscle group reacts badly to stress, particularly to mental overload, so it needs support with the B complex vitamin group, vitamin E, zinc, magnesium, safflower oil, apple cider vinegar, poppy seed and tarragon.

S Avoid all spicy foods, refined sugars, caffeine and alcohol. You may also find milk products difficult to digest, and there may be a temporary hypersensitivity to many foods.

E Nervous/restful, injustice/justice, sour/agreeable, defeated/success, unwilling/willing, irritated/tranquil, upset/calm, depressed/cheerful, confused/confident, barrier/clear.

Hamstrings. There are three muscles in this group. All three start on the bottom back of the pelvis (on the bones you sit on), and hold it down towards the back of the knee. They cramp easily because the muscles on the front of the leg *(quadriceps)* tend to be more developed, and because they cross two joints they tend to contract in waves rather than ends to middle (like most other muscles). Cellists have difficulty sitting on chairs with seats that slope back, as the front edge then tends to cut into this muscle group most uncomfortably. These muscles, together with the calf muscles, also become permanently shortened in women who habitually wear high heels for performance and do not stretch afterwards. This eventually causes chronic knee, back and neck pain. Because of the meridian association, there are frequently accompanying symptoms of fatigue, restlessness, toxic headache and constipation, colitis or haemorrhoids, the last things you need on tour!

TP (1) The Testee lies face down and bends one knee 60 to 70°. The buttocks are stabilised while the lower leg is pushed straight down to the table. If there is a tendency to cramp, then stabilise mid-thigh instead. (2) The Testee lies face up, knee bent. The knee is stabilised while the lower leg is pulled away from the buttock to straighten the limb. Other muscles to test if weak: gluteals, abdominals, *TFL* and adductors.

A Quadriceps.

MP (1) On the inside of the thigh as high as you can near the groin, yet still be on the thigh. (2) The bones of the pelvis at the back that you sit on. (3) The most prominent bumps on the top back of the pelvis (PSIS) – put your hands on your hips and slide them round to the back of the pelvis until you find them.

M Large intestine.

HP (1) Draw an imaginary line from the corner of each eye, which

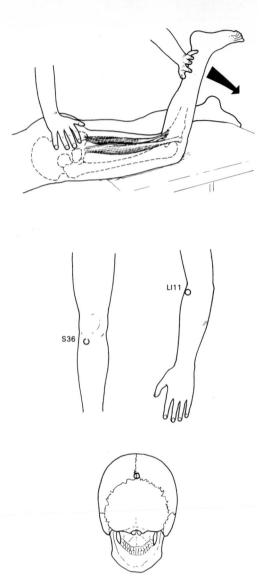

Hamstrings

passes through the top of each ear and goes round to the centre back
of the head (one inch (2.5cm) above the posterior fontanel). This
point is often in the hair whirl. (2) Acu-points LI-11 and S-36. LI-
11 is at the outer end of the elbow crease. Hold it with S-36 which is

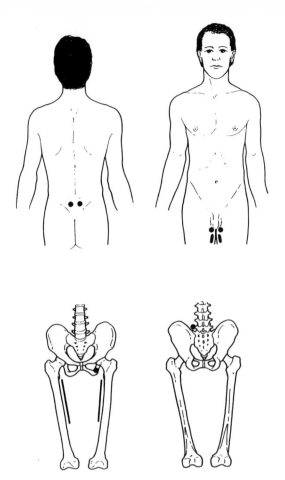

Hamstrings continued

one inch (2.5cm) below the knee cap and one and a half inches (3cm) out to the side in a little dip.

N Avoid laxatives if possible by eating a high-fibre diet and avoiding refined sugars and starches. Foods rich in vitamins B complex and E, zinc, alfalfa, garlic, parsley, kelp, lecithin, paprika, ginger, dill seed are good. Drink lots of plain pure spring water.

S Carrots.

E Unwilling/willing, restless/calm, nervous/restful and peaceful, concerned/trust, self centred/kind, irritated/tranquil.

BF Pine.

Tensor fascia lata (TFL). This muscle runs down the outside of your thigh (exactly under the seam of your jeans) and stabilises the hip and the side of the knee joint. As a musician, your only interest in it is as a postural muscle. However, weakness is often accompanied with low-back and knee

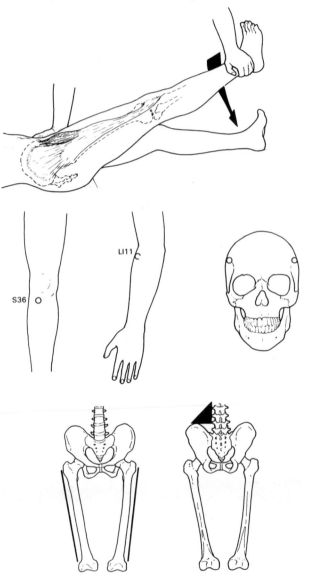

Tensor fascia lata

problems, constipation and colitis, diarrhoea, menstrual problems and breast soreness because of its meridian association.

TP The Testee lies face up with straight leg raised about 45°, and taken out to the side about 30°. The foot is turned in. The other hip is stabilised, as pressure is put on the outer ankle to push the leg back down next to the other leg. Sort out your test position in your mind before testing as the leg feels very heavy in this position and will tire easily before you have even tested it if you are inefficient, especially if it is weak! Other muscles to test, if weak: *quadriceps, gluteus medius* and *g. minimus, psoas.*

A Adductors.

MP (1) Along the entire length of the outer thigh from one inch (2.5cm) below the knee, to above the hip joint. (2) A triangular area either side of the bottom of the spine, just above the pelvis.

M Large intestine.

HP as Hamstrings.

N This is another muscle which reacts badly to dehydration, so no diuretics (no caffeine, dandelion coffee or alcohol), and increase intake of vitamins B complex and D, magnesium.

S Garlic, rice, pecans

E Confused/confident, unsociable/sociable, cut off/united.

Adductors. Yet another group of muscles. They are all attached to the bottom of the pubic bone, and at the succeeding places along the inner side of the thigh bone, which means they all pull the legs inwards. They are used by cellists to hold the lower bouts and by women wearing short black skirts, viol, tuba and euphonium players and others, to hold the knees together or to make a platform for the instrument. The saphenous nerve and vein pass through the lower part of the adductor muscles and can therefore become crushed by gripping the cello (or viol) too hard; this causes burning inner thigh, knee or calf pain often occuring at night, and there may be loss of feeling during the day. Pain in the area may also be due to a low-back problem, so if it doesn't clear with a reduction in grip pressure, go and see a chiropractor or osteopath. Weakness can cause leg length difference, low backache, walking difficulty especially in moving legs forward, groin pain, pubic bone pain and pain during intercourse.

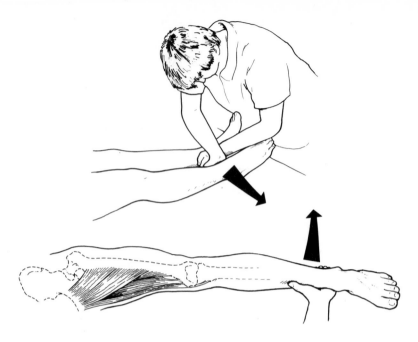

Adductors

TP The Testee lies face up, legs together. One ankle is stabilised while pressure is put on the inside of the other to pull that leg away. Watch for hip rock as the Testee tries to use other muscles. Other muscles to test, if weak: Quadriceps and Hamstrings.
A Gluteals and *TFL*.
MP (1) The middle top of the pubic bone. (2) The most prominent bumps on the top back of the pelvis.
M Pericardium (Cx).
HP (1) The parietal eminence which is three inches (7.5cm) above the ear at the widest part of the head. (2) Draw an imaginary line from the corner of the eye to the top of the ear, extend it two inches (5cm) behind the ear and hold this point. (3) Acu-points Cx-9 and Lv-1. Cx-9 is on the nailbed of the middle finger. Hold it with Lv-1 which is on the nailbed of the big toe, on the side nearest the other toes.
N Foods rich in vitamins A, B complex, E, iron, calcium, magnesium, banana, slippery elm, mint, kelp.

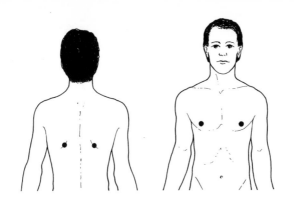

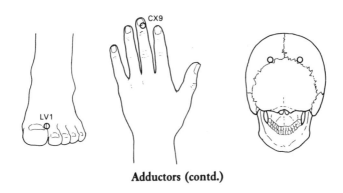

Adductors (contd.)

S Melon, cabbage family.
E Self-centred/kind, grief for self/fellow feeling, sorrow/joy, irresponsible/responsible, unfulfilled/fulfilled, confused/confident, deceiving/truth, sad/glad, nervous/peaceful, tongue-tied/expressive.
BF Holly.

Calf and foot muscles

Gastrocnemius and *Soleus*
Tibials and *Peronei*

Gastrocnemius and *soleus* pull on the Achilles tendon, and point the foot. To point the toes up and in, you use *anterior tibial,* to point down and in you use *posterior tibial.* To point the toes up and out you use *peronius tertius,* and down and out you use the other *peronius* muscles.

These are the two main calf muscles and lie one under the other. They share the Achilles tendon. *Gastrocnemius* crosses the knee joint, *soleus* doesn't. They are part of the chain of muscles which pulls from the head downwards to counteract the forward flop of the body that would otherwise occur due to gravity. They both react badly to the habit of wearing high heels, by cramping and leg twitch, unless stretched when you take those shoes off. They are both very strong, and singly they have to lift your entire weight when you walk. Weakness will cause a forward-leaning posture; spasm will cause a chain of events that may start as calf pain and progress to low-back pain and neck pain as each part of the body tries to compensate for this basic postural fault. Because of the meridian association there may also be poor digestion. *Soleus* and *gastrocnemius* are used by any musician who has pedals on their instrument i.e. harp, organ, timps, vibraphone, harmonium, as well as the more common keyboards.

TP (1) Mainly *gastrocnemius:* the Testee stands on the ball of one foot. Pressure is put on the shoulders to pull the heel back to the floor. (2) Mainly *soleus:* the Testee lies face down and the knee is bent 90° toes pointed. The heel is pulled up while downward pressure is put on the ball of the foot to bend the ankle. Other muscles to test, if weak: thigh muscles.

A *Tibials* and *peronei.*

MP (1) One inch (2.5cm) out and two inches (5cm) up from the tummy button.(2) Between the lowest three ribs on the back, either side of the spine.

M Triple warmer.

HP (1) Draw an imaginary line each side, from the corner of each eye passing through the top of the ear. Hold the point where the continuation of these two meet at the back of the head. (2) Acupoints TW-3 and GB-41. TW-3 is found on the back of the hand between the ring and little finger, and halfway between the base of the fingers and the wrist crease. Hold it with GB-41 which is on a similar place on the top of the foot – between the base of the last two toes and the ankle crease.

N Vitamin C, potassium, lecithin, manganese, alfalfa, apricot,

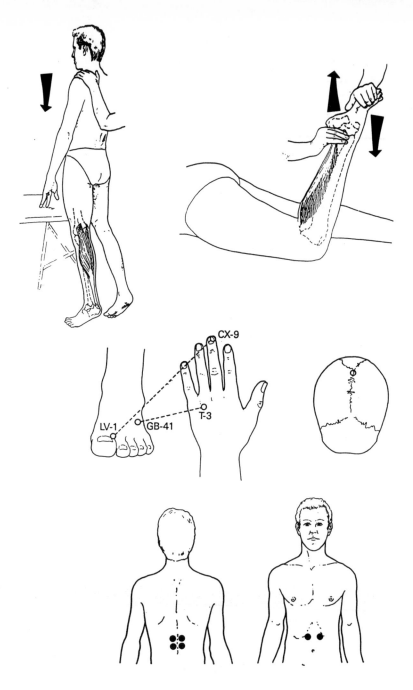

Gastrocnemius and soleus

357

banana, garlic.

S Tobacco, excess vitamin A, plastics, PVC, polystyrene, and polythene, cellophane and rubber.

E Unwilling/willing, restless/calm, confused/confident, cut off/united, not needed/needed, ungiving/cooperative, forsaken/accepted, incapable/understandable, disappointed/satisfied, forced/helpful.

BF Mustard.

Anterior tibial and *peronius tertius*. These two muscles work against *gastrocnemius* and *soleus* in pedalling (see above); *posterior tibial* and *peronius longus* (and *brevis*) work with them. All of them are important to organists (and some harpsichordists) to manipulate and move from one pedal to the

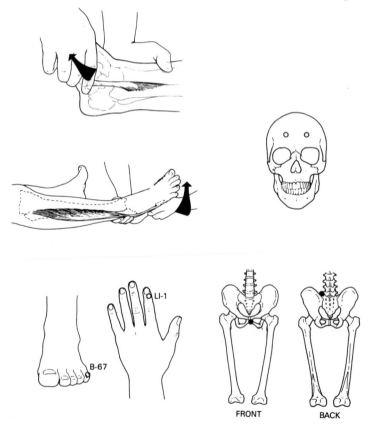

Peronius longus and brevis and peronius tertius

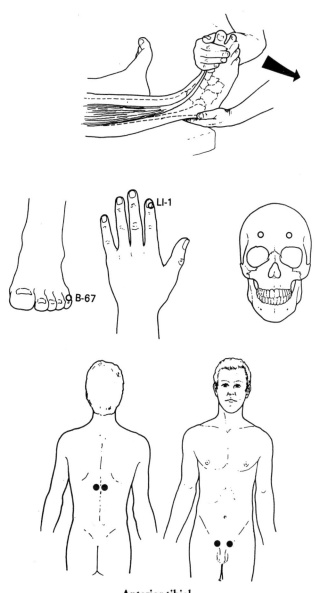

Anterior tibial

next. All but one of the muscles cross the ankle joint, running from the shin bones to the foot. They are very strong and proportionately short, therefore they tend to cramp. Weak shin muscles may cause flat feet, and because of their meridian association are frequently indicators of bladder

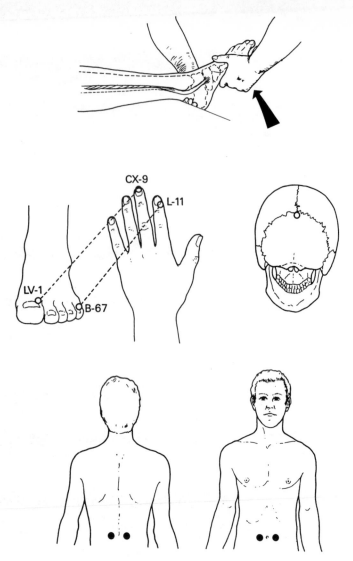

Tibialis posterior

problems and 'foot-drop' which trips you up. Weak *peronei* may also pre-dispose to twisting or turning the ankle over. There may also be foot and knee pain and poor balance.

TP All are tested with the Testee lying face up. (1) *Ant. tibial* The ankle is maximally flexed, with the toes up and in, the heel is supported underneath, while pressure is put on the top of the foot to point the big toe. (2) *Peroneus tertius* The ankle is maximally flexed with the toes up and out. The heel is supported underneath and pressure is put on the top outside of the foot to point the toes. (3) *Post. tibial* The toes are held pointed down and in. The heel is supported underneath and pressure is put on the ball of the foot to push it up and out. (4) *Peroneus longus* and *brevis* The toes are pointed down and out. The heel is supported underneath and pressure is put on the ball of the foot under the toes to push the foot up and in. Other muscles to test if weak: *piriformis, psoas, gastrocnemius* and *soleus*.

A Muscles tested in (1) and (2) above work as antagonists to those in (3) and (4).

MP (1) The tummy button and one inch (2.5cm) either side. (2) Upper and lower edges of the pubic bone. (3) The most prominent bumps on the top back of the pelvis (PSIS). (4) Either side of the lower spine above the previous points.

M Bladder.

HP (1) The frontal eminences – over the centre of each eye and halfway between eyebrows and hairline. (2) The glabella – between the eyebrows. (3) Acu-points B-67 and LI-1. B-67 is on the nailbed of the little toe. Hold it with LI-1 which is on the outer edge of the nailbed of the index finger.

N Vitamins B complex and E, calcium, magnesium, buckwheat, sunflower seeds, cayenne, lentils, rice, tarragon and lemon grass.

S Wood smoke, apples and cider, grapes and raisins.

E Nervous/restful, forgotten/remembered, unwilling/willing, wasted/invigorated, confused/confident, arrogant or defensive/listening, too much responsibility/responsible, hopeless/trusting, unsupportive/supportive, defeated/success, undesireable/pleasant, paranoid/secure, disorganised/organised, impatient/patient.

BF Impatiens

Please realise that although the above muscles may seem many and various, they are only the most important few, which are relevant to musicians.

REFERENCES (Chapters 10 to 14)

1. **Barton J.** (1981) *The Atlas* Vols. 1-7; *Encyclopedia of Body and Mind* Vol.4, Biokinesiology, 461 Sawyer Rd, Shady Cove, Oregan 97539, USA

2. **Caillet R.** (1982) *Hand Pain and Impairment,* Davis, California

3. – (1988) *Soft Tissue, Pain and Disability,* Davis, California

4. – (1991) *Neck and Arm Pain,* Davis, California

5. **Kendall F.** and **McCreary E.** (1983) *Muscle Testing and Function,* Williams and Wilkins

6. **Thie J.** (1973) *Touch for Health,* De Vorrs, Marina del Rey, CA 90291, USA

7. **Walther D.** (1983) *Applied Kinesiology* Vol.2; *Head, Neck and Jaw Pain and Dysfunction – the Stomatognathic System,* Systems DC Colorado USA

CHAPTER 15

More useful Techniques

More useful Techniques

Emergency mid-concert self-help; Warm-up and warm-down; Stretching without tears; Keeping fit; Types of massage; Anti-cramp; Hypertonic muscles; Origin/insertion and spindle cell technique; Reactive muscles; Pain chasing; Aerobic/Anaerobic; Injury reversal technique; Spontaneous positional release; Scars; Carpal and Guyon tunnel syndromes; Meridian running; Other useful acu-points; Right/left brain coordination; Reflexology points; Rehabilitation ladders.

Emergency mid-concert self-help

Emergencies shouldn't happen. But they do. They usually occur as the straw that breaks the camel's back, because the warning signs have been ignored and because of a chronic 'just one more' attitude. Obviously they are less likely, and less dire with good preparation. We are not talking here about fainting or falling off the stage. Such problems are a matter for the St John's Ambulance or Red Cross personnel present and the concert hall management, and you should not consider continuing to play unless they clear you. Having said that, there's nothing to stop you learning First Aid, and *all orchestral managers accompanying orchestras* should be proficient in at least the basic course. But suppose someone bumps into you as you bend to lift your instrument case, causing you to stumble awkwardly and strain a muscle? Suppose your pre-concert meal threatens to resist the digestive process? What if the dull ache around your left thumb suddenly becomes a shooting pain?

Much of what follows would not apply if you were a rank-and-file string player in a large symphony orchestra, because there are other players on the same part. However, here we are mainly talking about small ensemble work, or the wind or brass section of an orchestra, where each player is a soloist.

'It' has happened, and you have a very short time before going on stage. What to do? The first thing to decide is *can you continue,* not do you want to continue. Typically problems are *mental* (panic), *physical* (pain or muscle strain), *chemical* (nausea, dizziness), *environmental* (too hot/cold, no air, no room), *instrumental* (I leave that one to your lurid imagination).
1. Remember that people will want to help you, and will want you to

continue. But *the final decision is yours, not theirs*.

2. *Ask for what you want and need.* If it is to do with the venue, get hold of the top person available who can actually do something about it, (usually the stage manager). As time is short, don't waste time complaining to anyone else. When you are performing, you are king – the whole outfit (both back stage and front-of-house audience) is there because of you, so don't be shy. Act like a king, but be polite. You always have the sanction of not going back on stage.

3. *Be specific.* People cannot be expected to read your mind.

4. You've had a shock. For that take Arnica 6 (two tablets every hour for six doses, then three times a day until you feel normal again), or Rescue Remedy as below. Later, when you have finished playing, re-assess the situation. Realise that so far you have been 'symptom treating'. The cause of the breakdown must be found and treated ASAP after the concert if you don't want it to recur and become a chronic problem.

Mental problems – you panic. (1) Sip water with four drops of Rescue Remedy per glass. (2) Sit down, hands on lap, and breathe deeply and quietly in and out. (3) Visualise a time of success. (4) When you get out there on stage, concentrate on what you want the music to say as you play each bit. Trust all the hours of work you have done. Remember that living for approval is just another way of dying; do it for you; go out and give the audience yourself, the person they came to hear, not a load of 'oughts and shoulds'.

Physical problems. These are the most common you may encounter:

Cramp. 'Feather' the muscle. Brush it very lightly and fast backwards and forwards with your hand till the cramp goes. This disperses the excess energy stuck in the muscle. Now gently stretch the muscle.

Muscle strain (pain that gradually gets worse as you play). (1) Ask for ice. (2) While you wait for it to arrive, rub the massage points (MPs) for that muscle hard for 30 seconds (not more!). (3) Pinch the muscle belly together and gently pull its ends apart (see **Origin/Insertion** later in this chapter). (4) Wrap the ice in a hanky and hold it over the muscle. You may also massage it gently with the ice-cube. Do not continue with the ice beyond ten minutes, less if it starts to hurt from the cold. (5) Take Rhus tox 6.

Muscle weakness (weakness and/or lack of feeling, which comes on slowly during performance). (1) Rub the MPs for that muscle. (2) Push the ends of the muscle together. (3) Massage it from body (centre) to extremity, to help blood flow. (4) Keep it warm. (5) Make sure all the joints of the limb that are nearer the heart are working well, and that your head and neck posture is the best it can be. (6) Take Arnica 6.

Muscle tear (pain usually happens suddenly, with immediate decrease in function). (1) If you *must* continue, realise you do so at the risk of being unable to play for a while afterwards (maybe one or two weeks depending on severity). (2) Ask for a paramedic if available, ice and a crepe bandage (or other type of flexible strapping) or borrow a limb support. Meanwhile, hold the muscle under a running cold tap. (3) Use the ice wrapped in a hanky over the painful area for ten minutes to stop it swelling. (4) Bind it gently so that you can move but it feels supported, taking care not to cut off its blood supply (i.e. make sure it doesn't turn blue). This is much easier for a paramedic to do than you, unless you are trained already in bandaging and strapping. (5) Take Rhus tox 6. (6) Rearrange the programme to lessen physical stress. (7) After the concert, see a trained therapist ASAP.

Blinding headache. (1) Make sure you are not staring into spotlights on stage. Get them properly angled by the lighting manager (before he goes home, usually about 4.30 pm.). (2) Do some palming (see Chapter 4). (3) Use Acu-point GB31. Press in hard for ten seconds on a point on the outside of the thighs where the end of your straight arm and middle finger would touch the seam of your jeans (if you were wearing them). This point can be excruciatingly tender. Press for ten, rest for ten – do this three times. (4) Search in the webbing between thumb and index finger for a sore point and squeeze it for 30 seconds. (5) Massage hard all round the base of your skull at the top of the neck from ear to ear, giving extra to all the sore spots. This will help your neck muscles relax. (6) Hold your frontal eminences (see Chapter 8), and give the pain your complete attention. Stop when it has gone. This is a good technique for any pain anywhere in the body that originates in tension.

Chemical problems – **Nausea.** Decide if it's caused by food or fear. If from *food* (1) allow yourself to be sick if possible, to get rid of the poisons and excesses. (2) Take Arsen Alb. 6 if it's mild food poisoning and diarrhoea,

Nux Vom. 6 if it's indigestion. If the nausea stems from *fear*, sip some cold (not iced) water, into which you've put four drops of Rescue Remedy or Arnica.

Allergy. Asthma is the only one that needs instant help, and you will probably know already what to do. However (1) Ask that the cause (scent or smoke) be removed and ask for a straw. (2) Sit quietly, calm yourself as best you can and breathe through the straw. If it hasn't settled in two minutes don't go back on stage. Ask the paramedic for help. You will know if you are going to collapse. Demand a doctor, and don't even think about continuing to perform. Lumps and bumps that come up can be covered with Rescue Remedy cream and covered against friction until after the performance. All allergic reaction is increased by mental stress, so breathe as deeply and as slowly as you can, visualising peaceful situations in all breaks, and don't be tempted to have any caffeine.

Dizziness. (1) Breathe deeply and get your feet above your head by lying on the floor with your feet on a chair. (2) If you haven't eaten for more than three hours ask for a lump of sugar. (3) If neither of these work, don't go back on stage. You may trip and hurt yourself seriously, and probably smash your instrument too.

Environmental problems. Find out who has real control in the building (usually the stage manager) and be specific, polite and firm about your needs and why it's essential something is done *now* rather than next week. If necessary, get back-up from your concert manager.

Instrumental emergencies. Decide to (1) Borrow what you need. (2) Invent – maybe the house technician can help. (3) Change the programme order or swap parts with someone capable. (4) Change the programme and play what is possible, given the limitations you now have, and tell the audience so that they can sympathise. (5) Never travel without your spares kit again.

Post mortem. While you are nursing yourself back to health, be responsible for your future, and make a written assessment. The breakdown occured. Why?

1. The losses and gains and long-term effects accruing from the emergency – what I did too much/too little of that predisposed me to breakdown?

2. What I can do/change technically to forestall another such

emergency, such as less technical crowding, or more stamina building?

3. Given the risks, what must I now know/learn/do/delegate, or do some things need to be delayed or reprogrammed?

4. Who can be trusted in such circumstances to help/take over?

5. To what expense am I prepared to go to keep my health/job/instrument going now and in the future?

6. What should I now add to my Emergency pack?

7. Who are the local experts for this problem? Who would be available on tour?

8. Who will come to *me* if I'm incapacitated (doctor, dentist, physio, chiro, osteo, instrument repairer)? Who does emergency repair work, who does the best work, and who has an instrument like mine that I can borrow?

9. What exactly does my insurance cover (read the small print)?

Warm-up and warm-down

The purpose of warm-up and warm-down is injury avoidance. Obvious to athletes, yet most muscians assume it's never going to happen to them. Unless they are playing in a cold church, most instrumentalists don't bother to do more than tune their instrument, and make sure it's properly set up, and waggle a finger or two in a rather bored way, before they launch into playing. Even then, they give more attention to their replaceable instrument than to their irreplaceable selves. They may have had it dinned in to them in early days that 'bandroom concerti' are frowned upon, not realising that this is quite different from constructive warm-up exercises. Some people do nothing because they are pathetically frightened to let anyone hear them alone in case they hear how less than adequate they now have become. Mostly they have little imagination as to how to make it fun, or that it's possible to warm-up without making a huge din.

The benefits of warming-up are flexibility and control, speed and sensitivity; and because less is taken out of you, there is stamina and room to spare rather than playing to the limits of your capability (which is when accidents happen). Muscles that are cold, tight, weak, and inadequately conditioned are more susceptible to over-use injuries. Contributors to strain are (a) changing instrument size, or to an instrument with a stiffer action or tighter springs; (b) an abrupt increase in playing time or repertoire change; (c) a new teacher or playing with excessive tension; (d) tension in normal life – gripping steering wheels, telephones, pens, knives, hammers.

A cold muscle is a slow muscle. Nerve conduction is slower, and the fibres of the muscle are less elastic and more liable to tear. The throughput of blood and nutrients is poor, as is clearance of waste products. A cold muscle has more resistance and will cramp more easily. Slow nerve conduction also contributes to reduced sensitivity in the fingers. Most top athletes take about 20 minutes to warm-up properly before an event. Musicians should do the same.

Obviously each person has different warm-up and warm-down needs, depending on physique, instrument and technique, so I can only make general suggestions here. My remarks are addressed mainly to, and in terms of, string, piano and wind players, as statistically they are the musicians most likely to have physical problems. **Warm-up** should be aimed at recreating the conditions where you play best (see Chapter 7).

1. Start with whole-body movements to get the general circulation going. Easiest is to do some cross-crawl (see below) and improve coordination at the same time.

2. Do some general stretches (see below) and get loose. You may be sitting on a chair for the next couple of hours, so wake your body up!

3. Begin to be more specific and work on your shoulders, then elbow, then wrist and finally fingers, using loosening, shaking and stretching.

4. Massage the main muscle groups you will use, starting on the main part of the body and working down to the fingers, by picking up the muscle belly and shaking it gently, and rubbing it in a circular fashion, ending up with extra massage between the bones of the hand, front and back of the palm (these muscles are too small to pick up, yet they do the most speed work).

5. Do some deep breathing (perhaps at the same time as the massage).

6. Get your instrument out and do some gentle stretching and breathing exercises with it to introduce yourselves to each other again. Now include another essential technique or two, string

369

crossing or tonguing or whatever, gradually getting faster and louder as you become more supple and your coordination improves.

7. Now concentrate on your sense of touch, and how lightly you can hold the instrument and play with balance and ease. Reach out and feel for the intonation, embouchure, depth of key.

8. Next play something normally – improvise perhaps – play something technically demanding that you play well and easily, but not the same piece every time, and no 'band room cadenzas' which only antagonise everyone else and impress no-one, particularly not the more experienced players. Now is not the time to practise that awkward 'bit' – that should have been done before in private; nor is it the time to test yourself on memory.

9. If you are a soloist, now is the time to do some more deep breathing and go within. Think of calmness, reassurance, trust, and of all your past successes, and recreate a mind-set where everything works well for you.

10. Go out on stage and enjoy yourself.

Warm-down should be more or less the reverse of warm-up. Conscious cooling down time after playing almost never happens amongst musicians. When the concert is over, either it's an express pack-up and out the door to catch the last train, or say 'yes' and 'no' in the right places to the right people in the green room so that you get the next job. No professional athlete would dream of such mistreatment of his body. This attitude harks back to the genteel days when one was not supposed to perspire in polite company! A true warm-down should be a mirror image of the warm-up, gradually decreasing the blood-flow back to normal, preventing the chill-factor, stiffness and cramp setting in, and making sure all the waste products are removed.

1. Congratulate yourself on what went well.

2. Breathe deeply and enjoy the applause. That applause is not only for now, but for all the years of hard work you've put in.

3. While your heart is still beating fast, whizz about on your instrument and use up the spare adrenalin. Do some celebratory improvising.

4. Gradually slow down and play gently at the extemities of the instrument, coming back to the centre and the easy bits of the

instrument.

5. Clean up and put away your instrument, making a note of any repairs or spares needed, and thank it.

6. Now do mirror image exercises, starting with your fingers and working up to whole-body movements, doing the opposite of what is required to play. Where joints bend and muscles contract to play, stretch them; where they twist, twist the other way.

7. Do some gentle but deep massage, 'reaching through to the bone', and iron out all the tender places and knots you find with a firm pressure over the knot while you stretch and flex the muscle till the knot melts. Be kind to your hard working body. If you find there is a feeling of skinburn or hair pull as you massage, use a very little oil, talc or, as a last resort, soap.

8. Know the places you tend to hold static as you play and give them a stretch as well. They've worked just as hard, even though they were not necessarily directly involved in manoeuvring your instrument. Don't forget to stretch and undo your calf muscles if you were wearing high heels! Keep a pair of flatties in your car or case.

9. Do some whole-body stretches in reverse order to your warm-up.

10. Go in peace with yourself and your body.

The constraints of last trains and shared cars, family needs and house managers wanting to lock up, make warm-down time almost an impossibility for most orchestral musicians but, even so, it is an ideal to aim for where possible. At the very least keep moving gently to help undo the knots, wrap up so you don't get chilled, and make a habit of warm-down after practising at home.

Sometimes venues are so cold that warming-up is necessarily a continuous affair, as the cold seems to creep up your legs from the stone floor. This is worse if you are not playing continuously. The only remedies are thick-soled shoes, insoles or fleecy-lined boots, a hand warmer in each pocket, fingerless mittens and long-johns. Specific finger warm-up with hot water works best if you can let the hot water run over your wrists (where the blood runs near the surface),and then vigorously massage from there to the fingertips. A quick 'run round the block', which would be recommended to athletes to stimulate the general circulation, is not so easy in long black!

There are also suggestions in Chapter 3, but, if you can't manage any of these, all you can do is to put your hands in your armpits or sit on them alternately, as you blow warm air on the fingerboard, or down the bore with all the keys covered, or ask for hot-water bottles to be put on the keyboard in the interval (like Roselyn Tureck; this isn't very good for a piano, and may affect its tuning, but then the concert organisers should have done something about it beforehand). You can play in overcoats like the Amadeus did at Jordans once, and you are also absolutely entitled to refuse to play on health grounds if it's that cold.

Stretching without tears

The purpose of stretching is to wake muscles up gently to remind them of their full range of movement. This is particularly important when we use a muscle professionally only within certain less-than-full parameters. Clothing must be loose and free of restrictions, absorbent and warm, even when damp.

When you are doing a stretch, the temptation is to bounce because muscles are elastic. However this simply activates the recoil mechanism and doesn't stretch muscles usefully. The best way to extend the range of movement of a muscle, is to stretch it as far as it will go comfortably, as you breathe out, and hold the stretch for ten seconds. This resets the nerve endings *(proprioceptors)* which give the brain feedback on the state of the muscle; you can now stretch a little further. This technique will only work twice or, at most, three times in a row effectively, with a little gain each time. After that you will gain nothing but pain and micro-tear damage so STOP. The amount of increase you have gained is all that the body can take – which may be more than some people and less than others. Don't judge yourself by them, this is not Stretch Olympics but a preparation for playing. You don't need to stretch every muscle in the book separately, work in groups. When you finish, your body should feel ready, eager and alert, not wrung-out and exhausted.

Do not attempt these stretches if you have any kind of back or neck problem without full consultation with your therapist. Neither I nor the publishers will take responsibility if you misuse or overdo these exercises. Your health is your responsibility, not ours.

The main areas to stretch are postural muscles in a general stretch, followed by specific muscles for all musicians. Those specific to your instrument you will do as part of your warm-up routine. You can do isometric muscle-work in a car as a last resort if you are stuck in a traffic jam, but this doesn't really stretch the full range of movement.

General stretch

1. *Low back*. Curl up with your knees on your chest and hug them to you as you breathe out. You can do this before getting out of bed as a wake-up exercise too. If you want to loosen up the pelvis do this on a hard surface and gently rock back and forth, side to side for a minute or so. If you get stiff sitting try the following: Lie face up, knees together and bent at 90°, feet on the floor. Pretend you have a balloon with the string held between your knees so it won't fly away. Bounce it on your abdomen. Let it go and then polish the floor under you with your bottom, going side to side and both clockwise and anti-clockwise. Now draw huge letters of the alphabet with each knee in turn. Finally stand up, hands on hips and pretend you have a hula hoop or do belly dancing. These will all loosen the lower back and pelvic joints and could improve your sex life!

2. *Low abdomen*. Stand one leg forward one back as far apart as is comfortable, feet facing forward. Hands on hips. Keep the back leg straight, lean back as you bend the front leg. Swap legs.

3. *Side stretch*. Feet shoulder-width apart. Right hand on hip, left hand over the head, bend to the right as far as possible while still facing front. Swap hands and sides.

4a. *Full Twist*. Feet shoulder-width apart, hands on hips, twist as far as possible one way without moving your feet. Twist the other way.

4b. *Half Twist*. Sit or hold the hips facing front, while you twist the shoulders as far round one way as you can. Now twist the other way.

5. *Thigh stretch*. Stand on one leg, lean back and grab the other ankle. Straighten your back and keep it vertical as you pull your ankle up behind your buttocks. Do not lean forward, it negates the stretch. Do the other thigh.

6. *Hamstring stretch*. Hands on waist, cross one straight leg over the other. Bend forward from the hip joint, (not the waist) to stretch the back leg. Swap legs.

7. *Foot stretch.* Walk about on tip toe, then on your heels, then on the outsides and insides of your feet. Wriggle your toes. If you haven't got room to do that in your shoes they are too tight, and will give you neck weakness.

8. *Arm stretch.* Lift straight arms up and back behind the head, then down and back up behind your back, then lift them to shoulder height and cross them in front, then behind as far as possible. Finally twist the arms palm in and palm out as far as you can.

9. *Neck stretch.* Drop the head on to the chest and hold, then look up and as far back as you can and hold that. Next get your ear as near your shoulder as possible, not forgetting the other side; next look over each shoulder as far as you can, and finally stick your chin out and then pull it in as far as you can. Now replace your head normally.

More specific flexibility exercises and stretches

1. Shoulder joint. Hands on shoulders. Write your full name in capital letters as large as as possible with the point of one elbow (or do both together if you like). You can write what you like, the letters will give you every possible range of motion.

2. Wrist stretch. With fingers vertical, stretch your wrist and flex it up and down as far as possible, ten seconds each way. You can do both hands together. Put palms together at chest height and, lowering both hands, then turning the hands so that they are backs together at waist height, raise them up to chest height. (Abilities will vary enormously here. STOP if you have any pain, tingling or loss of feeling, and turn to the advice on carpal tunnel syndrome below.) Next put the forearm and hand on a flat surface and stretch the little finger side by bending then hand and wrist towards the thumb, and the thumb side by bending the hand sideways towards the little finger. Finally, keeping the forearm flat, lift first the thumb side away then the little finger side away. In all these there will only be a small amount of movement, except in the forward and backward stretches.

3. Now complete the wrist flexibility by holding the forearm and, by way of a change, write half the alphabet in lower case letters as large as possible with your right knuckles and the other half with your left.

4. Hand, finger and thumb sideways stretch. First stretch the fingers as far apart as you can. Then with the right hand, using thumb and middle finger, stretch and hold the stretch for ten seconds between the left thumb to index, thumb to middle, thumb to ring and thumb to little fingers. Next stretch and hold index to middle, index to ring and index to little fingers. Continue with middle to ring and middle to little fingers and finally ring to little fingers. Now swap hands.

5. Hand, finger and thumb front-to-back stretch. Use the wrist of one hand between the fingers of the other successively to gently push and stretch one finger back and the other forward. End with a stretch of the thumb across the palm to the base of the little finger.

6. Finger and thumb flexibility. Hold the right wrist with the left hand to prevent it helping. Keeping tip-to-tip contact between thumb and each finger of the right hand, successively do some more alphabet writing, and then swap hands. It's not as easy as it seems!

7. I'll bet by now you have forgotten all about breathing! It is important for everyone to keep the breathing muscles stretched, not just those of you who blow. Start sitting hunched up and bent forward with elbows crossed and down between your legs. Fill your 'stomach' with air and let it push your arms out of the way. Unfold your body enough so that your hands can go to the side of your ribs. Fill with air and push your ribs out against your hands. Next use your hands to fight the breast bone as it rises as you fill up with air. Finally fling your arms up, out and back, and as wide as you can, to take in the last scrap of air you can, and then relax before you either levitate or explode! (This exercise takes far more time to explain than to do.)

8. Face stretch. Singers, wind and brass players will each have their own version of this. However, in general, begin by puffing out the cheeks and then sucking them in, next protrude the lips to whistle, next bring the lower jaw as far forward and back as possible, then yawn and finally smile as wide as you can.

9. For facial flexibility mouth the letters of the alphabet, and if you are singing in a foreign language do it in that language too.

10. Don't forget the eye exercises in Chapter 4.

More hand and whole-body stretching, and exercises relevant to musicians, can be found in Schneider et al. (1994) and Anderson (1980). Both are really excellent books (see References at end of chapter).

Keep fit (KF)

Many talented musicians were actively discouraged from sports at school because they might damage their hands, or because their gentler nature hated combat and contact sport. Taken sensibly, with proper precautions, sport is no more dangerous than cutting bread with a sharp bread knife or crossing the road. However, little or no sport means that musicians mostly live in their heads except when playing their instrument, are bodily very unaware, and often become short in team spirit, which can cause problems in orchestras. Musicians are short of spare time, sit about a lot, and use some muscles disproportionatly more than others. They are well coordinated and well motivated in the muscles they use and lazy about the rest because of mental and emotional fatigue, since a three-hour rehearsal is said to have a similar energy output to a rugby match. This unbalanced unfitness is not specific to musicians. Many sports professionals are just as unfit and unbalanced! Doing something to keep fit generally is therefore very much more important than most people realise.

1. General fitness actually improves your playing, your feeling of well-being and your ability to cope with stress of all types.
2. It redresses over-use imbalance.
3. It keeps your spine straight.
4. It improves your coordination.
5. It releases endorphins in the brain, helping you to feel positive about life.
6. It keeps your weight nearer to normal.
7. It balances the meridians.

As a musician, your inclination, patience and time are likely to be in short supply, so you are probably reduced to three options:
1. Do ten minutes KF a day in a graded way until you reach optimum fitness for your age, maintaining it thereafter with sessions three times a week (see References). This is good if you are shy, or are embarrassed about your slothful body. However it needs a lot of discipline to keep it up . You might find it easier to:
2. Have a personal coach, who will supply you with motive and

drive, and will cost you quite a bit, or you can:

3. Join a gym or a club and do dance aerobics, or go swimming, especially backstroke, do some form of yoga, or learn t'ai chi. All will get you meeting people who are not musicians. Swimming, yoga and t'ai chi are more 'portable' when touring, but will lose you less calories. All of the above are properly balanced in body use, but golf, tennis and other racquet sports are one-sided, and may actually compound an existing problem due to the occupational hazards of the instrument you play.

For burning calories fastest and making you leaner, the top three exercises are jogging (can be hard on the knees), dance aerobics, and fast walking (cheapest and best). For undoing a squashed chest, swimming is good, but won't use so many calories. Indoor bikes and ski-machines are surprisingly only slightly better at burning calories, no matter what their sales people say.

When you get home after a hard day, it's often pleasant to have an Epsom salts soak. Not a couple of tablespoons of scented bath salts, but as much as three cups or one pound (half a kilo) of dissolved Epsom salts. Don't drink the water! This is an old Rugby players' remedy for easing out aches and stiffness.

Massage

There are many types of massage: Swedish, remedial or sports, aromatherapy, reflexology and shiatsu, as well as erotic 'with extras', and books are available on all of them. I shall not discuss the last, I leave that to you. Straight, Swedish or remedial massage can be either invigorating or calming, and to some extent depends on the practitioner and on your personal likes and dislikes. Some people do not feel they have had their money's worth unless they feel tired afterwards, and equate heavy pressure and pummelling with getting in touch with and straightening out parts of their body they normally ignore, because they live in their heads. For them massage is a lazy form of passive exercise. Others would be shattered by this, and only want the lightest of esoteric strokes to lead them into a relaxed meditative state. Sports people often only want the parts they have exercised worked on as part of a warm-down regime because they know it will lessen stiffness later. Some only want their back worked on or hate having their head or feet touched. Whatever you choose, when you go for a massage, realise that it is *your* time and you do not have to have any 'extras' you don't want.

To find a reputable practitioner, apply to one of the massage schools offering a certificated course, and ask for their best student. All others will have full diaries if they are any good. Alternatively you and your spouse or best beloved could learn together, and then you are set up for life. The ideal for a soloist on a concerto tour might be an invigorating massage before, and a calming one after the performance as part of the warm-up/down procedures from a tame travelling masseur, but that is as expensive as taking your own grand piano with you and can't be done on the bandroom floor! Some have been known to research and carry a list of all the Turkish baths on tour, or Japanese massage parlours. Top hotels may have a resident masseur if they have a fitness centre. It's worth an enquiry at the reception desk.

Shiatsu incorporates the important acu-points relevant to your condition, and brings about both relaxation and healing. Very often acu-points coincide with areas of muscular tension that a chiropractor, osteopath, or physiotherapist will work on using trigger point therapy. Many muscle facilitation techniques are available (see below).

Tougher than trigger point massage is *Rolfing,* which can be exquisitely painful, and works on releasing and stretching the fascia (the sort of sausage skin which encases each muscle), thereby having dramatic effects on posture, and allowing muscles which for years have been held in contraction, to relax. Generally this is done as an integrated course of ten treatments, concentrating on specific areas each session.

Self Massage. You know your own areas of cramp, spasm and tension. Find the places and use deep, firm, but gentle and slow circular motion on these (making sure the rest of you doesn't become tense while you do it!).

A useful execise is to massage the entire scalp with your outstretched fingers, really moving the skin against the bone, also going gently round the eye sockets. Next, working with your thumbs, pay particular attention to the jaw joint in front of your ears, and the top of the back of the neck under the skull. Follow this by clasping hands behind the neck and squeezing between fingers and palm down one side; then change hands and squeeze down the other. For awkward places on your back you can use a golf ball, positioniong it so that it rests under the centre of a tight muscle when you lie on it. Relax in this position until the muscle tension goes.

Aromatherapy is at the gentle end of the massage scale. Essential flower essences are added to a plant oil which acts as a carrier, and the volatile oils are absorbed through the skin. They work through their subtle chemistry and through emotional associations, likes and dislikes. Lavender is one of the most popular because of its many healing and relaxing properties, but you will find a full list in Raymond Lautie's book (see References). Sometimes it is very pleasant to have just your face done by someone else, to melt away the world's tension, and finish with a hot towel over you to help soak in the oils.

Reflexology as a form of foot massage, can be extremely relaxing as well as usefully diagnostic in a general way. Similarly a head, hand and jaw massage. It all depends where you hold tension or screw up in knots with playing, or which area you ignore in normal daily living.

Tired muscle or 'over-use' injury? How do you know the difference? Fry (1986) has defined five categories which should act as alarm bells and stop you playing. (1) Pain at one site only. (2) Pain at multiple sites. (3) Pain that persists beyond the time of playing, with some loss of coordination. (4) All of the above, plus pain in normal activities of daily life (ADL). (5) All the above, where all activities using the affected body part cause pain.

You should never let things get to this state, and you will not if you throw out the notion of 'No pain, no gain'. Instead of bashing on, hoping the pain will go away, use your brains for silent practice and thoughtful consideration of your technique.

Anti-cramp

Cramp is usually due to trying to force a cold muscle to work before it is properly warmed up, or lack of warm-down after a lot of exertion. Night-cramp is said to be due to calcium imbalance. When a muscle cramps, it is because mechanically the microscopic ratchet system of fibres is jammed in contraction. Chemically the waste products are clogging the electrical control of the muscle ratchet, and meridian energy-wise cramp is interpreted as too much energy in one place.

The traditional method of release is to stretch the muscle forcibly or massage it deeply and, as a last resort, inject it with botulinum toxin (which is a very drastic remedy). However, where there is ordinary cramp (and not a serious incurable problem like Motor Neurone disease), the most effective method is 'feathering', which is painless, better than heavy massage, often far faster, and can relieve all cramp symptoms. Simply disperse the excess energy by brushing the muscle with your fingers very fast and very lightly, backwards and forwards and end to end, as though you were brushing off the dust. It usually only takes ten seconds, but may need to be repeated after using the muscle again till it settles down.

I recommend re-reading Chapter 10 before proceeding further, to familiarise yourself with basic muscle testing. If, when you have worked on all the MPs and HPs there is still a problem (such as pain, spasm, twinges or stiffness, the posture looks distorted but the muscles test strong, there is a restricted range of movement or there are over-enlarged flabby muscles, there is persistant recruiting of muscles that shouldn't normally be used to carry out a specific function), the problem may lie in the balance between the relative tension settings of those muscles. For instance, one muscle may be chronically contracted because you habitually use it that way. Typical of this is the raised left shoulder of so many violinists. It causes 'switch off' of all the muscles that work against it, because they then have to work at half strength, and can cause joint malfunction. The first technique to work on is:

Hypertonic muscles, muscle energy techniques, neuro-muscular relaxation

This is a simple muscle technique with many names, often used by physiotherapists, osteopaths and chiropractors, but with the addition of breathing and indicator muscle testing, as discovered by Frank Mahoney DC, which vastly increases its effectiveness. Use it when you find a muscle that feels tight, sore, and doesn't want to relax when you finish playing.

1. Find a strong indicator muscle (see Chapter 10).
2. Put the sore muscle into extension by stretching it as far as it will go, or to the point where pain starts. Then bring it just back from that.
3. Hold it there, while you retest the indicator muscle which will now be weak if this technique is needed.

4. Keeping the problem muscle in extension by holding it, ask the Testee to take a deep breath and, *while exhaling,* gently and slowly contract the muscle against the resistance the Tester is providing over a count of eight to ten seconds.

5. The Testee then relaxes the muscle gently and the Tester can now take up the slack, to reach a new starting position.

6. Stages 3 to 5 are repeated twice more.

7. Retest stages 2 and 3 but now the indicator muscle will stay strong.

It is particularly important that the muscle is only worked on with resistance when the Testee breaths *out.* Many people stop breathing or push when inhaling and this will only worsen the problem and may jam the muscle completely. This technique is particularly successful where problems recur as a result of repetitive movements, requiring specific muscle contraction. The muscles will have a greater potential than is being used in this repetitive action. It is as if the brain thinks that the small range of movement used repetitively is the maximum range of movement, and erroneously resets other muscles accordingly.

Origin/insertion and spindle cell technique
These techniques always work, but the effect can be short lived as you are working on the sensory cells of the muscle itself. There are two ways to strengthen a muscle mechanically. The first is to push the two ends of the muscle (the origin and insertion) together. This has the general effect of shortening the muscle artificially and thus strengthening it. (The reverse is also true – if you pull the two ends of a strong muscle apart, it will then test as weak.)

The second technique (seemingly opposite to the first) is to pull apart the fibres (spindle cells) in the belly of the muscle so they are not overcrowded and can work more efficiently. This will strengthen the muscle (naturally the reverse is true – if you push the belly of a muscle together it will weaken a strong muscle). These effects will not last if you haven't sorted out the underlying problem of how the muscle got in that state. However, the technique is particularly useful to switch a muscle off temporarily when working with Reactive muscles (see below) and in emergency, mid-concert.

Reactive muscles

If the deisred result is achieved with the use of the two techniques described above, but the effect lasts only for a few seconds, you may have a reactive muscle syndrome. This usually occurs in muscles which are very frequently used (as in playing), or in a combination of a muscle and its antagonist. It can also apply where a muscle affects its twin on the opposite side of the body, e.g. right *latissimus dorsi* affecting left *latissimus dorsi*. The syndrome occurs because one of the two is set too high (i.e. is too contracted) and thereby inhibits or weakens the other. The way to find this syndrome is to test the two suspect muscles in very quick succession. If they are both strong if tested singly, but when tested quickly one after the other one now becomes weak, then the balance between them needs re-setting.

1. Work on the muscle which remains strong.

2. Switch it off by reversing normal origin/insertion technique (see above), or by 'misusing' the relevant MPs by feathering them instead of massaging firmly (NB the MPs are not usually on the problem muscle itself), or by gently hitting the HPs (not the acu-points!).

3. The muscle that was weak will now have strengthened since it is no longer inhibited. Contract it gently several times to reset it.

4. Tap on the Testee's forehead in a small clockwise circle. This will reset the muscle you purposely weakened.

5. Test the two muscles again in quick succession. Both should now remain strong.

6. Any pair of muscles can get 'hooked up' like this, and for musicians a frequent occurence involves the eye muscles and feet, causing tripping up over kerb stones (see Chapter 4).

Pain Chasing

This technique is useful when there are shooting pains that come and go and seem to wander or progress from muscle to muscle.

1. Start with the muscle that is giving pain now.

2. Find a strong indicator muscle.

3. Bit by bit, feel the territory of muscle that hurts, retesting the indicator muscle as you do so.

4. The point you touch which causes the strong indicator muscle suddenly to test weak is the next point to work on.

5. Firmly pinch together either side of that spot several times for a few seconds.

6. If you have been successful, touching the spot will now no longer cause the indicator muscle to weaken.

7. Go through the entire muscle and remove any other points.

8. Tap clockwise in small circle on the Testee's forehead to reset the mind-muscle connection and ask where the pain has now gone; chase the pain from the new muscle in the same way. When there is no further pain, stop. This technique often unravels old injury patterns and compensatory tension chains built by the body in order to try to solve the problem itself.

Aerobic/anaerobic

Playing often involves repetitive use of a muscle which becomes fatigued or weak sooner than expected, after sustained or repeated action.

1. Test the suspect muscle. It will be strong.

2. Now test it lightly but quickly ten times in succession and it becomes weak.

3. If it now becomes and remains strong when the Testee holds the MPs or HPs for that muscle (see Chapter 10), these points need working on for at least three to four minutes as there has been inadequate lymphatic clearing of the muscle. Waste products are clogging it, causing shortage of oxygen and consequent weakness.

Injury reversal technique

Just as you retain a mental memory of the accidents that happen to you, so there is also a tissue memory. At its most basic level, the self-preservation mechanism of the body remembers at a subconscious level that when you got in *that* position, something nasty happened and there was injury. It therefore resists that position, and goes into a 'switch-off' protection mode, even when the danger is long past, every time that position is repeated. It is that subconscious memory which will cause hesitancy and lack of confidence, incomplete healing, or delayed return to normal use when there is no other apparent reason for it. Typical injuries are an old forgotten whiplash, falling on your hands, breaking or dislocating a limb (especially the shoulder), and tooth extraction etc.

1. Find a strong indicator muscle.

2. The Testee must describe the accident in as lurid a detail as possible, physically getting into the positions they were in, with instrument too, if that is relevant. What matters is not so much mental recall as body recall.

3. Test the indicator muscle, which will now be weak if this technique is relevant and the event still active in the subconscious.

4. You may need to support the Testee in this position with cushions and furniture. It doesn't matter what the support is made of, it's the position and contact points with other structures that's important.

5. Hold the Testee's Frontal Eminences – over each eye and mid-way between the eyebrows and hairline, while the story of the accident is retold three times.

6. Retest the indicator muscle which should now be strong. If not, there may be further positions with stored memories.

This technique may uncover defensive 'switch-off' reactions – patterns which have been affecting the body for years which it built up as a safety measure. These remain unhelpfully active, when all they are actually doing is holding back progress and confidence. If the accident is recent, obviously the Testee *must* be checked by a competent physician. More often than not, however, the body may be reflecting the last stages of healing from surgery, and you will have been told that you will now just have to live with the lesser function.

Spontaneous positional release

Although this technique is useful on many large muscles, the greatest use to a musician is probably to undo the tensions in the small intrinsic muscles of the spine which are otherwise difficult to negotiate or feel. Symptomatic might be a sharp pain or tenderness at one spot, a 'crick in the neck', or sudden inability to turn the head.

1. The Testee lies face up. The Tester then holds the head, taking its weight, and placing a firm finger over the painful spot (usually somewhere on the neck).

2. While receiving *continous* feedback from the Testee, Tester and Testee together find the most comfortable and pain-free position of

the erstwhile painful spot by moving the head. This can be *any* and often extraordinary position of the head and neck! Search till you find it.

3. Holding the position, pressure is then placed on the crown of the head to push the head 'into' the base of the neck, and held for 30 seconds. The principle behind the method is to contract the muscle more, so that its natural release mechanism comes into play, not unlike undoing a hook and eye – the more you pull it the more it holds, but push it together and it releases easily.

4. The same technique may be used on any of the small muscles of the spine, by moving the torso until the pain disappears, and then applying pressure.

Scars

Scars can have an extraordinary effect, even keyhole surgery and stitch scars, particularly if they happen to cut across a meridian. This is because scar tissue is different from normal skin and hasn't the same stretch or conductive properties. Scars also often contract, pucker and itch, pulling on muscles in an abnormal way. When they occur internally they can also cause adhesions, with an occasionally very disruptive effect. There is nothing that can be done here about internal scars (so talk to your GP); external ones can be easily helped, however. Post-operative carpal tunnel scars (see below) are typical of these.

1. Immediately after the operation dressings are permanently removed, smooth vitamin E cream all over the site. It will help skin healing and reduces puckering.

2. Do not work on a scar that has not properly healed yet. When the scar is *really* strong and well healed, say six months later, find a strong indicator muscle and

3. Work along the scar bit by bit, testing the indicator muscle as you go. Any weakness indicates that that place is out of synch. with the rest of the surrounding tissue, and needs treatment.

4. Use PR (a pain relieving spray that contains fluro-methane available at the chemist) or an ice cube to freeze that spot, so that there is light frosting over it (this should take two or three minutes only – you don't want to cause frostbite!).

5. While it is intensely cold, gently stretch the scar tissue as if to pull the wound apart four or five times. Stretch round scars from the centre out.

6. Warm it up and retest. The indicator muscle should now be strong.

Carpal tunnel and Guyon tunnel syndromes

These are both nerve compression syndromes described in Chapter 9. They cause weakness, tingling and pain in the hand. Carpal tunnel syndrome is often associated with an over-flexed wrist position, such as when playing above the tenth position on the violin or viola. It may also be made worse by the shape of the upper bouts of the instrument, the set of the neck and the height of the bridge, all of which affect the amount of pressure needed to depress the strings. Diabetics, young women with slender wrists, pregnant women and small people are most at risk, due to overuse and lack of space within the wrist. Overuse causes irritation to the nerve sheath and it swells, leaving even less room for the nerve. The median nerve passes through the carpal tunnel and affects working of the thumb, index and sometimes part of the middle finger.

The ulnar nerve passes between the pisiform and the hook of the hammate – two wrist bones at the base of the little finger, which make the tunnel of Guyon, causing problems with the ring and little fingers. If either of these syndromes keeps recurring, the sufferer should buy a wrist splint or support from the chemist, seriously look at their playing hand position and/or consider a smaller size fingerboard or instrument. To correct these conditions, first do the **General Hand Test:**

1. The Testee holds the tip of the thumb and little finger together, making a ring. The Tester then gently tests them by pulling them apart, using single fingers only, by hooking one finger round the Testee's thumb and one round the little finger.
2. There may be some 'give' because there are so many joints involved. However the muscles should still lock.
3. Correct any weakness as follows (refer to Chapter 10). **MP** (1) Under the pubic bone on the front of the pelvis. (2) Between the seventh and eighth ribs in the cartilage on the left side of the breastbone. (3) The most prominent bumps on the top back of the

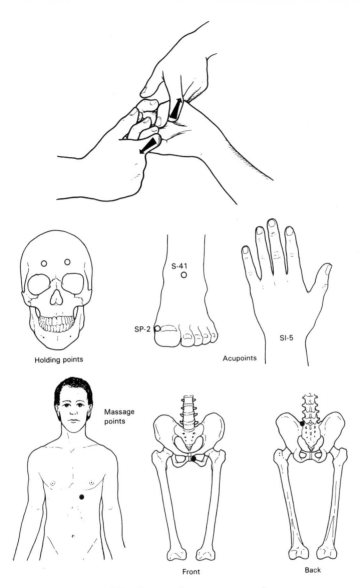

Holding points

S-41
SP-2

Acupoints

SI-5

Massage
points

Front

Back

General hand test and opponens muscles

pelvis. (4) Either side of the spine, level with the bottom of the
shoulder-blades. **HP** (1) The frontal eminences – above the centre
of each eye half-way between the eyebrows and the hairline. (2)
Centre back of the head on a straight line that starts at the corner of

the eye, and passes through the top of the ear, both sides. (3) Acupoints Sp-2 and H-8. Sp-2 is on the nail side of the large joint at the base of the big toe. Hold it with H-8 which is on the palm, on the crease under the ring finger. This will eliminate confusing weakness of the intrinsic muscles of the hand.

4. The Testee now encircles the wrist with thumb and index finger of the other hand, holding it very gently as though it were very precious, fragile and not to be squeezed, and the muscle test is performed as above again, both with palm up and again with palm down.

5. Watch to see whether the thumb or little finger weakens most, and with palm up or palm down. Thumb weakening means carpal tunnel, little finger weakening means Guyon tunnel. If weakness is caused only in the palm down position (as it frequently is in pianists), check that the hand muscles are not reactive to *pronator teres*. If there is weakness only in the palm up position (as in upper strings) then the hand muscles may be reactive to *supinator* (see Reactive muscles technique above).

With **carpal tunnel syndrome** it is the median nerve which is impinged under the tough *flexor retinaculum* or ligament that binds the wrist bones together. Correction of weakness is effected by altering the relationship between the bones which tension this ligament. A definitive test is if pressure on the base of the palm just beyond the wrist crease causes a worsening of the problem in the fingers. (There may also be signs of muscle wasting in the ball of the thumb.)

1. The Tester holds the Testee's hand palm up in the fingers of his two hands, and with his thumbs above the wrist joint along the forearm.

2. Establish the direction of adjustment by lightly brushing the thumbs together and retesting, or brushing thumbs apart and retesting. If thumbs together strengthens the general hand test, then the correction needed is to squeeze the two splayed forearm bones together. However, I have found far more frequently that the forearm bones are jammed together, and need to be eased apart with pressure from the Tester's thumbs on the inside edges of the Testee's forearm bones, pushing them out sideways all the way to the elbow. An over-

tight watch-strap may well be the cause of the problem.

3. Helpful acu-points are LI-4 and H-3. LI-4 is on the back of the hand half-way along the thumb side of the bone below the index finger. Hold it with H-3 which is at the inner end of the crease on the inside of the elbow.

4. If the wrist is sensitive, support it for two weeks with a support bandage, splint or 'Tubigrip'. Don't make it too tight, and release it several times a day, to let the area breathe and re-establish good blood-flow.

5. Eating foods high in vitamin B complex and B6 will help.

6. Gentle use rather than a complete cessation of playing can speed return to normal use. However, if there is a lot of swelling and inflammation, do some ice massage before and after attempting any stage in the Rehabilitation Ladder (see below). *After* the swelling has gone, then use heat before and ice afterwards. Careful use of this technique may prevent the necessity for surgery.

The ring and little finger malfunction and weakness associated with **Guyon tunnel syndrome** is corrected as follows:

1. The general hand test is strong (see above).

2. With the Testee's hand palm up, pressure is put on the base of the palm, little-finger side, to push the nobbly pea-sized pisiform bone away from the thumb and against the hammate bone.

3. Repeat with the Testee's hand palm down. Pressure is now put just inside the bump at the end of the forearm bone, little finger side.

4. Correction is in whichever direction causes the general hand test to become strong (little-finger side).

5. Take hold of the two sides of the Testee's hand, palm up or palm down as just decided above, and place both thumbs on the bone you are correcting at the little finger side of the wrist. The Testee's arm should be totally relaxed as you pull very gently and press sharply with your thumbs, giving the arm a quick flick like a small whip from the contact point of your thumbs. Speed is more important than pressure.

6. Retest with the general hand muscle test, which should now be strong. This syndrome will benefit also from an increase in intake of vitamin B. Pushing heavy swing doors and leaning on outstretched

palms should be avoided for two weeks.

Meridian running

To 'run' each meridian accurately, a complete map is needed. However a wonderful energiser, and particularly useful mid-concert 'perk up' is achieved by running the hands over the body in large sweeps as follows:

1. Run one hand down the inside of your arm from the front of the shoulder, past the armpit to inside elbow, palm and fingers. Do the other arm.

2. Run one hand up the back of the other arm from fingers, past the elbow point, round the back of the shoulder to the back of the ear. Repeat with the other arm.

3. Place your hands on your big toes and sweep up the inside of your legs. Continue up the front of the body to the collar bones.

3. Place your hands on your ribs and sweep down the sides of your body and outsides of your legs to the little toes.

4. 'Zip up' the front of your body from crotch to lower lip, and up the back from the tailbone, up the spine, over the top of the head and down the nose to the upper lip.

Each sweep, except the last zip up, enhances and emphasises the correct flow of three meridians at once. Ending on the lips will remind you to finish with a smile. The whole exercise takes less than ten seconds to do.

Other useful acu-points

These are points to hold or rub gently to relieve the specified problem. Each point is valid on its own.

Migraine. Lu-7 – on the inner forearm, four finger widths up from the wrist crease, thumb side.

Frontal headache and sinus pain. GB-14 – above the centre of each eye, half-way between the eyebrow and hairline; also IGV-23 – one inch (2.5cm) above the natural hair line on the mid-line of the head.

Headache. Bl-67 – on the outer edge of the nail of the little toe.

Head and neck pain. LI-4 – at the end of the crease when the thumb and index finger are held together.

Headaches in the back of the head and neck. GB-20 – on the base of the skull half-way between the back of the ear and the small dip centre top of the neck.

Infections. St-36 – a hand's width below the kneecap, two finger widths to the outer side of the leg.

Hormone and menstrual problems. Sp-6 – on the inside calf, one hand's width above the inside ankle.

Emotional stress. Ht-3 – at the inside end of the elbow crease.

Hearing, tinnitus and jaw problems. SI-19 – just in front of the ear in the dip that appears when the mouth is open; and GB-2 – in front of the ear and level with the lowest part of the earhole above the ear lobe.

Eye problems. Bl-1 – immediately above the inner corner of the eye; and GB-1 – at the outer corner of the eye.

Low back and leg pain. Bl-60 – half-way between the outer ankle bone and the Achilles tendon; and GB-30 – in the dimple in the middle of each buttock.

Chronic pain and hypertension. K-1 – on the sole of the foot, at the heel end of the crease between the ball of the big toe, and the other toes.

Stress from fear and neurosis. Cx-6 – three fingers above the inner wrist crease, thumb side, between forearm bone and tendons.

Shoulder, elbow, wrist and finger problems. Tw-5 – three fingers above the wrist crease on the back of the forearm, between the two forearm bones.

General muscle relaxing point. Lv-2 – where the skin joins the big toe and the toe next to it.

Right/left brain coordination
Adults as well as children can become subject to minor neurological disorganisation. In children, the most common symptoms are reading and learning difficulties, dyslexia and clumsiness. It is commonly thought to be because the child missed a stage in neurological development between six months and one year, such as the crawling stage between shuffling along on the bottom and walking. However this is not the only cause. Upsets in neurological organisation can be caused by opposing brain-hand, brain-ear and brain-eye dominance, an unbalanced bite and heavy dental work, as well as foot problems and allergy .

In adults, who mostly have found a way to manage without obvious dyslexic symptoms, it shows up as clumsiness, inability to march in step

with others (or lifting the same leg as arm when marching, instead of opposite arm and leg, consequently having a rolling instead of a straight gait).
There may also be unsynchronised arm/leg swing, or even no arm swing at
all. Channelled thinking is another symptom. People with this problem are
either thinking spatially *or* analytically, and are unable to integrate the two
skills. They may be very good at one and very poor at the other: good at
sport, for example, but unable to spell or write a reasoned essay/letter,
despite obvious intelligence and having received a similar level of tuition in
both. They may also fail to understand an instruction properly.

In Chapter 4 the problems of a dyslexic child learning a musical
instrument were discussed. However, we can all benefit from movements
that will integrate the two sides of the brain, and de-stress areas of difficulty due to neurological disorganisation caused by playing a one-sided
instrument, recent dental work, new shoes or acquired food sensitivity.

Cross-crawl patterning was introduced into applied kinesiology by
George Goodheart from Doman and Delacato's work. It is a way of
reasserting the normal pattern and integrating right and left brain into
good coordination and clear thinking. It raises energy levels because you
are not always fighting yourself to achieve good coordination.
1. With a strong indicator muscle, look at a cross (as in noughts and
crosses) and then at vertical parallel lines. If the indicator muscle
goes weak when looking at the cross and stays strong when looking
at the parallel lines then you need this technique. Any other
combination is fine.
2. The Testee lies face up, legs straight.
3. Assess side of weakness by turning both feet in. The side that turns
in most is the side to which the head needs to be turned at stage 5.
4. *Simultaneously* lift right arm and bend up left leg. Lower both
limbs and repeat the other side.
5. Turn the head to the chosen side when the same-side arm is lifted.
When the opposite arm is lifted, the head should face up normally
(e.g. if stage 3 indicated that the head should be turned to the right,
then it will be right arm lift plus head turn to right; left arm lift plus
face up normally).
6. 30 cycles a day is a good number, until it becomes second nature.
It is also helpful to do this when tired, and before practising a

Cross-patterning using both sides of the brain

particularly difficult technical passage.

7. If the problem persists or you still feel worse after a month of daily cross-crawl, see an applied kinesiologist to sort out the underlying cause.

8. Cross-patterning can also be done standing (marching on the spot), but it is far easier (until you are used to it) to lose the sense of coordination when upright.

9. Another, less obvious way to help yourself with integration of complicated comprehension is to draw an infinity sign (infinity or 'lazy eight' – an eight on its side with the right 'end' open), making sure you draw up the middle and round the sides (not down the middle and up the sides). This also integrates right and left brain. Finish by holding the frontal eminences – points over the centre of each eye half-way between the eyebrow and hairline – for 30 seconds.

Reflexology points

Reflexology points are well worth working on even though you may not be a skilled practitioner. The relevant places will be sore. If you have problems in any of the areas listed below, rub deeply with the tip of your thumb for about 30 seconds at the specified point on the foot. The area listed are those particularly useful to musicians:

1. Eyes – between the second and third toes in the webbing.
2. Ears – between the third, fourth and fifth toes in the webbing.
3. Shoulder points – on the outside of the little toe where it meets the foot.
4. Neck and jaw – all round the base of the big toe where it meets the foot, and the next joint away.
5. Sinuses – the tops of all the toes.
6. Spine – from the neck points on the base of the big toe, which represents the top of the neck, all the way down the inside of the longitudinal arch of the foot, to the inner ankle, which represents the sacrum and coccyx.
7. Lungs – on the ball of the foot except under the big toe.
8. Chest – on the top of the foot near the toes. This will be puffy and tender if the chest is congested.

The rest of the points are either harder to find, or relate to organs and thus require some knowledge of their function. They should only be worked on by a practitioner or under instruction.

Rehabilitation ladders

Rehabilitation ladders are extremely useful to show you how bad the injury is, and to show your progress back to health as a musician. If you have to stop playing for any reason, even an extended holiday, you may need to remedy the disuse with strengthening exercises. Return to health

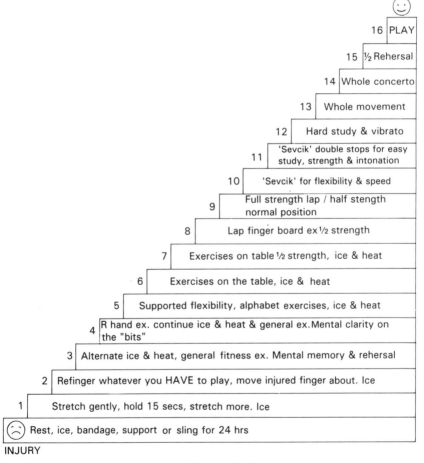

16 PLAY
15 ½ Rehersal
14 Whole concerto
13 Whole movement
12 Hard study & vibrato
11 'Sevcik' double stops for easy study, strength & intonation
10 'Sevcik' for flexibility & speed
9 Full strength lap / half stength normal position
8 Lap finger board ex ½ strength
7 Exercises on table ½ strength, ice & heat
6 Exercises on the table, ice & heat
5 Supported flexibility, alphabet exercises, ice & heat
4 R hand ex. continue ice & heat & general ex. Mental clarity on the "bits"
3 Alternate ice & heat, general fitness ex. Mental memory & rehersal
2 Refinger whatever you HAVE to play, move injured finger about. Ice
1 Stretch gently, hold 15 secs, stretch more. Ice
Rest, ice, bandage, support or sling for 24 hrs
INJURY

Rehabilitation ladder

rarely occurs in a steady progressive line, and playing is no exception. Far more common is a small progression, then what seems to be a plateau, then a sudden new progression, then another plateau and so on. It's important to remember this, in your impatience to get back to playing, so that you don't push yourself too fast and too far, and undo all the good already done.

A rehabilitation ladder is a graded series of exercises that can be used for general fitness or for specific injuries. Both are useful to musicians, but each instrument will have its own set of likely injuries and therefore its own specific rehabilitation ladder. It is of no use for me to give one for each instrument, as age, style and amount of playing as well as technique vary enormously. All I can do is give you examples, principles and rules so that you can devise your own. Think *for* yourself, and *of* yourself in terms of a beginner. What basic exercises would you teach? Then make a progress chart, bridging the gap between the 'beginner' and the level of professional proficiency you wish to attain. Think of it as a form of accelerated learning. Plan your work, and then work your plan with tender care. If pain reappears after progressing to the next level, drop back at least two levels, lengthen rest periods or stop for a day. Expect setbacks due to over keenness, but don't look for them. Keep *positive*.

1. Always begin with gentle stretching exercises (see p369 under **warm-up**).

2. Start at the bottom of the ladder, even if you can do better, as it will act as a form of warm-up for what follows.

3. At the first sign of pain, STOP. If the pain goes within 20 seconds you may continue, but with caution.

4. If the pain doesn't go, leave it for 24 hours and start at the bottom again.

5. Progress from gross or whole-body movements, through strength or speed, to stamina or fine movement.

6. Put the lot together.

7. While you are stuck on the lower rungs of the ladder *do not neglect the mental side of playing* – do plenty of score reading and visualisation, and attend rehearsals so that you don't miss out on the camaraderie of your section, and the chance of marking your part, even if you are paying someone to stand in for you. And don't neglect

your general fitness.

General sports and fitness ladder
1. After injury rest, use ice in a cloth ten minutes on ten minutes off, three times round, support the area with a bandage and hold it up with a sling or similar for 24 hours to stop swelling.
2. Stretch gently. No bouncing! Stretch until it just starts to hurt. Hold just less than that level and then in 15 to 20 seconds stretch a little more. Healing muscles scar. Scars shorten muscles. Shortened muscles tear again, so always stretch first before you exercise, even when fit.
3. Isometrics using the muscle in the middle of its range only. Isometrics mean that you push against the opposite hand/arm/leg, without either one winning. That way you won't go beyond your natural strength. Hold ten seconds, relax ten seconds. Repeat for two to three minutes only. *Do not push through pain!*
4. Isometrics using normal muscle length and contraction.
5. Isometrics using full range of motion.
6. Use light weights – this means light enough to produce no pain, while moving the weight from one extreme range of the muscle to the other over a five-second time span, and back over the same time. Rest for ten seconds and repeat exercise for two to three minutes.
7. As above with a slightly increased weight.
8. Start technical skills slowly e.g. running, swimming etc.
9. Increase force, practising techniques at half maximum effort.
10. Use maximum effort in practice only.
11. Start to play in easy low-grade matches with easy opposition.
12. Back to normal grade playing.

Injured finger ladder
1. If you are not a string player, translate this ladder into your own terms, using the same principles. If you see someone else in trouble, share what you have learned and tactfully, privately, suggest they do the same.
2. For an injured left finger, start with 1 and 2 as above. Wear a sling or immobilise the finger by strapping it to an adjacent one for a few

days, to prevent you using it in normal daily living.

3. Move it about gently meanwhile re-fingering everything for when and if you absolutely *have* to play. Recognise the risk of re-injury if you do.

4. Concentrate on right-hand exercises and mental practice, also attend rehearsals. Alternate ice and heat over the area. Keep up your general fitness levels by swimming, t'ai chi or whatever you usually do.

5. While supporting the left hand with the right, do gentle exercises, miming in the air without your instrument. Stop at the first sign of pain or tiredness. Work on flexibility not strength. Using the injured joint, write the alphabet in the air with letters as large as possible.

6. Do some five-finger exercises (or similar, as appropriate to your instrument) on a table – still without your instrument, and still 'miming' without any strength. You may still need to use ice afterwards for ten minutes to stop any swelling.

7. When you can mime number 6 above quickly and easily with no strength, then use half strength. Meanwhile, build general strength either by squeezing a squash ball or a ball of newspaper, or putting a rubber band round the outsides of all the fingers and thumb and stretching it out wide, depending on the direction of weakness. Keep exercise times shorter than the rests between them.

8. Now use the finger board but with the instrument resting in your lap so there is minimum twist, and still with only half strength (keyboard players could use a light-action pianissimo). Keep doing exercise 7.

9. Full strength in your lap, half strength in normal playing position, do five minutes at a time and rest five.

10. Do some easy Sevcik, Czerny or other 'tongue twister-type' exercises for flexibility and speed. Use a metronome to build speed gradually and a video slow-motion playback, to analyse your technique and postural errors. Keep having frequent breaks, playing 10 to 15 minutes, resting five.

11. Do some harder exercises, some double-stops and an easy study for strength and intonation. Begin to build playing time.

12. Do a harder study and use some vibrato, going for coordination

and strength.

13. Play through a whole movement – choose easy ones at first.

14. Play through a whole concerto to build stamina.

15. Do half a rehearsal, or a whole one if the programme is not taxing.

16. Return to normal playing.

After each session do some 'warm-down' exercises!

GOOD LUCK

REFERENCES

1. **Anderson R.** (1980/1992) *Stretching: Exercises for everyday fitness for 25 individual sports*, Pelham Books

2. **Corvo J.** (1981) *The Miracle of You (Reflexology or Zone Therapy)*, Villiers Publications

3. **Downing G.** (1972) *The Massage Book*, Wildwood House Ltd. London

4. **Feitis R.** ed. (1978) *Ida Rolf Talks About Rolfing and Physical Reality*, Harper Colophon

5. **Fry H.** (1986) *Overuse Syndrome in Musicians: prevention and management in Occupational Health* (The Lancet, 27.9.86, pp728-731)

6. **Gelb H.**(1983) *Killing Pain Without Prescription*. Thorsons, Harper Collins

7. **Lautie R.** and **Passebecq A.** (1982) *Aromatherapy, The Use of Plant Essences in Healing*, Thorsons, Harper Collins.

8. **Prudden B.** (1977) *Pain Erasure the Bonny Prudden Way*, Ballentine Books NY, USA

9. **Read M.** (1984) *Sports Injuries A Unique Guide to Self-diagnosis and Rehabilitation*, Breslich and Foss

10. **Royal Canadian Airforce Exercises** (1953) *Physical fitness 5BX 11 Minute-a-day Plan for Men, XBX 12 Minute-a-day Plan for Women, A get fit/stay fit course for town dwellers*, Penguin

11. **Schneider M.** (1994) *The Handbook of Self-Healing*, Penguin Arkana

12. **Smith B.** and **Stevens G.** (1980) *The Emergency Book. You Can Save a Life*, Fireside, Simon Schuster

13. **Walther D.** (1980) *Applied Kinesiology Synopsis, Ch.7 Meridian*

Therapy, p14-240, Systems DC, Pueblo Colorado USA

ORGANISATIONS
Remedial Massage. The Churchill Centre, 22 Montague St, London
W1H 1TB. *Tel:* 0171-402 9475

CONCLUSION

In this book I have aimed at a producing a manual which gives musicians a choice in the area of their own health. To take charge, be responsible and, while using all aspects of medicine as they are relevant, leave behind the attitude of 'Mother NHS always knows best'. Sometimes she does, sometimes she doesn't; there are often other options. Barring accidents that fall upon us from outside, there is often a lack of personal resonsibility, forethought and planning, which is essential if you are to get the best out of yourself and the people you ask for help. Only this way can you give your best in your chosen life. Trust only your instinct and reason, and, where the two clash, follow the former, for your instinct is the greatest expert on *you* that ever lived. I have aimed at the centre: between lay and medical knowledge; between the scientific attitudes of dry, logical reductionism, and 'whole-istic' artistic, unquantifiable lateral thinking and intuition. To use one without the other amounts to medical dyslexia. Science is not so much a matter of proof, statistics and quantity, so beloved of many, as of doubt, questioning quality and discovery.

There is so much that could be done in music colleges, as part of the curriculum, to prolong and glory in musical life. I would like to see a video recorder used as much as a tape recorder as a learning tool, to show students physical misuse, as well as musical and instrumental mistakes. Such teaching has a far greater positive self-motivational impact.

We unrealistically train too many people to be soloists, whereas so few ever reach that state. Inevitably this fosters the attitude that being an orchestral musician is a compromise and second best, as noticed by Beecham who described a distinguished orchestra as 'this collection of disappointed soloists'. In the prospectuses of orchestral training schemes there is much laudable musical variety, but nothing on the physical needs and stamina required by musicians.

I would recommend inspiring aspiring students to learn about themselves in the basics of anatomy, physiology, ergonomics, nutrition, personal and group social management skills. They should aim at understanding injury prevention, in order to enjoy and prolong their playing life. I would be happy if this book provided an outline for a simple course, Norwegian style, where such subjects were mandatory in the first-year college curriculum, with advanced studies arranged into a module contributing to a final teaching degree. This would self-motivate musicians to see themselves as whole, integrated people who communicate on all levels, and not just as sophisticated performing monkeys.

Where problems have gone beyond self-help, it is crucial for medical practitioners to observe the patient *in actual performance* as part of their rehabilitation programme, in the same way as they do in top sports medicine. Players can at least make a start by taking their instrument with them to consultations, although playing under stress is quite different from playing a few notes in a private surgery.

It would be wonderful if each orchestra could have not only a GP, but a homeopath, naturopath, kinesiologist, osteopath and chiropractor, somewhat in the way that Martina Navratilova built a winning support team around her. They handled everything from diet training and equipment repair to promotions, putting her in first class condition and leaving her free to go out and be a world beater so many times over.

There needs to be a better definition of what 'value for money' and 'productivity' mean in musical terms, both for players and audiences alike. An informed definition should take into account the good and bad effects of programme repetition and recording, of down-sizing, and of involvement of all parties at all levels.

Music exports in 1995 were over £1.5 billion, according to Adam Shaw (on 'Working Lunch' BBC2, Mon. 11th Dec. 1995), with the top musicians' earnings far outstripping those of the 'Fat Cats' of industry. In my dream of a perfect musician's world, I would like a sense of pride about the profession as with top football clubs. This would entail supporters' clubs that had great pride in their chosen orchestra and did more than just attend 'meet the players' evenings. With the growing popularity of the classics from Classic FM and similar stations, how about supporters' clubs sponsoring aspiring orchestral members, thus balancing the ever-popular sponsorship for soloist child prodigies? Why not have orchestral physical training schemes for young orchestral players, open to amateurs and supporters also? It is all a matter of how it is presented to the public.

Only soloists, leaders and conductors have any real say in negotiating their pay rates and the job of a rank-and-file player tends to be looked down on by the rest of the social world almost as it was in Mozart's day. It would be nice if British orchestras had a bit of a swagger – but first there must be more to swagger about physically. An orchestra's greatest assets are its players: their motivation, enthusiasm and skill.

Inevitably, in this book, there are unconscious biases and omissions as it comprises the garnered ideas, sentiments and experiences of the lifetime of one person. I am not 'pro' or 'anti' anything if that's what works for you as a musician, but I find it hard to bear watching people haplessly and needlessly destroying themselves in a very tough profession, because they are unaware of the possibilities and solutions which exist to help them, let alone the variety of options from which they can choose. Anyone with any positive suggestions for additional material along these lines, should write to me, c/o Rhinegold Publishing. Suitable material will be acknowledged and included in subsequent editions.

Index

muscle (A), 248

Antiperspirants, 58

AP *see Adductor pollicis*

APB *see Abductor pollicis brevis*

'A pill for every ill', 142-5

APL *see Abductor pollicis longus*

Applied Kinesiology, 11, 13-14
    and ileocaecal valve syndrome, 134-5
    for visual inhibition, 71-2

Arm, blood and nerve supplies to, 225-6
    elbow, 218
    forearm, bones of, 218
    growth, 36
    muscles of, 219-20
    referred pain in, 228
    upper, bones of, 218

Arm supplies, 225-6

Aromatherapy, 379

Arthritis, 232-4
    and fatigue, 202
    diet for, 233
    rheumatoid, 128, 136, 232
    triggered by double-jointedness, 25

Arts Psychology Consultants, 185

Aspirin, 233

Assessing the Problem (muscle testing), 240-41

Asthma, 128, 171, 367

Aural inhibition, 79-80

B

Bach flower remedies (BF), 14, 172-3, 211, 249

Back, muscles, 330-35
    pain, 211, 391

Bags (for valuables), 113

BAPAM *see* British Association for Performing Arts Medicine

Barton, John, 249, 362

Basic body awareness, 21

Bates, W.,15, 67, 69-70

Bechstein, 25

Bed boards, 116

Behavioural barometer, 176-8

Being Tired all the Time (TATT), 201-3

Beta blockers, 155, 156

BF *see* Bach Flower remedies

Digestion, 128-30
Digitorum, 298
Digits, 34
Dizziness, 367
DJD *see* Degenerative joint disease
Don't Do, Delegate, 197, 215
Double-jointedness, 24-5
Draughts, 57-8
Driving, 68-9
Drugs, 9, 143-5
Du Pré, Jacqueline, 154-5, 222
Dynamics of the Singing Voice, 169, 184
Dyslexia and music, 73-4

E

E *see* Emotionally relevant words
Ears, The, 75-80
Eating, 121-4
    and arthritis, 233
Eczema, 59, 136
E for additives, 128, 152
E Numbers, 127-8
Ehlers-Danlos disease, 22
EK for Kids, 74, 89
Elbow, 218, 391
    golfer's, 219
    movement of, 224
    muscles of, 219
    nerves, 229
    tennis, 219
Emergency mid-concert self-help, 364-8
    mental problems, 365
    physical problems, 365-7
Emotional stress release (ESR) points, 176-8
Emotionally relevant words (E), 249
Enemas, 151
EPB *see* Extensor pollicis brevis
EPL *see* Extensor pollicis longus
Epilepsy, 68
Epsom salts, 377
Erector spinae (Sacrospinalis), 332-5, *333*
Erhard, 162
ESR *see* Emotional stress release
Ethmoid, 32

410

411

Levator, anguli oris, 253-4
    labii superioris, 253
    scapulae, 266-8, 267
Lifting, *110*, 111
Ligaments, 222-3
Lindlahr, H., 147-8
Lips, 24
Listening, 205-6
Lists, 101-6
Long- and Short-term Help, 169-73
Long hand muscles, 306-9
Long sight, 66
Long Thumb Muscles, The, 310-14
Lumbar muscles, 355-40
Lumbricales, 321, 321-2
Lungs, 24
Lupus, 128
Lymphatic drainage points, 16

M

M *see* Chinese acupuncture meridian
Magnesium, 126
Mahoney, Frank, 380
Malocclusion, 84-5
Mandel, S., 4, 17
Mandela, Nelson, 159
Mandible, 33
Manganese, 126
Marfan's disease, 22-3
Massage, 377-9
    points (MP), 244-5, 248-9
    Remedial, 400
    self, 378-9
Masseter, 256-7
Maxilla, 32
MBS Medical Ltd, 90
McColl, Anthony, 77, 89, 90
McCormack, Mark, 205, 215
ME *see* Myalgic encephalomyelitis
Medline, 4
Memory, 16, 50-55
Memory, sight-reading and practice, 50-52
Menier's disease, 76, 78
Menstrual problems, 391

N

415

416

Repetitive strain injury, 21
Rescue Remedy, 172, 180, 182, 365, 367
Rhomboids, 219, 277-9, *278*
Ribs, 33-4
Richter, Sviatoslav, 201
Risoris, 253
Rolfing, 378
ROM *see* Normal Range of Movement
Room sharing and strange beds, 106-7

S

S *see* Substances to avoid
Sacrospinalis (Erector spinae), 332-5, *333*
SADs *see* Seasonally affective disorders
Samples for diagnosis, 12
Saphenous nerve compression, 27
Saying 'No' to work, 183-4
Scalenes, 257-60
Scapulae, 34, 218, 219
Scars, 385-6
Schaffer, Jo, 131, 152
Schoenberg, 154
School of Tropical Medicine, 97
Schumann, 23
Sciatic Nerve, The, 232, 340
SCM *see Sterno-cleido mastoid*
Sea-band Ltd, 116
Seasonally affective disorders (SADs), 200-201
Secrets of Musical Confidence, The, 169, 184
Segovia, 156
Self-criticism, 166
Self-help, 13-15
Self-talk, 179
Selye, Hans, 146-7
Selye, Lindlahr and Naturopathy, 146-8
Semispinalis, 260-61
Serratus anterior, 324-6, *325*
Shaw, Adam, 403
Shiatsu, 378
Shields and ear plugs, 27, 77-8
Shoes, formal, for women, 100-101
Short sight, 66
Short-term help with stress, 170-73
Shoulder, 218, 391

U

V

W

X

Z